A ROOSTER ONCE CROWED

*A Commentary on the
Greatest Story Ever Told*

BRYANT CORNETT

Carpenter's Son Publishing

A Rooster Once Crowed: A Commentary on the Greatest Story Ever Told

©2013 by Bryant Cornett

Published by Carpenter's Son Publishing, Franklin, Tennessee

Published in association with Larry Carpenter of Christian Book Services, LLC
www.christianbookservices.com

Scripture taken from the NEW AMERICAN STANDARD BIBLE®, Copyright ©
1960, 1962, 1963, 1968, 1971, 1972, 1973, 1975, 1977, 1995 by The Lockman Foundation.
Used by permission.

Cover Design by Kent Weakley

Interior Design by Suzanne Lawing

Editing by Andrew Toy, Gail Fallen, and Cheryl Lewis

Published January, 2014

Printed in the United States of America

978-1-940262-07-9

This book is dedicated to my lovely wife, without whom I do not know where I would be and who sacrificed more for this than anyone. And to William, Mary Dudley, and Hudson— three of the best kids I've ever known.

Acknowledgements

"*A Rooster Once Crowed* helped me understand the Gospel more clearly and love our Savior more dearly. Bryant has shown a new facet to the diamond which is the Gospel and readers will see the beauty of Jesus and His loving sacrifice in a way that will change the lives of new believers and committed Christians."
    - Len Sykes, Reflections Ministries, Atlanta Georgia

"*A Rooster Once Crowed* is a study which is broad in scope, accessible to seekers and – from my perspective as a Messianic Jewish rabbi – sensitive to the nuances of Yeshua (Jesus). Take your time with this material. You won't be disappointed."
    - Rabbi Richard Nichol, Needham, Massachusetts

"My friend Bryant Cornett has crafted a compelling way to tell the old old story by integrating a wide variety of scriptures with illustrations and narratives that press for a decision. This story speaks to the mind, the heart and the will reminding us that revelation requires a response."
    – Dr. Ken Boa, author, Atlanta, Georgia

"This book is for building disciples. If you want to be one or are building them, read this book."
    – Jerry Leachman, former chaplain for the Washington Redskins, Washington, DC.

Contents

Introduction

This book demands a decision.

In Jesus' last hours, He said Peter would deny Him before the rooster crowed twice. Peter replied, "No way. Not even facing death will I deny You." But a few hours later in the midst of a big commotion, pressure from the world, and three denials, the rooster crowed once.

"What was that?"

It seemed familiar. "Where did I just hear someone mention a rooster?"

See, Peter was getting by, doing what needed to be done, staying close in case opportunity presented itself. But that first crow of the rooster found Peter warming himself on the porch.

The second crow of the rooster sounded and Peter was shattered. Tears rolled down his face as he realized that his time with Jesus was over. What Jesus told them was happening and Peter's own denials made him feel ineligible. Alone in the moment with the sun peeking

> AND JESUS SAID [TO PETER], "TRULY I SAY TO YOU, THAT THIS VERY NIGHT, BEFORE A ROOSTER CROWS TWICE, YOU YOURSELF WILL DENY ME THREE TIMES." BUT PETER KEPT SAYING INSISTENTLY, "EVEN IF I HAVE TO DIE WITH YOU, I WILL NOT DENY YOU!" AND THEY ALL WERE SAYING THE SAME THING ALSO. ...
>
> BUT HE DENIED IT, SAYING, "I NEITHER KNOW NOR UNDERSTAND WHAT YOU ARE TALKING ABOUT." AND HE WENT OUT ONTO THE PORCH. THE SERVANT-GIRL SAW HIM, AND BEGAN ONCE MORE TO SAY TO THE BYSTANDERS, "THIS IS ONE OF THEM!" BUT AGAIN HE DENIED IT. AND AFTER A LITTLE WHILE THE BYSTANDERS WERE AGAIN SAYING TO PETER, "SURELY YOU ARE ONE OF THEM, FOR YOU ARE A GALILEAN TOO." BUT [PETER] BEGAN TO CURSE AND SWEAR, "I DO NOT KNOW THIS MAN YOU ARE TALKING ABOUT!" IMMEDIATELY A ROOSTER CROWED A SECOND TIME. AND PETER REMEMBERED HOW JESUS HAD MADE THE REMARK TO HIM, "BEFORE A ROOSTER CROWS TWICE, YOU WILL DENY ME THREE TIMES." AND HE BEGAN TO WEEP.
>
> - MARK 14:30-31, 68-72

over the horizon, Peter felt outside and unworthy even while he experienced that what Jesus said was true.

We are living in those few moments between the rooster's first crow—familiarity, worldliness, getting by, chores, provision, warming ourselves on the porch—and the second crow—shame, realization, loss, despair, weeping.

Because a rooster once crowed is an opportunity to turn around, to change our course, to reclaim, and to run home. But the second crow, the second crow is the realization of truth.

You may feel like you're on your hundredth crow or that you haven't yet heard the sound, but this is it. This is the rooster first crowed. This is an opportunity to engage the material and to make a decision about what you believe and how you will live that belief out from this moment onward. Because there is a second crow coming. The rooster always crows twice.

***

This book began with a vision I received one night planning a lesson for my Sunday school class at Family Ties at Peachtree Road United Methodist Church. For the first time without a written note, I gave this lesson to a packed class of about 40 folks, and it was, by far, the best lesson I'd ever given.

I knew immediately that I had to share this as far as I could. It was a gift that required stewardship.

As of this writing, people in 54 countries have downloaded a version of the 38-minute talk nearly 8,000 times—if you'd like to hear it go to www.fullporchpress.com. That some have found it valuable enough to forward it to their friends, and those friends have sent it to their friends, is a great encouragement. The response to this Gospel story is a testament to the power of the Gospel. We're all hungry for its truth, authenticity, love, and depth.

I've borrowed heavily from great thinkers throughout this book. Without the Bible, Lon Solomon's background in biology and faith, Tim Keller's sermon series "King's Cross" on the Gospel of Mark, Ken Boa's depth, Len Sykes' patience, C. S. Lewis' musings on everything else, Rabbi Rich Nichol's view of history, or Cheryl Lewis' kind eye, I would never have been able to put into words what I saw.

Indeed, I put each of these on level with Moses, Matthew, Mark, Luke, John, and Paul because, like these heroes of the Bible, God spoke through them in miraculous ways exactly when I needed to hear them. I can't tell you how many times I felt lost and afraid that I had nothing to say, and God's Word came to me like manna through them with exactly what I needed. Thank you.

***

Peter was wrong, you know.

Standing on Caiaphas' porch, Peter thought that he was finished. But he chose the right path and his story didn't end there. Peter went through forgiveness and on to become the rock on which the church was built.

It doesn't end here for you, either. No matter if you believe or are hostile toward Jesus, the central tenant of our faith is that we all fall short of the standard. Not one of us is up to snuff.

> FOR ALL HAVE SINNED AND FALL SHORT OF THE GLORY OF GOD,
> - ROMANS 3:23

But from here, from wherever you are, in this time, you have a chance to make a decision. After enough time, indecision is a decision. The rooster has crowed, so let those with ears to hear, hear and eyes to see, see.

This is a commentary on the Gospel of Jesus Christ, the greatest story ever told.

CHAPTER 1

A View from the Porch

Imagine you're a parent, and you have two children—a boy and a girl.

Your boy is a high school all-American and an honor student who loves and serves you unconditionally. He has a heart for others and from a young age, every person he has met left conversations with him thinking he will own the world someday. And you agree. He goes to college on a full scholarship, playing a sport you love like you've never seen anyone play it before. He chose that college because it was where he thought you wanted him to go. He graduates, works for a while, and gets married. You love his wife, and when the three of you are together, you orbit around each other. Each of you competes to love the other two more. Then, he quits his job to go back to law school in a faraway city for admirable reasons. You're proud of him and just can't believe you're connected to this person. Knowing that he loves you nearly breaks you in two.

You have a daughter, too. She is strong and beautiful, but from an early age, has shown an uncanny ability to make wrong decisions. If you've been around someone like this, you know that after a while, they're choosing only from a menu of bad choices. There are no good choices left. She steals from you and curses at you. Things get so bad that her presence in your home hurts you, and she feels the exact same way. In the last couple of years, you've become estranged.

One day, you're in the kitchen when the phone rings. The conversation goes something like this: "You won't remember me, but I'm a friend of your daughter and we're into some really bad stuff. The worst kind of stuff, and she's been sold to some really bad people. They're moving us around a lot, and I heard them say they're taking her overseas tonight. I didn't have anyone else to call. We're at this address and, if you want to see her again, she'll be here for the next four hours, but..."

The line goes dead.

As you hang up the phone, you realize that the address she has given you is in the same distant city where your son is attending law school. There is no way for you to make it there in four hours—but your son could.

Do you send him? Do you send your only son to save your daughter?

But what if you know—and I can't tell you how you know, but you know—that your son will not make it out alive, will you send your son to save your daughter?

If you know—and I can't tell you how you know, but you know—your son will die an unspeakably painful death that would not necessarily save her, will you still send him? Will you send him if his sacrifice only guarantees her three steps outside the door, and that once there, she can make a choice?

Would you make that sacrifice knowing that she may walk back into that house? Would you make that sacrifice to give her the chance to run home to you? Could you even take her back? She might decide to stay there, on the porch, managing her life—understanding the sacrifice made on her behalf, but just too scared or attached to run home? Will she accept the sacrifice, but deny its cost and choose to live closer, but not altogether back with you?

This story became real to me once I realized that each morning when I wake up, I'm that girl on the porch, three steps outside the door, deciding which of those choices I'm going to make. Will I honor the sacrifice that allowed me to see the light of day, or will I choose to walk back into that house?

What is it that makes us repeatedly go back inside? An addiction or vice? Family or charity? It doesn't have to be a bad thing that keeps us there.

In the end, where I move from that porch tells me and my God whether I am a person that "couldn't not" enter into the love and care of Him, or a person who just won't.

Through the next chapters we will begin to look at this story and uncover the truth and love woven into the Gospel. This story, God's love letter to humanity, is real, and it's OK to believe it. In fact, I'd strongly encourage it.

***

At the end of each chapter, you'll see a box like the one on the next page with suggested reading. Choose one of the four Gospels (Matthew, Mark, Luke or, John) with which you are least familiar and commit to reading through it over the course of this book. Following along with this will greatly enhance your experience. If you're overly ambitious, pick two, three, or even all four. You can even mix and match as you go along. Just make sure you read at least one. It's worth it.

Also, throughout the book you will see boxes containing Scripture that is referenced within the text or supports a thought. It will be tempting to skip or read past them, but I encourage you to start by reading all the Scripture in the chapter and maybe even look back over them after you finish. There is something excellent about these that is enhanced by reading them together with the text, too. I guarantee that you'll come away from the exercise with a new understanding of what has been done for you. Each one is a seed created with you in mind, planted thousands of years ago and set to sprout within you at this very moment.

Before you go on to the next chapter, take a few moments to read one or more of the following:
Matthew Chapters 1 & 2
Mark Chapter 1
Luke Chapters 1 & 2
John Chapter 1

CHAPTER 2

In the Beginning, God . . .

To say that these four words changed the world is a massive understatement. To say that these four words set the rails which defined time and the direction of the universe before either existed, is closer. In. The. Beginning. God. In the beginning God created the universe in community with Jesus and the Holy Spirit establishing all that was right and the rhythm of the Great Dance. This has massive ramifications on us today and gives us a look into the very being of God. God created the heavens, the earth, and man and it was only the beginning.

All great stories have a beginning, but do you know why? Because this one did.

Not only did this story have a beginning, it had *THE* beginning. Because of it, authors and storytellers until the end of time are forced to compete earnestly for second place. When it comes to beginnings, first place was secured a long time ago.

"In the beginning, God..."

Four more powerful words have never been written. "In the

> IN THE BEGINNING GOD . . .
> - GENESIS 1:1A

beginning, God..." contains a course of events so large that it defies explanation.

To tell the story of the Gospel, to share a perspective of the greatest story ever told—a story that has been clipped, stolen, borrowed, or used in every great piece of literature since—to tell a story that contains this much excellence we must start at the beginning.

And in the beginning, God was.

In this chapter, we will explore three questions:

> AND THE SPIRIT OF GOD WAS MOVING OVER THE SURFACE OF THE WATERS.
>
> - GENESIS 1:2B

What was in the beginning?

What does heaven tell us about God?

What does that mean for us today?

Indeed, **WHAT WAS IN THE BEGINNING?**

> IN THE BEGINNING WAS THE WORD, AND THE WORD WAS WITH GOD. HE WAS IN THE BEGINNING WITH GOD. ALL THINGS CAME INTO BEING THROUGH HIM, AND APART FROM HIM NOTHING CAME INTO BEING THAT HAS COME INTO BEING. IN HIM WAS LIFE, AND THE LIFE WAS THE LIGHT OF MEN. THE LIGHT SHINES IN THE DARKNESS, AND THE DARKNESS DID NOT COMPREHEND IT.
>
> - JOHN 1:1-5

We know from Genesis 1 that the Spirit of God was moving over the surface of the waters of creation. And we know from John 1 (and if you're a student of the Bible, you'll know that the Word is code for Jesus) that Jesus was there in the beginning, too. John 1 backs up Genesis 1 that God spoke to affect Creation.

The fact that God created the world by speaking it into being, instead of the myriad of other means at His disposal—He could have formed it, blasted it, molded it, manipulated it—reinforces the evidence of Jesus' presence at the time of Creation. And this provides evidence of the existence of the Trinity from the beginning.

We have writings, composed within 100 years after the death of Christ, mentioning prayer "to Christ, and to the Father and to the Spirit." It is not clear in Scripture, but entirely possible that the apostles began to teach about the Trinity directly after Pentecost. Paul links the three in 2 Corinthians, but he doesn't really try and define Their nature.

> THE GRACE OF THE LORD JESUS CHRIST, AND THE LOVE OF GOD, AND THE FELLOWSHIP OF THE HOLY SPIRIT, BE WITH YOU ALL...
>
> - 2 CORINTHIANS 13:14

Various official councils and beliefs about the relationship and entity of the Trinity cropped up over the years. Then, in 325 A.D., the Council of Nicaea settled the issue as it sits today:

—from before the beginning, the Trinity represents the three persons of the Godhead: God, the Father; Jesus, His only begotten Son; and the Holy Spirit and that together They are One God in three Persons, no more One than Three and no more Three than One.

For such a fundamental teaching, I wish that Jesus had spelled it out a little clearer, but He talked often about the Father and, from time to time, about the Holy Spirit. In Matthew 28, Christ's final words of this account of the Gospel, Jesus links the three inexorably.

> GO THEREFORE AND MAKE DISCIPLES OF ALL THE NATIONS, BAPTIZING THEM IN THE NAME OF THE FATHER AND THE SON AND THE HOLY SPIRIT, TEACHING THEM TO OBSERVE ALL THAT I COMMANDED YOU; AND LO, I AM WITH YOU ALWAYS, EVEN TO THE END OF THE AGE.
>
> - MATTHEW 28:19-20

I bristle at trying to quantify this relationship between the three. The greatest part of them and their relationship is beyond our comprehension and, if our knowing of the nature and relationship of the Trinity is necessary, Jesus would have explained it in greater detail. So I recommend holding this part loosely. In other words, don't try to cram them or their relationship to each other into a human understanding.

Simply rest in the knowledge that the few clues Jesus does give us provide depth and texture to the relationship that is fundamental to knowing God.

> IN THOSE DAYS JESUS CAME FROM NAZARETH IN GALILEE AND WAS BAPTIZED BY JOHN IN THE JORDAN. IMMEDIATELY COMING UP OUT OF THE WATER, HE SAW THE HEAVENS OPENING, AND THE SPIRIT LIKE A DOVE DESCENDING UPON HIM; AND A VOICE CAME OUT OF THE HEAVENS: "YOU ARE MY BELOVED SON, IN YOU I AM WELL-PLEASED." IMMEDIATELY THE SPIRIT IMPELLED HIM TO GO OUT INTO THE WILDERNESS.
>
> - MARK 1:9-12

Aside from Creation, in Genesis 1, the greatest example of the presence of the Trinity (and the only one where man is actually present) is in Mark 1:9-12.

So, from our earliest accounts, from the creation of the heavens and the earth, we have a sense that God, singular in power, lived in community with Jesus and the Holy Spirit.

Tim Keller is the pastor at Redeemer Presbyterian Church in New York City. In 2006 he started a sermon series titled "King's Cross" where he distilled for me three things that we can discern from these interactions:

First, if the heavens and the earth were created by a triune God, then ultimate reality is relational. Said another way, the ultimate focus of the world and our lives, in order to use them both within warranty, is within community.

Second, the nature of the Trinity is *LOVE*. This is shown in the singular example of the Three being in the same place in the presence of man, where Jesus is literally covered in love—*You are My Son Whom I love*—and the Spirit fills Him with power. Each honors the other with love and service.

> THE ONE WHO DOES NOT LOVE DOES NOT KNOW GOD, FOR GOD IS LOVE.
>
> - 1 JOHN 4:8

And third, this community among the three, sharing in love from all time, is Their essence. It is why we can say that God is love.

I love how Cornelius Plantinga puts it:

At the center of the universe, self-giving love is the dynamic currency of the trinitarian life of God. The persons within God

> MY PRAYER IS NOT FOR [THE DISCIPLES] ALONE. I PRAY ALSO FOR THOSE WHO WILL BELIEVE IN ME THROUGH THEIR MESSAGE, THAT ALL OF THEM MAY BE ONE, FATHER, JUST AS YOU ARE IN ME AND I AM IN YOU. MAY THEY ALSO BE IN US SO THAT THE WORLD MAY BELIEVE THAT YOU HAVE SENT ME.
>
> - JOHN 17:20-21

exalt each other, commune with each other, defer to one another. Each person, so to speak, makes room for the other two. I know it sounds a little strange, but we might almost say that the persons within God show each other divine hospitality. After all, John's Gospel tells us that the Father is 'in' the Son and that the Son is 'in' the Father (17:21), and that each loves and glorifies the other. ... each of the divine persons harbors the others at the center of His being. In a constant movement of overture and acceptance, each person envelops and encircles the others.[1]

Later in the same sermon series, Keller points out the excellence of the Trinity, and that its existence is one of the most powerful examples of the truth of Christianity. No one would ever come up with it; the Trinity's complexity overloads the brain, and yet it fits perfectly within the framework of the Gospel.

Without the Trinity, we run into all kinds of problems. Consider love. Love exists between one being and another. Without the other, love cannot exist. So if God is fundamentally love—true love— then without the Trinity, without the others, before Creation, there could have been no love. God created us to love out of love, and the existence of the Trinity makes that possible.

If God is One, and not Three, then He would have sought love from us. If that had been the case, then His essence would be something other than love. But the dynamic of the Trinity is off the spectrum. It represents the unity of absolute truth that comes from One (Three in One), but the diversity of community involvement that comes from the Three (One of Three).

Those cultures that worship one god celebrate the individual, but polytheistic cultures (those that worship many gods) tend to look to the family as the ultimate object of worship. The Trinity transcends a linear scale and honors individual sacrifice toward each member of an extended family unit (all of humanity). So begins the great dance of each orbiting around the other.

> IN THE BEGINNING GOD CREATED THE HEAVENS AND THE EARTH.
>
> - GENESIS 1:1

In this, we see that God created the heavens and the earth with such precision and perfection that all still function today, magnifying His glory and being born, uniquely, out of labor. All religions have some account of the beginning, but none begin with an all-powerful God reaching down to labor in creation.

In creation, with an understanding of Tri-unity, we can liken it to a couple who toil together to painstakingly build a home, brick by brick, out of love for one another. Once the house is built and everything is to their liking, there is nothing the couple can do to increase their love any more than bring a child into it.

Here, in the world, we can never get this quite right, but the Trinity, with perfect love, could. That is the Spirit with which God created man. Can't you feel it here, in this first account of Creation provided in the Bible?

It is easy for us to see the excellence that God created on earth, but He didn't just create earth. He created heaven, too. What we think about heaven, how you think about heaven, and when you think about heaven has an enormous impact on our lives, because it guides and shows us the nature of God.

So, **WHAT DOES HEAVEN TELL US ABOUT GOD?** Have you ever really thought about heaven? Do you thirst for it? Does the realization of it spur you on to greater and greater service? Is it real to you?

Early in my walk, it wasn't real to me. I didn't have a picture of what heaven was and, quite frankly, hanging out on a cloud while strumming a harp didn't sound that appealing. I just didn't think much about heaven.

I felt that the reward of knowing God in this life was enough. When Christ became a real force in my life and entered into my daily decision-making, the joy and freedom that I felt from His presence seemed an unbelievable reward. I looked at heaven like a freshly minted college graduate looks at a 401(k)—with the biggest paycheck of my life and the promise of another one in two weeks, putting money away for retirement down the road just seemed like a bonus.

That changed about a year into my walk when I spent a day in prayer focused on heaven with Len Sykes, a missionary based in Atlanta. Initially, considering the fullness of heaven seemed a little crass, like "countin' up our winnin's 'fore the dealin's done,"[2] but I trusted Len and waded in.

Those few hours developed into one of the critical pillars of my faith. The idea and concept of heaven, the realness of it, and a physical thirst for it have grown in me an unshakeable faith in what is to come.

Through these three sections, my prayer is that you will grow to yearn for heaven as much as I do, that together we'll yearn for it even more and that the mere mention of the word will begin to evoke a physical reaction in you—a savoring in your mouth that melts for the sweetness of heaven.

So what do we really know about heaven? From here, I'll make no differentiation between the heaven that God created, heaven as it sits today, and the new heaven that will exist at the end of time. We know a good deal about these realities from the Bible (and there are a number of good books on the subject),[i] but I'm going to focus on the most cohesive vision that we have of heaven. In Revelation 21, John is given a vision of the new heaven and the new earth that is to come. Revelation

> THEN I SAW A NEW HEAVEN AND A NEW EARTH; FOR THE FIRST HEAVEN AND THE FIRST EARTH PASSED AWAY, AND THERE IS NO LONGER ANY SEA.
> - REVELATION 21:1

---

i Randy Alcorn's 2004 book, *Heaven*; Joni Eareckson Tada's 1995 book, *Heaven: Your Real Home*; Don Piper's 2007 book, *90 Minutes in Heaven*; and Todd Burpo's 2010 book, *Heaven is for Real* are several really great places to start.

> GOD BLESSED THE SEVENTH DAY AND SANCTIFIED IT, BECAUSE IN IT [THE DAY] HE RESTED FROM ALL HIS WORK WHICH GOD HAD CREATED AND MADE.
>
> - GENESIS 2:3

> THE LORD GOD PLANTED A GARDEN TOWARD THE EAST, IN EDEN; AND THERE HE PLACED THE MAN WHOM HE HAD FORMED.
>
> - GENESIS 2:8

21:1 packs a lot into it.

Genesis 1:1 through Genesis 2:3 introduces the first Creation account with, "In the beginning, God created..." It encompasses the sixth day, when He creates man, and then, in Genesis 2:3, the account of Creation is concluded.

Genesis 2:4 picks up with another view of the same creation. It's where we get the account of a more detailed creation of man and woman, and are told more about the ecosystem of the earth, and shown, in Genesis 2:8, that Eden was placed apart.

Genesis 2:10-14 gives us coordinates for the location of Eden. If not for a massive flood 1,500 years later, they might have proved helpful in finding it.[ii]

Eden was in the world, special, and separated from the world. It was a little bit of heaven on earth—paradise. But Eden wasn't paradise due to the lush vegetation (which it had), nor the bounty it provided (which it did). Eden was paradise because of the physical, available presence of God there.

Toward the end of Revelation, after the rapture and the plagues and all the gnashing of teeth, we discover a Scripture that says the first heaven—where our beloved saints are now—and the first earth (not Eden, which was set apart, but this old ratty place in which we now live) will have been used up and discarded. It describes what's next: a new place, a better place. It is a place that I'm dying to attend—even now, as I sit in a nice, warm house with an

---

ii Jewish tradition states that the foundation stone of Creation—where man was made and Eden—was on Mt. Moriah, the site of the modern day Dome of the Rock, a Muslim mosque, in Jerusalem.

incredible family. I'm ready to go.

I really love Revelation 21:2-3. Imagine being able to eradicate the terrible side of living in any city (trash, poverty, crime, pollution, homelessness, isolation from community, traffic, etc.) and magnify only the positives (culture, luxury, food, drink, theater, art, architecture, diversity, etc.). This will be a city unlike any we've ever seen!

In verses 18-21, John describes the brilliance of the city. What is missing from that description? The harshest material in a city, the material that is literally glue to an earthly city, is completely absent. Instead of concrete, there are costly stones, crystal-clear jasper, and gold so pure it's like glass.

Imagine a bride, your own daughter, walking down the aisle. I'm not sure how a city could be made that beautiful but, to John, standing below and seeing this city being dropped down to earth, the ugliest part of it must have been the part John was seeing. Yet what came to his mind was a bride.

We don't know much

> AND I SAW THE HOLY CITY, THE NEW JERUSALEM, COMING DOWN OUT OF HEAVEN FROM GOD, MADE READY AS A BRIDE ADORNED FOR HER HUSBAND. AND I HEARD A LOUD VOICE FROM THE THRONE, SAYING, "BEHOLD, THE TABERNACLE OF GOD IS AMONG MEN, AND HE WILL DWELL AMONG THEM, AND THEY SHALL BE HIS PEOPLE, AND GOD HIMSELF WILL BE AMONG THEM...
>
> - REVELATION 21:2-3

> THE MATERIAL OF THE WALL WAS JASPER; AND THE CITY WAS PURE GOLD, LIKE CLEAR GLASS. THE FOUNDATION STONES OF THE CITY WALL WERE ADORNED WITH EVERY KIND OF PRECIOUS STONE. THE FIRST FOUNDATION STONE WAS JASPER; THE SECOND, SAPPHIRE; THE THIRD, CHALCEDONY; THE FOURTH, EMERALD; THE FIFTH, SARDONYX; THE SIXTH, SARDIUS; THE SEVENTH, CHRYSOLITE; THE EIGHTH, BERYL; THE NINTH, TOPAZ; THE TENTH, CHRYSOPRASE; THE ELEVENTH, JACINTH; THE TWELFTH, AMETHYST. AND THE TWELVE GATES WERE TWELVE PEARLS; EACH ONE OF THE GATES WAS A SINGLE PEARL. AND THE STREET OF THE CITY WAS PURE GOLD, LIKE TRANSPARENT GLASS.
>
> - REVELATION 21:18-21

about John, except that he was one of the twelve apostles and the only one who died of natural causes at an old age. He was likely over 80 years old when he died, and he wrote Revelation in the last 4 to ten years of his life. We don't know if he was married, had a daughter, or escorted her down an aisle, but it is safe to assume that, in such a full life, he saw a few brides. It's incredible that this beauty of "a bride, adorned for her husband" is what came to his mind in what surely must be the least flattering view of this marvelous city.

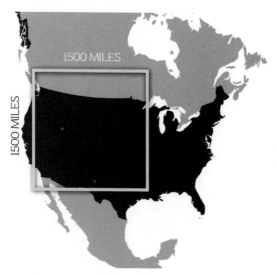

Later in Revelation 21:15-16, John also gets a chance to document the size of this city when an angel pulls out a measuring rod and measures it in front of him. When I tell you that this city will make New York City, Paris, London, and Tokyo combined look like the four great suburbs of Minot, North Dakota, it is not an understatement.

We can't even imagine a city of such size. If it was stacked atop the United States, it would cover over 60 percent of the entire United States.[iii]

> THE ONE WHO SPOKE WITH ME HAD A GOLD MEASURING ROD TO MEASURE THE CITY, AND ITS GATES AND ITS WALL. THE CITY IS LAID OUT AS A SQUARE, AND ITS LENGTH IS GREAT AS THE WIDTH; AND HE MEASURED THE CITY WITH THE ROD, FIFTEEN HUNDRED MILES; ITS LENGTH AND WIDTH AND HEIGHT ARE EQUAL.
> - REVELATION 21:15-16

But that's not the whole story.

Read closely: Revelation 21:16 says that the city's "length and width *AND HEIGHT* are equal." There is nothing remotely like this on our planet. The earth isn't an exact sphere, so it varies a bit, but, generally, if you started digging at the North Pole and kept digging, you'd hit the South Pole after 7,900 miles.

The New Jerusalem will be 1,500 miles high—just about 20 percent of the width of the entire planet. The highest thing on earth is Mount Everest and that's only 5.5 miles high! New York City, arguably the greatest city we've ever seen, would be the equivalent of a one stop-sign town—not even worth a blinking light.

What about nature? Well, if you took off in a plane and flew straight up, over the clouds, do you know how high you'd be? At an extreme, you'd be about 7 miles high. Imagine the nature in a space 1,500 miles high covering 60 percent of the United States. I can't wait to ski there in the morning and hit the beach at night.

Remember, this place will exist without any of the negatives of any city we know. The culture, food, and art generated from a city this great has to dwarf anything we can even imagine today. Take any of the hassles of such a place (reservations, traffic, petty jealousy), and the possibilities are endless. This will be a city of a size

---

iii I've shown the New Jerusalem over the United States here to give the reader an idea of scale. There is nothing to support that the New Jerusalem will actually be in this location and plenty to support that it will be placed in the location of the modern-day Jerusalem. These images are only rendered to convey scale.

> THEN HE SAID TO ME, "IT IS DONE. I AM THE ALPHA AND THE OMEGA, THE BEGINNING AND THE END. I WILL GIVE TO THE ONE WHO THIRSTS FROM THE SPRING OF THE WATER OF LIFE WITHOUT COST. HE WHO OVERCOMES WILL INHERIT THESE THINGS, AND I WILL BE HIS GOD AND HE WILL BE MY SON.
>
> ...
>
> I SAW NO TEMPLE IN IT, FOR THE LORD GOD THE ALMIGHTY AND THE LAMB ARE ITS TEMPLE. AND THE CITY HAS NO NEED OF THE SUN OR OF THE MOON TO SHINE ON IT, FOR THE GLORY OF GOD HAS ILLUMINED IT, AND ITS LAMP IS THE LAMB. THE NATIONS WILL WALK BY ITS LIGHT, AND THE KINGS OF THE EARTH WILL BRING THEIR GLORY INTO IT. IN THE DAYTIME (FOR THERE WILL BE NO NIGHT THERE) ITS GATES WILL NEVER BE CLOSED; AND THEY WILL BRING THE GLORY AND THE HONOR OF THE NATIONS INTO IT...
>
> - REVELATION 21:6-7, 22-26

and scale and talent that we couldn't even imagine—and with room for full-fledged nature.

In Revelation 21, excerpted here, I see two more parts to this perfection. First, consider that joy is (another) currency of heaven. Here on earth, we need a certain amount of joy to live well, but, if we're quiet and honest long enough, we'll admit that even the best of us are barely getting by. We mimic greatness on earth in everything from automobiles to hotels to cinema, but even excellent examples of these are still missing something. The difference between the joy we currently experience and the most joy we could possibly stand is miles wide.

Those who have experienced Jesus know there is a deeper longing for something that we have yet to taste. All men seek it earnestly, but are willing to settle for something that only resembles it. The satisfaction is flimsy and fleeting from the substitutes. They take many forms, such as drugs, fame, or luxury. We can even pursue fulfillment through work, companionship, or immersing ourselves into our children's lives.

Heaven spans that gap in us. It takes the shortfall and covers an exponential multiple of the difference. The catalyst, the difference, is the presence of God in heaven. God will literally illuminate the city there. No power bills, no light bulbs—God will light the city. His closeness will bring, finally, the greatest joy we can experience.

Second, if you consider that moment-to-moment joy your nut, as in the amount of currency you crave to live a full life, then there is one other problem—debt. In the thousands of years that man has just been getting by, parsing out joy in small amounts, we have racked up a significant amount of debt. It is common to look at sin

> AND HE WILL WIPE AWAY EVERY TEAR FROM THEIR EYES; AND THERE WILL NO LONGER BE ANY DEATH; THERE WILL NO LONGER BE ANY MOURNING, OR CRYING, OR PAIN; THE FIRST THINGS HAVE PASSED AWAY. AND HE WHO SITS ON THE THRONE SAID, "BEHOLD, I AM MAKING ALL THINGS NEW."
>
> - REVELATION 21:4-5

as debt, and I think that's a part of this, but let's also include all forms of tragedy, unhappiness, and loss. Bad things that happen to good people, crimes against children, loss of any kind all add to this increasing debt. If we're going to spend countless units of joy day after day in heaven, then this debt must be satisfied, too.

In heaven, along with ultimate joy, God will make all the wrong things right. Things that shred us now, whether we caused them or were complicit or played no role at all, will all be made right and turned for God's great glory. Again, Plantinga, quoted by Keller:

> Cornelius Plantinga says in his book "Engaging God's World" that the second coming is good news for people whose lives are filled with bad news. If you are a slave in Pharaoh's Egypt or in the southern United States in the early nineteenth century, or if you are an Israelite exiled in Babylon, or a Kosovar exiled in Albania, if you are a woman in a culture where when your husband is mad at you he can lock you in a closet or call up his buddies and threaten to have

> THEREFORE YOU TOO HAVE GRIEF NOW; BUT I WILL SEE YOU AGAIN, AND YOUR HEART WILL REJOICE, AND NO ONE WILL TAKE YOUR JOY AWAY FROM YOU.
>
> - JOHN 16:22

them rape you, if you are a Christian in sub-Saharan Africa today where AIDS is devastating whole populations, you don't yawn when someone mentions the return of Jesus. The coming of the kingdom depends on the coming of the King, and the coming of the King means justice will at last fill the earth.[3]

If there is something that you hate in the world, the coming of the King Who ushers in a new heaven and a new earth will turn that shame into glory.

Heaven is for Real is a compelling book about a child who comes back from a healthcare emergency with scripturally-correct explanations for what he saw in heaven. In it, Colton Burpo says that, in heaven, "Jesus has markers." There's a cute discussion that follows, but it becomes clear that this four-year-old is talking about and identifies the locations of the wounds in Jesus' hands and feet. Colton's dad is a minister, but he's adamant that their Sunday school curriculum doesn't include a discussion of nails into the hands and feet of Jesus. That's why Colton didn't recognize these as wounds, but markers. For me, this account reinforced my certainty that our shame on earth will become our glory in heaven.

Another example of this can be found near the end of C. S. Lewis' *The Great Divorce*. Certainly fiction, it's a great account of some issues dealing with heaven. The book starts out in hell as ghosts (men and women who have died) board a bus headed to a waiting room (of sorts) in heaven. A series of characters are met there by folks from their past to plead with them to make the trip into heaven. It's a succession of failures—each one clinging to something that is totally insignificant. (It cut me as I realized I'd held on to something just like that.)

The story depicts three or four ghosts, until we meet one with a red lizard on his shoulder. Unlike the rest of the ghosts, this one is met by an angel, literally on fire, and called the Burning One. The angel offers to kill this lizard (in this story, representing lust) if the ghost gives him permission. Disturbingly, the ghost prefers to just manage the lizard better. Not surprisingly, the lizard agrees that's a better course, saying, "...I'll be so good. I admit I've sometimes gone too far in the past, but I promise I won't do it again. I'll give you nothing but really nice dreams…"

The angel and the ghost go back and forth, and the conversation is agonizing until the ghost finally concedes and allows the angel to kill the lizard.

"God help me," the ghost whimpers, "God help me," as the angel chokes the lizard.

Then, the ghost who had been so wispy and insignificant under the yoke of lust just moments before, begins to change.

For a moment I could make out nothing distinctly. Then I saw, between me and the nearest bush, unmistakably solid but growing every moment solider, the upper arm and the shoulder of a man. Then, brighter still and stronger, the legs and hands. The neck and golden head materialized while I watched, and if my attention had not wavered I should have seen the actual completing of a man—an immense man, naked, not much smaller than the Angel. What distracted me was the fact that at the same moment something seemed to be happening to the Lizard. At first I thought the operation had failed. So far from dying, the creature was still struggling and even growing bigger as it struggled. And as it grew it changed. Its hinder parts grew rounder. The tail, still flickering, became a tail of hair that flickered between huge and glossy buttocks. Suddenly I started back, rubbing my eyes. What stood before me was the greatest stallion I have ever seen, silvery white but with mane and tail of gold. It was smooth and shining, rippled with swells of flesh and muscle, whinnying and stamping with its hoofs. At each stamp the land shook and the trees dwindled. The new-made man turned and clapped the new horse's neck. It nosed his bright body. Horse and master breathed each into the other's nostrils. The man turned from it, flung himself at the feet of the Burning One, and embraced them. When he rose I thought his face shone with tears, but it may have been only the liquid love and brightness (one cannot distinguish them in that country) which flowed from him. I had not long to think about it. In joyous haste the young man leaped upon the horse's back. Turning in his seat he waved a farewell, then nudged the stallion with his heels. They were off before I well knew what was

*happening. There was riding if you like! I came out as quickly as
I could from among the bushes to follow them with my eyes; but
already they were only like a shooting star far off on the green
plain, and soon among the foothills of the mountains. Then, still
like a star, I saw them winding up, scaling what seemed impossible steeps, and quicker every moment, till near the dim brow
of the landscape, so high that I must strain my neck to see them,
they vanished, bright themselves, into the rose-brightness of that
everlasting morning on into heaven...*

In heaven, the worst things that happen to the least of us will be
made right, and our tears will be wiped away. I'm sure I haven't
even scratched the surface of heaven, but how great does that place
sound? How would you like to luxuriate in the fullness of that kind
of perfection? How great is it to know that every need will be met
and every wrong will be made right?

What does this tell us about God?

God, the triune God, created man out of community and in
Love for one purpose: to increase love through worship, honor,
and praise. From a human perspective, this seems selfish, but do
we call parents selfish for bringing a child into the world? No. It is
at incalculable cost that parents bring a child into the world, but
they do it, at their best, in a spirit of seeking to increase their love
by sharing it.

God knew that man's highest calling was to enter into His
home (heaven), to get into the rhythm of heaven and to be a fully
functioning member (with meaningful work) there. That's why
C.S. Lewis described the Trinity as a "cosmic dance,"[4] and Dante
penned heaven a flurry of movement and song around a point "enclosed by a circle whose motion is so rapid because of burning love
which spurs it on."[5]

This visual of heaven being a cosmic dance—with God, Jesus,
and the Holy Spirit at the center, and all the heavenly host and the
chosen orbiting around them—is a glance of what we can expect
and prepare to enter.

In any dance, to be really great, there are three things that one
must master: **Step, Beat,** and **Tune**.

You must know the step, feel the beat, and breathe the tune. If you've only got the step and the tune down, you'll never make it out of high school drama class. Pick up the beat, but lose the tune, and you're back to touring in a regional company.

To make the Great Dance, you must have a real relationship with all three. We can see hints of that on earth. In heaven:

The Step is Service. This is not the service that you want to provide, but the service the recipient requires. I am willing to feed a man, but he needs my time, too, and that might be too much. Real, sacrificial service is the step of the Kingdom of God. We discuss this in greater detail in *Chapter 7*.

> FOR EVEN THE SON OF MAN DID NOT COME TO BE SERVED, BUT TO SERVE, AND TO GIVE HIS LIFE A RANSOM FOR MANY.
>
> - MARK 10:45
>
> AND HE SAID TO THEM, "THE KINGS OF THE GENTILES LORD IT OVER THEM; AND THOSE WHO HAVE AUTHORITY OVER THEM ARE CALLED 'BENEFACTORS.' BUT IT IS NOT THIS WAY WITH YOU, BUT THE ONE WHO IS THE GREATEST AMONG YOU MUST BECOME LIKE THE YOUNGEST, AND THE LEADER LIKE THE SERVANT. FOR WHO IS GREATER, THE ONE WHO RECLINES AT THE TABLE OR THE ONE WHO SERVES? IS IT NOT THE ONE WHO RECLINES AT THE TABLE? BUT I AM AMONG YOU AS THE ONE WHO SERVES.
>
> - LUKE 22:25-27

The Beat is Love. Try dancing without a beat. Without Love, you can't join the Great Dance, and the Bible, the whole canon of Scripture affirms this. Love is the center of the Shema (Deuteronomy 6:4–9, 11:13-21, and Numbers 15:37–41) and love is the very essence of God. Without love, we are noisy, bankrupt, wisps of smoke. We discuss this in greater detail later in *Chapter 8*.

> IF I SPEAK WITH THE TONGUES OF MEN AND OF ANGELS, BUT DO NOT HAVE LOVE, I HAVE BECOME A NOISY GONG OR A CLANGING CYMBAL. IF I HAVE THE GIFT OF PROPHECY, AND KNOW ALL MYSTERIES AND ALL KNOWLEDGE; AND IF I HAVE ALL FAITH, SO AS TO REMOVE MOUNTAINS, BUT DO NOT HAVE LOVE, I AM NOTHING. AND IF I GIVE ALL MY POSSESSIONS TO FEED THE POOR, AND IF I SURRENDER MY BODY TO BE BURNED, BUT DO NOT HAVE LOVE, IT PROFITS ME NOTHING.... LOVE NEVER FAILS... AND NOW THESE THREE REMAIN: FAITH, HOPE AND LOVE. BUT THE GREATEST OF THESE IS LOVE.
>
> - 1 CORINTHIANS 13:1-3, 8A, 13
>
> ABOVE ALL, KEEP FERVENT IN YOUR LOVE FOR ONE ANOTHER, BECAUSE LOVE COVERS A MULTITUDE OF SINS.
>
> - 1 PETER 4:8

The Tune is Belief. We're besieged by a culture of individualism telling us that we're all to follow our hearts and find our own truth. Jesus brings us a different message. It's not just important that you believe, but what you believe and how you believe are also critical. We'll address this more in *Chapter 9*. Belief is as important to entering the Kingdom as the tune is to a dance.

> THE TIME IS FULFILLED, AND THE KINGDOM OF GOD IS AT HAND; REPENT AND BELIEVE IN THE GOSPEL.
>
> - MARK 1:15
>
> DO NOT BE AFRAID ANY LONGER, ONLY BELIEVE.
>
> - MARK 5:36B
>
> AS MOSES LIFTED UP THE SERPENT IN THE WILDERNESS, EVEN SO MUST THE SON OF MAN BE LIFTED UP; SO THAT WHOEVER BELIEVES WILL IN HIM HAVE ETERNAL LIFE. "FOR GOD SO LOVED THE WORLD, THAT HE GAVE HIS ONLY BEGOTTEN SON, THAT WHOEVER BELIEVES IN HIM SHALL NOT PERISH, BUT HAVE ETERNAL LIFE.
>
> - JOHN 3:14-16

So within this center of the Great Dance, in community and out of love, God—no more One than Three nor Three than One—designed and built this world with an incredible amount of precision and excellence. For God to have built a thing so alive, real, and magnificent for every human, I'm convinced that there is something each and every one of us must do here, while we still can. There is something we must learn, something we must understand, or some skill we must develop.

WHAT DOES THAT MEAN FOR US TODAY?

The skill we must attain and the knowledge we must develop is a correct view of the Great Dance. In consistent steps of service to the other, beating to the rhythm of love and moving in the belief in Jesus, heaven pulsates with life—1, 2, 3—1, 2, 3—1, 2, 3. Heaven heaves and gasps in a great rhythm of constant movement, loving service, meaningful work, and worship.

> MY PRAYER IS NOT FOR [THE DISCIPLES] ALONE. I PRAY ALSO FOR THOSE WHO WILL BELIEVE IN ME THROUGH THEIR MESSAGE, THAT ALL OF THEM MAY BE ONE, FATHER, JUST AS YOU ARE IN ME AND I AM IN YOU. MAY THEY ALSO BE IN US SO THAT THE WORLD MAY BELIEVE THAT YOU HAVE SENT ME.
> - JOHN 17:20-21

For God to have built so much excellence into this world, and to have paid so dearly for it, I believe we are to use our time here to practice these key parts of heaven, because there, our ability to learn these pieces is diminished.

Why practice sacrificial service? We've talked about the perfection in heaven that will provide for your every need, but won't my needs be met, too? If our needs are provisioned, then won't everyone have their needs met? In heaven, there will no longer be any in need of our service, yet we will nevertheless happily serve.

This is a tough concept to understand, but Dickens does a pretty good job in *A Christmas Carol*. In the following scene, Marley, Scrooge's deceased business partner, has just left Scrooge through the bedroom window:

Scrooge followed to the window: desperate in his curiosity. He looked out. The air was filled with phantoms, wandering hither and thither in restless haste, and moaning as they went. Every one of them wore chains like Marley's Ghost; some few (they might be guilty governments) were linked together; none were free. Many had been personally known to Scrooge in their lives. He had been quite familiar with one old ghost, in a white waistcoat, with a monstrous iron safe attached to its ankle, who cried piteously at being unable to assist a wretched woman with an infant, whom it saw below, upon a door-step. The misery with them all was, clearly, that they sought to interfere, for good, in human matters, and had lost the power for ever.[6]

To join the Great Dance, you must really know the step, and that comes from service to others for God, honoring and glorifying Him. That leads to a great need in our souls: meaningful work in heaven. But it's not all technique. There's heart, too.

Why practice love? This one is the most important. If you had to choose one of the three to lean into, to really practice, it would be this one. We know that God is love and that His every motivation is with all knowledge to increase love. We'll talk a lot more about this as we go along. That said, I'll give these two reasons now:

> IF I SPEAK WITH THE TONGUES OF MEN AND OF ANGELS, BUT DO NOT HAVE LOVE, I HAVE BECOME A NOISY GONG OR A CLANGING CYMBAL. IF I HAVE THE GIFT OF PROPHECY, AND KNOW ALL MYSTERIES AND ALL KNOWLEDGE; AND IF I HAVE ALL FAITH, SO AS TO REMOVE MOUNTAINS, BUT DO NOT HAVE LOVE, I AM NOTHING. AND IF I GIVE ALL MY POSSESSIONS TO FEED THE POOR, AND IF I SURRENDER MY BODY TO BE BURNED, BUT DO NOT HAVE LOVE, IT PROFITS ME NOTHING.
>
> - 1 CORINTHIANS 13:1-3

If you want to begin a relationship with someone—not even a God/worshiper relationship, but merely a friendly one—then it has to be built on something you have in common with that person. It might be hard to develop a relationship with Mario Andretti based on your love of floral arrangements, or with Bill Clinton based on your love of entomology. They may be indifferent or willing to try to care about those things, but in the end, it is not their passion or the drive of their life.

To establish a relationship with someone, you have to have access, mutual interest, and commonality. For that relationship to grow into a deep one, that commonality would need to be a central and core value or interest for both parties. If God is love, then to strengthen a relationship with Him, I must be seeking a greater role for love in my life.

I start a lot of fires in our fireplace over the winter. I've gotten pretty good at it and know there is a tipping point: those few minutes when your fire goes from vulnerable and potentially extinguishable—when everything's still a little cool and nothing has really caught fire yet—to the point where it is unquenchable. In the beginning, a strong breeze, a glass of water, or just leaving it alone might squelch the fire. But after the tipping point, there is virtually no way to stop it cleanly. Even turning the hose on it would leave some hot embers. The fire is unquenchable.

Our love is like that in heaven. I can't tell you much more than this, but I believe that passing over into heaven with a small amount of love is extremely precarious. It's not that something there will extinguish it, but all the other things we carry with us—hatred, jealousy, greed, worry—are like buckets of water that we're pulling along and at any moment could slosh over and extinguish our love.

Lastly, there's a head part of the Great Dance. **Why practice belief?**

Well, because Jesus said to. All parts of the Bible are littered with scripture on the importance of belief. Abraham believed God, and it was credited to him as righteousness.

Just like a dancer who is technically perfect and owns the beat, but cannot really feel the

> FOR WHAT DOES THE SCRIPTURE SAY? "ABRAHAM BELIEVED GOD, AND IT WAS CREDITED TO HIM AS RIGHTEOUSNESS." NOW TO THE ONE WHO WORKS, HIS WAGE IS NOT CREDITED AS A FAVOR, BUT AS WHAT IS DUE. BUT TO THE ONE WHO DOES NOT WORK, BUT BELIEVES IN HIM WHO JUSTIFIES THE UNGODLY, HIS FAITH IS CREDITED AS RIGHTEOUSNESS.
>
> - ROMANS 4:3-5

music deep in her heart, we have seen how insufficient those are who serve earnestly and love honestly, but do not believe. In the

> THEREFORE EVERYONE WHO CONFESSES ME BEFORE MEN, I WILL ALSO CONFESS HIM BEFORE MY FATHER WHO IS IN HEAVEN. BUT WHOEVER DENIES ME BEFORE MEN, I WILL ALSO DENY HIM BEFORE MY FATHER WHO IS IN HEAVEN.
>
> - MATTHEW 10:32-33

end, without belief in the sacrifice and resurrection of Jesus, service and love just can't bridge the gap. The service becomes onerous and efficient and the love feeds on itself for fuel, like a mansion that's slowly dismantled, piece by piece, to be burned in the fireplace for heat. As we'll see, fundamental belief in Jesus is the only way to fuel service and love without cannibalizing each.

In heaven, we will no longer have the opportunity to believe. Most Disney movies in the last 20 years, tell the story of someone who is placed in a land where they're not fully known. The entire movie hinges on a set of characters, some good and some bad, who do not know the true worth of this one character. In the end, the true worth of the one is known, and everything is set right. Those that disregarded or mistreated the one are punished or ostracized, and those that loved the one in spite of the circumstances get to live in the castle or are welcomed into the inner circle.

> JESUS SAID TO HIM, "BECAUSE YOU HAVE SEEN ME, HAVE YOU BELIEVED? BLESSED ARE THEY WHO DID NOT SEE, AND YET BELIEVED."
>
> - JOHN 20:29

That story—in fact, every piece of credible literature over the last few thousand years—is the Gospel story. We are living within it; but soon, the full worth of the One will be revealed, and there will no longer be an opportunity to express belief.

I understand that, for some of you, there are significant barriers to belief. We'll address some of those throughout this book, but some of them sit right here, "In the beginning..."

If science doesn't accost your belief, then feel free to skip ahead a few pages to the paragraph that starts with, "So if this..." But if it does, consider the following:

In earlier drafts of this book, I had several chapters on evolution and barely scratched the surface. If this is an impediment to your faith, know that there are countless resources for researching this subject yourself—it's too big a decision to just hitch your wagon to someone else's opinion. But for now, I'll provide two of the most compelling pieces of information that I found.

> BUT WHOEVER CAUSES ONE OF THESE LITTLE ONES WHO BELIEVE IN ME TO STUMBLE, IT WOULD BE BETTER FOR HIM TO HAVE A HEAVY MILLSTONE HUNG AROUND HIS NECK, AND TO BE DROWNED IN THE DEPTH OF THE SEA.
> - MATTHEW 18:6

All credible science now agrees that the universe had a **point of beginning**. Stephen Hawking (no friend to the biblical Creation account) said, "All the evidence seems to indicate that the universe has not existed forever, but that it had a beginning, about 15 billion years ago. This is probably the most remarkable discovery of modern cosmology. Yet it is now taken for granted."[7]

To concede an event of Creation, but still deny a Creator, takes an extreme amount of mental gymnastics. We know of hundreds of variables that, if altered in even the smallest amount, would make the universe unstable and collapse upon itself. For instance, the ratio of electrons to protons, which is extremely important to our survival, can only deviate a little—and I mean VERY little. For every 10 to the 37th power, meaning for every 10 with 37 zeros behind it, you can vary ONE of them and still exist. If you vary two, the universe rips apart.

Consider this great example from Dr. Hugh Ross, an astrophysicist and apologist, on how small one for every 10 to the 37th power is:

Cover the entire North American continent in dimes all the way up to the moon, a height of about 239,000 miles. (In comparison, the money to pay for the U.S. federal government debt would cover one square mile less than two feet deep with dimes.) Next, pile dimes from here to the moon on a billion other continents the same size as North America. Paint one dime red and mix it into the billions of piles of dimes. Blindfold a friend and ask him to pick out one dime. The odds that he will pick the red dime are 1 in 10 to the 37th power. [8]

Or consider the genetic code. We are still unraveling the genetic code of man but, for the first cell of man to have been created out of nothing would be similar odds of hitting the cherry on a three-billion-reel slot machine with 22 pictures on each reel. If 10 to the 37th power seems like long odds, try one in 22 to the three billionth power.

Consider these two quotes:

"To suppose that the first cell originated by chance is like believing that a tornado could sweep through a junkyard filled with airline parts and form a Boeing 747." [9]

"To suppose that the eye with its ability to adjust its focus, admit different amounts of light, and correct for chromatic aberrations, could have been formed by natural selection seems, I freely confess, absurd in the highest degree." [10]

Someone with a different academic degree than mine could refute these facts, and yet another could rebut that, but the fact is that science has an extremely bad track record. New discoveries disprove old discoveries, but society never fails to believe that it—whether in the first, twelfth or twenty-first century—has finally grasped truth by the throat.

> HE IS LIKE A MAN BUILDING A HOUSE, WHO DUG DEEP AND LAID A FOUNDATION ON THE ROCK; AND WHEN A FLOOD OCCURRED, THE TORRENT BURST AGAINST THAT HOUSE AND COULD NOT SHAKE IT, BECAUSE IT HAD BEEN WELL BUILT.
>
> LIKE A MAN WHO BUILT A HOUSE ON THE GROUND WITHOUT ANY FOUNDATION; AND THE TORRENT BURST AGAINST IT AND IMMEDIATELY IT COLLAPSED, AND THE RUIN OF THAT HOUSE WAS GREAT.
>
> - LUKE 6:48, 49B

So if this or additional research brings you to a point of realizing that what has been presented as fact may not actually be the full story—that, at best, we're playing with 10 or 100 of what must be a million facts—then I ask you: What would you like to be true? Is there any benefit to leaning into science if its foundations seem shaky? Or, standing in heaven, in the presence of God, angels trumpeting, which of these would you want to say?

a) Oh, really? I'm sorry. I didn't know. I thought every word in the Bible was true.

or

b) Oh, really? You mean it was entirely true, after all? Really? Even Jonah and the whale? Yes, I'm afraid that I did tell some folks not to bother with that part.

Everything that we've talked about up to this point has enormous implications on our lives. If it is true—if a triune God created us from a community of Three, born of labor (read service in Genesis 1 and 2) and out of love for Another, and that the focus of our lives is relationships—then the practice we get here (through imperfect relationships in a broken world) is practice for the perfected relationships we will have in heaven.

Are you thirsty, yet? Did an understanding of the greatness of heaven, the excellence of God's plan, and His Love for you awaken something inside of you to make you hunger and thirst for the righteousness that heaven will bring? Well, there's more.

The realization of this prize, along with the price paid for it, has driven me into a life that is absolutely fearless. It has given me a perspective on pain and suffering that is a comfort to me and those around me. I'm still growing into this (and lose it at times when I focus on myself), but this faith in the greatness of heaven, and that one day all things will be made right, has moved mountains in my life and is allowing me to move mountains on this earth.

> REJOICE ALWAYS; PRAY WITHOUT CEASING; IN EVERYTHING GIVE THANKS; FOR THIS IS GOD'S WILL FOR YOU IN CHRIST JESUS.
> - 1 THESSALONIANS 6:16-18

I have begun to see and experience pieces of heaven on this earth that push me on, like a boy eying the bike he's earnestly saving to purchase. If I am successful in guarding and stoking this flame, this fledgling thirst for heaven, then one day, that for which I long will be mine. And it will be even greater than I can imagine.

Each of us has a thing (or things) to which we look for our security or significance. I call it your Fundamental, and what each of us selects as our Fundamental is of extreme importance. Choose something great, that can never be taken away and will fill you, and you're like a man who builds his foundation on a rock. But choose poorly, or choose something that can be taken away or that is too superficial to actually fill you, and the risk is enormous.

Know that in heaven rests a Fundamental so big it will wholly fill us, and it is so fine that it cannot disappoint, and is guaranteed that it will never go away. By orienting my days and time toward heaven, I have literally ushered pieces of it into my life here—today.

Lastly, if you are fortunate enough to live in those extremely rare times and even more rare places (or homes) where your life isn't dominated by bad news, then cultivating a thirst for heaven gives us a chance to be compassionate. In fact, to be a Christian demands this type of compassion.

Do you merely accept God's commission, or are you excited to fulfill it? Do you regard the Kingdom of God to come as basically good, or do you thirst and yearn for it? If you don't thirst for it for yourself, compassion requires us to thirst for it for our neighbors.

A greater view of the coming heaven has pushed me toward a higher joy than I've ever known. At my best, I'm freed to serve others, knowing there is greatness and rest coming. It inspires me to move away from my worst self, where I sought new and creative ways to get others to serve me. It has given me a view of relationships that is no longer consumer-based: I can serve others, even when they are not meeting my needs at an acceptable cost to me.

It has given me the energy to carry on, when I'm tired or run down or at the end of my rope. You would think that knowing that this world is a shadow of what's to come would make me value it less, but instead of eating hamburger and trying to imagine that it is steak, I'm now actually enjoying the burger. In shooting for heaven, the world has been thrown in for free. But shoot for the world, and you'll miss both as you focus on yourself.

There is a blessing beyond belief in knowing that I will spend all eternity in a place that will truly satisfy. It has made the troubles of today light and momentary. With this step of service, beat of love, and tune of belief, I'm given the opportunity, even within the fall, wherever I am, to be an example of Jesus Christ. In Him, I can

> FOR MOMENTARY, LIGHT AFFLICTION IS PRODUCING FOR US AN ETERNAL WEIGHT OF GLORY FAR BEYOND ALL COMPARISON, WHILE WE LOOK NOT AT THE THINGS WHICH ARE SEEN, BUT AT THE THINGS WHICH ARE NOT SEEN; FOR THE THINGS WHICH ARE SEEN ARE TEMPORAL, BUT THE THINGS WHICH ARE NOT SEEN ARE ETERNAL.
> - 2 CORINTHIANS 4:17-18

live the life of service and love through belief in the One who has always existed, but in our Gospel story, is still to come. Cover all of this in worship of God, prayers of repentance, and a spirit of thanksgiving, and we begin to bring heaven into focus, here on earth. Today.

Get a picture of heaven because, when you make *that* blessed hope the frame of all your experience on earth, then even the worst of our current circumstances can be joyful.

Before you go on to the next chapter, take a few moments to read one or more of the following:
Matthew Chapters 3 & 4
Mark Chapters 2 & 3
Luke Chapter 3 through 4:13
John Chapter 2 through 3:21

CHAPTER 3

The Fall

Things work out great for a while. But in time, Adam brings sin into the world, and there is a definitive break. While God remains in this loving relationship that brought man about, man sometimes walks, and sometimes edges and sometime runs from God. For thousands of years, each sin layers on the next and pushes man further and further away from God.

After Creation, Adam and Eve lived in Eden's perfection—essentially heaven on earth. Genesis 2 ends with the creation of Eve and, without any time stamp at all, the next chapter details man's fall.

In the course of five verses, we've covered the facts of the second most important event in the history of humanity: the Fall. Without the Fall, there would be no Gospel, no need for redeeming love, no account to settle. **THIS EVENT, OUR PARTICIPATION IN IT**, and **ITS EFFECTS** are some of the hardest things to reconcile in the Gospel, so we'll look at each of them in that order.

THIS EVENT

The Fall was the end of the beginning. It represented such a pe-

> NOW THE SERPENT WAS MORE CRAFTY THAN ANY BEAST OF THE FIELD WHICH THE LORD GOD HAD MADE. AND HE SAID TO THE WOMAN, "INDEED, HAS GOD SAID, 'YOU SHALL NOT EAT FROM ANY TREE OF THE GARDEN'?" THE WOMAN SAID TO THE SERPENT, "FROM THE FRUIT OF THE TREES OF THE GARDEN WE MAY EAT; BUT FROM THE FRUIT OF THE TREE WHICH IS IN THE MIDDLE OF THE GARDEN, GOD HAS SAID, 'YOU SHALL NOT EAT FROM IT OR TOUCH IT, OR YOU WILL DIE.'" THE SERPENT SAID TO THE WOMAN, "YOU SURELY WILL NOT DIE! FOR GOD KNOWS THAT IN THE DAY YOU EAT FROM IT YOUR EYES WILL BE OPENED, AND YOU WILL BE LIKE GOD, KNOWING GOOD AND EVIL." WHEN THE WOMAN SAW THAT THE TREE WAS GOOD FOR FOOD, AND THAT IT WAS A DELIGHT TO THE EYES, AND THAT THE TREE WAS DESIRABLE TO MAKE ONE WISE, SHE TOOK FROM ITS FRUIT AND ATE; AND SHE GAVE ALSO TO HER HUSBAND WITH HER, AND HE ATE. THEN THE EYES OF BOTH OF THEM WERE OPENED, AND THEY KNEW THAT THEY WERE NAKED; AND THEY SEWED FIG LEAVES TOGETHER AND MADE THEMSELVES LOIN COVERINGS.
>
> - GENESIS 3:3-7

riod of great destruction and separation that we can hardly fathom it. For thousands of years, all mankind has been affected.

The idea of original sin—one action—that would change the course of all time for all men is an idea that is too big to even contemplate. To get close, we need to understand three things:

First, take into account the **context of the universe** at that point.

According to the Heritage Foundation, in 2007 the federal government had "at least 4,450 crimes"[11] that you could commit. Total city, county, state, and other jurisdictional laws, and you would easily triple that number to an estimated 12,000 infractions. We're accustomed to living under rules. The Hebrew Torah, which God gave man, was 613 laws, but to whom did God give the Law? Moses, and he wouldn't appear on the stage of history for thousands of years.

Adam had one rule given to him in Genesis 2:16-17. He had been given everything: meaningful work, sustenance, companionship in Eve, and fellowship with God.

You know that feeling we all have in our hearts? That we're missing something or not living up to our true potential or are somehow inauthentic? It's a gnawing, low-level fear that we really don't matter. Adam didn't

> THE LORD GOD COMMANDED THE MAN, SAYING, "FROM ANY TREE OF THE GARDEN YOU MAY EAT FREELY; BUT FROM THE TREE OF THE KNOWLEDGE OF GOOD AND EVIL YOU SHALL NOT EAT, FOR IN THE DAY THAT YOU EAT FROM IT YOU WILL SURELY DIE."
> - GENESIS 2:16-17

have that. He never had that. He never once knew that feeling before the Fall. He was a part of the community with a great triune God and that filled him. Adam had all kinds of great things in front of him, and yet he was willing to undo it all for a bite of fruit. I'm doubtful that Adam could have known the full consequences of his actions but, even if he did, Adam and I are cut from the same cloth.

How long did it take Adam to eat the fruit? I've mentioned this at the open of this section, but while there is a significant recording of time throughout Genesis—days and years are meticulously cataloged—it is curious to me that there is no mention of a timeframe between the creation of man and the Fall. We go straight from the creation of Eve and into the snake's craftiness in the garden. Genesis 5 gives us some clues, but it appears that Adam (fully grown

> THIS IS THE BOOK OF THE GENERATIONS OF ADAM. IN THE DAY WHEN GOD CREATED MAN, HE MADE HIM IN THE LIKENESS OF GOD. HE CREATED THEM MALE AND FEMALE, AND HE BLESSED THEM AND NAMED THEM MAN IN THE DAY WHEN THEY WERE CREATED. WHEN ADAM HAD LIVED ONE HUNDRED AND THIRTY YEARS, HE BECAME THE FATHER OF A SON IN HIS OWN LIKENESS, ACCORDING TO HIS IMAGE, AND NAMED HIM SETH. THEN THE DAYS OF ADAM AFTER HE BECAME THE FATHER OF SETH WERE EIGHT HUNDRED YEARS, AND HE HAD OTHER SONS AND DAUGHTERS. SO ALL THE DAYS THAT ADAM LIVED WERE NINE HUNDRED AND THIRTY YEARS, AND HE DIED.
> - GENESIS 5:1-5

and with all his mental faculties) was likely an adult in the garden for at least 100 years. And, as we will see in a little bit, without death or deterioration of his body, Adam had tens of thousands of days (at least several lifetimes) to enjoy God's presence, but also to break the one rule that he was not to break.

Adam was a human like you and like me, so I ask you: Would you have eaten the fruit from the one tree that God asked you to leave alone? I'd like to think that I wouldn't; that I could enjoy the days in paradise with my mate and be content with meaningful work and the presence of God, walking with us in the garden. Still, I know that's not how it would have happened. Without death or deterioration to slow me down, I might have lasted another day or 10 days or 10,000 days but, at some point, I would have listened to the half-truths that the serpent spoke, or I would have followed Eve's lead. In a weak six minutes, I would have eaten the fruit.

I know this because I don't live everyday grateful for the gifts I've been given. I often want what God knows I'm not supposed to have. I've been in situations where I was willing to gamble it all away on the hope that I wouldn't get caught, and for what? Temporary pleasure.

Some of you are probably living with consequences of your own six-minute decisions or those of others. Maybe your father made one of those decisions or your grandfather did. Sometimes these choices are small and seemingly insignificant, but sometimes they literally change the course of the world for you or four or 40 or 40,000 others.

Lastly, it matters who Adam was. Adam, designated as the first, made clean in God's image, was the federal head of humanity.[12] As Americans, we really don't like this. Individualism, the idea that each individual must determine his own truth and that institutions (such as the state or family or a church) should not be able to impose its truth on the individual, is so ingrained in Americans that it seems like an ultimate truth. We hold up the separation of church and state alongside the freedom-of-religion doctrines and declare that even the founding fathers believed the individual is responsible for discerning his own truth.

We believe this in the face of significant evidence to the contrary, and Americans are nearly alone in this ideal. No other culture in the world has such a rabid culture of individualism as America. In Europe, Asia, and Africa, there is a deep understanding that the sins of the father diminish the tribe. In America, while we would bristle at that, we can still see its truth. Can a Madoff get a job on Wall Street again? He never had a son, but would Donny Hitler be a welcome candidate for your son's private school? If the world is indeed a series of small towns, we all know that small towns never forget.

If we begrudgingly concede that, as the federal head of humanity, we are part of the Fall through our participation in mankind and nature, then so what?

What is the real **EFFECT OF THE FALL** on our lives?

The effect of the Fall was legion.

But buried inside the punishment that comes as a result of the Fall is a promise. I don't pretend to know the ultimate truth on this, but I can see three things peeking through.

First, in the curse on the serpent, God speaks to Satan through the serpent saying, "And I will put enmity between you and the woman, and between your seed and her seed; he shall bruise you on the head, and you shall bruise him on the heel." Remember, Moses wrote Genesis under God's instruction. In the following chapters, Moses begins to discuss the genealogy of Adam and, in every case, history is always passed

> "Because you have done this, Cursed are you more than all cattle, And more than every beast of the field; On your belly you will go, And dust you will eat All the days of your life; And I will put enmity Between you and the woman, And between your seed and her seed; He shall bruise you on the head, And you shall bruise him on the heel."
>
> To the woman He said, "I will greatly multiply Your pain in childbirth, In pain you will bring forth children; Yet your desire will be for your husband, And he will rule over you."
>
> - Genesis 3:14-16

from father to son. A few wives are mentioned, but names, property, and lines all pass from fathers to sons *THROUGH* women.

Isn't it curious that God would address Satan in a context of woman's seed? What does Scripture say? It says that this seed (of a woman) shall bruise or crush the serpent on the head—a potentially lethal blow to a serpent. Yet it also says that the serpent shall bruise or crush the seed (of a woman) on the heel—a potentially lethal blow to a man from a poisonous serpent.

I believe that this is God speaking to evil, saying that one day—that very day that humanity can bear it—He will send One, tiny as a seed, to earth through a woman who is untouched by any man. That seed will crush evil just as evil tries to crush the seed.

The second is the "thorns and thistles." In a modern world, this seems like a strange thing to bring up. No one likes them, but by and large, we seem to have overcome them, right? Perhaps. Go to New York City, and thorns are likely contained to a few small places in Central Park. But watch a movie about the end of the world, and what literally scales the buildings and brings them down? You got it.

> THEN TO ADAM HE SAID, "BECAUSE YOU HAVE LISTENED TO THE VOICE OF YOUR WIFE, AND HAVE EATEN FROM THE TREE ABOUT WHICH I COMMANDED YOU, SAYING, 'YOU SHALL NOT EAT FROM IT'; CURSED IS THE GROUND BECAUSE OF YOU; IN TOIL YOU WILL EAT OF IT ALL THE DAYS OF YOUR LIFE. "BOTH THORNS AND THISTLES IT SHALL GROW FOR YOU; AND YOU WILL EAT THE PLANTS OF THE FIELD; BY THE SWEAT OF YOUR FACE YOU WILL EAT BREAD, TILL YOU RETURN TO THE GROUND, BECAUSE FROM IT YOU WERE TAKEN; FOR YOU ARE DUST, AND TO DUST YOU SHALL RETURN."
> - GENESIS 3:17-19

With labor and activity, I can keep thorns and thistles out of my yard. But if I stop, if I cease my labor, they will creep back in. Jesus talked about seed planted among thorns, and the thorns (the world) came up and choked out the Word of God from the listeners' grasp.

Where is the next most famous thorn in the Bible? In our story, there comes a day when the thorn will be turned, literally bent,

> OTHER SEED FELL AMONG THE THORNS, AND THE THORNS CAME UP AND CHOKED IT, AND IT YIELDED NO CROP ... AND OTHERS ARE THE ONES ON WHOM SEED WAS SOWN AMONG THE THORNS; THESE ARE THE ONES WHO HAVE HEARD THE WORD, BUT THE WORRIES OF THE WORLD, AND THE DECEITFULNESS OF RICHES, AND THE DESIRES FOR OTHER THINGS ENTER IN AND CHOKE THE WORD, AND IT BECOMES UNFRUITFUL.
> - MATTHEW 4:5, 18-19

> PILATE THEN TOOK JESUS AND SCOURGED HIM. AND THE SOLDIERS TWISTED TOGETHER A CROWN OF THORNS AND PUT IT ON HIS HEAD, AND PUT A PURPLE ROBE ON HIM; AND THEY BEGAN TO COME UP TO HIM AND SAY, "HAIL, KING OF THE JEWS!" AND TO GIVE HIM SLAPS IN THE FACE.
> - JOHN 19:1-3

into a crown. In that day, this unceasing, grasping, unbeatable force of the world will be tamed and turned into His glory. Man's curse, overcome, will become God's glory.

The last blessing, buried in the effects of the Fall, is death itself. Really? How exactly is death, stalking us as we just discussed, a blessing? With the Fall came a change in path. With the Fall, we went from walking in perfection with God to walking away from God. How long can mankind walk away from God? How far can you or I walk away from God? Each and every one of us has cancers within us that are so slow growing that they will never kill us. We would die of 100 other things before one of these cancers became lethal, so they go untreated.

> THE LAST ENEMY THAT WILL BE ABOLISHED IS DEATH.
> - 1 CORINTHIANS 15:26

But what about other things that death keeps from growing too fierce within us? What about anger? Laziness? Hatred? After the Fall, all types of sin came into our lives, into the world, and into our hearts. If death had not come too, and if our time here in a fallen world had not been limited, what kind of a horror could I become, given 10,000 years? How much (un-repented) anger could

> THE NURSING CHILD WILL PLAY BY THE HOLE OF THE COBRA, AND THE WEANED CHILD WILL PUT HIS HAND ON THE VIPER'S DEN.
>
> - ISAIAH 11:8

> AND HE WILL WIPE AWAY EVERY TEAR FROM THEIR EYES; AND THERE WILL NO LONGER BE ANY DEATH; THERE WILL NO LONGER BE ANY MOURNING, OR CRYING, OR PAIN; THE FIRST THINGS HAVE PASSED AWAY.
>
> - REVELATION 21:4

> THERE WILL NO LONGER BE ANY CURSE; AND THE THRONE OF GOD AND OF THE LAMB WILL BE IN IT, AND HIS BOND-SERVANTS WILL SERVE HIM; THEY WILL SEE HIS FACE, AND HIS NAME WILL BE ON THEIR FOREHEADS.
>
> - REVELATION 22:3-4

I hold? How much (remorseless) hate could I bear before I tore myself open in agony, begging for death to save me?

The beautiful thing in all of this is that it is completely beyond man to have established any of this. No one could have ever imagined it. To have Moses compose even the beginning of the book of Genesis and convey truths that are alive today is absolutely inconceivable without a Creator.

My favorite part is that even in the midst of what must have been an incredible betrayal, God's love is already planning a day—That Day—when all will be made right. Each of these curses, problems, issues, dangers, and losses will be undone.

From the Fall, God had a plan to make even this right, and your part in that plan is more important than you can imagine. It was written in at Creation, prepared for this day, and is waiting on your response. Want to know how?

THEREFORE, JUST AS THROUGH ONE MAN SIN ENTERED INTO THE WORLD, AND DEATH THROUGH SIN, AND SO DEATH SPREAD TO ALL MEN, BECAUSE ALL SINNED—FOR UNTIL THE LAW SIN WAS IN THE WORLD, BUT SIN IS NOT IMPUTED WHEN THERE IS NO LAW. NEVERTHELESS DEATH REIGNED FROM ADAM UNTIL MOSES, EVEN OVER THOSE WHO HAD NOT SINNED IN THE LIKENESS OF THE OFFENSE OF ADAM, WHO IS A TYPE OF HIM WHO WAS TO COME. BUT THE FREE GIFT IS NOT LIKE THE TRANSGRESSION. FOR IF BY THE TRANSGRESSION OF THE ONE THE MANY DIED, MUCH MORE DID THE GRACE OF GOD AND THE GIFT BY THE GRACE OF THE ONE MAN, JESUS CHRIST, ABOUND TO THE MANY. THE GIFT IS NOT LIKE THAT WHICH CAME THROUGH THE ONE WHO SINNED; FOR ON THE ONE HAND THE JUDGMENT AROSE FROM ONE TRANSGRESSION RESULTING IN CONDEMNATION, BUT ON THE OTHER HAND THE FREE GIFT AROSE FROM MANY TRANSGRESSIONS RE-SULTING IN JUSTIFICATION. FOR IF BY THE TRANSGRESSION OF THE ONE, DEATH REIGNED THROUGH THE ONE, MUCH MORE THOSE WHO RECEIVE THE ABUNDANCE OF GRACE AND OF THE GIFT OF RIGHTEOUSNESS WILL REIGN IN LIFE THROUGH THE ONE, JESUS CHRIST. SO THEN AS THROUGH ONE TRANSGRESSION THERE RESULTED CONDEMNATION TO ALL MEN, EVEN SO THROUGH ONE ACT OF RIGHTEOUSNESS THERE RESULTED JUSTIFICATION OF LIFE TO ALL MEN. FOR AS THROUGH THE ONE MAN'S DISOBEDIENCE THE MANY WERE MADE SINNERS, EVEN SO THROUGH THE OBEDIENCE OF THE ONE THE MANY WILL BE MADE RIGHTEOUS. THE LAW CAME IN SO THAT THE TRANSGRESSION WOULD INCREASE; BUT WHERE SIN INCREASED, GRACE ABOUNDED ALL THE MORE, SO THAT, AS SIN REIGNED IN DEATH, EVEN SO GRACE WOULD REIGN THROUGH RIGHTEOUSNESS TO ETERNAL LIFE THROUGH JESUS CHRIST OUR LORD.

- ROMANS 5:12-21

Before you go on to the next chapter, take a few moments to read one or more of the following:
Matthew Chapters 5 through 7
Mark Chapter 4
Luke 4:14 through the end of Chapter 5
John 3:22 through the end of Chapter 5

CHAPTER 4

Those Who Can't Not

Immediately after the Fall, in persons number three and four, Cain and Abel, we see the archetypes of two different attitudes we possess today. Abel, who gives his first and finest to God, typifies us at our best, when we just can't NOT be part of this Great Dance. Even when there seems no way to achieve it, we answer the call and know that getting into step is our heart's deepest desire. But then there's Cain who, under no requirement to sacrifice to God, provides one for which God has no regard. At our worst, sometimes out of greed or jealousy or lust or some kind of hardness, we refuse the offer and joy of entering this Great Dance. Whether we choose it or just don't choose anything else, we live there, on the outside of the Great Dance.

Of all the chapters, this one has endured the greatest amount of writing, rewriting, and editing because it is important to me that this Gospel story is a true representation—an accurate portrayal of the Word—and not merely a clever one.

In Cain and Abel, we see the course of an empire and struggle

> FOR THIS IS THE MESSAGE WHICH YOU HAVE HEARD FROM THE BEGINNING, THAT WE SHOULD LOVE ONE ANOTHER; NOT AS CAIN, WHO WAS OF THE EVIL ONE AND SLEW HIS BROTHER. AND FOR WHAT REASON DID HE SLAY HIM? BECAUSE HIS DEEDS WERE EVIL, AND HIS BROTHER'S WERE RIGHTEOUS.
>
> - 1 JOHN 3:11-12

> NOW THE MAN HAD RELATIONS WITH HIS WIFE EVE, AND SHE CONCEIVED AND GAVE BIRTH TO CAIN, AND SHE SAID, "I HAVE GOTTEN A MANCHILD WITH THE HELP OF THE LORD."
>
> - GENESIS 4:1

> BEHOLD, CHILDREN ARE A GIFT OF THE LORD,
> THE FRUIT OF THE WOMB IS A REWARD.
> LIKE ARROWS IN THE HAND OF A WARRIOR,
> SO ARE THE CHILDREN OF ONE'S YOUTH.
> HOW BLESSED IS THE MAN WHOSE QUIVER IS FULL OF THEM;
>
> - PSALM 127:3-5B

and pain and strife. In some ways, their story seems more relevant to us. Sure, we get that it's a shame about Adam and Eve, but quite frankly, we've only known a fallen world and so can only grasp at wisps of what they actually lost. But this—brother versus brother, labor, sweat of the brow, sacrifice, anger, rebuking, murder—is something with which we all can identify. This story is a realization of the Fall.

Genesis 4 tells us that Adam and Eve had Cain after their fall from grace. I think it is interesting that God only gave Adam a child then. We consider children such a miracle and a blessing, and that is certainly reinforced throughout the Bible. Indeed, our children truly are blessings in our lives and a prism through which we can understand our heavenly Father.

But, for anyone in the midst of raising children and honest about the labor of it, the process of having and raising children is a humbling task that will break the back of the proud. Even if you manage to muddle through their formative years, we sow seeds that will literally bring us to our knees.

If you're God, and anything is possible—children could appear when fully grown like Adam and Eve, or they could be sun-baked in bean pods—everything is on the table, here—then there must be some excellence designed into this process. How great is God that even in the blessing of receiving a child, there is growth, hard lessons, and a breaking of self and individualism all baked into a cuddly package that is literally irresistible? Even the most shallow among us would wail at not getting one of these little back-breakers.

> I WILL GREATLY MULTIPLY YOUR PAIN IN CHILDBIRTH, IN PAIN YOU WILL BRING FORTH CHILDREN...
> - GENESIS 3:16A

Here are a few scriptures to investigate and ponder. In Genesis 3:16, read about Eve's punishment. Then, consider Genesis 4:2. Cain comes first and then Abel.

> AGAIN, SHE GAVE BIRTH TO HIS BROTHER ABEL. AND ABEL WAS A KEEPER OF FLOCKS, BUT CAIN WAS A TILLER OF THE GROUND.
> - GENESIS 4:2

Keep going. Genesis 4:3-5a is interesting on a couple of levels. First, why are they providing offerings to the Lord? Why *do* we bring offerings to the Lord?

Under Mosaic Law, Jews gave a tenth to the Levites, the priests of Israel (Leviticus 27:30-33); another tenth to be set aside for a colossal party in Jerusalem or in some other more convenient city that the Lord determined (Deuteronomy 14:22-27); and a third tenth, which was only due every three years, to the widows, orphans, and aliens in the country (Deuteronomy 14:28-29).

> SO IT CAME ABOUT IN THE COURSE OF TIME THAT CAIN BROUGHT AN OFFERING TO THE LORD OF THE FRUIT OF THE GROUND. ABEL, ON HIS PART ALSO BROUGHT OF THE FIRSTLINGS OF HIS FLOCK AND OF THEIR FAT PORTIONS. AND THE LORD HAD REGARD FOR ABEL AND FOR HIS OFFERING; BUT FOR CAIN AND FOR HIS OFFERING HE HAD NO REGARD.
> - GENESIS 4:3-5A

But in this scripture, Moses wasn't coming around for another few thousand years. Neither Cain nor Abel was under any obligation to provide an offering to God. So why did they do it? Why

> THE LORD GOD MADE GARMENTS OF SKIN FOR ADAM AND HIS WIFE, AND CLOTHED THEM.
> - GENESIS 3:21

offer *anything*? The language here reflects something different than I'm conveying, so I want to be true to that. The phrase "So it came about in the course of time..." or "At the designated time..." (as the NET Bible translates it) could convey that Adam and Eve had laid down family rules requiring an offering at a certain time.

While there was no legal requirement at that time for this type of sacrifice, God may have set an example for blood-atoning sacrifice that covers sin when He killed animals to cover Adam and Eve as they left the Garden. In the end, both Cain and Abel, likely of age, offered sacrifices with no clear requirement of the law.

So not because it was required, but likely because it was what they wanted, two men brought the fruit of their labor to God. The farmer brought grain and the shepherd brought flesh and blood.

Some men I respect feel that Cain's offering was not acceptable, because it was not a blood offering. That could be true, but I'm inclined to disagree. There is a word, *minkah*, (translated "offering") that is the same Hebrew word used in Leviticus 2 to discuss an offering.[14] In the Leviticus text, the context of the offering is grain, so I'm inclined to believe that it wasn't the fact one offering was grain and the other contained blood that put off God, but the issue is not totally settled.

Scholars disagree on this and maybe this is why: Cain's offering is described as simply "fruit of the ground," which seems to convey run-of-the-mill stuff or just whatever was lying around. Abel's offering was, by one translation, the fattest firstborn of his lambs. To give the fattest of the flock was a pretty big deal back then. A fatted lamb was like a great Roth IRA investment. All the taxes had been paid in feed and water that the ewe had eaten when she birthed a live lamb—a quasi-miracle, since some just don't survive. Nourishment required a lot of the mother's milk (that could have been sold) to get extremely fat, and represented the full potential of Abel's labor when he slaughtered it and presented it to God. Abel's offering was exceptional in that it was the best he had to give.

If there is one theme visited over and over in the Bible (and visited first and foremost here in Genesis 4), it is that God honors those who take something they should have loved (in fact, likely do love), and put it on an altar to Him.

Abel should have looked to the greatest of his flock as his provision. He should have been counting their worth. Livestock, if you can grow them faster than they die or you harvest them, grow exponentially. David should have worried about his head and not stepped onto the battlefield to face that Philistine. Jeremiah should have backed down and shut up. I should have gotten back to work and quit messing with this manuscript a long time ago.

The world tells us that holding onto the best is necessary in order to survive, but when we orchestrate opportunities to sacrifice those things for Him, He honors us. He honored Abel with His great regard.

Cain realized that God had no regard for his offering and Scripture says his countenance fell. Do you know what that's like? Do you know how it feels when God seems to have no regard for your offering?

I do. Last week, my countenance fell when God's provision felt far from me and I had noticeably fewer touches by Him. It all seemed to begin after I became so enthralled in my son's football game that I cared more about what I wanted than anyone else's needs. (Those of you who get passionate about sports know exactly what I'm describing.) Just that

> So CAIN BECAME VERY ANGRY AND HIS COUNTENANCE FELL. THEN THE LORD SAID TO CAIN, "WHY ARE YOU ANGRY? AND WHY HAS YOUR COUNTENANCE FALLEN? IF YOU DO WELL, WILL NOT YOUR COUNTENANCE BE LIFTED UP? AND IF YOU DO NOT DO WELL, SIN IS CROUCHING AT THE DOOR; AND ITS DESIRE IS FOR YOU, BUT YOU MUST MASTER IT."
> - GENESIS 4:5B-7

> BY FAITH ABEL OFFERED TO GOD A BETTER SACRIFICE THAN CAIN, THROUGH WHICH HE OBTAINED THE TESTIMONY THAT HE WAS RIGHTEOUS, GOD TESTIFYING ABOUT HIS GIFTS, AND THROUGH FAITH, THOUGH HE IS DEAD, HE STILL SPEAKS.
> - HEBREWS 11:4

morning, I had been pondering whether the loss of God's presence in my life would be the worst thing I could imagine. Somehow, those two occasions came together and changed something in me.

By the end of the week, I realized I was feeling a distance from God, though I knew He was there. I began to frantically search for what had gone wrong, like a man who has lost his wallet retraces his steps. As I recalled my selfish emotions earlier in the week, I realized that, like Cain, I felt that I'd failed to provide a worthy sacrifice of my time, focus, and actions, and so of them, God felt "no regard."

A relationship is like a masterpiece. While destruction of a building or loss of a year at college can be difficult, they can be repaired or redeemed. But for a relationship or a masterpiece, you can work on it for ten years, and one mistake—one slip of the hand or one sly word—can irreparably damage it. With other humans, we say things to each other that will blot out all other assurances for decades to come.

Disappointing your great Creator feels disorienting and terrible, and saying that your "countenance fell" doesn't quite seem to cut it.

But I've also felt like Abel. When I first finished reading the Bible, and whenever I give this lesson, I've felt the joy and love of meaningful service to God. It is also extraordinary to be within His slipstream when I'm serving my family or giving thanks. It is the credibility of being named righteous by God—not self-righteous, but righteous. This is addressed directly in Hebrews 11.

Aleksandr I. Solzhenitsyn wrote in *The Gulag Archipelago*:

> *If only it were all so simple! If only there were evil people somewhere insidiously committing evil deeds, and it were necessary only to separate them from the rest of us and destroy them. **But the line dividing good and evil cuts through the heart of every human being.***[14]

Whether in prayer, giving sacrificially or in service, it is easy for me to forget how great it is to meander in the soft garden of Abel's sacrifice, inside the warm confines of God's regard.

I warm myself there. I get comfortable there. I might even build myself a little house to stay in, but eventually, sooner or later, like Adam fully grown with days upon days upon days to falter, I fail. I step back into the heat of Cain's desert, of my own will, but I hate it.

> FOR WE KNOW THAT THE LAW IS SPIRITUAL, BUT I AM OF FLESH, SOLD INTO BONDAGE TO SIN. FOR WHAT I AM DOING, I DO NOT UNDERSTAND; FOR I AM NOT PRACTICING WHAT I WOULD LIKE TO DO, BUT I AM DOING THE VERY THING I HATE. BUT IF I DO THE VERY THING I DO NOT WANT TO DO, I AGREE WITH THE LAW, CONFESSING THAT THE LAW IS GOOD.
> — ROMANS 7:14-16

I begin to feel the heat of the air and the dryness of the soil. It may take longer than it should, but I begin reaching and grasping backward to return to God's favor.

This isn't me saving myself. I'm already saved by God's grace first and then by my belief in the price paid for me, but I also have a responsibility: I repent. I repent in front of men. I renew my commitment to arm myself with Scripture which, had I been doing it all along, would have warned me against venturing astray in the first place. I pray and, while still shaking off a little bit of the desert sand, the point of return comes when I earnestly offer up something that I truly treasure—a sacrifice of monumental importance to me. It is at that point that I truly feel the return of God's regard for my work/time/worship. I believe that I have done well, and therefore my countenance is lifted up.

It's not my only choice. That is not what Cain chose.

Cain felt that with his offering, but with a side of regret. He knew that he had held back, despite putting up some great parts of his harvest. Getting a C- on your work hurts. Afterward, he was mad that he'd even bothered. He was angry that he hadn't put in the additional effort. He was furious that he'd been humiliated. Then, when he spoke to the Teacher, he was told that he didn't do a good job. And on top of that, it's not just that you didn't do a good job, but there's a bigger issue behind this specific work product. Cain didn't take it well. Not only did he have a bad project, if he didn't master this, he was a dead man.

We're pretty detached from true horrors crouching at our door, but in the wild, as he was, this was fear-inducing. Something crouching at his door, after what happened to his parents, must have been maddening: "You mean it could get worse than this? I already have to live with my parents chewing my ear off about how You kicked us out of the greatest place I could ever imagine. I've got these cherubim with flaming swords over here to remind me that I'll never get in, and now the same thing (read: sin) that caused all that carnage is crouching at my door to take me down even further?"

> SO HE DROVE THE MAN OUT; AND AT THE EAST OF THE GARDEN OF EDEN HE STATIONED THE CHERUBIM AND THE FLAMING SWORD WHICH TURNED EVERY DIRECTION TO GUARD THE WAY TO THE TREE OF LIFE.
>
> - GENESIS 3:24

Cain, mad at the rebuking, called his brother out to the field and told him exactly what God said. Shouldn't Cain have been elated to have heard from God?

Job endured unimaginable distress and trial, and in the end, because of his response, he was redeemed. When he got all his stuff back, what do you think Job counted as his true treasure—all the material things restored, or the fact that God knew his name and crossed that chasm to speak with him?

I don't blame Cain, because I was Cain just last week. I gave up all manner of God's presence and fruit for nothing. If we see ourselves for what we truly are, we will often see evidence of Cain. I'm certain that, when he spilled his guts to Abel, he was hoping for righteous indignation.

Instead, Abel probably told him, "That's about right, Cain. It's not just this offering that you flubbed, but you've been disrespectful to Mom. Your wife has mentioned it, too. We all love you, but God's right. If you don't change, that lizard crouching at your door is going to consume you."

> CAIN TOLD ABEL HIS BROTHER. AND IT CAME ABOUT WHEN THEY WERE IN THE FIELD, THAT CAIN ROSE UP AGAINST ABEL HIS BROTHER AND KILLED HIM.
>
> - GENESIS 4:8

The greatest risk we face today—the veritable lizard crouching at our door—is that we spend so much of our time managing sin, explaining it, making it worthy (or trivial) in men's eyes that we never cross back over into the warmth of God's favor. Instead of serving, loving, and strengthening our belief, we sow seeds of lust, greed, sloth, pride, envy, gluttony or—in the case of Cain—hatred.

Wracked with anger, Cain killed Abel there in the field.

Whether salvation can be lost by venturing too far afield into sin or is locked into a soul upon the moment of belief is a topic that has twisted theologians and split congregations for thousands of years. Where Cain or Abel went after they died is beyond a characterization that I can make. I like what Tozer said:

> God will not hold us responsible to understand the mysteries of election, predestination and the divine sovereignty. The best and safest way to deal with these truths is to raise our eyes to God and in deepest reverence say, 'O Lord, Thou knowest.' Those things belong to the deep and mysterious profound of God's omniscience. Prying into them may make theologians, but it will never make saints.[15]

> SO THEN EACH ONE OF US WILL GIVE AN ACCOUNT OF HIMSELF TO GOD.
> - ROMANS 14:12

> [JESUS] CAME TO HIS OWN, AND THOSE WHO WERE HIS OWN DID NOT RECEIVE HIM. BUT AS MANY AS RECEIVED HIM, TO THEM HE GAVE THE RIGHT TO BECOME CHILDREN OF GOD, EVEN TO THOSE WHO BELIEVE IN HIS NAME...
> - JOHN 1:11-12

> THEN [ABRAHAM] BELIEVED IN THE LORD; AND [GOD] RECKONED IT TO HIM AS RIGHTEOUSNESS.
> - GENESIS 15:6

In persons number three and four on earth, I see the archetype of two people whom I know in me. At times, I have been Abel—one who, since the beginning, even when there appeared no way for him to be part of this, couldn't imagine a scenario where he would not be included in this Great Dance called heaven. At my best, I put in the time and learn the steps. Fully knowing that Jesus' sacrifice will justify these accounts, I recognize my role in the process and love recklessly. I recognize that God counts me as righteous through my belief in Jesus—a belief that drives my service and love to extreme limits. I set my heart on settling my account the best I can, even while recognizing that on my own, I'll never bridge the gap. But in spite of my circumstances and failings, I couldn't not be part of that Great Dance hosted in heaven.

Then, at my worst, I become Cain, refusing to admit my shortcomings or lean into God's grace. I refuse or (at best) delay getting my arms around the sin that falls to my account. I feel awkward going through the steps and eventually give up. I see serving myself as my highest and best use. The list goes on. I ignore my role in it and I get a taste of the punishment visited on Cain. Because of my circumstances and failings (mine and others, writ large), I just won't be part of that Great Dance hosted in heaven.

What does that mean for you? If you look at this as a spectrum, on one end is Abel with his unyielding desire to please God with his best and greatest. It is a place in your heart that, while fully realizing free will, you sacrifice to a higher One, a Fundamental big enough to bear it, so there is nothing that will keep you from it. Think Mary of Bethany wiping Jesus' feet with oil costing a year's wages or Paul's mission work or Joshua entering the Promised Land. It doesn't have to be a sacrifice, but it is something that burned within them so hot, there was no way they weren't going to complete their mission.

> MARY THEN TOOK A POUND OF VERY COSTLY PERFUME OF PURE NARD, AND ANOINTED THE FEET OF JESUS AND WIPED HIS FEET WITH HER HAIR; AND THE HOUSE WAS FILLED WITH THE FRAGRANCE OF THE PERFUME.
>
> - JOHN 12:3

On the other end of the spectrum is Cain and his attitude to check the box on the religion imposed on him by his parents. It is a dark place where selfishness rules, and despite knowing and seeing that happiness lies within the walls of the Great Dance, you'd rather stand outside in the cold.

When you say something that is true but extremely hurtful to a loved one, or when you cut a corner because the benefit to you is too great, you're squarely within this end of the spectrum.

Want to reclaim the legacy of Abel?

If you still have the small flame or ember of Abel within you, you can feed it with service, love, and real belief. You can enjoy the pleasure of God's regard and look for it in every interaction, smile, or ray of sunlight. You can decide today that you'll set your heart on a Fundamental big enough to deserve love.

> DO NOT FEAR, FOR I HAVE RE-
> DEEMED YOU;
> I HAVE CALLED YOU BY NAME;
> YOU ARE MINE!
> - ISAIAH 43:1B

If you don't feel even an ember of Abel within you, don't despair. You can ask for it!

We took our kids to New York City a few years ago and couldn't wait to take them to FAO Schwartz, a huge toy store that's like parents remember toy stores from time past. We looked around for about an hour, and I was dying for them to choose that special toy that we would always remember. They thought the store was interesting, but, in the end, they didn't pick anything. We walked down the street to a Toys"R"Us and bought a Lego set that I could have purchased back home and now sits broken down at the bottom of a drawer in the basement. I was dying to get them something great, but they needed to want it, too.

God has been calling you by name, and if you will take the initiative to ask for that ember—it's enough for you to want to want Him—then it is His absolute pleasure to give it to you. His call for you is real, but it requires an affirmative response.

> NOT EVERYONE WHO SAYS TO ME,
> 'LORD, LORD,' WILL ENTER THE
> KINGDOM OF HEAVEN, BUT HE WHO
> DOES THE WILL OF MY FATHER
> WHO IS IN HEAVEN WILL ENTER.
> MANY WILL SAY TO ME ON THAT
> DAY, 'LORD, LORD, DID WE NOT
> PROPHESY IN YOUR NAME, AND IN
> YOUR NAME CAST OUT DEMONS,
> AND IN YOUR NAME PERFORM
> MANY MIRACLES?' AND THEN I
> WILL DECLARE TO THEM, 'I NEVER
> KNEW YOU; DEPART FROM ME,
> YOU WHO PRACTICE LAWLESSNESS.
> - MATTHEW 7:21-23

> BUT WHEN THE SON OF MAN COMES IN HIS GLORY, AND ALL THE ANGELS WITH HIM, THEN HE WILL SIT ON HIS GLORIOUS THRONE. ALL THE NATIONS WILL BE GATHERED BEFORE HIM; AND HE WILL SEPARATE THEM FROM ONE ANOTHER, AS THE SHEPHERD SEPARATES THE SHEEP FROM THE GOATS; AND HE WILL PUT THE SHEEP ON HIS RIGHT, AND THE GOATS ON THE LEFT. THEN THE KING WILL SAY TO THOSE ON HIS RIGHT, 'COME, YOU WHO ARE BLESSED OF MY FATHER, INHERIT THE KINGDOM PREPARED FOR YOU FROM THE FOUNDATION OF THE WORLD.'
> THEN HE WILL ALSO SAY TO THOSE ON HIS LEFT, 'DEPART FROM ME, AC-CURSED ONES, INTO THE ETERNAL FIRE WHICH HAS BEEN PREPARED FOR THE DEVIL AND HIS ANGELS;
> THESE WILL GO AWAY INTO ETERNAL PUNISHMENT, BUT THE RIGHTEOUS INTO ETERNAL LIFE.'
>
> - MATTHEW 25:31-34, 41, 46

Answering this call and setting your heart toward God promises eternal life. Not doing it brings extreme consequences. Paul wrote to folks he'd never met in Romans 1 to address those who lived like Cain, vacationing so long in the desert of God's disfavor that they'd begun to build homes there. Paul said that, eventually, God will give them what they want—He will leave them alone.

Cain, receiving a double portion of his father's legacy, consisting mainly of pain and strife, walks the earth. No person administers final judgment—that is the business of our Lord. But we know that one day—That Day—One will come Who will make it all right again. He will separate all of mankind to His right and to His left, burn off the dross, and deliver an overflowing portion to all those who can't not be part of this wonderful, cosmic Great Dance.

FOR THE WRATH OF GOD IS REVEALED FROM HEAVEN AGAINST ALL UNGODLI-NESS AND UNRIGHTEOUSNESS OF MEN WHO SUPPRESS THE TRUTH IN UNRIGH-TEOUSNESS, BECAUSE THAT WHICH IS KNOWN ABOUT GOD IS EVIDENT WITHIN THEM; FOR GOD MADE IT EVIDENT TO THEM. FOR SINCE THE CREATION OF THE WORLD HIS INVISIBLE ATTRIBUTES, HIS ETERNAL POWER AND DIVINE NATURE, HAVE BEEN CLEARLY SEEN, BEING UNDERSTOOD THROUGH WHAT HAS BEEN MADE, SO THAT THEY ARE WITHOUT EXCUSE. FOR EVEN THOUGH THEY KNEW GOD, THEY DID NOT HONOR HIM AS GOD OR GIVE THANKS, BUT THEY BECAME FUTILE IN THEIR SPECULATIONS, AND THEIR FOOLISH HEART WAS DARKENED. PROFESSING TO BE WISE, THEY BECAME FOOLS, AND EX-CHANGED THE GLORY OF THE INCORRUPTIBLE GOD FOR AN IMAGE IN THE FORM OF CORRUPTIBLE MAN AND OF BIRDS AND FOUR-FOOTED ANIMALS AND CRAWLING CREATURES. THEREFORE GOD GAVE THEM OVER IN THE LUSTS OF THEIR HEARTS TO IMPURITY, SO THAT THEIR BODIES WOULD BE DISHONORED AMONG THEM. FOR THEY EXCHANGED THE TRUTH OF GOD FOR A LIE, AND WORSHIPED AND SERVED THE CREATURE RATHER THAN THE CREATOR, WHO IS BLESSED FOREVER. AMEN. FOR THIS REASON GOD GAVE THEM OVER TO DEGRADING PASSIONS...

AND JUST AS THEY DID NOT SEE FIT TO ACKNOWLEDGE GOD ANY LONGER, GOD GAVE THEM OVER TO A DEPRAVED MIND, TO DO THOSE THINGS WHICH ARE NOT PROPER, BEING FILLED WITH ALL UNRIGHTEOUSNESS, WICKEDNESS, GREED, EVIL; FULL OF ENVY, MURDER, STRIFE, DECEIT, MALICE; THEY ARE GOSSIPS, SLANDERERS, HATERS OF GOD, INSOLENT, ARROGANT, BOASTFUL, INVENTORS OF EVIL, DISOBEDIENT TO PARENTS, WITHOUT UNDERSTANDING, UNTRUSTWORTHY, UNLOVING, UNMERCIFUL; AND ALTHOUGH THEY KNOW THE ORDINANCE OF GOD, THAT THOSE WHO PRACTICE SUCH THINGS ARE WORTHY OF DEATH, THEY NOT ONLY DO THE SAME, BUT ALSO GIVE HEARTY APPROVAL TO THOSE WHO PRACTICE THEM.

- ROMANS 1:18-26A, 28-32

Before you go on to the next chapter, take a few mo-
ments to read one or more of the following:
Matthew Chapters 8 through 10
Mark Chapters 5 & 6
Luke Chapters 6 & 7
John Chapter 6

CHAPTER 5

The Prophets

So man continues down a path away from God. And sin lays on sin until there was one burning question of the day among those that couldn't NOT. The thing that Ezekiel and Jeremiah and Hosea and all the prophets are really asking in the last 1,000 years before the year zero is, "How can the God we know ever justify our accounts and wipe away the sins we and our families and our tribe committed?"

They understood that God was not feudal, but a God of truth, and He stood in the gaps for all those that stood on the truth. But if no one was left to stand on truth, then what was left but the gap?

And so God, full of love and joy as host of this Great Dance, chose to leave heaven to see and walk with us, even in our sin. He chose the possibility of our reciprocated love over His greatest love, because He has always had a plan. The cost of this time away from heaven, and the time that Jesus walked the earth, and the time that the Spirit is with us is unknowable. But we can know that whatever the cost, He endured it FOR us and out of love.

> THEN [ADAM] AND [EVE] HEARD THE SOUND OF THE LORD GOD WALKING IN THE GARDEN...
>
> - GENESIS 3:8A
>
> THEN ENOCH WALKED WITH GOD ...
>
> - GENESIS 5:22A
>
> NOAH WAS A RIGHTEOUS MAN, BLAMELESS IN HIS TIME; NOAH WALKED WITH GOD.
>
> - GENESIS 6:9B
>
> NOW THE LORD APPEARED TO [ABRAHAM] BY THE OAKS OF MAMRE, WHILE HE WAS SITTING AT THE TENT DOOR IN THE HEAT OF THE DAY. ...
>
> THEN THE MEN ROSE UP FROM THERE, AND LOOKED DOWN TOWARD SODOM; AND ABRAHAM WAS WALKING WITH THEM TO SEND THEM OFF.
>
> - GENESIS 18:1, 16
>
> THEN JACOB WAS LEFT ALONE, AND A MAN WRESTLED WITH HIM UNTIL DAYBREAK. ...
>
> SO JACOB NAMED THE PLACE PENIEL, FOR HE SAID, "I HAVE SEEN GOD FACE TO FACE, YET MY LIFE HAS BEEN PRESERVED."
>
> - GENESIS 32:24, 30
>
> BUT HE SAID, "YOU CANNOT SEE MY FACE, FOR NO MAN CAN SEE ME AND LIVE!"
>
> - EXODUS 33:20
>
> NO ONE HAS SEEN GOD AT ANY TIME...
>
> - JOHN 1:18
>
> IN THE YEAR OF KING UZZIAH'S DEATH I SAW THE LORD SITTING ON A THRONE, LOFTY AND EXALTED, WITH THE TRAIN OF HIS ROBE FILLING THE TEMPLE.
>
> - ISAIAH 6:1

Mankind is a hard case. There's no record of any pleading or requests for mercy from Adam when he was expelled from the Garden of Eden. There's no record of Eve sobbing at the gates or of their children repenting in dust and ashes. Perhaps they did, but it's not recorded in Genesis.

Genesis 3:8 implies that Adam had walked with God in Eden before. We also know from scripture that the mysterious high priest Enoch walked with God. Noah walked with God, Abraham walked with God, and Jacob wrestled God. Over the next almost-500 years, mankind's sin had increased to such a fevered pitch that no human, even the righteous Moses, could be in God's presence or see His face and live.

Opinions on my conclusion here vary; men

I respect have suggested that "walking with God" was just an expression Moses used from the time and that it conveyed no special closeness or relationship with God above others called righteous by God (such as David, Jeremiah, etc.). Indeed, the Gospel of John clearly states that "No one has seen God at any time," despite Isaiah making a pretty clear description of God in the temple.

Still, I think even the most conservative among us would agree that enough accumulated sin changes things for everyone. Sin stacked upon sin from the beginning of time likely had an effect to change the way mankind interacted with God and the way He handled us.

In Genesis 6, God sees the wickedness of man. Paul tells us in Romans that as far as sin goes, those before Moses had a high-limit credit card, but as we can see, there was a limit. Consider Cain and this note from the *NET Bible*:

"The Hebrew verb (sha'ah) simply means 'to gaze at, to look on with favor or with devotion for.' The text does not indicate how this [regard or no regard] was communicated, but it indicated that Cain and Abel knew immediately. Either there was some manifestation of divine pleasure given to Abel and withheld from Cain (fire consuming the sac-

> THEN THE LORD SAW THAT THE WICKEDNESS OF MAN WAS GREAT ON THE EARTH, AND THAT EVERY INTENT OF THE THOUGHTS OF HIS HEART WAS ONLY EVIL CONTINUALLY. THE LORD WAS SORRY THAT HE HAD MADE MAN ON THE EARTH, AND HE WAS GRIEVED IN HIS HEART. THE LORD SAID, "I WILL BLOT OUT MAN WHOM I HAVE CREATED FROM THE FACE OF THE LAND, FROM MAN TO ANIMALS TO CREEPING THINGS AND TO BIRDS OF THE SKY; FOR I AM SORRY THAT I HAVE MADE THEM."
> - GENESIS 6:5-7

> FOR UNTIL THE LAW SIN WAS IN THE WORLD, BUT SIN IS NOT IMPUTED WHEN THERE IS NO LAW.
> - ROMANS 5:13

> ABEL, ON HIS PART ALSO BROUGHT OF THE FIRSTLINGS OF HIS FLOCK AND OF THEIR FAT PORTIONS. AND THE LORD HAD REGARD FOR ABEL AND FOR HIS OFFERING; BUT FOR CAIN AND FOR HIS OFFERING HE HAD NO REGARD. SO CAIN BECAME VERY ANGRY AND HIS COUNTENANCE FELL.
> - GENESIS 4:4-5

rifice?) or there was an inner awareness of divine response."

Sunday school classes far and wide paint Cain as a forsaken man, whose sin pushed him farther into a broken world and away from God—indeed, as a hateful person marked by God. But in this picture of immediacy of feeling God's regard (or lack thereof), it is possible that his relationship with God was one that even the holiest among us only achieve momentarily—if ever. At my best, with repentance, fasting, Scripture, and service, I can only feel the slightest touch (like a blown kiss or the weight of the wind) of God's pleasure.

Maybe you're better, but at far less than Cain's best and in the midst of sin, he heard from, understood, and responded to the very regard of God. I believe this is a peek into how man interacted with God thousands of years ago, before chronic sin really changed the dynamic of the chasm.

Over the course of thousands of years, Noah built an ark and God reset humanity in a second Creation story. Abraham left his home and went to the Promised Land, where he had Isaac, who had Jacob. Jacob had 12 sons who (more or less) launched the 12 tribes of Israel. Joseph was sold into slavery and eventually rose to become the second-highest ruler in the then-greatest country in the world. Though that went well, eventually all of his and his brothers' descendants fell into 400 years of slavery.

Moses came along and led the people out of slavery, delivering the Law to them. Because of his temper, he was only allowed to gaze upon the Promised Land. Joshua led the people into Israel and began a period where Israel was ruled by quasi-military judges such as Deborah, Gideon, Samson, Eli, and a few others (who aren't so famous).

Samuel was the last judge of Israel when the people demanded a king. King Saul didn't work out and was replaced by David. In David's son, Solomon, Israel came its closest (even to this day) to fulfilling God's potential for them but, toward the end of Solomon's life, he failed. In one generation, by 931 B.C., the Kingdom was taken away and split into two nations.

The Northern Kingdom of Israel lasted for 219 years and was

then conquered by the Assyrians. The Southern Kingdom of Judah lasted for 355 years and was conquered by the Babylonians. The temple was sacked and all of Judah was deported to Babylon, where they were exiled for 50 years. During the exile, great portions of the Old Testament were put together, written down, and ordered. Then, 70 years after the exile, the temple was rebuilt and the sacrifices, as required by the Law, were resumed.

On paper, this looks like redemption, but in reality, from the fall of Judah in 586 B.C. until 1948 A.D., when the United Nations declared the nation of Israel, the Promised Land was never under its own control. It was controlled by a series of vassal rulers, who bought or traded their way into kingship over an area rife with tribal loyalties and competing religious views. Sometimes with gold and sometimes with blood, agendas were waged and settled over the city of Jerusalem.

With this view of history, and with the understanding that God created us in relationship out of love—to increase His own love by giving it away, by including us in this Great Dance—we gain new perspective on the major and minor prophets throughout the Old Testament.

Before we jump in, let's look once more at the timing and layout of the Old Testament:

1. Genesis through 2 Chronicles covers biblical history through 800 B.C. It conveys most of the sequential stories of the Bible and carries through the era of the divided kingdoms. Let's skip Ezra, Nehemiah, and Esther for the moment.

2. We now get to the wisdom literature in the Bible. Job (which is a story that likely happened before Joseph's rule in Egypt), Psalms, Proverbs, Ecclesiastes, and the Song of Solomon provide a brief cushion before some of the most punishing portions of the Bible.

3. The major prophets pick up the story, but in a completely different way than what was just mentioned in 1, above. If (1) was the front page of the newspaper, then this is the editorial page. There is an increase in the shrillness of the warnings and judgment delivered by these prophets. Gone is the instruction

and on comes the discipline.

4. All of this culminates in the stories we skipped: Ezra, Nehemiah and Esther, plus Malachi and Joel to close out the linear stories of the Bible.

5. The next 400 years, sometimes called the intertestamental period, are marked by a silence from God similar to the 400 years of silence in slavery in Egypt. Texts were certainly written during this time, and some of them make up the Apocrypha in the Catholic Bible.

So how can God hold men in 586 B.C. accountable for sins that compounded over the years and justify such incredible ruthlessness?

I believe the answer lies in this idea of the Great Dance and a proper understanding of the importance of knowing the step (sacrificial service) and the beat (love) of the dance. If it was really just a high-school dance, there wouldn't be much harm in not learning the steps. But if the Great Dance is heaven and the alternative is hell, then it becomes critically important to get the step and the beat right.

Christians believe that when we die, God stands in eternal judgment of us. We believe that we all fall short, but through the blood of Christ, our sins are covered and debt is paid in full. First, we must believe in Him. We must believe and accept this great and free gift that Jesus has given us. Christians also believe that there is an alternative. Both testaments are full of references to hell and chronicle the horrors of spending eternity there.

My understanding of Scripture is that God views the whole of humanity like a parent views the life of a child. When given a child, a parent knows to vaccinate him. Nearly naked and cold, the child is mercilessly held down and given shots. The pain can be excruciating. If his entire life consisted only of the seconds during those appointments, plus a spanking or

> BUT DO NOT LET THIS ONE FACT ESCAPE YOUR NOTICE, BELOVED, THAT WITH THE LORD ONE DAY IS LIKE A THOUSAND YEARS, AND A THOUSAND YEARS LIKE ONE DAY.
>
> - 2 PETER 3:8

two and the week he deservedly spent grounded, then it would be fair to call his life terrible.

But that's not the whole story, is it? The shots helped the child avoid terrible diseases that could have debilitated him, and the discipline that his parents leveled against him forced him to rethink decisions that would have led to catastrophe in his life.

While it was excruciating for entire generations in slavery, exile, and the dark of God's Word (the intertestamental period and slavery in Egypt), these trials were necessary. Each one of us carries a responsibility to the life cycle of mankind. We learn something about thirst from Moses' trek in the desert and about faithfulness from Daniel's trip to the lion's den. We learn about the depravity of men's hearts from the horrors of war. This accumulation of knowledge—not abstract knowledge, but knowledge based upon real experience, bought with blood and sweat, borne proportionately greater by some—is required in order for us to achieve the greatness planned for us.

It was rumored that, on his deathbed, Pancho Villa said, "Don't let it end like this. Tell them I said something."

That desperation of wanting our lives to mean something is familiar to us. So as we read these experiences—not fiction, but real experiences that some lived and bled and cried through—find some way in your life to let the legacy end better. We will never be able to achieve this fully, but when we can take another's tragedy, loss, or holocaust and enter into that pain to learn from it or resolve never to allow it to happen again or see a path that we're on and turn from that path, then we—I, you—become part of the redemption and happy ending.

The prophets knew something about God. They didn't see all that Jesus brought us, but they knew, like the child found in the discipline from his parents, that God would withhold nothing in the pursuit of a right relationship with His children. God was unwilling to favor or spoil His children at the cost of ruin or to set aside the pain of a vaccine. The risk of the alternative is too high.

When I look at the arc of humanity over this time and the tenor of the prophets, I don't see a wrathful God, full of vengeance, throwing a tantrum because mankind can't figure out the step or the beat.

I see a parent at His wit's end, who knows how great a life can be, in spite of all these mistakes. I see a parent willing to leave perfection—the Great Dance—to travel the lonely road into prison, only to be told that the inmate won't see Him today.

I see a parent who knows the alternative and will do anything to keep that child, conceived in love, away from impending flames.

I see a parent, fully knowing, willing to move heaven and earth if that child will only turn back and choose Him.

I see a parent way past hoping for a child that can't not be in our family, and now, desperately fighting, at all costs, to pull a child up from a nosedive.

Today, we look at those throughout the Old Testament who were punished, killed, or dropped into wells. Good and bad men throughout the Bible met ends that seem unfair. But we overlook that God never gave up on us. Even when He had the chance, like a mother's prayer, God never stopped pleading and working out an excellence in each of us.

C. S. Lewis, in *The Problem of Pain,* said it well:

> We are, not metaphorically but in very truth, a Divine work of art, something that God is making, and therefore something with which He will not be satisfied until it has a certain character. Here again we come up against what I have called the 'intolerable compliment.' Over a sketch made idly to amuse a child, an artist may not take much trouble: he may be content to let it go even though it is not exactly as he meant it to be. But over the great picture of his life—the work which he loves, though in a different fashion, as intensely as a man loves a woman or a mother a child—he will take endless trouble—and would doubtless, thereby give endless trouble to the picture if it were sentient. One can imagine a sentient picture, after being rubbed and scraped and re-commenced for the tenth time, wishing that it were only a thumb-nail sketch whose making was over in a minute. In the same way, it is natural for us to wish that God had designed for us a less glorious and less arduous destiny; but

then we are wishing not for more love but for less.[16]

God cannot give less. Heaven cannot accept less. And we cannot function, without voiding our warranty, with any less.

Before you go on to the next chapter, take a few moments to read one or more of the following:
Matthew Chapters 11 through 13
Mark Chapters 7 & 8
Luke Chapters 8 through 10
John Chapters 7 & 8

CHAPTER 6

The Wait of the Gospel

The wait must have been excruciating. At least seven factors existed in the time of Jesus that had never existed before, but there are probably hundreds of others. For thousands of years, humanity suffered under the weight of our sin, but we did not suffer alone. God had a plan to redeem humanity, and the minute that we could bear its weight, Jesus came with a message of how we, too, can enter into this Great Dance.

THEN THE LORD RAINED ON SODOM AND GOMORRAH BRIMSTONE AND FIRE FROM THE LORD OUT OF HEAVEN, AND HE OVERTHREW THOSE CITIES, AND ALL THE VALLEY, AND ALL THE INHABITANTS OF THE CITIES, AND WHAT GREW ON THE GROUND.

- GENESIS 19:24-25

WHEN GOD SAW THEIR DEEDS, THAT THEY TURNED FROM THEIR WICKED WAY, THEN GOD RELENTED CONCERNING THE CALAMITY WHICH HE HAD DECLARED HE WOULD BRING UPON THEM. AND HE DID NOT DO IT.

- JONAH 3:10

Throughout the Old Testament, any discerning reader is struck by how much blood is actually spilled. God brought fire down on Sodom and Gomorrah, but spared Nineveh. Sometimes judgment came and sometimes judgment waited. Over the course of time, man suffered incalculable atrocities. The Holocaust, with millions of Jews killed, is still too fresh a wound to prod, but it's on par with other destruction perpetrated against God's people: the Flood, 400 years of slavery in Egypt, 40 years in the desert where likely two million Israelites died (see Numbers 14:25-35), exile in Babylon, the horrors of Hellenization, and life under Christian-hating Roman emperors.

In our house, we have a rule borrowed from an old Jerry Leachman lecture: **No one suffers alone.** For us, it means that if a member of our family is unhappy or unable to come to the table of joy that we set, we will not eat the meal there. We will not put our happiness or comfort or joy over another's pain or sorrow. If you cannot enter into mine, then I reduce myself to enter into yours.

The U.S. military has the same rule: "Leave no man behind." My family hasn't been tested like a serviceman who puts himself in harm's way to save a comrade, or God, who spent thousands of years broken-hearted with man. But, in each of these examples, we can see that while the punishment was leveled against one (or One), others suffer.

The degree to which God suffered due to mankind's judgment is unknowable, but there must have been some cost to God to leave the perfection of His Great Dance to come to earth and deal with us. From the Beginning, and until Christ, God was continually with us, speaking to us, speaking through us (except for 400 years during slavery in Egypt and around 430 years after the death of Nehemiah), sometimes walking with us, and warning us.

This period of mankind walking away from God, Who created us to dance with Him, must have been excruciating to Him. We can identify with earthly loss or tragedy, but for God, Who created time, Who is outside of time, for Whom "one day is like a thousand years, and a thousand years like one day" (2 Peter 3:8), it is possible that this ancient period of separation is just as raw for Him today as 9/11 or the Holocaust has been for those that experienced it. It is clear to me that none of us suffer alone.

From the beginning, through the Old Testament, and even into today—this very moment—God has had the power to snap His fingers and say, "We're good. Don't worry about all the sin. Don't worry about whatever you did. Your accounts are paid. You're free to enter into My love." The very definition of omnipotence demands it. Yet, He doesn't and

> ENTER THROUGH THE NARROW GATE; FOR THE GATE IS WIDE AND THE WAY IS BROAD THAT LEADS TO DESTRUCTION, AND THERE ARE MANY WHO ENTER THROUGH IT. FOR THE GATE IS SMALL AND THE WAY IS NARROW THAT LEADS TO LIFE, AND THERE ARE FEW WHO FIND IT.
> - MATTHEW 7:13-14

didn't. He knows humanity has to be prepared to bear the weight of the pardon. Humanity has to be able to understand it.

Think for a minute about the last time you knew you had to do something that you really didn't want to do. Maybe you had to pay a debt or have a conversation with a loved one or a family member. Maybe you needed to confront a friend or give up something in your life that you enjoyed. Whatever it was, you did it. We're Americans, and part of being an American is getting done what needs doing. You got it done.

How much harder would it have been if you had to wait? What if you needed to deal with an aging parent, but had to let the situation linger for another five years? How about if you needed to settle a debt with your neighbor or brother whom you knew you could fully forgive, but to really love them you had to let the debt sit there, like rotting milk stinking up everything between you for another six months? What if you had a son who was addicted to drugs, but to really love him, you knew you had to leave him to his own devices?

I have a vision of Jesus bursting into the throne room the moment Eve broke the skin of the fruit and hurling Himself at the Father's feet, low and pleading, begging, "Can I go now? Will you throw a cross

> FOR WHILE WE WERE STILL HELPLESS, AT THE RIGHT TIME CHRIST DIED FOR THE UNGODLY.
> - ROMANS 5:6

into the middle of that garden and let Me climb onto it? Will you let My blood cover her and redeem mankind?" And God leans down, pulling his Son off the ground, looks Him full in the face, sort of smiling, but also fully recognizing there's pain ahead, and says, "No, Son. Man cannot yet bear the weight of the Gospel." So They wipe away Their tears, and watch, and wait, and help where They can.[iv]

But thousands of years later, the very second that man can bear the Gospel, Jesus comes.

There were probably hundreds of things that came together for the first time in the world in the few hundred years before Christ, but I've only come up with seven factors that changed the world and gave it, even in its weakness, the strength to bear the weight of the Gospel. Consider:

1. **Roman Roads.** Beginning in about 500 B.C., the Romans began building roads in an effort to unite their territories. I couldn't find any data on the amount of roads built by the time of Christ but, by 100 A.D., Rome had built over 258,000 miles of roads throughout the world.[17] That is five times the mileage of the United States' entire interstate highway system. If you grew up in a rural area, 258,000 miles of road is 25 percent of every single unpaved road in the entire United States. That's also about 55 percent more than every mile of interstate and major road in the United States today.[18] Roman roads cut through hills and filled in ravines to provide reliable transportation between cities. These roads weren't like our roads that shut down every few years for maintenance. Starting with compressed dirt, they set large stones below smaller stones— and lime below an even finer grain of pounded stone below large rounded stones—that gave these roads an arc to drain water and keep dry.[19] Some of these roads are still in use today.

---

iv I would ask that you treat the scene in this paragraph very carefully. While it may have actually occurred and I did see it, it is not directly supported by Scripture. There is no description of this happening. This may have happened and it may have not happened, but there is also, more likely, a third option that we just can't see yet. In this, use with care.

2. **Safe Seas.** Wide expanses of earth require a government that can police it. Like Africa today, where weak governments fertilize some of the worst atrocities we've ever seen, the Mediterranean was a place where anarchy reined. Alexander the Great conquered most of the known world by the year he died in 323 B.C. Over the next 250 years, a series of his commanders and their heirs fought over the lands from Egypt to Greece, but kept the seas generally safe. In the transition to Roman rule from Ptolemaic and Seleucid rule, piracy flourished in the open seas. Coastal towns with no defense became havens for pirates or victims.

"Consequently, the pirates remained the only considerable naval power in the Eastern Mediterranean with bases throughout the sea."[20] Like any criminal enterprise, its success was its downfall. Attacks became more brazen and finally, in the summer of 66 B.C., the Roman Senate granted Pompey extraordinary leeway in dealing with piracy on the Mediterranean and in 89 days, he destroyed 1,300 pirate vessels on the Mediterranean. This virtually ended piracy on the Mediterranean for 1,200 years.

3. **Greek.** Following the death of Alexander the Great, Israel and the rest of the known world went through a period of Hellenization. To varying degrees over that period, those under Greek rule were forced to dress, sing, appreciate, and speak Greek. Sometimes encouraged, and sometimes forced with blood, Greek culture was mandated throughout most of the known world. I've heard a preacher mention that 30 percent of the known world spoke Greek at this time, but I couldn't confirm that statistic. However, "thanks to Alexander, Greek was the international language; now, for the first time, the Bible could be ready by virtually everyone."[21]

4. **Pax Romana.** Beginning 30 years before the birth of Christ and ending about 150 years afterward, the Roman Empire experienced a period of relative peace. Wars were still waged on the borders, but during this period there was no major invasion, piracy, or great civil war. This period of stability gave

those living under Roman rule a rare opportunity to answer questions and submit to activities that are often pushed aside in times of great conflict.

5. **No Borders.** For the first time in history, one could travel to virtually all the land that the Mediterranean touched—all of Eastern Europe, and the habitable portions of the Middle East and Northern Africa—without a passport. Within the lifetime of those who saw Jesus (117 A.D.), the empire reached its peak and one could travel for 2.5 million square miles[22] without passing through customs or immigration.

6. **Unity.** While it may seem strange to call a Roman occupation unity, consider Jerusalem's history. Since Solomon's death in 931 B.C., which we have called the closest that mankind ever got to a realization of the covenant, the nation of Israel has been either split (divided kingdoms), at war (with Assyria or Babylon), occupied by a series of warring kings (Seleucids vs. Ptolemies), or at war with itself (Maccabean Revolt) until 64 B.C. when the Pharisees begged Pompey (a Roman leader, consul, and militarist with a big army) to save them from the Maccabees (essentially themselves).[23] The next 134 years, while painful for those under the yoke of Roman law, would be characterized as a slow news day in Israel. This unity was broken in 70 A.D. when Romans leveled Jerusalem, and Jesus' prediction from around 37 years earlier came true.

7. **The Pride of Herod.** Herod the Great was a ruler of epic proportions. His great-grandfather was a convert to Judaism by force in a type of Maccabean reverse discrimination and his mother was an Arab. Herod the Great had a troubled relationship with his people. His wife, whom he adored and later killed (only to call after her throughout his palace for the rest of his life), hated him and openly belittled him in court. With over 500 concubines, he denied himself no pleasure, but this pursuit built a home of danger and deceit. Yet, through cunning, blood, and ruthlessness, in 40 B.C., this incredibly unlikely Herod stood between Marc Anthony and Octavian (nephew of Caesar) and was named by the Roman Senate King of Ju-

daea and Roman ally.

Standing between "the two pillars of the world," this "half Jew, half Arab" descendent of Esau knew that back at home, among the people, "he would have to fight for every inch of his kingdom, and then Jerusalem."[24] He did, and over the next 40 years, he built Jerusalem into the center of the world. Rome was still Rome, like Washington, D.C., where the laws were made. But Jerusalem and the temple complex, out of Herod's pride, were built into the center of the world. Jerusalem became New York City—the center of culture, architecture, literature, and the arts. It was said, "Whoever did not see Jerusalem in her glory has never seen a beautiful city" and "Ten measures of beauty descended to the world, Jerusalem took nine."

> AS FOR THESE THINGS WHICH YOU ARE LOOKING AT, THE DAYS WILL COME IN WHICH THERE WILL NOT BE LEFT ONE STONE UPON ANOTHER WHICH WILL NOT BE TORN DOWN.
> - LUKE 21:6

Again, there are probably hundreds, but these seven events meant, for the first time in history that if you sent someone out to spread the Gospel, there was a good road to lead them there. And if you put someone on a ship with a letter or an alm, barring weather, the seas were safe enough to carry them. If you wrote a book or a letter, then most of the known world could hear it because, with blood and sweat, chances were great that they now spoke Greek. Government forces were aligned so that one man could walk for three years in an area a little bit larger than Puerto Rico and the entire world would take notice.

Most scholars believe that Jesus was 28 or 29 when He started His ministry and that it took three years, but we're examining an ancient story spanning thousands of years from the Garden of Eden to the cross.

Why a cross? We know from history that death on a cross was laden with symbolism:

> MY SOUL IS DEEPLY GRIEVED TO THE POINT OF DEATH; REMAIN HERE AND KEEP WATCH. AND HE WENT A LITTLE BEYOND THEM, AND FELL TO THE GROUND AND BEGAN TO PRAY THAT IF IT WERE POSSIBLE, THE HOUR MIGHT PASS HIM BY. AND HE WAS SAYING, "ABBA! FATHER! ALL THINGS ARE POSSIBLE FOR YOU; REMOVE THIS CUP FROM ME; YET NOT WHAT I WILL, BUT WHAT YOU WILL.
>
> - MARK 14:34-36

Crucifixion, said Josephus, was "the most miserable death," designed to demean the victim publicly. Hence Pilate ordered Jesus' placard to be attached to His cross—KING OF THE JEWS. Victims could be tied or nailed. The skill was to ensure victims did not bleed to death. The nails were usually driven through the forearms—not the palms—and ankles: the bones of a crucified Jew have been found in a tomb in north Jerusalem with a 4 1/2-inch iron nail sticking through the skeletal ankle. ...Victims were usually crucified naked—with men facing outwards ... [25]

So why this? Jesus, in Gethsemane, clearly didn't want to take on this ordeal.

I would ask that you hold my next few paragraphs loosely because we will not fully know this until that day when we see Him fully, but here is what I believe: **The cross was the sacrifice that we demanded.** It's hard to imagine that the debtor would get to choose the method by which a creditor forgives the debt. But if the purpose of the payment was to woo and win the debtor, then a debt paid too easily only pays the debt. Gethsemane proves that this debt was not paid easily.

When I was a teenager, I thought my parents were about as rich as anyone else. For them to cover tuition at the Johns Hopkins University was just the freight for being my parents. I knew it was a lot of money, but if I'd even taken the time to think about it (which I don't think I did), I would have thought they had plenty more. Looking back, I know it was a sacrifice for them. They tried to guide me to a state school at 10 percent of the cost, but it wasn't what I wanted.

Arian Foster grew up differently. He made the news in 2012 by signing a five-year, $43.5 million contract with the Houston Texans. In a news conference, he said this deal was significant to him because it meant that his family would never struggle again.[26] Crying, he recounted growing up in New Mexico with a single mom. Arian said he and his siblings struggled and one day his mother "pawned her wedding ring to give us some food that night and I just told myself that I wanted to do something with my life to make sure that when I had a kid he never had to worry about the lights being on."

Do you see that? Arian has a different understanding of the sacrifice that his parents made for him. My parents paid many tens of thousands of dollars per year and his mother sold a wedding ring that likely cost a few thousand dollars. Yet his appreciation for her sacrifice greatly outweighed mine.

This says something unfortunate about me, but the illustration is meant to illuminate that it matters who is paying the debt. If you're trying to win over the debtor, then the sacrifice has to

> THERE IS ONE WHO SCATTERS, AND YET INCREASES ALL THE MORE, AND THERE IS ONE WHO WITHHOLDS WHAT IS JUSTLY DUE, AND YET IT RESULTS ONLY IN WANT.
> - PROVERBS 11:24

be big and understandable. And if you're God, Creator of heaven and earth, owner of everything, how can anything possibly be a sacrifice?

In my humble opinion, the cross does it perfectly. For you and for me, God scattered His glory with shards of skin and blood strewn through the streets, so that we may be gathered. This very act was the

> BUT JESUS WAS SAYING, "FATHER, FORGIVE THEM; FOR THEY DO NOT KNOW WHAT THEY ARE DOING." AND THEY CAST LOTS, DIVIDING UP HIS GARMENTS AMONG THEMSELVES.
> - LUKE 23:34

pinnacle of service. For you and for me, Jesus did that thing that he didn't want to do. It embodied service, yes, but in a way that bled love, saying, "Forgive them..." as they gambled away his clothing.

For you and for me, Jesus believed. He believed all that His Father told Him, but also, He believed that it was worth it. My parents and Arian's mom must have decided that it was worth it, too. But if they had not—if He had not—where would we be?

In the end, the debt has to be paid, but the goal isn't to merely pay the debt. For God, paying the debt is just a nice consequence. The real goal is bringing the debtor back from the brink and into the Great Dance. So no matter how great the sacrifice or how long the wait or how heavy the burden, no risk is too great to achieve the realization of God's plan for us.

Service. Love. Belief. Service. Love. Belief.

Before you go on to the next chapter, take a few moments to read one or more of the following:
Matthew Chapters 14 & 15
Mark Chapter 9
Luke Chapter 11 through 13:21
John Chapters 9 & 10

CHAPTER 7

Step this Way

Jesus brought us a way that, in order to go up to join that Great Dance, we have to go down. This wasn't a prescriptive way, but a demonstrative way. It is exactly what He did.

God sent Jesus the minute that humanity could bear this Good News, and, with Him, Jesus brought us three things. We'll look at those three things over the next three chapters, but let's start with the way right where you'd begin to share the Gospel: Haggai.

Really. Five hundred and twenty years before

> ON THE TWENTY-FOURTH OF THE NINTH MONTH, IN THE SECOND YEAR OF DARIUS, THE WORD OF THE LORD CAME TO HAGGAI THE PROPHET, SAYING, "THUS SAYS THE LORD OF HOSTS, 'ASK NOW THE PRIESTS FOR A RULING: IF A MAN CARRIES HOLY MEAT IN THE FOLD OF HIS GARMENT, AND TOUCHES BREAD WITH THIS FOLD, OR COOKED FOOD, WINE, OIL, OR ANY OTHER FOOD, WILL IT BECOME HOLY?'" AND THE PRIESTS ANSWERED, "NO." THEN HAGGAI SAID, "IF ONE WHO IS UNCLEAN FROM A CORPSE TOUCHES ANY OF THESE, WILL THE LATTER BECOME UNCLEAN?" AND THE PRIESTS ANSWERED, "IT WILL BECOME UNCLEAN."
>
> - HAGGAI 2:10-13

Jesus came, Haggai the prophet was hearing from and speaking for God to us. He was old and part of a small contingent that came back from Babylon to rebuild the temple after Babylon sacked it. During his ministry, he emphasized four things, but the third is especially relevant here.

I can hear you now: "Wait a minute... 500 years is a long time. A lot can change in that period of time."

It didn't. His message might have been delivered the day before Mary and Joseph arrived in Bethlehem. Since the beginning of time, just as light always overcomes darkness (try as it may, even the darkest darkness cannot consume the faintest candle), when an unclean thing touches a clean/holy thing, the clean thing becomes unclean. No amount of cleanliness—not the high priest, not a holy sacrifice, nothing—could be clean enough that, when it came into contact with uncleanliness, it remained clean, much less could make the unclean item clean.

> THE LIGHT SHINES IN THE DARKNESS, AND THE DARKNESS DID NOT COMPREHEND IT.
>
> - JOHN 1:5

Haggai made a pronouncement on the people, saying that their sin had separated them from God. Even in the midst of that era's most important work, their labor and role in accomplishing this great project did not excuse sin. Keep this in mind as we think about the way that Jesus brought us.

The first thing that Jesus brought us was a way.

From just after the beginning, there wasn't a way for mankind to enter back into the presence of God. Eternal life was a bridge too far. There were multiple men whom God called faithful or righteous but, as sin laid upon sin, it became impossible for even those gifted with God's Word (the prophets who heard from and loved God) to imagine a scenario where God could redeem anyone.

The best of them knew something about God. They knew that He wasn't a tribal leader. They knew He wouldn't take Israel, set them behind His back, and lay siege to nations that stood in Israel's way, although He had certainly done that. They knew He was a God of the Law and of truth. That meant He would take Israel, and put all those behind His back that followed the Law and protect them from all who were in front of Him—those who wouldn't follow the Law.

What scared them—what really put their backs into cries for repentance—was a realization that no one was left standing behind God. The entirety of humanity stood in front of God, within the path of His wrath.

So this way was no small thing. The fact that it was even possible when, for thousands of years, it had appeared impossible, is in itself a miracle. This way was ground breaking, because there was now a performance for God's people to achieve what they never could previously under the Law.

This way was descriptive, not prescriptive. When you go to the doctor, he checks you out and says that, based on your symptoms, you need to take certain medicines. He prescribes a course of treatment for you because you need it. It would never dawn on you that the doctor should undergo a similar treatment, because he didn't carry your symptoms. That's a prescriptive way. A descriptive way says, "Watch me," or "Do as I do," or "Walk the walk I'm walking."

Jesus' descriptive way was this:

If you want to go up, you must go down.

If you want to be exalted, you must humble yourself.

If you want to be increased, you must be diminished.

If you want to realize righteousness, you must first realize your sin.

It was exactly the opposite of what they had in mind. Even today, we answer like they did 2,000 years ago: "Got it. Is there another option?" Mankind waited 4,000 years, suffering at the hands of sin and under the yoke of the law, only to come out the other side with this difficult command. It was hard then, and it is still hard today.

It was difficult then, because Jesus preached to religious rulers who came from 2,500-year

> FOR YOU KNOW THE GRACE OF OUR LORD JESUS CHRIST, THAT THOUGH HE WAS RICH, YET FOR YOUR SAKE HE BECAME POOR, SO THAT YOU THROUGH HIS POVERTY MIGHT BECOME RICH.
> - 2 CORINTHIANS 8:9

> REPENT, FOR THE KINGDOM OF HEAVEN IS AT HAND.
> - MATTHEW 4:17

Levitical dynasties. For 50 generations, some hung their significance and livelihoods on the backs of their fathers, who were all temple priests. That meant something. It meant that they got kind greetings from folks in the markets and the best seats in the temple. That was something about which they had been proud of for a very long time. Then along came a child, only 12 years old, to show them differently (or later a man from the countryside to tell them that a molester or scumbag was in line for heaven—ahead of them). That was tough to take. They figured they might be in line behind Moses and the prophets, but not far behind. Their focus had been to the extreme on their own righteousness for hundreds of years, but Jesus and John the Baptist came with another message—the same message: Repent.

This is just as hard for us today. There are two Americas. There is one America that is sound asleep within its own dream and fully realizing all the fruits that this country has to offer. It is the America about which Christmas carols and love songs are sung. Citizens of this America have jobs and retirement accounts. They buy plane tickets with about as much thought as movie tickets. They move to new cities for better opportunities and finance a lifestyle that fits their station in life. I'm part of this America. For those of us in this America, this way—Jesus' way—is extremely difficult.

> TWO THINGS I ASKED OF YOU,
> DO NOT REFUSE ME BEFORE I DIE:
> KEEP DECEPTION AND LIES FAR FROM ME,
> GIVE ME NEITHER POVERTY NOR RICHES;
> FEED ME WITH THE FOOD THAT IS MY PORTION,
> THAT I NOT BE FULL AND DENY YOU AND SAY, "WHO IS THE LORD?"
> OR THAT I NOT BE IN WANT AND STEAL, AND PROFANE THE NAME OF MY GOD.
> - PROVERBS 30:7-9

It is challenging because I can make 12 bad decisions and still not be down. My life, my choices, my family, and my environment all conspire to keep me up. My parents and in-laws love this, and I'm not saying it is bad to make good decisions. But when I am up, it is difficult to acknowledge God's hand in these present circumstances and easy to consider them a fruit of my own labor.

There's a second America. There's an America that sits bolt upright nightly and unable to rest for a moment from the harshness of their reality. Keeping heat and

> THE RICH AND THE POOR HAVE A COMMON BOND,
> THE LORD IS THE MAKER OF THEM ALL.
> - PROVERBS 22:2

food and bills at bay is a constant juggling act where releasing just one ball ends in catastrophic consequences. It might mean a return to addiction, jail, homelessness, or another broken promise to a child, but every day is met with challenge and vice. The bounty of those who live a few miles away is nothing more than a dream to residents of this second America. They buy groceries with the precision of a surgeon. Credit is beyond their reach and they get stuck, sometimes left, in cities that are entirely foreign to them. I'm part of this America, too, but as a visitor. When I've talked with those who live on the streets, I can see they have a quicker grasp on the Way.

They don't have to walk two steps to go down. They wake up down. Their lives, choices, family, and environment all work with Six Sigma efficiency to keep them down. These are mothers, veterans, children, and entire families that live throughout this country and within your community and across every ethnicity. They wake up every day with no one to bear them up but Jesus.

Becca Stevens is a minister who has preached at our church with an incredible story. For years, she has selflessly run shelters in Nashville for women who have been assaulted by a culture of prostitution. She has an amazing ministry and story. She says, "If you want to see the face of Jesus, go to jail."

I've seen this myself. If you've ever gotten a chance to really interact with homeless men—not just feed them or serve them—but just talk, introduce yourself, and ask them about their day, you'll see something different from the conversations you have in the hallways at your church. I don't have an exhaustive study or years serving the poor, but this anecdote is consistent each and every time I visit.

I know a group of real-estate men who love to cook. They've got all the great toys for chili and BBQ competitions, so they thought they could put that to use feeding the poor in downtown Atlanta each Saturday. I've volunteered with my family a few times. Once setup is complete, I typically just wander back and talk to the men who are standing in line. (Women are invited to the front of the line, so they're always through before I can chat with them.) Every time I've walked that line, sharing bottled waters or coffee or just making small talk, I've had Jesus shared with me many times. Think of a guy who just bought a Ferrari and is sitting alone in a bar at three o'clock in the afternoon. These men are exactly like that—looking for any opportunity to talk about their great love.

I don't mean to paint the picture that every homeless person is faithful and every churchgoer is not, but in that line, on any given Saturday morning, I'll have more conversations initiated with me about the Gospel than I will in an entire month of idle chitchat at church. God is breaking out of them, bleeding out of their eyes, and they just love to share God's message, despite their daily hardships.

> IN THE BEGINNING WAS THE WORD, AND THE WORD WAS WITH GOD AND THE WORD WAS GOD. HE WAS IN THE BEGINNING WITH GOD. ALL THINGS CAME INTO BEING THROUGH HIM, AND APART FROM HIM NOTHING CAME INTO BEING THAT HAS COME INTO BEING. IN HIM WAS LIFE, AND THE LIFE WAS THE LIGHT OF MEN.
>
> - JOHN 1:1-4

Jesus models this.

The Creator of heaven and earth went down. It is unfathomable what the true cost was, but we know from history that God chose to send Jesus to Bethlehem in the womb of a virgin of no standing and into a family that was only able to make the minimum of sacrifice for the birth of the Son of God. They offered two young pigeons. He grew up not in the center of the world, but in a backwater town.

How hard must this have been? The Creator of the universe chose this way, this family, and this time to serve us. This lowest of circumstances is how God chose to show us we should go down. Over 33 years, Jesus continued that solemn march to the cross. He humbled himself so

> WHEN THE DAYS OF HER PURIFICATION ARE COMPLETED, FOR A SON OR FOR A DAUGHTER, SHE SHALL BRING TO THE PRIEST AT THE DOORWAY OF THE TENT OF MEETING A ONE YEAR OLD LAMB FOR A BURNT OFFERING AND A YOUNG PIGEON OR A TURTLEDOVE FOR A SIN OFFERING. ... BUT IF SHE CANNOT AFFORD A LAMB, THEN SHE SHALL TAKE TWO TURTLEDOVES OR TWO YOUNG PIGEONS, THE ONE FOR A BURNT OFFERING AND THE OTHER FOR A SIN OFFERING; AND THE PRIEST SHALL MAKE ATONEMENT FOR HER, AND SHE WILL BE CLEAN.
> - LEVITICUS 12:6, 8

that He could be exalted. He scattered His power so that He could consolidate it. The realization of the purpose of man, to worship God, was finally achieved by Jesus' humiliation at the hands of those for whom He died.

In the Great Dance, in heaven, this way is the step that we must learn to enter into the dance. It is the step of service—not just convenient service, but sacrificial service. It is a type of service that says, "How can I serve you?" or "How would you like to be served?" instead of "Here's what I'm able to do for you," or "I will serve you by..."

> BUT GOD DEMONSTRATES HIS OWN LOVE TOWARD US, IN THAT WHILE WE WERE YET SINNERS, CHRIST DIED FOR US.
> - ROMANS 5:8

> WHOEVER WISHES TO BECOME GREAT AMONG YOU SHALL BE YOUR SERVANT; AND WHOEVER WISHES TO BE FIRST AMONG YOU SHALL BE SLAVE OF ALL. FOR EVEN THE SON OF MAN DID NOT COME TO BE SERVED, BUT TO SERVE, AND TO GIVE HIS LIFE A RANSOM FOR MANY.
> - MARK 10:43B-45

> AND A LEPER CAME TO JESUS, BESEECHING HIM AND FALLING ON HIS KNEES BEFORE HIM, AND SAYING, "IF YOU ARE WILLING, YOU CAN MAKE ME CLEAN." MOVED WITH COMPASSION, JESUS STRETCHED OUT HIS HAND AND TOUCHED HIM, AND SAID TO HIM, "I AM WILLING; BE CLEANSED." IMMEDIATELY THE LEPROSY LEFT HIM AND HE WAS CLEANSED. AND HE STERNLY WARNED HIM AND IMMEDIATELY SENT HIM AWAY, AND HE SAID TO HIM, "SEE THAT YOU SAY NOTHING TO ANYONE; BUT GO, SHOW YOURSELF TO THE PRIEST AND OFFER FOR YOUR CLEANSING WHAT MOSES COMMANDED, AS A TESTIMONY TO THEM." BUT HE WENT OUT AND BEGAN TO PROCLAIM IT FREELY AND TO SPREAD THE NEWS AROUND, TO SUCH AN EXTENT THAT JESUS COULD NO LONGER PUBLICLY ENTER A CITY, BUT STAYED OUT IN UNPOPULATED AREAS; AND THEY WERE COMING TO HIM FROM EVERYWHERE.
>
> - MARK 1:40-45

> AS FOR THE LEPER WHO HAS THE INFECTION, HIS CLOTHES SHALL BE TORN, AND THE HAIR OF HIS HEAD SHALL BE UNCOVERED, AND HE SHALL COVER HIS MUSTACHE AND CRY, 'UNCLEAN! UNCLEAN!' HE SHALL REMAIN UNCLEAN ALL THE DAYS DURING WHICH HE HAS THE INFECTION; HE IS UNCLEAN. HE SHALL LIVE ALONE; HIS DWELLING SHALL BE OUTSIDE THE CAMP.
>
> - LEVITICUS 13:45-46

Consider this in the story of the leper in Mark 1.[27]

Leprosy was a terrible cocktail of problems for those afflicted with it. It is a physically debilitating disease, with bacteria entering the body and producing skin lesions that progressively and permanently damage the skin, nerves, and eyes, leaving the body open to secondary infections that can cause the skin to fall off and/or deteriorate painfully. The disease was untreatable and highly contagious.

Because of this, leprosy was socially debilitating, too. Mosaic Law (in Leviticus) dictated that those presented to the priest as having leprosy would be set aside from the people. Religious leaders, being who they were by the time of Jesus, had added several other laws to the heap. A leper couldn't come within five miles of a Jew. A priest or citizen standing under a tree whose shade was breached by a leper became ceremonially unclean. Some have reported that babies will die without touch, but lepers were required to live without any human contact.

Lastly, it was spiritually debilitating, too. In those days, Jews came to the temple to worship, and being excluded from worship meant that they were excluded from God. For a leper, ceremonial uncleanliness permeated every inch of their lives.

Mark 1 shares the story of a leper, presumably a Jew. A Greek or Roman leper would have said, "...You can make me well," but only a Jew would say, "...You can make me clean." The leper knew that he needed more than healing; he needed to be made clean in the eyes of his community and in the eyes of God. He needed help that only Jesus could give him. So what did he do?

It is possible that Jesus was out in the country and away from all others at this point, but based on his success in Capernaum, it's unlikely He was alone. Jesus was standing among those of the community when this leper made a mad dash for life. He came into the inhabited places, and to the feet of Jesus and begged Him, "If You are willing, You can make me clean." His actions broke all the rules, but what he said was even more scandalous.

He didn't say, "You have to make me clean," or "Make me clean so that I do not die," because there is no question that others were preparing to strike dead this frontal assault on public health. He was really saying, "If You see fit to save me, I have risked everything to come to You. I won't define my needs, but if You are willing, I respectfully ask that you make me clean. I have presented no conditions to my service to You. I have indeed risked everything in advance, and if You are willing..."

From this man, the leper, we get a picture of the way, the step that is required for the Great Dance, of unconditional service and how we can go down. How different is this from your walk to Christianity? What are the questions you get from friends considering coming to Jesus? "If I become a Christian, do I have to support...?" or "If I'm a Christian, can I still...?"

Essentially, we're asking if Jesus can address our needs without too high a cost on our end. Those are the questions of someone who is up. The leper's mad dash toward salvation is the action of someone who knows down, puts himself unconditionally at God's service, and looks to God to meet whatever needs that God defines.

What does Jesus do? He feels compassion. He touches the leper. He heals him. He provides him salvation. We know from the Gospels that Jesus didn't *have* to touch the leper to heal him. Jesus' willingness to heal the leper[v] was His own and required neither touch nor compassion, but God doesn't heal us that way. God heals us in the way we need to be healed. With His touch, Jesus healed the leper's wounds, his estrangement from community and his heart.

Salvation, redemption, and community all in one.

Remember Haggai? For the first time, in all of history, something clean, the right thing, came into contact with something unclean, and the clean made the unclean become clean. It was a game-changer. Along the way, through the leper's unconditional service, he reversed an ancient curse. Not only did the clean (Jesus) stay clean, but the unclean became clean.

Through Jesus, we can all become ceremonially clean, no matter what we've done.

Keller calls the leper's dash and Jesus' response of unconditional love scandalous. Jesus' mission was literally to save the world by spreading His Word, but, because of the leper's response to Jesus' instructions, they trade places.

Jesus instructs him to tell no one, but the leper can't help it. He tells everyone that he's clean and no longer has to live in the hillside. Because of that, everyone wanted to see Him and Jesus can no longer enter a city.

Cities represent ease and comfort. It was where culture and religion and academia occurred, but for a leper, Jesus left the cities and met mankind in the unpopulated areas.

Jesus can't become unclean, but for this man—one person below the bottom of the rung of society—Jesus lives the life of a man unclean and away from the cities. It is a picture of what also happens

---

v I can just hear him in heaven now, I HAVE A NAME, YOU KNOW!!! I'M NOT A LEPER ANYMORE—take that up with Mark, buddy!

to Jesus three years later when, for men living in the world and within community, Jesus is dragged outside the city gate and onto the garbage dump. He is taken to the place of the lepers and made a pariah.

> [GOD] MADE HIM WHO KNEW NO SIN TO BE SIN ON OUR BEHALF, SO THAT WE MIGHT BECOME THE RIGHTEOUSNESS OF GOD IN HIM.
> - 2 CORINTHIANS 5:21

God showed us the Way through Jesus, He takes our uncleanness at an extreme cost onto Himself so that we will be forever clean.

Bruce Waltke, a famous Bible scholar, read the entire Bible looking at the idea of what it means to be righteous (to live justly in the world). He determined that the just or righteous are those who "are willing to disadvantage themselves to advantage the community; the [unjust] are willing to disadvantage the community to advantage themselves."[28]

So where does this meet you today? Whether the world has you by the throat or you own half the city, what does it look like to go down and is it worth it to go up?

I've had a very real experience with this in September of 2012 with Jerry Leachman, a lover of Jesus and missionary on the ground in Washington, DC. Leachman ministers to men and came to Atlanta to speak to our church. I had the honor of taking him around and hearing every talk he gave in the city. Toward the end of our time together, some of the troubles facing our nation began to weigh on my heart.

For the first time, I really experienced the hopelessness of the hole we are digging. I saw, and almost experienced, that the only thing that can deliver our country was revival, and at the end of that weekend, I had a real thirst for it. I didn't even begin to work out what revival looked like, but I had a fire in me for revival.

> THE TIME IS FULFILLED, AND THE KINGDOM OF GOD IS AT HAND; REPENT AND BELIEVE IN THE GOSPEL.
> - MARK 1:15

With a little research, I found that all major revival begins with true repentance. I came across Jesus' first words

> THEREFORE, CONFESS YOUR SINS TO ONE ANOTHER, AND PRAY FOR ONE ANOTHER SO THAT YOU MAY BE HEALED. THE EFFECTIVE PRAYER OF A RIGHTEOUS MAN CAN ACCOMPLISH MUCH.
>
> - JAMES 5:16

of His ministry in Mark 1 and James 5.

With two brothers in Christ, we walked past the threshold of the sanctuary to repent. I'm not sure they were on board with repenting, and to be honest, I wasn't either. I remember that, as I put one foot in front of the other, I thought of reasons why I really didn't want to do this—things like, "I've been forgiven for these sins," and "I don't want them to know that," and "Is this really that important?" But a moment later, I was at the altar, praying.

> THE LORD SAID TO MOSES, "I WILL ALSO DO THIS THING OF WHICH YOU HAVE SPOKEN; FOR YOU HAVE FOUND FAVOR IN MY SIGHT AND I HAVE KNOWN YOU BY NAME." THEN MOSES SAID, "I PRAY YOU, SHOW ME YOUR GLORY!" AND HE SAID, "I MYSELF WILL MAKE ALL MY GOODNESS PASS BEFORE YOU, AND WILL PROCLAIM THE NAME OF THE LORD BEFORE YOU; AND I WILL BE GRACIOUS TO WHOM I WILL BE GRACIOUS, AND WILL SHOW COMPASSION ON WHOM I WILL SHOW COMPASSION."
>
> - EXODUS 33:17-19

What came out of me started slowly but, over the coming minutes, I let loose the worst sins I had—things that I'd only shared with God. I was humiliated there, with my two friends, but I wanted God more. Like a leper dashing through the crowd, I could almost feel the blows to my carefully curated self—but then something incredible happened.

I felt the presence of God. He'd been there all the time, but something about this humbling, this running to the feet of God, risking a lot, and laying aside any condition to my service, revealed Him to me in a much fuller way.

I went down that day, and He bore me up.

Though my nation didn't experience revival, I did. On that day, I felt a physical wrenching in me that I now consider an anointing.

Three days later, I was given the vision that became this lesson. For me, this is what it looks like to go down, and yes. Yes. EXTREME-LY, YES! It is worth it to go up.

I don't know if this works for everyone, but it works for me. Each time I make that walk to repent of my sins of the week and any others that come onto my heart, with my brothers in Christ or another that I pull into a prayer room—every single time, my eyes are opened to the very real presence of God within that room. I don't know if it will work for you. To be honest, I haven't found anyone willing to try it again with a group, but it's a big enough deal that I urge you to try it.

Wouldn't that be just like God to have put His Kingdom within the reach of anyone willing to make that long walk down the aisle and earnestly repent as Jesus asked 2,000 years ago? Try.

Regardless of your results, there is blessing in this model. Find a way this week—whether it's repentance or giving away some amount of money or time that you need or sharing something personal—to go down in sacrificial service to someone else and wait—no, expect—that if you do it for Christ, He will literally bear you up.

But do it like the leper, without any expectation or condition as to what that blessing will be.

I can't wait to hear your results!

Before you go on to the next chapter, take a few moments to read one or more of the following:
Matthew Chapters 16 through 18
Mark Chapter 10
Luke 13:22 through Chapter 14
John Chapters 11 & 12

CHAPTER 8

Truth Beats Love

Jesus brought us the truth that religion won't save us, that our works aren't sufficient, and our thinking they are sufficient negates them, anyway. Until we understand what God did to give us the opportunity to enter the Great Dance, even our works push us farther from Him. The Gospel is that God sacrificed His most Precious out of love for me and, therefore, it's my absolute pleasure to obey.

The second thing that Jesus brought us was a truth.

Within the context of the Great Dance, in Chapter 1, we drew a line between the beat of the dance and love. Love, sometimes termed grace, with its warm and fuzzy consequences, seems to be at the opposite end of the spectrum from truth, which is often associated with the law with all of its requirements and obedience. We must choose, mustn't we, whether to enforce the law (truth) or to administer grace (love)?

No, in fact, we don't have to choose. We will see throughout this chapter that when we choose between law and grace, or truth and love, we diminish and end up with a poor version of both. Jesus connected them in the specific truth He brought.

To whom did Jesus bring this truth?

What is this truth?

How can truth, mishandled, diminish our love?

How can truth and love work together as our Fundamental, a concept that we've discussed briefly but will fully work out here.

In those days, **JESUS BROUGHT THIS TRUTH TO** two major groups: the Sadducees and the Pharisees. The Sadducees were more liberal in their faith. They got along to get along, and were more willing to conform to the greatest power of the day. Because of that, they held most of the lucrative government offices and the best jobs in the temple. They were among the wealthy class and looked more Greek and Roman than the typical Israelite.

They believed only in the Law contained in the Torah (Genesis, Exodus, Leviticus, Numbers, and Deuteronomy) and rejected any other oral Law proposed by the Pharisees. Because the Torah contained little mention of life after death, they disregarded eternal life completely. This played out in their lives, as they were more likely to make decisions based on accommodating their present circumstances.

> HE WHO HAS MY COMMAND-
> MENTS AND KEEPS THEM IS THE
> ONE WHO LOVES ME; AND HE
> WHO LOVES ME WILL BE LOVED
> BY MY FATHER, AND I WILL
> LOVE HIM AND WILL DISCLOSE
> MYSELF TO HIM.
>
> - JOHN 14:21

The Pharisees were the faith conservatives of the day—sort of. They spent a lifetime memorizing and trying to live by each and every one of the 613 Laws in the Bible. They followed the rules.

When you get serious about following 613 laws, and you lay thousands of years of human interaction over it, you develop some well-thought-out interpretations that turn into laws themselves. These new laws compound on top of each other until an already impossible law can become an obsession. These guys were sometimes wealthy, but typically were from the working class. Some that took pride in their ability to follow the rules, exclude others, or weigh down their brethren were regular foils in Jesus' ministry. They would have looked extremely traditional.

They believed so strongly in a "world to come" and that the dead would be resurrected that failure to believe it as they did was one of the only three things that they thought would keep one from eternal life. Because of this, they were earnestly trying to earn reward and favor in this world to come. (A Pharisee didn't quite see it as heaven, so for now, we'll just refer to this as resurrection and eternal life.)

We have the same groups today. We may not be able to neatly stuff them into Republican and Democrat, rural or urban, lover or fighter—but we have pieces of each.

To be candid, I have been pieces of both.

I've been a Sadducee when I go along to get along—thinking that I'm doing good enough in this faith walk. I've changed my preferences toward the preferences of a client or a boss to make them like me. I have thrown out a coarse joke when it seemed appropriate or denied Christ when someone I want to impress also denied Him. I often looked, dressed, and acted like those that occupy this world, rather than those whom I am called to love. And I have made decisions that are convenient to my present circumstances, even when they result in a resounding "Atta boy" from the deepest evil. Jesus criticized the Sadducees, but they weren't his focus. His most scathing commentary was for the Pharisees.

I have been a Pharisee, too. I've been a student of the Word, which Jesus loves, but I've also been a rule-follower. Jesus loves obedience, too, but when I've looked to others and felt superior to them or when God has asked me to help someone cut away something with a scalpel and I've used an ax, I've been a Pharisee. I have tried to earn God's favor by obeying the rules I liked and failing to love. I've searched the Internet for a hair shirt. I've felt pride in things of God as if I'd been the one that initiated them. I have served others with a poor heart or hoped that others would see my labor and think better of me. I have judged others mercilessly.

Once you get outside yourself and begin to get serious about the Word, and start putting some action behind what you say you believe, there is an extreme risk of slipping into the trap of the Pharisees.

The risk is to get off the storyline of the Gospel—instead of curating it, we begin to interpret it and mold it around things that we can handle. We begin to say, "He couldn't have meant that," or, "How can that be true?" God leveled His greatest criticism against those that calcify here—that became hard in their conviction that their own works made them acceptable and their religion would save them. In the end, Pharisees 2,000 years ago and today build the Gospel around a set of rules they hope to achieve and encourage others to do the same.

WHAT IS THIS TRUTH? The truth that Jesus brought us is that our works will never save us and, if you believe they will, you're doomed. Throughout all history, no man except One has been able to accomplish works that stand up to the Law. The standard is too high. In the 21st century, here's how it plays out:

"Lord, I love You and I trust You. I obey all You tell me to do. I know that I take those additional deductions I didn't earn and I know I yell at my _____ and I know that I could have dealt differently with that person who's against me, but hey. What else have Ya got? There is no one else in my _____ that's half as committed to You as I am. So, You're welcome. And while we're on the subject, I've got a few requests. I can't wait to be with You and see You, but in the meantime, I need healthy _____, and a good _____ and how about throwing something in for me, too? You know what I like. Thanks. Amen." [29]

But God, on the other end, says, "Wait, wait, wait, wait, wait, wait. I have something I need to tell you..." Yet he's met by that long, loud dial tone of someone who has hung up to run off to work or carpool or _____.

Our response leaves the all-powerful Creator of heaven and earth sitting on the other end with fewer options than He had at the beginning of the discussion. Lay months upon months there and what choice does He have but to shake our very foundations?

We know something of this God by now, don't we? We know that He had the ability to snap His fingers and clear our accounts, but to do so would have been an insufficient amount of love and grace to win our hearts. Instead, of the simple solution, He chose love. God chose love for us, for His Son, and for the Holy Spirit in the way that love demanded it: the cross.

You know how this story progresses. Over time, because of our choices—choices that put other things in front of God in our hearts—we begin to lose these things (the healthy _____, the good _____, and the other pleasures). If your view of God is built on this—that I am accepted by God, because I obey— then whether you've actually drawn this out or not, you're really saying that God owes you. It's His end of the contract.

God owes you a good life, healthy kids, a loving/helpful spouse, a job, etc. And if He can't (*or doesn't or won't*) provide those for you, then you'll provide them for yourself.

I've taken a long time to get here, but the truth of Jesus turns this kind of thinking on its head. **The truth is that He came to give us everything—to scatter His power, to become poor, to give up all glory, humbly—out of love for us. The truth is that when I recognize that, when that becomes my Fundamental, it is my absolute pleasure to obey.**

When that truth goes deep into the center of our lives, things change.

I go from a guy ticking off 50 cents for every candy bar on a ledger like Ben Kingsley in a convenience store in *House of Sand and Fog* to Johnny Depp in *Blow* without the time to count transactions—I just weigh the money and put it in the spare bedroom. It goes from minutiae to Niagara. When the fact that the all-powerful Creator of heaven and earth came down to climb on a cross to be shredded and torn for me becomes my Fundamental, it is my absolute pleasure to obey in everything—things big and small.

Instead of obedience being a chore that keeps me from what I'd really like to be doing, my love courses through this fundamental truth, drives my obedience and replenishes my love. Like a heart beats blood, my truth beats love, pushing it into all corners of my life.

But the truth doesn't automatically work that way in our lives, does it? For most of us, our central truth (not God's truth or law, but the laws by which we live) doesn't grow our love and pleasure to obey. Our obedience is a furnace for which we earnestly search every corner of the house looking for any small bit of love to keep it running just a little bit longer. How can it become our pleasure to obey?

Before we look at this, let's examine two parables Jesus shared to explore **HOW TRUTH, MISHANDLED, DIMINISHES OUR LOVE.**

Two men, a rich young ruler and a lawyer, approach Jesus and ask him nearly identical questions. They're both weighing Jesus and trying to decide whether they should consider Him worthy to follow or instead begin a list of reasons to hate Him.

"What shall I do to inherit eternal life?"

How you respond to Jesus' answer to this question determines the tune your truth beats to. Does your truth beat love or does your truth beat hate, jealousy, comparison, rules, freedom, self…

Luke 10 is the only Gospel to report this incredible story of the Good Samaritan. It is so fundamental to our teaching that every child in Sunday school knows and can tell you the story.

Let me set the stage:

In that time, a lawyer wasn't like we might think of one today. His expertise was in Mosaic Law and, so he acted kind of like an arbiter and judge for faithful men when they got into a dispute or when they just wanted to know how something should be interpreted.

Christians have gotten away from this today but, for centuries, those seeking to be faithful to God would seek out wise counselors, like this lawyer, to tell them what is acceptable in a specific situation. The faithful Jew would lay out the facts and pose a question, then the lawyer would mine his extensive canon of mostly memorized Scripture and make a ruling.[vi]

---

vi Orthodox Jews still have something like this today http://www.nytimes.com/2012/07/19/world/middleeast/rabbi-y-s-elyashiv-master-of-talmudic-law-dies-at-102.html?_r=0

In this parable, the lawyer stands and asks the question perfectly. He doesn't ask, "What shall I do to *EARN* eternal life?" No, he uses the word "inherit." See the difference? Want to *earn* a fortune? Get an education. Get a job. Save a lot of money and then take some big risks—maybe six in a row—and then, maybe, you'll *earn* a fortune.

Want to *inherit* a fortune? If this option is even available to you (by being born into the right family), then there's one thing you've got to do: Don't mess up. At this point, the lawyer's looking good to the crowd—but Jesus sees his heart.

Jesus then turns the question back on him, but the lawyer was ready.

Perhaps the lawyer had heard Jesus' teaching and just parroted it back to Him, or it could have been a significant part of the teaching at the time. Either way, His response is profound, because it draws together two different scriptures from the depths of the Torah.

> AND A LAWYER STOOD UP AND PUT HIM TO THE TEST, SAYING, "TEACHER, WHAT SHALL I DO TO INHERIT ETERNAL LIFE?" AND HE SAID TO HIM, "WHAT IS WRITTEN IN THE LAW? HOW DOES IT READ TO YOU?" AND HE ANSWERED, "YOU SHALL LOVE THE LORD YOUR GOD WITH ALL YOUR HEART, AND WITH ALL YOUR SOUL, AND WITH ALL YOUR STRENGTH, AND WITH ALL YOUR MIND; AND YOUR NEIGHBOR AS YOURSELF." AND HE SAID TO HIM, "YOU HAVE ANSWERED CORRECTLY; DO THIS AND YOU WILL LIVE."
> - LUKE 10:25-28

> HEAR, O ISRAEL! THE LORD IS OUR GOD, THE LORD IS ONE! YOU SHALL LOVE THE LORD YOUR GOD WITH ALL YOUR HEART AND WITH ALL YOUR SOUL AND WITH ALL YOUR MIGHT.
> - DEUTERONOMY 6:4-5

> IT SHALL COME ABOUT, IF YOU LISTEN OBEDIENTLY TO MY COMMANDMENTS WHICH I AM COMMANDING YOU TODAY, TO LOVE THE LORD YOUR GOD AND TO SERVE HIM WITH ALL YOUR HEART AND ALL YOUR SOUL...
> - DEUTERONOMY 11:13

"You shall love the Lord your God with all your heart, and with all your soul, and with all your strength, and with all your mind," is a close interpretation of the Shema.[vii] The collection of verses called the Shema were of critical importance to Judaism by 100 A.D. and is still contained within Phylacteries (or Tefillin) and the Mezuzah outside Jewish homes today. They are the John 3:16 of Judaism.

> YOU SHALL NOT HATE YOUR FELLOW COUNTRYMAN IN YOUR HEART; YOU MAY SURELY REPROVE YOUR NEIGHBOR, BUT SHALL NOT INCUR SIN BECAUSE OF HIM. YOU SHALL NOT TAKE VENGEANCE, NOR BEAR ANY GRUDGE AGAINST THE SONS OF YOUR PEOPLE, BUT YOU SHALL LOVE YOUR NEIGHBOR AS YOURSELF; I AM THE LORD.
> - LEVITICUS 19:17-18

"And [love] your neighbor as yourself," is a little more problematic. It also comes from the Torah, but is buried in the middle of Leviticus 19 under the (much later-given and only in Protestant Bibles) title "Sundry Laws." Called the greatest commandment by Christ (Matthew 22:39 and Mark 12:31) and quoted by Paul (Romans 13:9 and Galatians 5:14) and James (2:8), it comes after some good rules for living and before guidelines on mixed breeding of cattle, seed, and clothing fibers.[viii]

This Law wasn't written on a tablet and brought down the mountain. Jesus and this lawyer pick these two scriptures out as two that define all Scripture and a roadmap to inherit eternal life.

Don't mess it up.

The lawyer got the answer he was seeking: Good job—do that and you'll get eternal life. Yes. Thank you. But, instead of stopping there, he pressed on.

Justify.

Jerry Leachman taught me that the word *justify* should be thought of as, "just as if I'd never..." or to settle accounts. When I owe AmEx $500, they will pursue me until I pay it, but once I pay

---

vii The Shema consists of Deuteronomy 6:4–9, 11:13-21, and Numbers 15:37–41

viii This verse is sometimes equated with the Golden Rule, stated in Matthew 7:12: "In everything, therefore, treat people the same way you want them to treat you, for this is the Law and the Prophets." Loving your neighbor as yourself is a higher standard than the Golden Rule. It is possible that you want to be left alone and not bothered by your neighbors. So you could fulfill the Golden Rule by disregarding your neighbor entirely. But in doing so, I would be far short of the standard of loving my neighbor as myself.

it, the account has been justified, settled, made just as if I had never incurred the debt. They're not mad at me. The account is paid.

What does Luke tell us that the lawyer is trying to do? He was trying to settle his own account—to justify himself. Standing in front of Jesus, he had been promised that he would inherit eternal life if he held to just two laws. The lawyer, in one beat, decided he would try to earn it. His truth marched to the beat of self, action, performance, and getting things done.

What comes next is that story that we all know: the Good Samaritan. As background, it's important to know who these characters represent in our current world. **The man** isn't really identified. Scholars speculate that this man was Jewish, but others suggest that he represents all of mankind.[30] **A priest** is a preacher or associate minister— a holy man. If you're active in your church, **the Levite** would have been one of us. In those times, he was of a special class that performed jobs around the temple, but today he would have been the guy on the finance committee, member of a Sunday school class, administrative board chair, or some

> BUT WISHING TO JUSTIFY HIMSELF, HE SAID TO JESUS, "AND WHO IS MY NEIGHBOR?" JESUS REPLIED AND SAID, "A MAN WAS GOING DOWN FROM JERUSALEM TO JERICHO, AND FELL AMONG ROBBERS, AND THEY STRIPPED HIM AND BEAT HIM, AND WENT AWAY LEAVING HIM HALF DEAD. AND BY CHANCE A PRIEST WAS GOING DOWN ON THAT ROAD, AND WHEN HE SAW HIM, HE PASSED BY ON THE OTHER SIDE. LIKEWISE A LEVITE ALSO, WHEN HE CAME TO THE PLACE AND SAW HIM, PASSED BY ON THE OTHER SIDE. BUT A SAMARITAN, WHO WAS ON A JOURNEY, CAME UPON HIM; AND WHEN HE SAW HIM, HE FELT COMPASSION, AND CAME TO HIM AND BANDAGED UP HIS WOUNDS, POURING OIL AND WINE ON THEM; AND HE PUT HIM ON HIS OWN BEAST, AND BROUGHT HIM TO AN INN AND TOOK CARE OF HIM. ON THE NEXT DAY HE TOOK OUT TWO DENARII AND GAVE THEM TO THE INNKEEPER AND SAID, 'TAKE CARE OF HIM; AND WHATEVER MORE YOU SPEND, WHEN I RETURN I WILL REPAY YOU.' WHICH OF THESE THREE DO YOU THINK PROVED TO BE A NEIGHBOR TO THE MAN WHO FELL INTO THE ROBBERS' HANDS?"
>
> - LUKE 10:29-36

lay person with a role in the church and doing some work there. The **Samaritan** was considered scum. When Nebuchadnezzar conquered Israel in 586 B.C., he took all the best families to Babylon, as was his custom. Those that remained were the lowest level workers. According to the elite sojourning in Babylon, Samaritans couldn't run the place and certainly didn't know the right way to pursue God.

The time in Babylon steeled the "good" guys and made them even madder when they returned to see the remnant Samaritans, now intermarried with some locals who moved in to fill the void—and were just as proud of their heritage in the land of Israel as the returning Israelite. Over the next 600 years, Samaritans and Jews fought like only brothers can. It was a long and dirty feud fed by militant Greek occupation, like gasoline feeds a fire. Conservatively, Jews hated Samaritans and the feeling was mutual.

> As He was setting out on a journey, a man ran up to Him and knelt before Him, and asked Him, "Good Teacher, what shall I do to inherit eternal life?"
>
> - Mark 10:17

Consider Jesus' question, "Which of these three do you think proved to be a neighbor to the man?" while we look at the next person, the rich young ruler in Mark 10, who asked this same question. It's the same exact wording, except this rich young ruler added the salutation, "Good Teacher," instead of the lawyer's, "Teacher."

Jason Lin suggested in a sermon that this addition to an already auspicious title was fawning, essentially trying to flatter Jesus—and He was having none of it. Jesus gave the same initial answer that He had given the lawyer: "Obey."

> And Jesus said to him, "Why do you call Me good? No one is good except God alone. You know the commandments, 'Do not murder, Do not commit adultery, Do not steal, Do not bear false witness, Do not defraud, Honor your father and mother.'" And he said to Him, "Teacher, I have kept all these things from my youth up."
>
> - Mark 10:18-20

If the rich young ruler had my Dad, he would have said, "Thank you. You are correct, sir." Jesus wouldn't have let that stand, though, because, "looking at him, Jesus felt love for him..." Love.

This prideful ruler, who chased after Him, fell at His feet and begged that the question we all pose deserved an answer, so Jesus gave him a different one. While He had told the lawyer to go and care for neighbors that hate him (or at least that he hated), this time, He told the ruler to sell all he had.

> LOOKING AT HIM, JESUS FELT A LOVE FOR HIM AND SAID TO HIM, "ONE THING YOU LACK: GO AND SELL ALL YOU POSSESS AND GIVE TO THE POOR, AND YOU WILL HAVE TREASURE IN HEAVEN; AND COME, FOLLOW ME." BUT AT THESE WORDS HE WAS SADDENED, AND HE WENT AWAY GRIEVING, FOR HE WAS ONE WHO OWNED MUCH PROPERTY."
> - MARK 10:21-22

Here in the stories of the lawyer and the rich young ruler, we have two who submit to the Law, but fail to connect it to their love. Instead of obeying because they love, they obey in order to be accepted. They hold their loves separate from the Law.

Let's look at this a little closer and see **HOW TRUTH AND LOVE CAN FUNDAMENTALLY WORK TOGETHER.** How can we connect our hearts' greatest love to fuel our obedience to the truth that Jesus affirmed?

First, notice how Jesus, in perfect wisdom, provided answers specific to each man, but also gave the same answer. **The answer was to obey out of your love.** Jesus told them to obey in the big things and to obey in the small things, but also to obey in the circle of things that each man considered impossible.

> GREATER LOVE HAS NO ONE THAN THIS, THAT ONE LAY DOWN HIS LIFE FOR HIS FRIENDS.
> - JOHN 15:13

Both men were disheartened, because they were focused on themselves and didn't see the others around them. When their obedience was fueled by their own needs, the level of obedience Jesus demanded was impossible. But when obedience is fueled by

> OWE NOTHING TO ANYONE EXCEPT TO LOVE ONE ANOTHER; FOR HE WHO LOVES HIS NEIGHBOR HAS FULFILLED THE LAW. FOR THIS, "YOU SHALL NOT COMMIT ADULTERY, YOU SHALL NOT MURDER, YOU SHALL NOT STEAL, YOU SHALL NOT COVET," AND IF THERE IS ANY OTHER COMMANDMENT, IT IS SUMMED UP IN THIS SAYING, "YOU SHALL LOVE YOUR NEIGHBOR AS YOURSELF." LOVE DOES NO WRONG TO A NEIGHBOR; THEREFORE LOVE IS THE FULFILLMENT OF THE LAW.
>
> - ROMANS 13:8-10

love, this type of obedience becomes a pleasure.

Let's look just below the surface in the parable of the Good Samaritan. The priest was headed away from Jerusalem into Jericho. The road is a 17-mile descent of about 3,300 feet—from the highest point in the area to the lowest point then known. It is treacherous and signifies a walk from heaven into hell. If the priest had touched that man, not because of nationality but because of his open wounds, he would have become ceremonially unclean. Since the ceremony would have happened in Jerusalem, it is not clear what relevance becoming unclean actually had to the priest, but it would have put him out of service for a period of time. The same goes for the Levite, but here, we're given no indication whether the Levite is ascending or descending. He is just going.

Their role within society is critical for these two characters. They were seen as the manifestation of piety and religious duty—their actual job was to serve God. If they were coming and going—whether ascending to or descending from Jerusalem—it was implied that they were in service to God, and yet their service lacked any love for this man.

How many times have I been en route to a Bible study and passed someone homeless or stranded on the side of the road? Does my obedience drive my love or does my love propel my obedience?

Said another way, in my heart, does the Law give me a way to prop up what I really love, or does my love push me to greater service through obedience to the Law? One leads to burnout, comparison, hatred, and standing outside of your father's party, cursing him.

The other may look to the world like the same thing, but instead of obedience diminishing you, feeling like a chore, or draining you, it becomes a spring of love that replenishes—a veritable fountain overflowing with water that runs through the streets and quenches the thirst of a city.

When the lowly Samaritan comes, everything changes because, "he felt compassion." He picked up someone that hated him and sacrificed his time and his provisions for this stranger. He proved to be a neighbor.

> BUT HE ANSWERED AND SAID TO HIS FATHER, 'LOOK! FOR SO MANY YEARS I HAVE BEEN SERVING YOU AND I HAVE NEVER NEGLECTED A COMMAND OF YOURS; AND YET YOU HAVE NEVER GIVEN ME A YOUNG GOAT, SO THAT I MIGHT CELEBRATE WITH MY FRIENDS...
> - LUKE 15:29

The Samaritan's truth beat love—his truth, obedience, and the law of his heart didn't run on rules and wasn't built to sustain another set of hidden loves. His truth was powered by his love. To the lawyer, Jesus' request, in that moment, was impossible. The lawyer's hate for his neighbor was so great that he

> AND HE SAID, "THE ONE WHO SHOWED MERCY TOWARD HIM." THEN JESUS SAID TO HIM, "GO AND DO THE SAME."
> - LUKE 10:37

couldn't even say the name Samaritan—he called him, "the one who showed mercy toward him."

Sa-mar-i-tan. It's pretty easy to say, but his truth beat a hatred so strong or he'd grown a pride so large that he couldn't even name the hero of this parable.

The rich young ruler, whom Jesus loved, got his answer—a true answer, which was evidence enough that his truth beat luxury or wealth or security or significance. In the presence of the Lord of the universe, he chose his stuff.

I've been there and I can tell you, when you get back home and look around at all that things you put in front of Jesus, it all looks like junk, anyway.

> FOR YOU KNOW THE GRACE OF OUR LORD JESUS CHRIST, THAT THOUGH HE WAS RICH, YET FOR YOUR SAKE HE BECAME POOR, SO THAT YOU THROUGH HIS POVERTY MIGHT BECOME RICH.
>
> - 2 CORINTHIANS 8:9

> YOU SHALL NOT HATE YOUR FELLOW COUNTRYMAN IN YOUR HEART; YOU MAY SURELY REPROVE YOUR NEIGHBOR, BUT SHALL NOT INCUR SIN BECAUSE OF HIM. YOU SHALL NOT TAKE VENGEANCE, NOR BEAR ANY GRUDGE AGAINST THE SONS OF YOUR PEOPLE, BUT YOU SHALL LOVE YOUR NEIGHBOR AS YOURSELF; I AM THE LORD.
>
> - LEVITICUS 19:17-18

These parables are ironic twists in a much larger Gospel story. Jesus was asking these two men to do the same impossible things that He was actually doing in their midst. This ancient story is one of an extremely wealthy man with centuries of reasons to be angry and with the ultimate credibility.

He travels across the universe into the land of those who hate Him. He reduces Himself by epic proportions in a Great Dance of Service. He keeps the commandments—all of them—perfectly in the Spirit that they were given and He is very good. He gives His time and treasure to the poor, but what He gives them is so much more than that—at a cost that is unspeakable. He loves God with every fiber of His being and exceeded Leviticus 19:18—finding the one narrow path toward loving His neighbor more than Himself.

And as this man ascended toward Jerusalem, Jesus was there before the priest. When the robbers lunged for the man, Jesus stood in his place, and took the beating. And as the man scurried away, and the priest moved to the other side of the road and the Levite passed by, Jesus knew that even though each one hated Him, it was His absolute pleasure to endure. Jesus' truth beat love like a heart beats blood.

Jesus didn't throw these parables around lightly. These parables told His great story, the Gospel story, to men who were reading from their own story, the wrong story. These parables were an opportunity for the scales to fall from our eyes and see the man that stands before them.

These parables aren't just examples. They were being lived out, in real time by Jesus Whose truth and love connected seamlessly into acts of service.

So **how can this connection become our Fundamental?**

Keller told a story[31] pretty soon after the 9/11 attacks on the World Trade Center, when the news media was full of pundits suggesting the real problem with the world was religious fundamentalism. Keller said that one night he heard his wife, Kathy, answer the pundits, "Well, it matters what your Fundamental is."

Your Fundamental is that thing at the center of your heart around which everything else orbits. It is the thing that you think about 10 or 100 times a day. It is that thing that you write books about in the form of checks and calendars. It is that thing that you plant and sow and, eventually, reap in your life. If that happens to be hatred and a feeling of superiority, then it's not too big a leap to consider flying a couple of planes into a building.

What is your Fundamental? You probably have a good idea what it is, but here's a way to confirm it. Think about the last time you walked into a room and felt less than everyone else there. They might have been richer, prettier, better dressed, more powerful, better athletes, or thinner. Hold that picture in your mind. Or, think about the last time you were in danger. Maybe you were in danger of losing your job, your house, a loved one, a child, your retirement—or maybe someone literally put a gun in your face.

Where you go next is your Fundamental. If you say, "Yeah, but I'm from a better family than all these folks," or "I'm OK, I've got a nest egg socked away," or "Yeah, but I drive a Mercedes."

Where you go next when your significance or security are threatened is your Fundamental.

And when that Fundamental

> BUT FROM THERE YOU WILL SEEK THE LORD YOUR GOD, AND YOU WILL FIND HIM IF YOU SEARCH FOR HIM WITH ALL YOUR HEART AND ALL YOUR SOUL.
> - DEUTERONOMY 4:29

> ASK, AND IT WILL BE GIVEN TO YOU; SEEK, AND YOU WILL FIND; KNOCK, AND IT WILL BE OPENED TO YOU.
> - MATTHEW 7:7

is that the all-powerful Creator of the universe came down from heaven at an unbelievable cost to break and tear His greatest love, because He loved you—when that becomes the center of your heart—then your heart switches over, love compels your service, and it is your absolute pleasure to obey.

But how do we do that? What does it look like to begin anew? Start with three things: a request, a warning, and a burial.

Start by **asking God** to increase your love. Earnestly pray for it and repent of those things that have muted it in your heart.

Remember the story of our trip to FAO Schwartz? We wanted to get our children a special toy there, but they needed to want it, too. This is like that. If you ask God for love, He will give it to you, because He's dying for you to have it. In fact, He has already paid for it, and all you have to do is choose it—to want it more than whatever your hand is clutching right now. With all the poetry you can muster, or even with a groan, reach up to God and ask Him to send His Spirit into your heart and to increase your love. Then, as you rise from prayer, walk out into the world as if your love has been exponentially increased. Even before you can see that it has, assume that God has loosened a wellspring of love within your heart.

C. S. Lewis talks about this at length:

> IN THE SAME WAY THE SPIRIT ALSO HELPS OUR WEAKNESS; FOR WE DO NOT KNOW HOW TO PRAY AS WE SHOULD, BUT THE SPIRIT HIMSELF INTERCEDES FOR US WITH GROANINGS TOO DEEP FOR WORDS...
> - ROMANS 8:26

> THEREFORE I SAY TO YOU, ALL THINGS FOR WHICH YOU PRAY AND ASK, BELIEVE THAT YOU HAVE RECEIVED THEM, AND THEY WILL BE GRANTED YOU.
> - MARK 11:24

Very often the only way to get a quality in reality is to start behaving as if you had it already. That's why children's games are so important. They are always pretending to be grown-ups—playing soldiers, playing shop. But all the time, they are hardening their muscles and sharpening their wits so that the pretense of being grown-up helps them to grow up in earnest.

Now the moment that you realize, "Here I am, dressing up as Christ," it is extremely likely that you will see at once some way in which at that very moment the pretense could be made less of a pretense and more of a reality. You will find several things going on in your mind, which would not be going on there if you were really the Son of God. Well, stop them. Or you may realize that, instead of saying your prayers, you ought to be downstairs writing a letter, or helping your wife to wash up. Well, go and do it.

... There are lots of things which your conscience might not call definitely wrong (specially things in your mind) but which you will see at once you cannot go on doing if you are seriously trying to be like Christ.

This prayer, assumption, and acting requires a **warning**: Jesus' truth to the lawyer and the rich young ruler were extremely costly to each. Jesus' love to us was costly. Any parent's love, if properly gifted to a child, is extremely expensive.

Yet somewhere along the way, we have decided that personal responsibility is our neighbor's job and doesn't have to cost us a thing.

> FOR IN THE WAY YOU JUDGE, YOU WILL BE JUDGED; AND BY YOUR STANDARD OF MEASURE, IT WILL BE MEASURED TO YOU. WHY DO YOU LOOK AT THE SPECK THAT IS IN YOUR BROTHER'S EYE, BUT DO NOT NOTICE THE LOG THAT IS IN YOUR OWN EYE? OR HOW CAN YOU SAY TO YOUR BROTHER, 'LET ME TAKE THE SPECK OUT OF YOUR EYE,' AND BEHOLD, THE LOG IS IN YOUR OWN EYE? YOU HYPOCRITE, FIRST TAKE THE LOG OUT OF YOUR OWN EYE, AND THEN YOU WILL SEE CLEARLY TO TAKE THE SPECK OUT OF YOUR BROTHER'S EYE.
>
> - MATTHEW 7:2-5

This even applies to the church, which is often outspoken about issues for which their stand on truth costs them little. Earnest churches have campaigned against accurate readable translations of the Bible, women's suffrage, abolition, civil rights, and other issues today—for which their stand on truth cost them nothing—while overlooking their own contribution (read: sin) to the issue entirely.

Society is no better. In the wake of the Sandy Hook massacre, those with no interest in owning or having a firearm see a solution in gun control. Those who own firearms but have no immediate connection to anyone who is mentally ill believe all can be solved by focusing on mental health. And those with children dealing with anti-social behaviors say we should not be too quick to point to a certain type of child as the problem. Somewhere along the way, we have decided that personal responsibility is our neighbor's job.

When we look past our own obvious sin to shine a light on the sin that we will never commit, we manipulate the Gospel. When we develop solutions to problems that lay the burden of compliance on our neighbors, we choose the lesser love of the lawyer. When we choose to focus our congregations on issues that do not affect our lifestyles in any way, we choose the rich young ruler's wealth over God.

The antidote to this is God's love letter to man. Sold more than any other book in history, the Bible is now universally available— and nearly unread in most of the developed world. Christians purport to build a life on it, but don't even bother to read it.

The Bible is the window to God and steady plodding through it, a chapter a day to start, will provide the protection and wisdom you need to avoid trouble as you move out into the world with love.

> THEN THE LORD GOD FORMED MAN OF DUST FROM THE GROUND, AND BREATHED INTO HIS NOSTRILS THE BREATH OF LIFE; AND MAN BECAME A LIVING BEING.
> - GENESIS 2:7

> AND JESUS UTTERED A LOUD CRY, AND BREATHED HIS LAST.
> - MARK 15:37

Finally, you must **bury the cross** deep within your heart. Read and work though the Gospels and this sacrifice until it melts you. Imagine what it must have been like to stand in Jerusalem. How did the blood of Jesus, mixed with dirt and sweat, smell? How did it feel to stand by and see 400 pounds of wood and flesh drop nine inches into the groove that had been cut to hold it?

There are innumerable ways to make this real to you, but draw close to the image of Adam, lifeless but held tenderly, and then the hot breath of God entering into His nostrils. It took days for God to create the world, and thousands of years for Him to fix it. From that first breath to Jesus' last, the Creator of the universe loved you in the most costly way anyone has ever seen. And the truth is, that even if everyone else had been spotless, He loved you enough to make the same choice of sacrifice, even while you waged rebellion against Him.

> GREATER LOVE HAS NO ONE THAN THIS, THAT ONE LAY DOWN HIS LIFE FOR HIS FRIENDS.
> - JOHN 15:13

When the fact that an all-powerful God of heaven and earth became a seed and was torn for you—when that becomes your Fundamental truth, then it is your absolute pleasure to obey.

Before you go on to the next chapter, take a few moments to read one or more of the following:
Matthew Chapters 19 & 20
Mark Chapter 11
Luke Chapters 15 & 16
John Chapters 13 & 14

CHAPTER 9

Tune into Life's Belief

Jesus brought us a life—His life. He left all He had ever known, all eternity in communion with God, to come to earth and be rejected by His Father for us. Could God have done it another way? I'm sure He could have—but this sacrifice was the sacrifice that WE demanded. How else could He demonstrate the depth of His love? The blood on the cross settled the accounts, but the resurrection was the receipt showing the debt was fully paid.

The prospect of writing this chapter frightens me.

Jesus brought us a way, and a truth. But He also brought us a life—His life. To weave a tapestry together of the ministry of Jesus seems a mountain too tall, but the

> SIMON PETER ANSWERED HIM, "LORD, TO WHOM SHALL WE GO? YOU HAVE WORDS OF ETERNAL LIFE.
> - JOHN 6:68

path back looks even more treacherous. So buckle your chinstraps. This chapter is longer than the previous ones, but is central to the Gospel. Let's begin with a review.

Chapter 1 gave us a new perspective on our role in the Cross. In the vision of heaven that we created in *Chapter 2*, we likened it to a heaving, pulsating, all-encompassing and fulfilling the Great Dance. *Chapters 3-6* connected the lines between the Fall, the prophets, and some of the most difficult passages in the Bible.

In *Chapter 7*, we explored the way that Jesus brought and equated it to the step a dancer must learn in order to participate in any dance. We drew that line toward our call to master sacrificial service here in the world.

In *Chapter 8*, we explored the truth that Jesus brought and likened it to the beat of the dance and the importance that we all have in feeling that lifeblood of humanity—love. We connected this love to our joy toward obedience in the truth of Scripture—the Law.

This chapter feels bigger. I'm not sure what you call a step and beat without a tune, but it probably isn't a dance. That's exactly how critical this part is to the faith of any Christian. Without the tune, service and love, ways and truths, steps and beats, God and Jesus become something else entirely. The two require a third.

In the words of Nathan Arizona, Sr., owner of Unpainted Arizona, "Eight hundred leaf-tables and no chairs? You can't sell leaf-tables and no chairs. Chairs, you got a dinette set. No chairs, you got [jack]..."[32]

No, the two require a third. In this chapter, we will draw out this third part of the Great Dance, and the most important of the three for each individual. We'll look at the life that Jesus gave us, connect it to the tune of the Great Dance, and show how here, in the world, we honor Him and accept salvation through our belief.

To do this, we'll look at this in three sections: **why believe, does the object of our belief matter, and what to believe.**

First, **WHY BELIEVE?** The easiest answer is that we believe because the Bible requires it over and over. Throughout this chapter, you have selections of Scripture from Genesis through the beginning of Acts, detailing some of the 259 instances that the word "believe" or "believed" is translated in the Bible—221 of them occur in the New Testament. Read through these periodically, looking for the promises that belief in Jesus brings. What does it say that failing to believe brings?

These are some of the biggest verses in the Bible. We know them, memorize them, and can quote them. But collected together, laid out like this, we get a clear view of the importance that God puts on our belief and clues of it from right near the beginning.

Abraham believed and it mattered. He became the father of a nation, and this wealthy, landless drifter became greater than any conqueror to come.

Pharaoh didn't believe the signs Moses brought to him, and he lost his life and the lives of many in his kingdom and household because of it.

Israel, in slavery, believed and they were led out of Egypt.

David believed and it saved him from despair.

God promised Isaiah, in the midst of turmoil, that while his people were scattered and buffeted, that He would send a Rock and that everyone who believed in it would not be disturbed.

The people of Nineveh believed in God, and they were spared the judgment of Sodom and Gomorrah.

The Centurion believed and his servant was healed.

Blind men believed that Jesus could heal them, and because of that, He did. Other men led children who believed away from their belief, and then wished they hadn't.

The least in a society believed, and that belief moved them to the front of the line for the Kingdom of God. The greatest in a society flaunted their unbelief, and will regret it for all time.

To those who believe, all things are promised by One who can actually deliver. The rewards of belief are offered to those who have yet to see—salvation awaits them. Those who wait until they see lose the opportunity to believe.

God blesses those who believe.

Those who fail to root their belief will not be saved and fall away.

Jesus came so that all might believe and, through that belief, we might become His brother, a fellow child of God.

Through Jesus, we have the opportunity to enter into eternal life, by way of belief. Our belief saves us from judgment that is laid up against all who fail to believe. It testifies to our love of God in the same way that unbelief testifies to our love of the darkness.

Many that would have called Jesus an enemy changed their hearts and believed. But others refused, even when presented with the physical presence and miracles of Jesus. They held tight to another Fundamental.

Our belief will feed and fill or starve and destroy us in ways we cannot imagine.

As we continue with this discussion, look at the full pages of Scripture on the pages following as a consistent reminder that God honors and promises much to those who believe. See how it reinforces that there is no greater message conveyed than the importance of belief. Christians believe because there is no alternative.

For the rest of the world, they must believe for the same reason. There is no alternative to belief for them, either. Atheists, nihilists, agnostics, and the lot all believe in something. Man has a hole in his heart and spends a lifetime looking for something big enough to fill it.

Even those focused on survival (say, in war) or those determined to waste their lives (maybe filling it with television or drugs) hang their belief on something. In fact, in life, there is no escaping belief, and whether one curates, criticizes, or just ignores their own, there is no alternative to belief.

Every one of us believes—*something*.

So **DOES THE OBJECT OF OUR BELIEF MATTER?**

Yes, it matters more than anything else one can choose.

In 1862, Victor Hugo published *Les Misérables*, the complex story of love, redemption, and grace. In it, he traced a large cast of extremely complex (fictional) characters over 30 years in pre-revolutionary France.

Jean Valjean, the main character, is released after being imprisoned for 19 years for stealing a loaf of bread to feed his sister's dying son. The world, he finds, has no tolerance for convicts. He is shown grace by a priest and eventually repents for all he had done and become, takes a new identity, and makes a prosperous life.

Inspector Javert, the antagonist in the story, was born in prison to gypsy parents and clawed his way up through the police force

THEN HE BELIEVED IN THE LORD; AND HE RECKONED IT TO HIM AS RIGH-
TEOUSNESS.

- GENESIS 15:6

IF THEY WILL NOT BELIEVE YOU OR HEED THE WITNESS OF THE FIRST SIGN,
THEY MAY BELIEVE THE WITNESS OF THE LAST SIGN.

- EXODUS 4:8

SO THE PEOPLE BELIEVED; AND WHEN THEY HEARD THAT THE LORD WAS
CONCERNED ABOUT THE SONS OF ISRAEL AND THAT HE HAD SEEN THEIR
AFFLICTION, THEN THEY BOWED LOW AND WORSHIPED.

- EXODUS 4:31

I WOULD HAVE DESPAIRED UNLESS I HAD BELIEVED THAT I WOULD SEE THE
GOODNESS OF THE LORD IN THE LAND OF THE LIVING.

- PSALM 27:13

THEREFORE THUS SAYS THE LORD GOD, "BEHOLD, I AM LAYING IN ZION
A STONE, A TESTED STONE, A COSTLY CORNERSTONE FOR THE FOUNDATION,
FIRMLY PLACED. HE WHO BELIEVES IN IT WILL NOT BE DISTURBED.

- ISAIAH 28:16

THEN THE PEOPLE OF NINEVEH BELIEVED IN GOD; AND THEY CALLED A
FAST AND PUT ON SACKCLOTH FROM THE GREATEST TO THE LEAST OF THEM.

- JONAH 3:5

AND JESUS SAID TO THE CENTURION, "GO; IT SHALL BE DONE FOR YOU
AS YOU HAVE BELIEVED." AND THE SERVANT WAS HEALED THAT VERY MO-
MENT.

- MATTHEW 8:13

WHEN HE ENTERED THE HOUSE, THE BLIND MEN CAME UP TO HIM, AND
JESUS SAID TO THEM, "DO YOU BELIEVE THAT I AM ABLE TO DO THIS?"
THEY SAID TO HIM, "YES, LORD."

- MATTHEW 9:28

ranks to a successful life on the strength of his own fierce belief in French justice. He knew Jean Valjean in prison, and after violating parole, Inspector Javert gives chase across France for years. The genius of Hugo's work is that both Jean Valjean, the repentant criminal, and Inspector Javert, the zealous keeper of the law, are likable.

In a dramatic twist, the tables are turned and Jean Valjean is tasked with killing Javert. Doing so would erase his own crimes forever and protect those he loved, but he doesn't do it. Jean Valjean spares Javert's life. Later, when Inspector Javert has the prisoner within his grasp, the inspector shows uncharacteristic mercy and lets Jean Valjean go free.

This twists the honor-bound inspector fiercely. He walks the streets of Paris and onto a bridge over the Seine River wracked with grief over his decision. On one hand, Jean Valjean needs to be turned over to the authorities, but on the other hand, the grace Javert had been given demands another thing. This hurts Inspector Javert because it puts a criminal above the law and puts himself under the galley and that just cannot be. Finally, Inspector Javert comes to this:

> ...He asked himself: "What has that convict done, that desperate fellow, whom I have pursued even to persecution, and who has had me under his foot, and who could have avenged himself, and who owed it both to his rancor and to his safety, in leaving me my life, in showing mercy upon me? His duty? No. Something more. And I in showing mercy upon him in my turn — what have I done? My duty? No. Something more. So there is something beyond duty? Here he took fright; his balance became disjointed; one of the scales fell into the abyss, the other rose heavenward, and Javert was no less terrified by the one which was on high than by the one which was below."[33]

For the first time, Inspector Javert saw that being good was not enough. Earlier in the story, Inspector Javert tried to resign to his superior for a mistake he'd made, but now, seeing his error in persecuting a the fallible French law, how was he to hand in his resignation to God? Inspector Javert was touched by God and he

BUT WHOEVER CAUSES ONE OF THESE LITTLE ONES WHO BELIEVE IN ME TO STUMBLE, IT WOULD BE BETTER FOR HIM TO HAVE A HEAVY MILLSTONE HUNG AROUND HIS NECK, AND TO BE DROWNED IN THE DEPTH OF THE SEA.

- MATTHEW 18:6

FOR JOHN CAME TO YOU IN THE WAY OF RIGHTEOUSNESS AND YOU DID NOT BELIEVE HIM; BUT THE TAX COLLECTORS AND PROSTITUTES DID BELIEVE HIM; AND YOU, SEEING THIS, DID NOT EVEN FEEL REMORSE AFTERWARD SO AS TO BELIEVE HIM.

- MATTHEW 21:32

HE SAVED OTHERS; HE CANNOT SAVE HIMSELF. HE IS THE KING OF ISRAEL; LET HIM NOW COME DOWN FROM THE CROSS, AND WE WILL BELIEVE IN HIM.

- MATTHEW 27:42

AND JESUS SAID TO HIM, " 'IF YOU CAN?' ALL THINGS ARE POSSIBLE TO HIM WHO BELIEVES." IMMEDIATELY THE BOY'S FATHER CRIED OUT AND SAID, "I DO BELIEVE; HELP MY UNBELIEF."

- MARK 9:23-24

THEREFORE I SAY TO YOU, ALL THINGS FOR WHICH YOU PRAY AND ASK, BELIEVE THAT YOU HAVE RECEIVED THEM, AND THEY WILL BE GRANTED YOU.

- MARK 11:24

THEY BEGAN REASONING AMONG THEMSELVES, SAYING, "IF WE SAY, 'FROM HEAVEN,' HE WILL SAY, 'THEN WHY DID YOU NOT BELIEVE HIM?'

- MARK 11:31

AFTERWARD HE APPEARED TO THE ELEVEN THEMSELVES AS THEY WERE RE-CLINING AT THE TABLE; AND HE REPROACHED THEM FOR THEIR UNBELIEF AND HARDNESS OF HEART, BECAUSE THEY HAD NOT BELIEVED THOSE WHO HAD SEEN HIM AFTER HE HAD RISEN.

- MARK 16:14

HE WHO HAS BELIEVED AND HAS BEEN BAPTIZED SHALL BE SAVED; BUT HE WHO HAS DISBELIEVED SHALL BE CONDEMNED.

- MARK 16:16

saw that the Gospel was contrary to the law that he had built a life upon. Everything was in vertigo.

Within a few pages, Inspector Javert takes his own life, plunging into the Seine.

> EVERYONE WHO HEARS THESE WORDS OF MINE AND DOES NOT ACT ON THEM, WILL BE LIKE A FOOLISH MAN WHO BUILT HIS HOUSE ON THE SAND. WHEN THE RAINS AND FLOODS COME AND THE WINDS BEAT AGAINST THAT HOUSE, IT WILL COLLAPSE WITH A MIGHTY CRASH.
>
> - MATTHEW 7:27

This is an extreme example, but when one's Fundamental is based on something that can prove untrue, one risks the crumbling of his foundation. Inspector Javert built a house on the foundation of French law. That doesn't sound like a terrible thing to build a foundation upon, but when the rains came and he realized there was a higher law than French, he was dismantled.

It matters what you believe.

Flannery O'Conner was a young, southern American, gothic writer and National Book Award winner, who died at the age of 39. In her short story, *A Good Man Is Hard to Find*, O'Conner paints a picture of a hardened criminal, called "The Misfit," who takes a family hostage on a country road. As all sorts of unspeakable atrocities are taking place against the family, the self-righteous grandmother tries to talk her way out of things. When things get entirely hopeless:

… [the grandmother] found herself saying, "Jesus, Jesus," meaning, Jesus will help you, but the way she was saying it, it sound as if she might be cursing.

"Yes'm," The Misfit said as if he agreed. "Jesus thrown everything off balance. It was the same case with Him as with me except He hadn't committed any crime and they could prove I had committed one because they had the papers on me… Jesus was the only One that ever raised the dead." The Misfit continued, "and He shouldn't have done it. He thrown everything off balance. If He did what He said, then it's nothing for you to do but throw away everything and follow Him, and if He didn't,

AND BLESSED IS SHE WHO BELIEVED THAT THERE WOULD BE A FULFILL-
MENT OF WHAT HAD BEEN SPOKEN TO HER BY THE LORD.

- LUKE 1:45

THOSE BESIDE THE ROAD ARE THOSE WHO HAVE HEARD; THEN THE DEVIL
COMES AND TAKES AWAY THE WORD FROM THEIR HEART, SO THAT THEY
WILL NOT BELIEVE AND BE SAVED. THOSE ON THE ROCKY SOIL ARE THOSE
WHO, WHEN THEY HEAR, RECEIVE THE WORD WITH JOY; AND THESE HAVE
NO FIRM ROOT; THEY BELIEVE FOR A WHILE, AND IN TIME OF TEMPTATION
FALL AWAY.

- LUKE 8:12-13

HE CAME AS A WITNESS, TO TESTIFY ABOUT THE LIGHT, SO THAT ALL
MIGHT BELIEVE THROUGH HIM.

- JOHN 1:7

HE CAME TO HIS OWN, AND THOSE WHO WERE HIS OWN DID NOT RECEIVE
HIM. BUT AS MANY AS RECEIVED HIM, TO THEM HE GAVE THE RIGHT TO
BECOME CHILDREN OF GOD, EVEN TO THOSE WHO BELIEVE IN HIS NAME,
WHO WERE BORN, NOT OF BLOOD NOR OF THE WILL OF THE FLESH NOR OF
THE WILL OF MAN, BUT OF GOD.

- JOHN 1:11-13

HE WHO BELIEVES IN THE SON HAS ETERNAL LIFE; BUT HE WHO DOES NOT
OBEY THE SON WILL NOT SEE LIFE, BUT THE WRATH OF GOD ABIDES ON
HIM.

- JOHN 3:36

FROM THAT CITY MANY OF THE SAMARITANS BELIEVED IN HIM BECAUSE OF
THE WORD OF THE WOMAN WHO TESTIFIED, " HE TOLD ME ALL THE THINGS
THAT I HAVE DONE."

- JOHN 4:39

SO JESUS SAID TO HIM, "UNLESS YOU PEOPLE SEE SIGNS AND WONDERS,
YOU SIMPLY WILL NOT BELIEVE."

- JOHN 4:48

then it's nothing for you to do but enjoy the few minutes you got left the best way you can—by killing somebody or burning down his house or doing some other meanness to him. No pleasure but meanness," he said, and his voice had become almost a snarl.

> FOR WHEN GENTILES WHO DO NOT HAVE THE LAW DO INSTINCTIVELY THE THINGS OF THE LAW, THESE, NOT HAVING THE LAW, ARE A LAW TO THEMSELVES, IN THAT THEY SHOW THE WORK OF THE LAW WRITTEN IN THEIR HEARTS, THEIR CONSCIENCE BEARING WITNESS AND THEIR THOUGHTS ALTERNATELY ACCUSING OR ELSE DEFENDING THEM, ON THE DAY WHEN, ACCORDING TO MY GOSPEL, GOD WILL JUDGE THE SECRETS OF MEN THROUGH CHRIST JESUS.
>
> - ROMANS 2:14-16

Javert had a great deal of belief in the wrong thing, and it was his undoing. But The Misfit slices the issue cleanly—believe in what Jesus did, or do not. This may seem like a line drawn too finely between good and evil, but—without Jesus and the sacrifice that He brought, without the call to obey from our great Creator, without the promise of eternal life—is it? Is The Misfit really that far off base?

If Jesus didn't do what He said He did, then what's to keep each and every one of us from following our own greatest pleasure at all times?

One might say yes, but in order for society as a whole to experience the greatest pleasure, we should come together to form rules for ethical living. The peace of the community is an ultimate goal, right?

Nope.

Who erected community peace as a goal? Without a set of standards that are above my own—the law, say—then each individual has no requirement to adhere to them. A group could break off, and decide that they want to live under a set of rules to benefit the community; but in the absence of the Law written on their hearts, the minute that one of the rules is counter to the individual, community begins to unravel. Before you know it, there's "nothing for you to do but enjoy the few minutes you got left the best way you can—by killing somebody or burning down his house or doing

IF I TOLD YOU EARTHLY THINGS AND YOU DO NOT BELIEVE, HOW WILL YOU BELIEVE IF I TELL YOU HEAVENLY THINGS? NO ONE HAS ASCENDED INTO HEAVEN, BUT HE WHO DESCENDED FROM HEAVEN: THE SON OF MAN. AS MOSES LIFTED UP THE SERPENT IN THE WILDERNESS, EVEN SO MUST THE SON OF MAN BE LIFTED UP; SO THAT WHOEVER BELIEVES WILL IN HIM HAVE ETERNAL LIFE. FOR GOD SO LOVED THE WORLD, THAT HE GAVE HIS ONLY BEGOTTEN SON, THAT WHOEVER BELIEVES IN HIM SHALL NOT PERISH, BUT HAVE ETERNAL LIFE. FOR GOD DID NOT SEND THE SON INTO THE WORLD TO JUDGE THE WORLD, BUT THAT THE WORLD MIGHT BE SAVED THROUGH HIM. HE WHO BELIEVES IN HIM IS NOT JUDGED; HE WHO DOES NOT BELIEVE HAS BEEN JUDGED ALREADY, BECAUSE HE HAS NOT BELIEVED IN THE NAME OF THE ONLY BEGOTTEN SON OF GOD. THIS IS THE JUDGMENT, THAT THE LIGHT HAS COME INTO THE WORLD, AND MEN LOVED THE DARKNESS RATHER THAN THE LIGHT, FOR THEIR DEEDS WERE EVIL.

\- JOHN 3:12-19

MANY MORE BELIEVED BECAUSE OF HIS WORD...

\- JOHN 4:41

JESUS SAID TO HIM, "GO; YOUR SON LIVES." THE MAN BELIEVED THE WORD THAT JESUS SPOKE TO HIM AND STARTED OFF.

\- JOHN 4:50

"TRULY, TRULY, I SAY TO YOU, HE WHO HEARS MY WORD, AND BELIEVES HIM WHO SENT ME, HAS ETERNAL LIFE, AND DOES NOT COME INTO JUDGMENT, BUT HAS PASSED OUT OF DEATH INTO LIFE.

\- JOHN 5:24

YOU DO NOT HAVE HIS WORD ABIDING IN YOU, FOR YOU DO NOT BELIEVE HIM WHOM HE SENT.

\- JOHN 5:38

HOW CAN YOU BELIEVE, WHEN YOU RECEIVE GLORY FROM ONE ANOTHER AND YOU DO NOT SEEK THE GLORY THAT IS FROM THE ONE AND ONLY GOD?

\- JOHN 5:44

some other meanness to him."

Well, there was law before Jesus, you'd say, and failure to believe in Jesus doesn't mean that we slide back into anarchy.

Yes, it does.

The Intertestamental Period, which we discussed earlier, is an example of just how bad things can get. By 332 B.C., Alexander conquered Israel, and within the next nine years took most of the known world. Instead of leaving a will, when he was asked who should preside over his kingdom, Alexander replied, "To the strongest." Then he died.

What ensued was a 300-year cage match fought in Jerusalem. Alexander's generals (and their descendants) didn't have the Law of Moses, but Israel did. Jews tried their best to keep it across a spectrum defined by two different poles:

The first group leaned into it, trusted in it, developed institutions for interpreting it, separated themselves from others who didn't, memorized the Word of God voraciously, and judged each other harshly depending upon their ability to creatively adhere to it. These folks eventually became known as Pharisees.[34]

The second group went along to get along, found or bought themselves into the great positions in the temple, flourished in trade, and lived with a focus on excellence in the world—as in "no life after death"—and codified what they considered the heart of the law to which they would (mostly) adhere. These came to later be called the Sadducees (see the beginning of *Chapter 8—Truth Beats Love*).[ix]

Before either group claimed that name, a priestly family, fed up with Greek rules, staged the Maccabean Revolt.

When a Greek general attempted to force an elderly Mattathias Maccabee to sacrifice a pig, Mattathias basically said, "If everyone else in the universe does this, I and my five sons will still walk with God."

---

ix It should be noted that although Pharisees and Sadducees were on opposite ends of the spectrum defined here, and were the two most visible Jewish sects in the New Testament, other sects existed (such as Zealots, Essenes, etc.) and many Jews of the time, much like today, would bristle at being labeled squarely within one group.

FOR IF YOU BELIEVED MOSES, YOU WOULD BELIEVE ME, FOR HE WROTE ABOUT ME. BUT IF YOU DO NOT BELIEVE HIS WRITINGS, HOW WILL YOU BELIEVE MY WORDS?"

- JOHN 5:46-47

JESUS SAID TO THEM, "I AM THE BREAD OF LIFE; HE WHO COMES TO ME WILL NOT HUNGER, AND HE WHO BELIEVES IN ME WILL NEVER THIRST.

- JOHN 6:35

BUT I SAID TO YOU THAT YOU HAVE SEEN ME, AND YET DO NOT BELIEVE.

- JOHN 6:36

FOR THIS IS THE WILL OF MY FATHER, THAT EVERYONE WHO BEHOLDS THE SON AND BELIEVES IN HIM WILL HAVE ETERNAL LIFE, AND I MYSELF WILL RAISE HIM UP ON THE LAST DAY.

- JOHN 6:40

TRULY, TRULY, I SAY TO YOU, HE WHO BELIEVES HAS ETERNAL LIFE.

- JOHN 6:47

"BUT THERE ARE SOME OF YOU WHO DO NOT BELIEVE." FOR JESUS KNEW FROM THE BEGINNING WHO THEY WERE WHO DID NOT BELIEVE, AND WHO IT WAS THAT WOULD BETRAY HIM.

- JOHN 6:64

BUT THIS HE SPOKE OF THE SPIRIT, WHOM THOSE WHO BELIEVED IN HIM WERE TO RECEIVE; FOR THE SPIRIT WAS NOT YET GIVEN, BECAUSE JESUS WAS NOT YET GLORIFIED.

- JOHN 7:39

NO ONE OF THE RULERS OR PHARISEES HAS BELIEVED IN HIM, HAS HE?

- JOHN 7:48

THEREFORE I SAID TO YOU THAT YOU WILL DIE IN YOUR SINS; FOR UNLESS YOU BELIEVE THAT I AM HE, YOU WILL DIE IN YOUR SINS."

- JOHN 8:24

When another villager stepped forward to sacrifice the pig, Mattathias killed him, and the general and Mattathias pulled down the altar.

For the next 98 years, the Maccabees alternated between a Seal Team 6 counter-government organization seeking freedom from Greek rule and rulers of Jerusalem and Judah (whose victories are so incomprehensible, they must have been divine).

Sounds great, right? The law is enough. If we all just follow the law, then we'll get along fine. There's no reason for "killing somebody or burning down his house or doing some other meanness to him," right?

Well, that's exactly what the Maccabees did. Toward the end of their rule, in the same way that the Greek generals had forced Hellenization (Greek culture, language, and religion) on Jews, Maccabean rulers like John Hyrcanus forcibly converted non-Jews in Israel under penalty of death. Toward the end of their rule, power corrupted them to such an extent that they looked more like Greek rulers than the Pharisees that initially supported them.[x]

> NO ONE CAN SERVE TWO MASTERS; FOR EITHER HE WILL HATE THE ONE AND LOVE THE OTHER, OR HE WILL BE DEVOTED TO ONE AND DESPISE THE OTHER.
> - MATTHEW 6:24A

Invariably, throughout the history of the Bible, man's inability to keep the Law proved that the law alone—the law without belief in something greater than ourselves—was insufficient to keep us good. And if the law is insufficient, then when you or I come to the end of it—when the law and our will are intractably at odds, without belief in something great enough, "then it's nothing for you to do but enjoy the few minutes you got left the best way you can."

---

x As a side note, Maccabean ruler's errors brought about two of the factors that paved the way for Jesus: 1) their mismanagement led to the formal request of help from Israel to the Romans to finally rid them of Greek rule. The thing about Romans is that once you invite them in, they never leave, and 2) one of those forced to convert to Judaism by John Hyrcanus was an Edomite descendant of Esau who became the grandfather of Herod the Great. This single conversion changed the face of Israel for a thousand years and put the country in the hands of a madman.

BUT BECAUSE I SPEAK THE TRUTH, YOU DO NOT BELIEVE ME.

- JOHN 8:45

WHICH ONE OF YOU CONVICTS ME OF SIN? IF I SPEAK TRUTH, WHY DO YOU NOT BELIEVE ME?

- JOHN 8:46

JESUS HEARD THAT THEY HAD PUT HIM OUT, AND FINDING HIM, HE SAID, "DO YOU BELIEVE IN THE SON OF MAN?" HE ANSWERED, "WHO IS HE, LORD, THAT I MAY BELIEVE IN HIM?" JESUS SAID TO HIM, "YOU HAVE BOTH SEEN HIM, AND HE IS THE ONE WHO IS TALKING WITH YOU." AND HE SAID, "LORD, I BELIEVE." AND HE WORSHIPED HIM.

- JOHN 9:35-38

BUT YOU DO NOT BELIEVE BECAUSE YOU ARE NOT OF MY SHEEP.

- JOHN 10:26

IF I DO NOT DO THE WORKS OF MY FATHER, DO NOT BELIEVE ME; BUT IF I DO THEM, THOUGH YOU DO NOT BELIEVE ME, BELIEVE THE WORKS, SO THAT YOU MAY KNOW AND UNDERSTAND THAT THE FATHER IS IN ME, AND I IN THE FATHER.

- JOHN 10:37-38

SO JESUS THEN SAID TO THEM PLAINLY, "LAZARUS IS DEAD, AND I AM GLAD FOR YOUR SAKES THAT I WAS NOT THERE, SO THAT YOU MAY BELIEVE; BUT LET US GO TO HIM." ... JESUS SAID TO HER, "I AM THE RESURRECTION AND THE LIFE; HE WHO BELIEVES IN ME WILL LIVE EVEN IF HE DIES, AND EVERYONE WHO LIVES AND BELIEVES IN ME WILL NEVER DIE. DO YOU BELIEVE THIS?" SHE SAID TO HIM, "YES, LORD; I HAVE BELIEVED THAT YOU ARE THE CHRIST, THE SON OF GOD, EVEN HE WHO COMES INTO THE WORLD." ... JESUS SAID TO HER, "DID I NOT SAY TO YOU THAT IF YOU BELIEVE, YOU WILL SEE THE GLORY OF GOD?" ... THEREFORE MANY OF THE JEWS WHO CAME TO MARY, AND SAW WHAT HE HAD DONE, BELIEVED IN HIM.

- JOHN 11:14-15, 25-27, 40, 45

It matters what you believe.

I hear you. These are all some pretty committed folks. In Inspector Javert, The Misfit, and the Maccabees, I have brought together a high-octane group of achievers who have committed to a path and followed it with gusto.

The problem here is the gusto. The rest of us aren't like them, are we? Surely we can manage with a few low-level Fundamentals without any of them having to crowd the other out, send us on a killing spree, forcibly convert a neighbor, or attempt suicide. Moderation in all things, right? *We* can be reasonable.

But can we? Before we go on, reread the scriptures listed in this section.

Inspector Javert was complacent in his single-mindedness until the moment that Jean Valjean released him. "Up to that moment he had lived with that blind faith which gloomy probity engenders. This faith had quitted him, this probity had deserted him. All that he had believed in melted away."[35]

In other words, it hit him quickly.

The Misfit killed, because of his realization that, without belief in Jesus, there wasn't much more for him to do than whatever he wanted. When we split our Fundamental, it takes us longer, but sooner or later, our preferences for the other or others becomes intractable with our belief in Jesus.

Like Adam in the Garden, we may hold out for a day or a thousand days, but there's a reason that our Fundamental is split. Sooner or later, we will murder for the other.

The Misfit, for all of his moral shortcomings, lived a life of integrity—his lowly actions were in line with his smallish morals. At some

> YOU HAVE HEARD THAT THE ANCIENTS WERE TOLD, 'YOU SHALL NOT COMMIT MURDER' AND 'WHOEVER COMMITS MURDER SHALL BE LIABLE TO THE COURT.' BUT I SAY TO YOU THAT EVERYONE WHO IS ANGRY WITH HIS BROTHER SHALL BE GUILTY BEFORE THE COURT; AND WHOEVER SAYS TO HIS BROTHER, 'YOU GOOD-FOR-NOTHING,' SHALL BE GUILTY BEFORE THE SUPREME COURT; AND WHOEVER SAYS, 'YOU FOOL,' SHALL BE GUILTY ENOUGH TO GO INTO THE FIERY HELL.
> - MATTHEW 5:21-22

THEREFORE THE CHIEF PRIESTS AND THE PHARISEES CONVENED A COUNCIL, AND WERE SAYING, "WHAT ARE WE DOING? FOR THIS MAN IS PERFORMING MANY SIGNS. IF WE LET HIM GO ON LIKE THIS, ALL MEN WILL BELIEVE IN HIM, AND THE ROMANS WILL COME AND TAKE AWAY BOTH OUR PLACE AND OUR NATION."

- JOHN 11:47-48

WHILE YOU HAVE THE LIGHT, BELIEVE IN THE LIGHT, SO THAT YOU MAY BECOME SONS OF LIGHT." THESE THINGS JESUS SPOKE, AND HE WENT AWAY AND HID HIMSELF FROM THEM.

- JOHN 12:36

NEVERTHELESS MANY EVEN OF THE RULERS BELIEVED IN HIM, BUT BECAUSE OF THE PHARISEES THEY WERE NOT CONFESSING HIM, FOR FEAR THAT THEY WOULD BE PUT OUT OF THE SYNAGOGUE; FOR THEY LOVED THE APPROVAL OF MEN RATHER THAN THE APPROVAL OF GOD. AND JESUS CRIED OUT AND SAID, "HE WHO BELIEVES IN ME, DOES NOT BELIEVE IN ME BUT IN HIM WHO SENT ME."

- JOHN 12:42-44

DO NOT LET YOUR HEART BE TROUBLED; BELIEVE IN GOD, BELIEVE ALSO IN ME.

- JOHN 14:1

BELIEVE ME THAT I AM IN THE FATHER AND THE FATHER IS IN ME; OTHERWISE BELIEVE BECAUSE OF THE WORKS THEMSELVES.

- JOHN 14:11

FOR THE FATHER HIMSELF LOVES YOU, BECAUSE YOU HAVE LOVED ME AND HAVE BELIEVED THAT I CAME FORTH FROM THE FATHER.

- JOHN 16:27

SO THE OTHER DISCIPLES WERE SAYING TO HIM, "WE HAVE SEEN THE LORD!" BUT [THOMAS] SAID TO THEM, "UNLESS I SEE IN HIS HANDS THE IMPRINT OF THE NAILS, AND PUT MY FINGER INTO THE PLACE OF THE NAILS, AND PUT MY HAND INTO HIS SIDE, I WILL NOT BELIEVE."

- JOHN 20:25

point in his life, he realized that his pleasure and Jesus' message were at odds, and he made a decision. However we hate his actions, there is a short list of those whose actions in the world can so closely align with their own truths.

The Maccabees likely never noticed the point at which their service to the law and to God began serving their hatred of the Greeks.

The fact is that it matters what you believe—more than you can possibly imagine. Scripture confirms that it is of eternal importance, and by the time you need it, it's too late to develop it. Whether you end up believing in something as deeply as Inspector Javert did, or getting as honest as The Misfit did, or wielding as much power as the Maccabees did, the fact is that you will need belief prior to death. Even if you don't, belief is the only thing that you'll take with you through death. When the time comes, what you believe matters.

So if we have laid out a case that everyone believes, and what we believe is of utmost importance, then the discerning reader sees that I have painted myself into a corner. It would be completely disingenuous for me to skip over here with a comment like, "Now we must each determine what to believe for ourselves, or to paint a picture of the cross on your heart."

I've paved the road this far, and honestly, I'm exhausted. I thought that the end of this topic was just ahead, but now I realize (or maybe always knew) that to complete this journey, a wide canyon must be bridged. And I am the least of these to span it.

IN WHAT ARE WE TO BELIEVE? I don't know if you've noticed it, but we have navigated the Gospel Story pretty well so far on experience and heart. We've avoided many of the unknowable theological issues that have plagued theologians for thousands of years and stuck to the fundamentals of the story, but that is only sufficient for so long. After a while, each of us has to decide, "What do I believe?"

NOW THEY HAVE COME TO KNOW THAT EVERYTHING YOU HAVE GIVEN ME IS FROM YOU; FOR THE WORDS WHICH YOU GAVE ME I HAVE GIVEN TO THEM; AND THEY RECEIVED THEM AND TRULY UNDERSTOOD THAT I CAME FORTH FROM YOU, AND THEY BELIEVED THAT YOU SENT ME. ... "I DO NOT ASK ON BEHALF OF THESE ALONE, BUT FOR THOSE ALSO WHO BELIEVE IN ME THROUGH THEIR WORD; THAT THEY MAY ALL BE ONE; EVEN AS YOU, FATHER, ARE IN ME AND I IN YOU, THAT THEY ALSO MAY BE IN US, SO THAT THE WORLD MAY BELIEVE THAT YOU SENT ME.

- JOHN 17:7-8, 20-21

JESUS SAID TO HIM, "BECAUSE YOU HAVE SEEN ME, HAVE YOU BELIEVED? BLESSED ARE THEY WHO DID NOT SEE, AND YET BELIEVED." THEREFORE MANY OTHER SIGNS JESUS ALSO PERFORMED IN THE PRESENCE OF THE DISCIPLES, WHICH ARE NOT WRITTEN IN THIS BOOK; BUT THESE HAVE BEEN WRITTEN SO THAT YOU MAY BELIEVE THAT JESUS IS THE CHRIST, THE SON OF GOD; AND THAT BELIEVING YOU MAY HAVE LIFE IN HIS NAME.

- JOHN 20:29-31

BUT MANY OF THOSE WHO HAD HEARD THE MESSAGE BELIEVED; AND THE NUMBER OF THE MEN CAME TO BE ABOUT FIVE THOUSAND.

- ACTS 4:4

AND THE CONGREGATION OF THOSE WHO BELIEVED WERE OF ONE HEART AND SOUL; AND NOT ONE OF THEM CLAIMED THAT ANYTHING BELONGING TO HIM WAS HIS OWN, BUT ALL THINGS WERE COMMON PROPERTY TO THEM.

- ACTS 4:32

AND ALL THE MORE BELIEVERS IN THE LORD, MULTITUDES OF MEN AND WOMEN, WERE CONSTANTLY ADDED TO THEIR NUMBER.

- ACTS 5:14

AS THEY WENT ALONG THE ROAD THEY CAME TO SOME WATER; AND THE EUNUCH SAID, "LOOK! WATER! WHAT PREVENTS ME FROM BEING BAPTIZED?" AND PHILIP SAID, "IF YOU BELIEVE WITH ALL YOUR HEART, YOU MAY." AND HE ANSWERED AND SAID, "I BELIEVE THAT JESUS CHRIST IS THE SON OF GOD."

- ACTS 8:36-37

THE APOSTLES' CREED

I believe in God, the Father Almighty,
    maker of heaven and earth.
And in Jesus Christ, his only Son, our Lord;
    who was conceived by the Holy Spirit,
    born of the virgin Mary,
    suffered under Pontius Pilate,
    was crucified, died, and was buried;
    the third day he rose from the dead;
    he ascended into heaven,
    and sitteth at the right hand of the Father Almighty.
    from thence he shall come again to judge the quick and
    the dead.
I believe in the Holy Spirit,
    the holy catholic Church,
    the communion of saints,
    the forgiveness of sins,
    the resurrection of the body,
    and the life everlasting. Amen.

> THE SERVANT-GIRL SAW [PETER], AND BEGAN ONCE MORE TO SAY TO THE BYSTANDERS, "THIS IS ONE OF THEM!" BUT AGAIN HE DENIED IT. AND AFTER A LITTLE WHILE THE BYSTANDERS WERE AGAIN SAYING TO PETER, "SURELY YOU ARE ONE OF THEM, FOR YOU ARE A GALILEAN TOO." BUT HE BEGAN TO CURSE AND SWEAR, "I DO NOT KNOW THIS MAN YOU ARE TALKING ABOUT!" IMMEDIATELY A ROOSTER CROWED A SECOND TIME. AND PETER REMEMBERED HOW JESUS HAD MADE THE REMARK TO HIM, "BEFORE A ROOSTER CROWS TWICE, YOU WILL DENY ME THREE TIMES." AND HE BEGAN TO WEEP.
>
> - MARK 14:69-72

The Apostles' Creed is one of those biblical traditions that has been around for a long time. Earliest records of it showed up in the first century around the time that the book of John was written. It has been changed, augmented, and edited over time, but it remains today as the central core of belief in Christianity and is read in churches around the world, in hundreds of languages, millions of times per week.

We profess it in church, and even those that don't actually believe it will stand and state their belief in the Apostles' Creed in front of the very altar of God.

So without taking away even the smallest word of that great Creed, I found that the theology of it and my lack of education left me feeling like a fraud. For this kind of belief—core, fundamental belief—I lean into the Gospel.

As Christians, **we're called to believe the story of the Gospel**. Keller gives a few great reasons that the Gospels must be true. First, they were written too soon after Jesus' death for the accounts to be fabricated. Scholars differ on when they were written, but of the spectrum of dates, Matthew is probably the earliest Gospel written. The earliest estimated date of the writing of Matthew is 37 A.D. and most believe that since the fall of Jerusalem in 70 A.D. is absent in all four Gospels, it proves they were written prior to that date. All credible historians believe that all four Gospels were completed by 100 A.D.[36]

If someone was going to fabricate an account or change a man's life to fit an agenda, it would be necessary to publish it after all the eyewitnesses had died off or didn't care. The Gospels were written much too early to serve an agenda other than the truth.

Second, the use of details that don't necessarily contribute to the storyline has been prevalent in fiction for the last 300 years, but prior to 1700, this type of literary form was completely non-existent. For one to believe that the Bible was written as fiction, one would have to believe that this literary style dropped into the hands of four liars around the turn of the century, permeated their four books, and did not appear again for 1,500 years.

Third, the Gospels were much too damaging to Christianity to have been fabricated. When the pillar of the church, Peter, denies Christ, that doesn't further an agenda—it begins another conversation. When Jesus censures his family, that doesn't play well for an audience that values family as its source of identity.[xi]

Lastly, most of the disciples died terrible deaths. Even if 12 (or really hundreds of) men could gather together to settle on a lie

143

> WHILE JESUS WAS STILL TALKING TO THE CROWD, HIS MOTHER AND BROTHERS STOOD OUTSIDE, WANTING TO SPEAK TO HIM. SOMEONE TOLD HIM, "YOUR MOTHER AND BROTHERS ARE STANDING OUTSIDE, WANTING TO SPEAK TO YOU." HE REPLIED TO HIM, "WHO IS MY MOTHER, AND WHO ARE MY BROTHERS?" POINTING TO HIS DISCIPLES, HE SAID, "HERE ARE MY MOTHER AND MY BROTHERS. FOR WHOEVER DOES THE WILL OF MY FATHER IN HEAVEN IS MY BROTHER AND SISTER AND MOTHER."
> - MATTHEW 12:46-50

> BELOVED, LET US LOVE ONE ANOTHER, FOR LOVE IS FROM GOD; AND EVERYONE WHO LOVES IS BORN OF GOD AND KNOWS GOD. THE ONE WHO DOES NOT LOVE DOES NOT KNOW GOD, FOR GOD IS LOVE. BY THIS THE LOVE OF GOD WAS MANIFESTED IN US, THAT GOD HAS SENT HIS ONLY BEGOTTEN SON INTO THE WORLD SO THAT WE MIGHT LIVE THROUGH HIM. IN THIS IS LOVE, NOT THAT WE LOVED GOD, BUT THAT HE LOVED US AND SENT HIS SON TO BE THE PROPITIATION FOR OUR SINS. BELOVED, IF GOD SO LOVED US, WE ALSO OUGHT TO LOVE ONE ANOTHER.
> - 1 JOHN 4:7-11

or a handful of half-truths, how many would die for it? Yet hundreds did. Other examples exist, too.[37]

We must believe that God, the Father, created heaven and earth in community with Jesus, His only born Son, and the Holy Spirit. This is something that we discussed at great length in *Chapter 1*. If you're still not clear, reread portions of those chapters for clarification.

We must believe that God created man out of love and for the purpose of loving and worshipping Him within the community of heaven—what we've called the Great Dance. Love cannot exist with one person. In order to love, one must have another. If God, alone, created man, then His center wouldn't have been love. He still could have created us to love and worship Him, but for God to be love, and for Him to create us out of love,

---

xi A great expansion of this can be found in Joy Davidman's letter printed in Lyle Dorsett's biography of her, *And God Came In* pgs. 112-116.

there must have been Three.

If every breath of Scripture from Creation through the cross and on to Revelation reinforces God's purest love for us, the essence of His being, we are assured of our unique purpose.

We must believe that because of our sin, we have been separated from God and the Great Dance, but that finding our way back is our greatest desire. Each of us is born with the Law written on our heart and so we feel guilt when we sin. Just like a child who has made a mistake and is full of shame runs away from the presence of her father, we sin and turn from God. What we turn toward makes the separation even greater.

But it is critical that we, created out of Love, realize our heart's greatest desire is to enter into community with Him. Sacrificial service covered in love built on a foundation of belief fills us here on earth and propels us to the ultimate goal of direct, experiential communion with God.

> BEHOLD, THE LORD'S HAND IS NOT SO SHORT
> THAT IT CANNOT SAVE;
> NOR IS HIS EAR SO DULL
> THAT IT CANNOT HEAR.
> BUT YOUR INIQUITIES HAVE MADE A SEPARATION BETWEEN YOU AND YOUR GOD,
> AND YOUR SINS HAVE HIDDEN HIS FACE FROM YOU SO THAT HE DOES NOT HEAR.
> - ISAIAH 59:1-2

We must believe that in each of us rests the ability to follow Him and thirst for the righteousness that He gives or the ability to turn from Him and deny God's presence in our lives. Inside each and every one of us is that ember to be like Abel and to live a life fully committed to God, to reach upward and join the ranks of those who couldn't *not* enter into the Great Dance. But the truth is that, to become one who can't not, one must choose that path, protect that ember, and grow it into a roaring, eternal flame. If the line between good and evil is drawn through men's hearts, we must choose which side to feed and which side to starve.

We must believe that even through hardship in this world, God's plan for our lives is working to a greater good. God doesn't promise believers a good life. God's promise is that when troubles come, a foundation of belief will allow each of us to weather them. Pair that with this hope we have developed in heaven and you will have an outlook on hardship, pain, and suffering in the world that will sustain you until that blessed day when each of us sees Jesus.

HE GIVES STRENGTH TO THE WEARY, AND TO HIM WHO LACKS MIGHT HE INCREASES POWER.

THOUGH YOUTHS GROW WEARY AND TIRED,

AND VIGOROUS YOUNG MEN STUMBLE BADLY,

YET THOSE WHO WAIT FOR THE LORD

WILL GAIN NEW STRENGTH;

THEY WILL MOUNT UP WITH WINGS LIKE EAGLES,

THEY WILL RUN AND NOT GET TIRED,

THEY WILL WALK AND NOT BECOME WEARY.

- ISAIAH 40:29-31

FOR BY THESE HE HAS GRANTED TO US HIS PRECIOUS AND MAGNIFICENT PROMISES, SO THAT BY THEM YOU MAY BECOME PARTAKERS OF THE DIVINE NATURE, HAVING ESCAPED THE CORRUPTION THAT IS IN THE WORLD BY LUST.

- 2 PETER 1:4

AND WE KNOW THAT GOD CAUSES ALL THINGS TO WORK TOGETHER FOR GOOD TO THOSE WHO LOVE GOD, TO THOSE WHO ARE CALLED ACCORDING TO HIS PURPOSE.

- ROMANS 8:28

AND MY GOD WILL SUPPLY ALL YOUR NEEDS ACCORDING TO HIS RICHES IN GLORY IN CHRIST JESUS.

- PHILIPPIANS 4:19

COME TO ME, ALL WHO ARE WEARY AND HEAVY-LADEN, AND I WILL GIVE YOU REST. TAKE MY YOKE UPON YOU AND LEARN FROM ME, FOR I AM GENTLE AND HUMBLE IN HEART, AND YOU WILL FIND REST FOR YOUR SOULS.

- MATTHEW 11:28-29

> BUT IN ALL THESE THINGS WE OVERWHELMINGLY CONQUER THROUGH HIM WHO LOVED US. FOR I AM CONVINCED THAT NEITHER DEATH, NOR LIFE, NOR ANGELS, NOR PRINCIPALITIES, NOR THINGS PRESENT, NOR THINGS TO COME, NOR POWERS, NOR HEIGHT, NOR DEPTH, NOR ANY OTHER CREATED THING, WILL BE ABLE TO SEPARATE US FROM THE LOVE OF GOD, WHICH IS IN CHRIST JESUS OUR LORD...
>
> - ROMANS 8:37-39

> FOR I KNOW THE PLANS THAT I HAVE FOR YOU,' DECLARES THE LORD, 'PLANS FOR WELFARE AND NOT FOR CALAMITY TO GIVE YOU A FUTURE AND A HOPE.
>
> - JEREMIAH 29:11

We must believe that Jesus was born to a virgin named Mary, walked the earth fully human, and was crucified on the cross, where He hung until He was dead for our sins. In order for Jesus to be the Christ, Scripture must be affirmed. Not one letter of the prophesy must go unfulfilled.

> THEREFORE THE LORD HIMSELF WILL GIVE YOU A SIGN: BEHOLD, A VIRGIN WILL BE WITH CHILD AND BEAR A SON, AND SHE WILL CALL HIS NAME IMMANUEL.
>
> - ISAIAH 7:14

For Jesus to be the Son of God and for Scripture to affirm His claims, Jesus must have been born this way, into the flesh. Jesus wasn't an idea or a spirit, but an actual person—fully human and fully God at the same time.

The cross was the most humiliating death available to man at the time and the death that we chose. I've stated that Jesus' death on the cross was the Person and the means that we, the debtor, required of God, the creditor, in order to win us. Said another way, on the cross, God bought our love in the costliest way possible.

If God had looked up from another hobby and said, "Sin, sure. That's fine. Clear the accounts," then He would look more like a billionaire with a universe of idle pursuits, raising kids to ignore

> NOW THE BIRTH OF JESUS CHRIST WAS AS FOLLOWS: WHEN HIS MOTHER MARY HAD BEEN BETROTHED TO JOSEPH, BEFORE THEY CAME TOGETHER SHE WAS FOUND TO BE WITH CHILD BY THE HOLY SPIRIT. AND JOSEPH HER HUSBAND, BEING A RIGHTEOUS MAN AND NOT WANTING TO DISGRACE HER, PLANNED TO SEND HER AWAY SECRETLY. BUT WHEN HE HAD CONSIDERED THIS, BEHOLD, AN ANGEL OF THE LORD APPEARED TO HIM IN A DREAM, SAYING, "JOSEPH, SON OF DAVID, DO NOT BE AFRAID TO TAKE MARY AS YOUR WIFE; FOR THE CHILD WHO HAS BEEN CONCEIVED IN HER IS OF THE HOLY SPIRIT. SHE WILL BEAR A SON; AND YOU SHALL CALL HIS NAME JESUS, FOR HE WILL SAVE HIS PEOPLE FROM THEIR SINS." NOW ALL THIS TOOK PLACE TO FULFILL WHAT WAS SPOKEN BY THE LORD THROUGH THE PROPHET: "BEHOLD, THE VIRGIN SHALL BE WITH CHILD AND SHALL BEAR A SON, AND THEY SHALL CALL HIS NAME IMMANUEL," WHICH TRANSLATED MEANS, "GOD WITH US."
>
> - MATTHEW 1:18-23

> ...JUST AS CHRIST ALSO LOVED THE CHURCH AND GAVE HIMSELF UP FOR HER...
>
> - EPHESIANS 5:25B

them. We'd never know He loved us. We'd never know He really cared about us and gave Himself up for us. It would be no big stretch for us to reciprocate a small love with a small devotion and to expect our provision. It would be easy to become indignantly angry when we didn't get our due. This is a scene played out in homes across the country and, to a smaller degree, in my home.

My kids are nine, seven and two. When they run to me asking to play and I tell them I have something else that I need to finish first, they die a little inside. If, when they come back and ask if they can do something questionable—eat a snack they're not supposed to eat at that time, drink a sugary drink, or watch TV—I tell them, "Sure. That's fine. Go ahead," they walk off glad to have the treat or the freedom, but they walk off alone. They know they've been sent away with a consolation prize. I won't give them me, so I give them something cheaper, and they know it.

God gave us every ounce of Himself.

And He died on the cross. Jesus' death was the atoning of our sin. He took hell and sin and death upon His shoulders in our stead. Death was required. From the beginning, in the Garden of Eden, life blood was required to cover sin. No one ever sacrificed a lamb that lived. Jesus wasn't a scapegoat.

He was *the Lamb.*

If believing that Jesus died on the cross is a stumbling block for you, then know this: Roman soldiers were killing machines. Not only did they kill men, they were students of it. The type of soldier that handled crucifixions was especially skilled at prolonging death. To say that anyone made it off the cross without death would be like saying that the president of the United States forgot who he was and booked a flight on Delta.com for his peace talks in Oslo. There was so much wrapped up in a soldier's identity and the institution of death that no one ever made it off a cross alive.

So if there was a birth, there was a life. And if that life was as reported, there was the cross. And if there was a cross, a Roman cross, there was a death.

> THE STONE WHICH THE BUILDERS REJECTED HAS BECOME THE CHIEF CORNER STONE.
> - PSALM 118:22

We must believe that this blood, spilled for us while we were still sinners, was the perfect sacrifice that covered our sins and that the resurrection of Jesus Christ was the receipt for that debt, stamped PAID. We've talked about how the rest of the world for all time has understood the idea that the sin of the father falls to the son and the tribe. We also talked about how, from the beginning of time, when an unclean thing touched a clean thing, the clean thing never made the unclean holy (see the beginning of *Chapter 7*). To clarify, from the beginning of time, no clean thing had made an unclean thing holy—but from near the beginning, God told us that it was possible.

Remember Abraham? In Genesis 18, Abraham walked with God and became the first intercessor. God revealed that He and His companions were going to destroy Sodom and Gomorrah.

ABRAHAM CAME NEAR AND SAID, "WILL YOU INDEED SWEEP AWAY THE RIGHTEOUS WITH THE WICKED? SUPPOSE THERE ARE FIFTY RIGHTEOUS WITHIN THE CITY; WILL YOU INDEED SWEEP IT AWAY AND NOT SPARE THE PLACE FOR THE SAKE OF THE FIFTY RIGHTEOUS WHO ARE IN IT? FAR BE IT FROM YOU TO DO SUCH A THING, TO SLAY THE RIGHTEOUS WITH THE WICKED, SO THAT THE RIGHTEOUS AND THE WICKED ARE TREATED ALIKE. FAR BE IT FROM YOU! SHALL NOT THE JUDGE OF ALL THE EARTH DEAL JUSTLY?" SO THE LORD SAID, "IF I FIND IN SODOM FIFTY RIGHTEOUS WITHIN THE CITY, THEN I WILL SPARE THE WHOLE PLACE ON THEIR ACCOUNT." AND ABRAHAM REPLIED, "NOW BEHOLD, I HAVE VENTURED TO SPEAK TO THE LORD, ALTHOUGH I AM BUT DUST AND ASHES. SUPPOSE THE FIFTY RIGHTEOUS ARE LACKING FIVE, WILL YOU DESTROY THE WHOLE CITY BECAUSE OF FIVE?" AND HE SAID, "I WILL NOT DESTROY IT IF I FIND FORTY-FIVE THERE." HE SPOKE TO HIM YET AGAIN AND SAID, "SUPPOSE FORTY ARE FOUND THERE?" AND HE SAID, "I WILL NOT DO IT ON ACCOUNT OF THE FORTY." THEN HE SAID, "OH MAY THE LORD NOT BE ANGRY, AND I SHALL SPEAK; SUPPOSE THIRTY

continued on next page

Abraham knew this city—his nephew lived there—and he began to question God.

Scripture doesn't say why Abraham stopped questioning God at 10 righteous men. Maybe he realized that he was questioning the all-powerful Creator of heaven and earth, or maybe he didn't want to know that Lot and his house were unrighteous. Scripture seems to indicate that God was finished speaking to Abraham, and He departed. But in this exchange, Abraham discovered the cornerstone of Christianity.

It took almost 1,500 years for God to answer the question that our belief pivots upon today. Remember *Chapter 5*? One of the prophets, Jeremiah, couldn't figure out how the God of truth that he knew could possibly justify all the accounts of man. He and God had a heated discussion in the first chapters of Jeremiah. God was determined in His course toward Israel and it wasn't pretty. But there, in Jeremiah 5, God answered the question without Abraham daring to ask: "If you can find one righteous man, I will spare Israel."

Although no one up until Jesus had accomplished it, there had always been a way for the clean to wash the unclean. If the sin of one could taint all, then the righteousness of one, the right One, could clean us all.

So Jesus was the One. But why all the blood and killing? Maybe we don't feel comfortable worshiping a God that is so bloodthirsty and gory. If sin needed to be covered, why choose a blood sacrifice?

All true love involves sacrifice.[38] We touched on it above, in the relationship between the billionaire father and his son, but let's look at a

continued from previous page

ARE FOUND THERE?" AND HE SAID, "I WILL NOT DO IT IF I FIND THIRTY THERE." AND HE SAID, "NOW BEHOLD, I HAVE VENTURED TO SPEAK TO THE LORD; SUPPOSE TWENTY ARE FOUND THERE?" AND HE SAID, "I WILL NOT DESTROY IT ON ACCOUNT OF THE TWENTY." THEN HE SAID, "OH MAY THE LORD NOT BE ANGRY, AND I SHALL SPEAK ONLY THIS ONCE; SUPPOSE TEN ARE FOUND THERE?" AND HE SAID, "I WILL NOT DESTROY IT ON ACCOUNT OF THE TEN." AS SOON AS HE HAD FINISHED SPEAKING TO ABRAHAM THE LORD DEPARTED, AND ABRAHAM RETURNED TO HIS PLACE.

- GENESIS 18:23-33

more typical parent-child relationship. If you believe Hollywood's version of kids, they're usually sweet and gentle, but if you have experienced the truth of parenting, you know a different story. They're hard and needy and time-consuming and require endless amounts of your resources.

For an adult to love a child, they have to pour out their lives for about 15 years. The parent has to bring their interests down and lay them at the feet of their child. The parent can't talk about what they want to talk about, they can't go where they want to go, and they can't eat what they want to eat.

This may be painting too harsh a picture of parenthood, but here's my point: Either the parent decides to completely fill their child's needs at the expense of their own, or the parent decides to continue to fill their own needs at the expense of their child. True love dictates that one must go down in order for the other to go up.

Without sacrifice, there can be relationship, but love requires more. It matters who the parent is, too. Parents with endless resources can meet their child's needs by hiring others to handle it for them, but to that child, the sacrifice isn't sufficient. When a parent says, "No, I won't sacrifice myself for you," then that child will never know his or her own worth.

> FOR GOD SO LOVED THE WORLD, THAT HE GAVE HIS ONLY BEGOTTEN SON...
>
> - JOHN 3:16A

Most action movies include this story line: Someone is safe. They aren't in any danger as they go through life, when their path is crossed by someone in danger. The other person is on the run from bad guys or war, or good guys who don't yet understand, but in order to pull that other person out of danger, someone has to enter into their danger. In order to love the other, someone has to sacrifice something big (their fortune, their safety, their reputation).

> BUT GOD DEMONSTRATES HIS OWN LOVE TOWARD US, IN THAT WHILE WE WERE YET SINNERS, CHRIST DIED FOR US.
>
> - ROMANS 5:8

> GREATER LOVE HAS NO ONE THAN THIS, THAT ONE LAY DOWN HIS LIFE FOR HIS FRIENDS.
>
> - JOHN 15:13

If they don't—if someone doesn't sacrifice self—then the other will perish.

Imagine that you love someone that has been hurt badly. Can you love them without entering into their pain? Can you love them from afar? Can you stay comfortable and exalted and high and still love someone that has been brought so low?

No. All true love requires sacrifice.

In biblical times, blood was a currency of sacrifice. To be honest, it still is. No great story has found a better example of complete, unadulterated, and absolute true love than this one.

Still, there is one part of this great story of the Gospel that is extremely hard to weave into a story. It is that He sacrificed his most Precious for us while we hated Him. We can never fully fathom His love for us.

After the death was a resurrection. If Jesus' death paid the penalty for our sin and bridged the chasm between man and God that we dug through our sin, then the resurrection is proof of God's acceptance of that sacrifice. As God had regard for Abel's sacrifice, Jesus' sacrifice fulfilled 4,000 years of prophesy in His perfect life, broken for us.

There is absolutely no denying that the resurrection happened. Brooke Foss Westcott said:

> *"Indeed taking all the evidence together, it is not too much to say that there is no single historic incident better or more variously supported than the Resurrection of Christ. Nothing but the antecedent assumption that it must be false could have suggested the idea of deficiency in the proof of it."*

His statement becomes tougher to understand toward the end, but he is saying that the fact that thousands and thousands of documents, letters, edicts, etc., WERE NOT written at that time denying that Jesus came back to life is yet more proof that this (admittedly hard to believe) story of resurrection happened.

Jesus rose from the dead and showed himself to hundreds—possibly thousands—of people.

Flannery O'Connor in *The Habit of Being: Letters of Flannery O'Connor* said:

> *"For me it is the virgin birth, the Incarnation, the resurrection which are the true laws of the flesh and the physical. Death, decay [and] destruction are the suspension of these laws."*

Finally, Andrew Murray in *Jesus Himself* said:

> *"A dead Christ I must do everything for; a living Christ does everything for me."*

"If He did what He said, then it's nothing for you to do but throw away everything and follow Him, and if He didn't, then it's nothing for you to do but enjoy the few minutes you got left the best way you can..."[39]

We must believe that Jesus, now in heaven, will return and bring a final judgment into this world along with a new heaven and a new earth for all eternity. Without judgment, there cannot be Christianity. This part is prickly for some, but have you ever had a job with no performance reviews? Or have you ever worked for a boss that was just passing the time and never gave you any instruction at all? In our DNA, we have a need to be encouraged, corrected, and finally acknowledged. The final judgment of Christ is littered throughout the New and Old Testaments, and is in itself a blessing. The fact that there will be a day when the board game will be put away, the money will go back into the slots, and the whole box of this world will be put back on a shelf means that we won't, like Adam, continue to go around the board forever, eventually failing.

> BUT WITH RIGHTEOUSNESS HE WILL JUDGE THE POOR, AND DECIDE WITH FAIRNESS FOR THE AFFLICTED OF THE EARTH; AND HE WILL STRIKE THE EARTH WITH THE ROD OF HIS MOUTH, AND WITH THE BREATH OF HIS LIPS HE WILL SLAY THE WICKED.
> - ISAIAH 11:4

> BEFORE THE LORD, FOR HE IS COMING,
> FOR HE IS COMING TO JUDGE THE EARTH.
> HE WILL JUDGE THE WORLD IN RIGHTEOUSNESS
> AND THE PEOPLES IN HIS FAITHFULNESS.
> - PSALM 96:13

The coming of God's judgment is designed to lead us to faith in Him for His sacrifice and to a life lived well here on earth. Without judgment, the world becomes an endless track of deeds and works that never measure up. In judgment, we find a great gift of finality, resolution, justice, and grace.

The Bible is clear that there is a place of eternal life and eternal death. One place leads to paradise and the presence of God; the other leads to emptiness, fire, and want. We've drawn heaven as the scene of a lively, pulsating Great Dance and hell as a place outside, cold and mad and unwilling to walk inside—but put that visual on steroids.

The Great Dance that is eternal life is infinitely more fulfilling and joyous and lively that we can imagine. But being outside that Great Dance is infinitely colder—so cold it burns—and the anger is heaped with regret, sorrow, and missed opportunities to a point that, in the world, each feeling would kill you instantly. There, inside eternal death, each eats and tears at you with its teeth, but you will not die.

This belief in judgment is not just useful for understanding what is to come. It is just as important for life today.

In 1998, at the age of 87, Czeslaw Milosz, a Polish Nobel Lauriat poet, wrote:

THEN ANOTHER ANGEL, A THIRD ONE, FOLLOWED THEM, SAYING WITH A LOUD VOICE, "IF ANYONE WORSHIPS THE BEAST AND HIS IMAGE, AND RECEIVES A MARK ON HIS FOREHEAD OR ON HIS HAND, HE ALSO WILL DRINK OF THE WINE OF THE WRATH OF GOD, WHICH IS MIXED IN FULL STRENGTH IN THE CUP OF HIS ANGER; AND HE WILL BE TORMENTED WITH FIRE AND BRIMSTONE IN THE PRESENCE OF THE HOLY ANGELS AND IN THE PRESENCE OF THE LAMB. AND THE SMOKE OF THEIR TORMENT GOES UP FOREVER AND EVER; THEY HAVE NO REST DAY AND NIGHT, THOSE WHO WORSHIP THE BEAST AND HIS IMAGE, AND WHOEVER RECEIVES THE MARK OF HIS NAME."
- REVELATION 14:9-11

BEHOLD, I AM COMING QUICKLY, AND MY REWARD IS WITH ME, TO RENDER TO EVERY MAN ACCORDING TO WHAT HE HAS DONE.
- REVELATION 22:12

Religion, opium for the people. To those suffering pain, humiliation, illness, and serfdom, it promised a reward in an afterlife. And now we are witnessing a transformation. A true opium for the people is a belief in nothingness after death—the huge solace of thinking that for our betrayals, greed, cowardice, murders we are not going to be judged.[40]

He had experienced the oppression by Nazis and the tyranny of Communist dictators. He had seen the horrors that man perpetrates when convinced that judgment is not forthcoming. Judgment is not a picture of violence, but a place of restraint.

What you believe determines whether you enter the Great Dance or stand outside, but how God's judgment manifests itself on any individual was most wisely answered by Ezekiel.

In the Valley of Dry Bones, God asked Ezekiel, who was looking over a valley filled with dried-out bones, "Can these bones live?"

> HE SAID TO ME, "SON OF MAN, CAN THESE BONES LIVE?" AND I ANSWERED, "O LORD GOD, YOU KNOW."
> - EZEKIEL 37:3

Can these bones that are clearly dead live? Can a man that served death all his life repent on his deathbed? Can a regular church-goer not believe? Can someone who has done unspeakable things, has run from God and cursed Him be forgiven and believe?

"Can these bones live?"

And Ezekiel answered, "O Lord God, You know."

Lastly, we must believe that until that day of judgment, we have been given the Holy Spirit to guide us toward righteousness, convict us of sin, and teach us of judgment with His wonderful gifts of love, joy, peace, patience, kindness, goodness, faithfulness, gentleness, and self-control. Against such there is no law.

Given on the day of Pentecost, the Holy Spirit came into the world to stay. The Holy Spirit is, to some extent, the Rodney Dangerfield of the Trinity—"can't get no respect." Hardly a child will pray to Him and yet He has done all the work here for the last few thousand years. He fills us, gives us power, teaches us to deny sin, witnesses for us, fills us with God's presence, guides us, teaches us what is good, reminds us what is evil, gives us joy, and tells us everything we know about

> BUT OF THAT DAY OR HOUR NO ONE KNOWS, NOT EVEN THE ANGELS IN HEAVEN, NOR THE SON, BUT THE FATHER ALONE.
> - MARK 13:32

God through Jesus and the prophets. It is hard to imagine what the world would be like without this extremely important member of the Trinity.

In Mark 13, Jesus is talking about His return to earth and that only God knows when that will be. John 16:13 gives us an interesting clue that the Holy Spirit also speaks what is told to Him by God, and that the Holy Spirit will be the one that will tell us what is to come.

When I was young, I thought the apostles had it easy. They got to see and learn directly from Jesus.

In this scripture from John 16, we get the feeling that these days now with the Holy Spirit are truly the good days. In this verse, Jesus implies that He has to go so that we can be given this great gift of the Helper—the Holy Spirit—almost as if the presence of the Holy Spirit is better for the time to come.

In all three synoptic Gospels, Jesus gives a cryptic warning against speaking against the Holy Spirit. Most commentators believe this is a warning against calling the works of God Satanic or claiming that God's miracles are not from Him.

As you progress into belief, try to develop a separate

> BUT NOW I AM GOING TO HIM WHO SENT ME; AND NONE OF YOU ASKS ME, 'WHERE ARE YOU GOING?' BUT BECAUSE I HAVE SAID THESE THINGS TO YOU, SORROW HAS FILLED YOUR HEART. BUT I TELL YOU THE TRUTH, IT IS TO YOUR ADVANTAGE THAT I GO AWAY; FOR IF I DO NOT GO AWAY, THE HELPER WILL NOT COME TO YOU; BUT IF I GO, I WILL SEND HIM TO YOU. AND HE, WHEN HE COMES, WILL CONVICT THE WORLD CONCERNING SIN AND RIGHTEOUSNESS AND JUDGMENT; CONCERNING SIN, BECAUSE THEY DO NOT BELIEVE IN ME; AND CONCERNING RIGHTEOUSNESS, BECAUSE I GO TO THE FATHER AND YOU NO LONGER SEE ME; AND CONCERNING JUDGMENT, BECAUSE THE RULER OF THIS WORLD HAS BEEN JUDGED. I HAVE MANY MORE THINGS TO SAY TO YOU, BUT YOU CANNOT BEAR THEM NOW. BUT WHEN HE, THE SPIRIT OF TRUTH, COMES, HE WILL GUIDE YOU INTO ALL THE TRUTH; FOR HE WILL NOT SPEAK ON HIS OWN INITIATIVE, BUT WHATEVER HE HEARS, HE WILL SPEAK; AND HE WILL DISCLOSE TO YOU WHAT IS TO COME. HE WILL GLORIFY ME, FOR HE WILL TAKE OF MINE AND WILL DISCLOSE IT TO YOU. ALL THINGS THAT THE FATHER HAS ARE MINE; THEREFORE I SAID THAT HE TAKES OF MINE AND WILL DISCLOSE IT TO YOU.
>
> - JOHN 16:5-15

relationship with each of the Persons of the triune. Ask God to lay their uniqueness on your heart, and try to imagine the image, personality and individuality of each. Pray to them individually. This may be difficult at first, but if God is no more One than Three and no more Three than One, then this dimension to your relationship helps you to better know Him.

WHOEVER SPEAKS A WORD AGAINST THE SON OF MAN, IT SHALL BE FORGIVEN HIM; BUT WHOEVER SPEAKS AGAINST THE HOLY SPIRIT, IT SHALL NOT BE FORGIVEN HIM, EITHER IN THIS AGE OR IN THE AGE TO COME.
- MATTHEW 12:32

AND EVERYONE WHO SPEAKS A WORD AGAINST THE SON OF MAN, IT WILL BE FORGIVEN HIM; BUT HE WHO BLASPHEMES AGAINST THE HOLY SPIRIT, IT WILL NOT BE FORGIVEN HIM.
- LUKE 12:10

TRULY I SAY TO YOU, ALL SINS SHALL BE FORGIVEN THE SONS OF MEN, AND WHATEVER BLASPHEMIES THEY UTTER; BUT WHOEVER BLASPHEMES AGAINST THE HOLY SPIRIT NEVER HAS FORGIVENESS, BUT IS GUILTY OF AN ETERNAL SIN"—BECAUSE THEY WERE SAYING, "HE HAS AN UNCLEAN SPIRIT."
- MARK 3:28-30

BUT THE FRUIT OF THE SPIRIT IS LOVE, JOY, PEACE, PATIENCE, KINDNESS, GOODNESS, FAITHFULNESS, GENTLENESS, SELF-CONTROL; AGAINST SUCH THINGS THERE IS NO LAW.
- GALATIANS 5:22-23

BUT WHEN THEY HAND YOU OVER, DO NOT WORRY ABOUT HOW OR WHAT YOU ARE TO SAY; FOR IT WILL BE GIVEN YOU IN THAT HOUR WHAT YOU ARE TO SAY. FOR IT IS NOT YOU WHO SPEAK, BUT IT IS THE SPIRIT OF YOUR FATHER WHO SPEAKS IN YOU.
- MATTHEW 10:19-20

"BRETHREN, THE SCRIPTURE HAD TO BE FULFILLED, WHICH THE HOLY SPIRIT FORETOLD BY THE MOUTH OF DAVID CONCERNING JUDAS, WHO BECAME A GUIDE TO THOSE WHO ARRESTED JESUS.
- ACTS 1:16

BUT YOU WILL RECEIVE POWER WHEN THE HOLY SPIRIT HAS COME UPON YOU…

- ACTS 1:8A

AND THEY WERE ALL FILLED WITH THE HOLY SPIRIT AND BEGAN TO SPEAK WITH OTHER TONGUES, AS THE SPIRIT WAS GIVING THEM UTTERANCE.

- ACTS 2:4

AND WE ARE WITNESSES OF THESE THINGS; AND SO IS THE HOLY SPIRIT, WHOM GOD HAS GIVEN TO THOSE WHO OBEY HIM."

- ACTS 5:32

SO THE CHURCH THROUGHOUT ALL JUDEA AND GALILEE AND SAMARIA ENJOYED PEACE, BEING BUILT UP; AND GOING ON IN THE FEAR OF THE LORD AND IN THE COMFORT OF THE HOLY SPIRIT, IT CONTINUED TO INCREASE.

- ACTS 9:31

YOU KNOW OF JESUS OF NAZARETH, HOW GOD ANOINTED HIM WITH THE HOLY SPIRIT AND WITH POWER.

- ACTS 10:38

FOR IT SEEMED GOOD TO THE HOLY SPIRIT AND TO US TO LAY UPON YOU NO GREATER BURDEN THAN THESE ESSENTIALS…

- ACTS 15:28

WHILE THEY WERE MINISTERING TO THE LORD AND FASTING, THE HOLY SPIRIT SAID, "SET APART FOR ME BARNABAS AND SAUL FOR THE WORK TO WHICH I HAVE CALLED THEM."

- ACTS 13:2

THEY PASSED THROUGH THE PHRYGIAN AND GALATIAN REGION, HAVING BEEN FORBIDDEN BY THE HOLY SPIRIT TO SPEAK THE WORD IN ASIA…

- ACTS 16:6

FOR THE KINGDOM OF GOD IS … RIGHTEOUSNESS AND PEACE AND JOY IN THE HOLY SPIRIT.

- ROMANS 14:17

FOR OUR GOSPEL DID NOT COME TO YOU IN WORD ONLY, BUT ALSO IN POWER AND IN THE HOLY SPIRIT AND WITH FULL CONVICTION; JUST AS YOU KNOW WHAT KIND OF MEN WE PROVED TO BE AMONG YOU FOR YOUR SAKE.

- 1 THESSALONIANS 1:5

FOR NO PROPHECY WAS EVER MADE BY AN ACT OF HUMAN WILL, BUT MEN MOVED BY THE HOLY SPIRIT SPOKE FROM GOD.

- 2 PETER 1:21

That's a lot of ground. I know.

To review, as Christians, we're called to believe the Gospel. We must believe:

- that God, the Father, created heaven and earth in community with Jesus, His only born Son, and the Holy Spirit.
- that God created man out of love and for the purpose of loving and worshiping Him within the community of heaven—what we've called the Great Dance.
- that because of our sin, we have been separated from God and the Great Dance, but that finding our way back is our greatest desire.
- that in each of us rests the ability to follow Him and thirst for the righteousness that He gives or the ability to turn from Him and deny God's presence in our lives.
- that even through hardship in this world, God's plan for our lives is working to a greater good.
- that Jesus was born to a virgin named Mary, walked the earth fully human, and was crucified on the cross, where He hung until He was dead.
- that this blood, spilled for us while we were still sinners, was the perfect sacrifice that covered our sins and that the resurrection of Jesus Christ was the receipt for that debt, stamped PAID.
- that Jesus, now in heaven, will return and bring a final judgment into this world along with a new heaven and a new earth.
- that until that day, we have been given the Holy Spirit to guide us and teach us with His wonderful gifts: love, joy, peace, patience, kindness, goodness, faithfulness, gentleness, and self-control; against which there is no law.

The truth of the Gospel is that belief matters. We all believe in something and the object of our belief sets us on a course for all eternity. Believe in something too small or too slippery or upon which you cannot rely, and you sow a fresh field with thorns. It may come up green at first, but there will be no harvest.

If you survive that winter and are given another season, then you will have a choice: Try it again and hope for a harvest, or literally turn around (the Bible would say, "repent") and tear up the thorns to plant real, life-sustaining crops.

The more seasons of thorns we plant, the harder it becomes to stop, but the wonderful thing about linear time is that we never have the opportunity to turn around toward the past. Our only opportunity to turn around, to repent, to plant different crops, and to believe is in *this very moment.* The winters are getting longer for all of us and the very wind, moon, sun, and stars all await your decision to repent and believe.

"But your salvation is not dependent on your commitment to God, but based on your belief in His perfect commitment to you."[41]

It is not the sowing and reaping that will save you, but your willingness to turn around, repent, and believe.

Imagine three people—a man and a couple—standing atop a cliff with a rope hanging down. The man tells the husband and wife that the rope is strong enough to save them if they were to fall off the cliff. The husband says OK, but the wife really studies the rope, gauges its thickness, checks its mooring, and determines with certainty that it would hold her.

If the man fell off the cliff, how much belief in the rope would he need to actually save him? Keller says only enough to grasp the rope.

This may seem like an escape hatch, but the truth is that the wife's additional certainty in the rope no more saves her than the husband's grasp. None of us are saved by the quality of our belief. All of us are saved by the quality of the rope.

This truth should help you in one of two ways.

First, if you're certain in the quality of your faith, don't be.

Those who spent years with God continually failed, looked to other things for their provision, and denied Him. The bit of belief that you have been given is a gift from God and nothing that you should boast about more than sight.

Instead of shining a light on your belief, shine that light on your unbelief. Find the things in your life that are crowding out your

Fundamental and seek to eradicate them. Every one of us has sown a crop or more of thorns, and because of that, no matter the quality of our belief, the thorns will show up from time to time.

Lean on belief in the sacrifice of Jesus to root out those thorns and to produce a bountiful crop for which the Lord will have much regard.

Or, if you're uncertain that you have even the smallest amount of belief, know that in this moment, you hold the power of the universe within your breath.

If you will turn from whatever you have placed your belief in and repent—if you will open your eyes and see yourself standing in front of the prison gate with God standing in front of you—if you will place your fears and love and actions into the hands of the One that has been there all along—then you will begin to feel your hand tighten around the rope and your descent will slow as the great Creator begins to move across the universe, into your heart, and bears you up.

Just as the extremely faithful cannot boast of the quality of their faith, you must not demur from the smallness of yours.

> IMMEDIATELY THE BOY'S FATHER CRIED OUT AND SAID, "I DO BELIEVE; HELP MY UNBELIEF."
> - MARK 9:24

Don't tarry there (the husband falling off the cliff certainly wishes that he'd seen and believed in the rope sooner), but don't think for a moment that God didn't die so that you would utter the words He's been dying to hear all along. He did.

This has been a long chapter, but I'll leave you with one thing we discussed at its beginning. In the *New American Standard Bible,* the word "believe" or "believes" or "believed" is translated 259 times. The word "belief" is translated zero times. You could argue that instead of using the word "belief" the translators used "faith" (378 times), but I think there is something else at play.

"Belief" is something that you can put on a shelf. "Belief" is a project that you look into, make a decision about, determine where you come down on it, and then move on. "Belief" is a noun.

"Believe" is a verb. It requires action. It doesn't sit idly by while you ignore your spouse or watch bad television. "Believe" follows you around like a tattoo on your face. It defines a house like its paint color on the outside AND the mantel on the inside.

You might have a lot of "beliefs," but what you "believe" defines you.

Put some action behind it. Jesus gave His life so that you might believe and the entirety of heaven moves to the tune of it.

Join us and believe.

Before you go on to the next chapter, take a few moments to read one or more of the following:
Matthew Chapters 21 through 23
Mark Chapters 12 & 13
Luke Chapters 17 & 18
John Chapters 15 & 16

CHAPTER 10

The Great-ceful Dance

God paid dearly for us and this world. The perfection that
He has laid into it tells me there is something that we're all
supposed to do here—something that each and every one of us
need in order to truly become one who can't not be with Him
in heaven. Getting into step with the Great Dance is something
that we can only do here by pulling the cross into our hearts
as our Fundamental. Practice the step, feel the beat, and own
the tune.

If you've ever driven with me, you know that I've spent a day or
two in traffic court. I've seen them in at least three states and tens
of jurisdictions, and they're all frighteningly similar.

Everyone gathers at the time written on their citation and is directed by name to a specific courtroom. Once there, the bailiff begins a roll call. As each name is called, he instructs the room that
there are two options. (There are three, really, but no one understands what nolo contendere means.) Each can claim to be guilty
or not guilty.

If you declare yourself guilty of the crime, you move to the front of the line. You get out sooner than everyone else, but leave bearing the full punishment of the crime. Some folks get a fine; others leave with jail time. For each and every crime in traffic court, there is a punishment attached, based on how much the community has been diminished.

The people in that line cut across every hedge we have built to separate us. There are Christians and atheists, black and white, short and tall, poor and rich, college graduates and the illiterate, Atlanta natives and Kenyans. It is a truly astonishing amount of diversity, but the scene always makes me sad.

There are a couple of folks for whom their traffic infraction, whether a DUI or a slow roll through a stop sign, is a very big deal. Four hundred dollars represents all they have saved or their kid's tuition or the seed money to buy tools to grow their business. Three days in jail is enough to send their whole family into homelessness, because no job waits for them. They may have committed the same crime I did, but for them, being judged guilty represents the end of the line.

I also see the men who have walked this road before them. They show up—they have to show up—because they didn't have the money for the fine. The judge calls them forward and asks if they now have funds to pay their fine. When they don't, they're given another day to show up and pay the fine. It is another opportunity to miss a half-day of work they can't afford to miss to tell the court they can't cover the fine. And if they miss that date, then they'll go to jail.

There's another group, though. I'm not typically part of this group, but I have been, and I know them a lot better. They show up too, but when their name is called, someone stands for them. An attorney they've hired speaks for them. He gets to go places in the courtroom and have discussions with the judge and the prosecution that the accused cannot. His advocacy makes a difference in a real-world courtroom.

We don't like to admit that having an advocate in court helps, but if you drive like me, you know that it does. I saw a man who felt so badly about the shame his DUI brought upon his family that he just wanted the whole thing to be over. He signed the paper stating he was guilty and the judge sent him to jail. He couldn't believe it. Instead of putting this behind him, he had cavalierly faced a shame that marked him forever.

Some judges are more patient than others, but I have felt the accused's fear and hopelessness there in the speed and efficiency of traffic court. For some, it's a new start, but for others, it feels like the beginning of the end.

Try and hold this scene of the traffic court in your mind as we close out this journey through the Gospel Story. Having traveled through antiquity, I'd like to bring the story to the doorstep of the heart and lay out how this begins to work in our lives as we seek to enter the Great Dance.

If you've ever been to a party or a dance, you know that it always begins with an invitation. Even public dances print an invitation in the newspaper. For the Great Dance, there is also an invitation.

In previous chapters, we got a peek behind the curtain to see what went on at this Great Dance, why we should thirst for it, and the cost of including us in it.

In this chapter, we're going to **look at the invitation, see how the invitation is delivered, consider how to respond to the invitation, and determine how we will wait until that great day of the Great Dance.**

LET'S TAKE A LOOK AT THE INVITATION. Even if you've never received one, consider yourself invited.

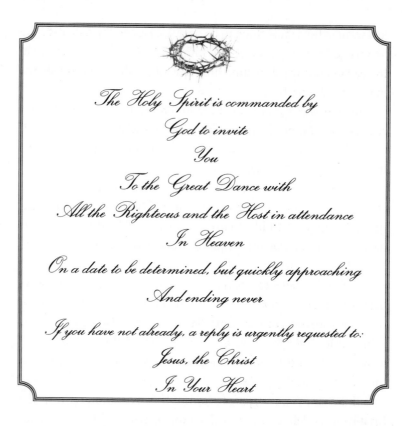

The Holy Spirit is commanded by
God to invite
You
To the Great Dance with
All the Righteous and the Host in attendance
In Heaven
On a date to be determined, but quickly approaching
And ending never
If you have not already, a reply is urgently requested to:
Jesus, the Christ
In Your Heart

What if you got this invitation one day, printed on heavy cardstock and wrapped in purple velvet—something akin to a British Royal Wedding invitation? What if, instead of an undetermined date, it had a specific date written on it for the Great Dance to begin? What if there was a phone number to call, or better yet, what if your response was required via writing? Not the pre-made kind:

_____ will attend, or
_____ will not attend

But just a blank sheet of paper on which you were to write out your response to this beautiful invitation. How would you indicate your attendance?

Go ahead and respond here:

Well, let's back up to about six hours before you actually get this invitation, retrace your day, and see **HOW THE INVITATION WAS DELIVERED.**

When I think of how I have viewed sin throughout my life, I have looked at it one of two ways. I have either considered sin no big deal or I have considered it forgiven by God's grace.

Both of my assumptions have been wrong.

For me, before I really believed, I figured that I was good enough. I followed the rules somewhat closely, and aside from my scrapes with traffic court, I'd put up a decent record.

But for my adherence to the law of God, the thoughts and actions of my heart, God had no regard. In many thousands of years, only One lived a life good enough and mine wasn't even close.

Looking past the lies, idolatry, gluttony, disrespect, greed, hatred, lust, and murder I'd committed on earth and/or in my heart, I still felt I was a pretty good guy. I measured my sin in inches while God saw it in acres. Not only was my unit of measurement too small, it didn't even begin to hold the dimension of my sin. I, the debtor, saw my sin as no big deal while He, the creditor, knew differently.

I grew up in the church and I believed in Jesus, but I never made a decision based on the cross. At work one day, I even scoffed at another Christian who purported to believe many of the things I've laid out here. I said that I believed; I may have even believed that I believed. Yet nothing in my life, when viewed through His light, would have proven or supported my belief.

I followed the rules because they served me, and even when I happened to follow the law, my obedience was insufficient in the light of the love God gave me.

> ...FOR ALL HAVE SINNED AND FALL SHORT OF THE GLORY OF GOD.
>
> - ROMANS 3:23

Once I believed in Jesus, despite my—sometimes best and sometimes mediocre—attempts, I still sinned. I began to follow the Law because I wanted to follow the example of Jesus—even though I constantly fell short.

But something was different.

I now had a realization that my sin fell to my account, that it separated me from God and that even the smallest sin in my life was a big deal. My view of it changed. I no longer wanted to be far from God or hurt the One I was orienting my heart toward.

> MY LITTLE CHILDREN, I AM WRITING THESE THINGS TO YOU SO THAT YOU MAY NOT SIN. AND IF ANYONE SINS, WE HAVE AN ADVOCATE WITH THE FATHER, JESUS CHRIST THE RIGHTEOUS; AND HE HIMSELF IS THE PROPITIATION FOR OUR SINS; AND NOT FOR OURS ONLY, BUT ALSO FOR THOSE OF THE WHOLE WORLD.
>
> - 1 JOHN 2:1-2

Still, I continued to sin. I was comforted that my acceptance of the sacrifice and my belief in Jesus covered my sin, but I thought it was God's grace that forgave me.

I was still wrong, or at least I'd skipped a major step.

I always had the vision of the unbeliever, standing in judgment in front of God without an Advocate in Jesus. I'd seen a hint of the destruction that causes and the crippling cycle that comes from the never-ending rotation of poverty, presence, and judgment in traffic court. But the court of God's judgment has infinitely worse consequences for those who present guilty without an Advocate.

Keller crystallized this for me.[42] I thought that the sin I had committed, laid bare in front of God, was an unwinnable case for Jesus. An all-knowing God didn't need evidence. He knew my guilt.

So Jesus, like all advocates with no case, laid Himself on the mercy of the court. He said:

> *"Yep, Bryant's back. I know we've been here a lot over the years, and there are a lot of charges pending here, sir, but can You give him another chance? I know Bryant personally and he is on our side. The evidence proves that he committed this crime and he has committed it previously a couple of times, but we know that You're a great Judge and that You have shown mercy to others, so I ask for Your grace again today."*

This is NOT how it works.

When we view God's grace as the forgiveness of sin, as ultimate patience from Him, and frankly, as charity, then we run into two problems.

The first is that a God of truth and ultimate justice would never convict one person for a crime and force them to endure judgment and allow another to commit the same exact crime (or a worse one) and go free. When this happens in traffic court, we hate it. We hate it that one who can afford an advocate gets different treatment from one who cannot. It happens, and it is unjust. Whether you or your advocate knows him, a just and righteous judge must rule the same for you as he would for another under the same circumstances.

The second problem is that, at some point, the accused assumes there is a line beyond which, if crossed, no forgiveness, patience, or charity can be given. Some Christians may bristle at that, but those on the front lines of helping the hurt can't go far without finding someone who feels their belief is too insufficient to receive forgiveness for the depth of their sin.

So know this: God's grace is not the forgiveness of sin. God's grace was His gift to us of Jesus to pay for the sin.

In court, many thousands of times, instead of throwing Himself on the mercy of the court, Jesus says:

"Lord God, You are a God of justice. Bryant has committed this sin and the punishment for that is established but, as You know, He knows Me, so I have paid for that sin. My account overflows—and it would be unjust for You to punish Him. I ask you to close this case."

> IF WE CONFESS OUR SINS, HE IS FAITHFUL AND RIGHTEOUS TO FORGIVE US OUR SINS AND TO CLEANSE US FROM ALL UNRIGHTEOUSNESS.
>
> - 1 JOHN 1:9

> FOR THE WAGES OF SIN IS DEATH, BUT THE FREE GIFT OF GOD IS ETERNAL LIFE IN CHRIST JESUS OUR LORD.
>
> - ROMANS 6:23

God does just that.

This may seem like a nuance, but if you're stuck thinking that something in your past is too big to forgive, or if you think that there is some work you need to complete before you can come to or be accepted by God or embark on belief, know that in Jesus, the law and grace fit like never before.

The Law must be followed, because if it is not, then I'm lost. I slide farther and farther away from that on which I've set my heart. This truth in the Law is hard and painful, but it is required in order to properly love.

The alternative is sin and sin widens the chasm.

But grace comes along and heals by bridging the vast gap. Not cheap grace, but grace paid for at an extreme cost—grace bought with blood and a scourging and on a cross. This kind of grace doesn't subvert the Law, but it affirms the Law. It points to the Law's eternal significance and then it instantly heals our inability to fulfill it.

In the courtroom, Jesus called sin out as sin—and then He paid for it. And as you walk out of the courtroom with Jesus, you marvel at Him, your head spinning from what has just been paid and the consequences you've just averted.

As you marvel, you remember how He said to "love one another." Could this have been what He meant? Being Jesus, He hears you, leans in close, and says,

"I don't condemn you. I want you to leave your life of sin and, if you don't, I love you; and if you can't, I love you; and if the woundedness and shrapnel of your sin leave you in a place where you're not even sure that you'll be able to walk away from the complexity of your sin, I love you; and if someone has sinned against you and it has sent you into a spiral of self-destructive behavior and you're not sure you'll ever recover, I love you.

"The truth is that you're a sinner, but through grace I don't condemn you and no one will ever love you any more than I do and I couldn't love you any more Myself."[43]

If you have been wounded, or if you're carrying righteousness around in a bag labeled self or if forgiveness seems a bridge too far, this view can be a game-changer.

> JESUS SAID TO HIM, "I AM THE WAY, AND THE TRUTH, AND THE LIFE; NO ONE COMES TO THE FATHER BUT THROUGH ME."
>
> - JOHN 14:6

The law is important, because disregarding it means moving farther away from God, but grace is important, too. We're already separated and without it—without God sending Jesus and Jesus actually going—there is no other way home.

So, you receive this invitation. If you believe, you'll receive it from the hand of Jesus on the way out of the courtroom, headed toward eternal life. If you've yet to believe, He hands it to you, sitting alone preparing your case at the defendant's table, as He leaves with a believer. He's glad one believer is

> WHAT MAN AMONG YOU, IF HE HAS A HUNDRED SHEEP AND HAS LOST ONE OF THEM, DOES NOT LEAVE THE NINETY-NINE IN THE OPEN PASTURE AND GO AFTER THE ONE WHICH IS LOST UNTIL HE FINDS IT? WHEN HE HAS FOUND IT, HE LAYS IT ON HIS SHOULDERS, REJOICING. AND WHEN HE COMES HOME, HE CALLS TOGETHER HIS FRIENDS AND HIS NEIGHBORS, SAYING TO THEM, 'REJOICE WITH ME, FOR I HAVE FOUND MY SHEEP WHICH WAS LOST!' I TELL YOU THAT IN THE SAME WAY, THERE WILL BE MORE JOY IN HEAVEN OVER ONE SINNER WHO REPENTS THAN OVER NINETY-NINE RIGHTEOUS PERSONS WHO NEED NO REPENTANCE.
>
> - LUKE 15:4-7

coming home, but would be extremely overjoyed, dancing in the street, if the other would respond with even the faintest, "yes."

Thus, the stage is set for two different people: one believes and one doesn't. Both must **DETERMINE HOW TO RESPOND TO THE INVITATION.**

The Bible is clear how judgment falls to those who fail to believe. Without an Advocate, the debt for sin must be paid by the sinner. The very act of RSVP'ing to the invitation brings Jesus running back to the court, vouching for the sin, and setting an additional place in heaven.

I've heard any number of reasons that folks deny Christ, but as virtually every person in the New Testament, The Misfit, and even modern-day scholars show, Jesus leaves you no room. Either you toss it all away and follow Him or you must kill Him. No one left Jesus to have a pleasant afternoon and see a matinee or said, "What a nice young man."

> HE WHO HATES ME HATES MY FATHER ALSO.
>
> - JOHN 15:23

Those who don't believe respond to this invitation in one of two ways. Either they spread everywhere the lies that they want to be true, making snide remarks and pushing others farther away from the truth—responding to Him with a loud and emphatic "NO," or they ignore His invitation, passing their time watching television or filling their mind with distraction. They wait and wait and wait—thinking they're keeping their options open until that final day comes—and it is too late. They are sent into the courtroom where those with no advocate go.

If you're this person, currently sitting at the defense table alone and preparing a case as best as you can;

if you're this person that just watched Jesus walk out of court and notice your teeth are clenched in anger; or,

if you're this person that's been so amused here on earth, making the best of it, trying to focus on happy things, and you've never really thought about it; or, if you're somewhere in between, but you want to accept this invitation you have just received, pray this prayer:

Jesus. Thank You for inviting me to this Great Dance. I have done nothing to deserve Your invitation. In fact, I have given You plenty of reason not to invite me. I have sinned against You, and I'm sorry. I turn from that life and I answer You now: Yes! I have counted the cost, and I know that You require me, my life, and my love and my will. I lift it all up to You now. Take me, Lord. I have no idea where this will go or where it will end, but I give my life over to You. Going forward, I will serve You. When You direct me, I will follow, and when I'm in the dark, I will use Your Word as a lamp. I will not stand on righteousness, because I know that I will fail. The fact that I believe I am following You does not mean that I am actually doing so, but I believe that a desire to please You does, in fact, please You. I ask that You lay in me a desire to serve oth-

> BUT WHEN THE SON OF MAN COMES IN HIS GLORY, AND ALL THE ANGELS WITH HIM, THEN HE WILL SIT ON HIS GLORIOUS THRONE. ALL THE NATIONS WILL BE GATHERED BEFORE HIM; AND HE WILL SEPARATE THEM FROM ONE ANOTHER, AS THE SHEPHERD SEPARATES THE SHEEP FROM THE GOATS; AND HE WILL PUT THE SHEEP ON HIS RIGHT, AND THE GOATS ON THE LEFT. THEN THE KING WILL SAY TO THOSE ON HIS RIGHT, 'COME, YOU WHO ARE BLESSED OF MY FATHER, INHERIT THE KINGDOM PREPARED FOR YOU FROM THE FOUNDATION OF THE WORLD
> THEN HE WILL ALSO SAY TO THOSE ON HIS LEFT, 'DEPART FROM ME, ACCURSED ONES, INTO THE ETERNAL FIRE WHICH HAS BEEN PREPARED FOR THE DEVIL AND HIS ANGELS;
> THESE WILL GO AWAY INTO ETERNAL PUNISHMENT, BUT THE RIGHTEOUS INTO ETERNAL LIFE.
> - MATTHEW 25:31-34, 41, 46

> I THANK CHRIST JESUS OUR LORD, WHO HAS STRENGTHENED ME, BECAUSE HE CONSIDERED ME FAITHFUL, PUTTING ME INTO SERVICE, EVEN THOUGH I WAS FORMERLY A BLASPHEMER AND A PERSECUTOR AND A VIOLENT AGGRESSOR. YET I WAS SHOWN MERCY BECAUSE I ACTED IGNORANTLY IN UNBELIEF; AND THE GRACE OF OUR LORD WAS MORE THAN ABUNDANT, WITH THE FAITH AND LOVE WHICH ARE FOUND IN CHRIST JESUS.
> - 1 TIMOTHY 1:12-14

ers as You did, covered in miles of love and built on a foundation of this belief in the sacrifice that You made for me. Help me grow all of this in me. Amen.

If you want to pray this prayer, but something is keeping you from it—if you lack belief or love or if you're holding on to something else too tightly—then it's enough to want to want Jesus. Jesus will start there.

Start by asking for belief. Earnestly pray for it. If you ask God for belief, He will give it to you, because He's dying for you to have it.

Do it now. *Don't wait.* You may not get another invitation, and even if you do, on that day, you'll wish you had done it sooner.

How does the believer respond to the very same invitation?

For the believer, the answer is yes. It can be, "sure," or it can be an overwhelming, loving, loud, and emphatic, "YES!" Each and every day, we are given an opportunity to respond to this invitation and turn from our own ways toward God's way.

In this invitation, eternity abounds.

> THEREFORE WE ALSO HAVE AS OUR AMBITION, WHETHER AT HOME OR ABSENT, TO BE PLEASING TO HIM. FOR WE MUST ALL APPEAR BEFORE THE JUDGMENT SEAT OF CHRIST, SO THAT EACH ONE MAY BE RECOMPENSED FOR HIS DEEDS IN THE BODY, ACCORDING TO WHAT HE HAS DONE, WHETHER GOOD OR BAD.
>
> - 2 CORINTHIANS 5:9-10
>
> BUT YOU, WHY DO YOU JUDGE YOUR BROTHER? OR YOU AGAIN, WHY DO YOU REGARD YOUR BROTHER WITH CONTEMPT? FOR WE WILL ALL STAND BEFORE THE JUDGMENT SEAT OF GOD.
>
> - ROMANS 14: 10B

Part of our response should be wrapped up in a surprisingly unknown part of our faith known at the Bema, or the Judgment Seat of Christ. In ancient times, the Bema was a meeting place in town where achievements were acknowledged.

Christians, those who believe and have answered yes to the invitation of Christ, will forgo God's judgment. Our names are on the list of the Lamb's Book of Life, and we will enter on the right into heaven directly, because Jesus paid for our sins. Just like my grandfather has never been summoned to traffic court, because he has no violations, Christians will skip God's judgment—our accounts are settled, justified (just as if they had never happened).

But once there and at the end of days, the entirety of Christendom across all geography and time will be given an audience with Christ where, through God's grace, we are given rewards for the work the Holy Spirit has done through us on earth.

This is a hard concept to nail down, but take a few minutes and imagine, on that day, and in the presence of thousands of years of believers, how would you want to be known? Would you want to be known for a tepid, "Sure," or a deathbed confession of faith? Or would you want to be known for sacrificing greatly, helping others, and using your love mercifully? With a video of your life showing overhead, for what would you want Paul or DL Moody or John Wesley to know you wept?

Staring into the eyes of the great Advocate, Creator and Christ, what would you want your greatest love to be? With your parents and all those whom you know, how or what or who do you want them to know that you served?

> NOW HE WHO PLANTS AND HE WHO WATERS ARE ONE; BUT EACH WILL RECEIVE HIS OWN REWARD ACCORDING TO HIS OWN LABOR. FOR WE ARE GOD'S FELLOW WORKERS; YOU ARE GOD'S FIELD, GOD'S BUILDING. ACCORDING TO THE GRACE OF GOD WHICH WAS GIVEN TO ME, LIKE A WISE MASTER BUILDER I LAID A FOUNDATION, AND ANOTHER IS BUILDING ON IT. BUT EACH MAN MUST BE CAREFUL HOW HE BUILDS ON IT. FOR NO MAN CAN LAY A FOUNDATION OTHER THAN THE ONE WHICH IS LAID, WHICH IS JESUS CHRIST. NOW IF ANY MAN BUILDS ON THE FOUNDATION WITH GOLD, SILVER, PRECIOUS STONES, WOOD, HAY, STRAW, EACH MAN'S WORK WILL BECOME EVIDENT; FOR THE DAY WILL SHOW IT BECAUSE IT IS TO BE REVEALED WITH FIRE, AND THE FIRE ITSELF WILL TEST THE QUALITY OF EACH MAN'S WORK. IF ANY MAN'S WORK WHICH HE HAS BUILT ON IT REMAINS, HE WILL RECEIVE A REWARD. IF ANY MAN'S WORK IS BURNED UP, HE WILL SUFFER LOSS; BUT HE HIMSELF WILL BE SAVED, YET SO AS THROUGH FIRE.
> - 1 CORINTHIANS 3:8-15

The Bema is not a place of judgment—all who see it have been saved—but there will be much rejoicing there and much regret. Those who are able to live life with a focus on that presentation and that day—those who have humbled themselves for that time— those who have made themselves poor for it—those who led out of weakness and yet believed because of that day, will rejoice greatly.

For each and every one of us, we can begin today, living this day in light of that day. This is where we come to realize the value of a life professionally lived. This is where our time, talents, and treasure grow extremely dim in the light of an even more real Jesus.

So, determined to attend, **HOW WILL WE WAIT UNTIL THAT DAY OF THE GREAT DANCE?**

If you were invited to a royal wedding, how would you wait for that? If you knew there would be dancing, how would you prepare? If you knew that an integral part of the festivity was a short film on the value of your life, how would you live?

I would think about it constantly. I would play out what it would look like and what to expect. I would research all I could find on it to make sure that I didn't embarrass myself, my wife, or other guests. I would buy things required for it—clothing, plane tickets, hotel accommodations. If we were to dance, I would learn the steps. I would practice and listen to the music and try to be as excellent as I could. If there was a film on my life, I would do all I could to make it the best life I could with the time I had.

Let's look at these things separately.

I would think about it constantly. We talked a lot in Chapter 1 about developing this thirst for heaven. If you still struggle with this, there are other resources. If you have that ember of longing for heaven, protect it.

A couple of years ago, I threw a surprise birthday party for my wife. It was a great time with a lot of friends, but after the party, she politely told me that she didn't want any more surprise parties. She said that part of the fun was looking forward to the party and imagining how it will be.

Christians can start off well without a picture of heaven, but when things get tough or consequences have big ramifications, it is extremely hard to stay faithful to the promise of God without an understanding of the promise of heaven. Said another way, it is hard to give your all without knowing that there will be a time, later, to enjoy the fruits of your labor. Without that in view, we all check up and rest along the way. If the journey is the reward, then one journeys differently. An Olympian journeys toward the Olympics differently than a spectator.

My prayer for those who read this and get a taste for heaven is that we all cross that line, into heaven, having left nothing on the field.

I would play out what it would look like and what to expect. I came across this quote attributed to A.W. Tozer:

> *I can safely say, on the authority of all that is revealed in the Word of God, that any man or woman on this earth who is bored and turned off by worship is not ready for heaven.*[44]

I'm not ready to draw the line that far, because it comes too close to final judgment, but I can say that, in my experience, when I went from believing that Jesus died to believing in Jesus—when this became real for me and I began to make hundreds of decisions daily with consideration of the cross—worship opened up for me. I became voracious in wanting to hear how God's Word was presented and to provide my praise to God, and this was the game-changer.

I stopped dragging myself into church on Sunday, looking for a nugget or a truth that would help me. I stopped treating our 8:45 worship service as a soup kitchen, where I went to get a little something warm to tide me over. I stopped saying things like, "I didn't really get anything out of that message." I stopped yelling at everyone to get ready in the morning because we had to be on time and I'd overslept.

I started seeing worship in

> YOU HUSBANDS IN THE SAME WAY, LIVE WITH YOUR WIVES IN AN UNDERSTANDING WAY, AS WITH SOMEONE WEAKER, SINCE SHE IS A WOMAN; AND SHOW HER HONOR AS A FELLOW HEIR OF THE GRACE OF LIFE, SO THAT YOUR PRAYERS WILL NOT BE HINDERED.
> - 1 PETER 3:7

our church as an opportunity to lift up an offering. I started treating our 8:45 service as a chance to show God how much I loved Him and to thank Jesus for His sacrifice and to love the Spirit of His community. I started saying things like, "Thank You." And mostly, I began to see Saturday night as a preparation to provide the sacrifice, so that Sunday morning, I could lift up my praise to God with a pure heart.

I would research all I could find on it to make sure that I didn't embarrass myself, my wife, or other guests. When you first fell in love (maybe as a teenager), what did you do? You surely thought about him or her constantly and did all the research you could on the object of your affection. You asked friends for details about possible interests and talked together on the phone for hours. You asked about family, so that you would know how to act. Each time you met, you would try to come up with some new thing to discuss that brought you closer together.

> YOUR WORD IS A LAMP TO MY FEET
> AND A LIGHT TO MY PATH.
> I HAVE SWORN AND I WILL CONFIRM IT,
> THAT I WILL KEEP YOUR RIGHTEOUS ORDINANCES.
> - PSALM 119:105-106

We do this same affection for God through study of the Word. God wrote a love letter to mankind and protected it throughout thousands of years. He put one in nearly every household and hotel room in America.[45] Six to eight billion copies of the Bible have been printed, making it the most printed and widely read book of all time.

The statistics are incredible, but the Bible is more important than just a book.

God has chosen to reveal more of Himself than ever before through the Word, and it enables me to constantly reorient my life toward Him. Without even the smallest amount of Scripture on a daily basis, my focus shifts off the Way, my grasp loosens from the truth, and I lose touch with the life I've been given. Things begin to crowd out my love and I begin to serve myself and the well of my belief drains low.

Scripture is the anchor that keeps me inside God's great regard.

I would buy things required for it—clothing, plane tickets, hotel accommodations. If we're honest, an invitation to a royal wedding would mean a disruption in our lives. It would take us away from our money, work, family, and what we've built at home. But that's OK, isn't it? Any one of us would weigh the cost and determine that the benefit is worth it. For all time, we would be able to tell our children that we attended the royal wedding. The experience would be an honor and the cost would be worth it.

Why don't we look at Jesus' invitation like that? Perhaps it's because the cost is so much greater. Maybe it's because the event seems to be decades away.

But it's a little more complicated than that. The truth is that your belief in the Groom has gotten you an invitation to this Great Dance and so a place has been set for you. But what you wear, how you're perceived, and everything about you is determined by how well you prepare for this Great Dance. If you wait until the last minute, you will present in front of the royal couple in tattered rags that fail to cover even your modesty. But if you begin now, using all that you've been given, your time and talents and treasure in preparation for this day, it will not only fulfill your greatest desire, but it will define you for all time to come.

> Do not store up for yourselves treasures on earth, where moth and rust destroy, and where thieves break in and steal. But store up for yourselves treasures in heaven, where neither moth nor rust destroys, and where thieves do not break in or steal; for where your treasure is, there your heart will be also. ... No one can serve two masters; for either he will hate the one and love the other, or he will be devoted to one and despise the other. You cannot serve God and wealth.
>
> - Matthew 6:19-21, 24

If there was dancing, I would learn the steps. I would practice

> YOU WILL KNOW THEM BY THEIR FRUITS. GRAPES ARE NOT GATHERED FROM THORN BUSHES NOR FIGS FROM THISTLES, ARE THEY? SO EVERY GOOD TREE BEARS GOOD FRUIT, BUT THE BAD TREE BEARS BAD FRUIT. A GOOD TREE CANNOT PRODUCE BAD FRUIT, NOR CAN A BAD TREE PRODUCE GOOD FRUIT. EVERY TREE THAT DOES NOT BEAR GOOD FRUIT IS CUT DOWN AND THROWN INTO THE FIRE. SO THEN, YOU WILL KNOW THEM BY THEIR FRUITS.
>
> - MATTHEW 7:16-20

> WHAT USE IS IT, MY BRETHREN, IF SOMEONE SAYS HE HAS FAITH BUT HE HAS NO WORKS? CAN THAT FAITH SAVE HIM? IF A BROTHER OR SISTER IS WITHOUT CLOTHING AND IN NEED OF DAILY FOOD, AND ONE OF YOU SAYS TO THEM, "GO IN PEACE, BE WARMED AND BE FILLED," AND YET YOU DO NOT GIVE THEM WHAT IS NECESSARY FOR THEIR BODY, WHAT USE IS THAT? EVEN SO FAITH, IF IT HAS NO WORKS, IS DEAD, BEING BY ITSELF. ... YOU SEE THAT A MAN IS JUSTIFIED BY WORKS AND NOT BY FAITH ALONE. IN THE SAME WAY, WAS NOT RAHAB THE HARLOT ALSO JUSTIFIED BY WORKS WHEN SHE RECEIVED THE MESSENGERS AND SENT THEM OUT BY ANOTHER WAY? FOR JUST AS THE BODY WITHOUT THE SPIRIT IS DEAD, SO ALSO FAITH WITHOUT WORKS IS DEAD.
>
> - JAMES 2:14-17, 24-26

and listen to the music and try to be as great as I could. We've talked about these in *Chapters 7—Step This Way, 8—Truth Beats Love,* and *9—Tune into Life's Belief,* but do you see how each is important? Do you see how they are no more three than one nor one than three?

Let's look at them, again.

Sacrificial service without love or belief is just a shame. It is a wasted opportunity. Imagine that a man saved a child from drowning, but in the process suffers an injury. Without love or belief, that sacrifice made for a child means everything to the child who is given another chance at life, but nothing to the man who spends the rest of his life nurturing a hatred for himself, the child, and the world.

Envision the same scenario, but this time, the man has love and no belief. Driven by his love, he continues to serve. He gives of his time and energy and spends his days looking for opportunities to save other children. This, admittedly, is better with love, but without belief, his only motivation of love diminishes over time. There's enough love to go around for a while, but when his love runs low, the service starts to sputter, and there's nothing else to recharge either.

A life lived loving and in sacrificial service without belief eventually is consumed, using its own mechanisms for fuel.

As I've said before, true love never exists without sacrifice. It's just a market transaction where one party exchanges something of worth for a good or a service of similar value.

Consider the love between a mother and a child—either the mother pours herself out for 15 years, giving up her needs or the child is poured out and lives the rest of his life in need. Love without service or belief is just a good start. There's no action to it—like a can of gasoline without a match or an engine.

> GREATER LOVE HAS NO ONE THAN THIS, THAT ONE LAY DOWN HIS LIFE FOR HIS FRIENDS.
> - JOHN 15:13

Imagine a young girl sitting alone in a cottage in the country with endless love in her heart, but who does nothing about it—she loves, but never shows it to another. She is overflowing with love, and yet has no one to love. Jesus and His brother James warned us about love and belief with no works to show for it.

Every dance starts with the tune—the music—and this one is no different. Scripture affirms that everything hinges on belief and the two without the third are useless. Service and love require belief. In fact, if you have none of the three, begin at belief and from there, nurture love.

Out of this growing belief and love, sacrificial service does seem a burden, but like your first love as a teenager, the opportunity to serve the One you love becomes an absolute pleasure.

IF I SPEAK WITH THE TONGUES OF MEN AND OF ANGELS, BUT DO NOT HAVE LOVE, I HAVE BECOME A NOISY GONG OR A CLANGING CYMBAL. IF I HAVE THE GIFT OF PROPHECY, AND KNOW ALL MYSTERIES AND ALL KNOWLEDGE; AND IF I HAVE ALL FAITH, SO AS TO REMOVE MOUNTAINS, BUT DO NOT HAVE LOVE, I AM NOTHING. AND IF I GIVE ALL MY POSSESSIONS TO FEED THE POOR, AND IF I SURRENDER MY BODY TO BE BURNED, BUT DO NOT HAVE LOVE, IT PROFITS ME NOTHING. LOVE IS PATIENT, LOVE IS KIND AND IS NOT JEALOUS; LOVE DOES NOT BRAG AND IS NOT ARROGANT, DOES NOT ACT UNBECOMINGLY; IT DOES NOT SEEK ITS OWN, IS NOT PROVOKED, DOES NOT TAKE INTO ACCOUNT A WRONG SUFFERED, DOES NOT REJOICE IN UNRIGH-TEOUSNESS, BUT REJOICES WITH THE TRUTH; BEARS ALL THINGS, BELIEVES ALL THINGS, HOPES ALL THINGS, ENDURES ALL THINGS. LOVE NEVER FAILS; BUT IF THERE ARE GIFTS OF PROPHECY, THEY WILL BE DONE AWAY; IF THERE ARE TONGUES, THEY WILL CEASE; IF THERE IS KNOWLEDGE, IT WILL BE DONE AWAY. FOR WE KNOW IN PART AND WE PROPHESY IN PART; BUT WHEN THE PERFECT COMES, THE PARTIAL WILL BE DONE AWAY. WHEN I WAS A CHILD, I USED TO SPEAK LIKE A CHILD, THINK LIKE A CHILD, REASON LIKE A CHILD; WHEN I BECAME A MAN, I DID AWAY WITH CHILDISH THINGS. FOR NOW WE SEE IN A MIRROR DIMLY, BUT THEN FACE TO FACE; NOW I KNOW IN PART, BUT THEN I WILL KNOW FULLY JUST AS I ALSO HAVE BEEN FULLY KNOWN. BUT NOW FAITH, HOPE, LOVE, ABIDE THESE THREE; BUT THE GREATEST OF THESE IS LOVE.

- 1 CORINTHIANS 13:1-13

AND HE SAID TO HIM, "'YOU SHALL LOVE THE LORD YOUR GOD WITH ALL YOUR HEART, AND WITH ALL YOUR SOUL, AND WITH ALL YOUR MIND.' THIS IS THE GREAT AND FOREMOST COMMANDMENT. THE SECOND IS LIKE IT, 'YOU SHALL LOVE YOUR NEIGHBOR AS YOURSELF.' ON THESE TWO COMMANDMENTS DEPEND THE WHOLE LAW AND THE PROPHETS."

- MATTHEW 22:37-40

BUT I HAVE THIS AGAINST YOU, THAT YOU HAVE LEFT YOUR FIRST LOVE.

- REVELATION 2:4

If there was a film on my life, I would do all I could to make it the best life I could with the time I had. This is where our analogy for the royal wedding breaks down. Time would limit this to no more than a mention, and it would be extremely unpopular to go out and give a bunch of money or feed a slew of homeless folks to have some good photos for the film. Only the most vain among us would attempt that type of polish job.

> HIS MASTER SAID TO HIM, 'WELL DONE, GOOD AND FAITHFUL SLAVE. YOU WERE FAITHFUL WITH A FEW THINGS, I WILL PUT YOU IN CHARGE OF MANY THINGS; ENTER INTO THE JOY OF YOUR MASTER.'
> - MATTHEW 25:23

But the only reason we can be cool about this is because, here on earth, a true documentary of my life is impossible. No one on earth will know my thoughts or my soul. But with the Great Dance, all of these impossibilities fade away. Scripture affirms that we will have this opportunity to review the life we have lived and the works that He accomplishes through us. With time taken off the table and a new ability to synthesize data, a total review of the lives in front of all Christendom is possible. To see the complete works of Paul or the unknown lady down the street, in a spirit of love at the Bema, will be absolutely incredible.

We're given time, too. We may have a day or a month or 70 years, but here on earth, with a heart turned toward God, it is nothing short of a pleasure to order a life centered around these ideas of service, love, and belief; practice the joy and peace that will consume us

> ANOTHER CAME, SAYING, 'MASTER, HERE IS YOUR MINA, WHICH I KEPT PUT AWAY IN A HANDKERCHIEF; FOR I WAS AFRAID OF YOU, BECAUSE YOU ARE AN EXACTING MAN; YOU TAKE UP WHAT YOU DID NOT LAY DOWN AND REAP WHAT YOU DID NOT SOW.' HE SAID TO HIM, 'BY YOUR OWN WORDS I WILL JUDGE YOU, YOU WORTHLESS SLAVE. DID YOU KNOW THAT I AM AN EXACTING MAN, TAKING UP WHAT I DID NOT LAY DOWN AND REAPING WHAT I DID NOT SOW? ... THEN HE SAID TO THE BYSTANDERS, 'TAKE THE MINA AWAY FROM HIM AND GIVE IT TO THE ONE WHO HAS THE TEN MINAS.' AND THEY SAID TO HIM, 'MASTER, HE HAS TEN MINAS ALREADY.' I TELL YOU THAT TO EVERYONE WHO HAS, MORE SHALL BE GIVEN, BUT FROM THE ONE WHO DOES NOT HAVE, EVEN WHAT HE DOES HAVE SHALL BE TAKEN AWAY.
> - LUKE 19:20-21, 23-26

in heaven; and manufacture three or four great things to talk about with your great love. Even if I only have six minutes left, wouldn't I use those to put at least two points up on the board? I could forgive or restore or refresh someone and at least guard against a shutout.

Christians will look to the Bema with eternal hope, to hear those great words, "Well done my good and faithful servant."

Or they will look to the Bema with regret at a life poorly lived. They'll still be in heaven, but as they march up those stairs, regret will slow their step, and as the years of their lives flicker by, they will be struck by the opportunity lost. The minutes they'd been given will be lost forever, and Jesus will remind them that they left their true love, but that their true love never left them.

If you can't wait to get started, great! Go out and create a life that you will be proud for your Great Love to see.

But if this seems like a burden to you, then don't start. This fire to live in the light of that day, to believe, to love others who aren't loveable, and to serve is something that God is dying to give you.

THEREFORE I SAY TO YOU, ALL THINGS FOR WHICH YOU PRAY AND ASK, BELIEVE THAT YOU HAVE RECEIVED THEM, AND THEY WILL BE GRANTED YOU.

- MARK 11:24

Start by asking Him for the light to build a fire inside you, and as you raise yourself from your knees, go out into the world knowing that all you have asked has been given to you.

> Before you go on to the next chapter, take a few moments to read one or more of the following:
> Matthew Chapters 24 & 25
> Mark Chapter 14
> Luke Chapters 19 & 20
> John Chapter 17

AFTERWORD

Questions from the Front

To round out this book, I will share with you two of the hardest questions I have been asked from those who have heard the story of the porch, shared in my introduction.

Q. Doesn't the fact that God knows Jesus will return to Him soften the blow of this sacrifice?

> NOW, FATHER, GLORIFY ME TOGETHER WITH YOURSELF, WITH THE GLORY WHICH I HAD WITH YOU BEFORE THE WORLD WAS.
> - JOHN 17:514:32-36

This one is a hard one. Jesus modeled service and love for us—and He certainly believed in His own story—but for Jesus, belief is different. It seems less accurate to call His faith in God "belief" and more accurate to call it *knowledge*. Because of His community with God for all time, and His experience with the Father and His presence at creation, Jesus wasn't given the opportunity to believe. He wholly knew. To us, He brought the opportunity to believe.

Throughout Jesus' ministry, He is the picture of calm. There is excitement (in His escape from temple elders, the Transfiguration,

> THEY CAME TO A PLACE NAMED GETHSEMANE; AND HE SAID TO HIS DISCIPLES, "SIT HERE UNTIL I HAVE PRAYED." AND HE TOOK WITH HIM PETER AND JAMES AND JOHN, AND BEGAN TO BE VERY DISTRESSED AND TROUBLED. AND HE SAID TO THEM, "MY SOUL IS DEEPLY GRIEVED TO THE POINT OF DEATH; REMAIN HERE AND KEEP WATCH." AND HE WENT A LITTLE BEYOND THEM, AND FELL TO THE GROUND AND BEGAN TO PRAY THAT IF IT WERE POSSIBLE, THE HOUR MIGHT PASS HIM BY. AND HE WAS SAYING, "ABBA! FATHER! ALL THINGS ARE POSSIBLE FOR YOU; REMOVE THIS CUP FROM ME; YET NOT WHAT I WILL, BUT WHAT YOU WILL."
>
> - MARK 14:32-36

> AND HE TOOK WITH HIM PETER AND THE TWO SONS OF ZEBEDEE, AND BEGAN TO BE GRIEVED AND DISTRESSED. THEN HE SAID TO THEM, "MY SOUL IS DEEPLY GRIEVED, TO THE POINT OF DEATH; REMAIN HERE AND KEEP WATCH WITH ME." AND HE WENT A LITTLE BEYOND THEM, AND FELL ON HIS FACE AND PRAYED, SAYING, "MY FATHER, IF IT IS POSSIBLE, LET THIS CUP PASS FROM ME; YET NOT AS I WILL, BUT AS YOU WILL." ... HE WENT AWAY AGAIN A SECOND TIME AND PRAYED, SAYING, "MY FATHER, IF THIS CANNOT PASS AWAY UNLESS I DRINK IT, YOUR WILL BE DONE."
>
> - MATTHEW 26:37-40, 42

and Satan's testing in the wilderness), miracles and drama, but He faces every turn as One Who knew this story and was prepared for it—until Gethsemane.

In Gethsemane, we see the picture of Jesus' panic—He was fully committed to God's will, but felt a moment of the flesh in outright rebellion. The detail in Luke, where the angel strengthens Him and Jesus sweat drops of blood, is a picture of duress. This condition, hematidrosis,[46] is rare and seen only in cases of extreme stress.

The begging and groveling in Gethsemane belies the argument that Jesus' sacrifice was lessened by His knowledge of eternity. If Jesus' knowledge that He would return to an eternity in heaven with God was a comfort, there must have been something else of immense consequence that wiped out this comfort.

Also, note that others died better than this. The account of the stoning of Stephen, the first Christian martyr after Christ, shows one whose belief was great (but certainly less than the knowledge of Jesus) and he died without fear.

Ignatius, in 110 A.D., was sentenced to die in Rome by being thrown to wild beasts. His Christian brethren wanted to plead for clemency, but he begged against it, writing, "May the wild beasts be eager to rush upon me. If they be unwilling, I will compel them. Come crowds of wild beasts; come tearings and manglings; wracking of bones and hacking of limbs; come cruel tortures of the devil; only let me attain unto Christ."[47]

At a time when being a Christian was dangerous, Polycarp led publicly in 155 A.D. In front of a Roman judge and facing death, Polycarp was given the option to deny Jesus and save his life. At each threat, he answered for Rome to bring its best. He stood defiant in the face of

> AND HE WITHDREW FROM THEM ABOUT A STONE'S THROW, AND HE KNELT DOWN AND BEGAN TO PRAY, SAYING, "FATHER, IF YOU ARE WILLING, REMOVE THIS CUP FROM ME; YET NOT MY WILL, BUT YOURS BE DONE." NOW AN ANGEL FROM HEAVEN APPEARED TO HIM, STRENGTHENING HIM. AND BEING IN AGONY HE WAS PRAYING VERY FERVENTLY; AND HIS SWEAT BECAME LIKE DROPS OF BLOOD, FALLING DOWN UPON THE GROUND
> - LUKE 22:41-44

> NOW WHEN [THE MEMBERS OF THE SANHEDRIN] HEARD THIS, THEY WERE CUT TO THE QUICK, AND THEY BEGAN GNASHING THEIR TEETH AT HIM. BUT BEING FULL OF THE HOLY SPIRIT, [STEPHEN] GAZED INTENTLY INTO HEAVEN AND SAW THE GLORY OF GOD, AND JESUS STANDING AT THE RIGHT HAND OF GOD; AND HE SAID, "BEHOLD, I SEE THE HEAVENS OPENED UP AND THE SON OF MAN STANDING AT THE RIGHT HAND OF GOD." BUT THEY CRIED OUT WITH A LOUD VOICE, AND COVERED THEIR EARS AND RUSHED AT HIM WITH ONE IMPULSE. WHEN THEY HAD DRIVEN HIM OUT OF THE CITY, THEY BEGAN STONING HIM; AND THE WITNESSES LAID ASIDE THEIR ROBES AT THE FEET OF A YOUNG MAN NAMED SAUL. THEY WENT ON STONING STEPHEN AS HE CALLED ON THE LORD AND SAID, "LORD JESUS, RECEIVE MY SPIRIT!" THEN FALLING ON HIS KNEES, HE CRIED OUT WITH A LOUD VOICE, "LORD, DO NOT HOLD THIS SIN AGAINST THEM!" HAVING SAID THIS, HE FELL ASLEEP.
> - ACTS 7:54-60

death, and as he was being led to a burning stake, Polycarp requested that they not bind him there, saying "Leave me as I am, for God will give me the strength to withstand your torments."

The soldiers did as he requested, and observers noted that Polycarp stood still as fire engulfed his entire body. It wasn't until a soldier stabbed Polycarp that the fire finally consumed him.[48]

This is merely three of thousands of examples of Christians dying with a view fixed on God. These were incredibly faithful men, but would anyone bet their belief against Jesus' knowledge?

Did Jesus' knowledge of an eternity with God provide some relief? It must have. But, while Stephen, Ignatius, and Polycarp were able to face death looking forward to a unity with God, Jesus' death meant a separation from God.

It is likely that Jesus knew that He would be reunited with God, but having been with God for all time, the separation that began in Gethsemane was absolutely excruciating. This separation, which we cannot fathom other than to imagine the earthly separation of a parent and son, was the true consequence of Jesus' sacrifice.

The death was terrible, but mere mortals have experienced that. Only One has experienced eternity with the Father, and then lost it.

> ENTER THROUGH THE NARROW GATE; FOR THE GATE IS WIDE AND THE WAY IS BROAD THAT LEADS TO DESTRUCTION, AND THERE ARE MANY WHO ENTER THROUGH IT. FOR THE GATE IS SMALL AND THE WAY IS NARROW THAT LEADS TO LIFE, AND THERE ARE FEW WHO FIND IT.
>
> - MATTHEW 7:13-14

This is yet another example of the greatness of heaven and an eternity spent with God. How great must something be that One endowed with perfect knowledge and perfect motives and perfect love—a veritable connoisseur and master of excellent things—can hardly bear a few hours or days without it? So precious is it that to lose it for even a moment changes His physiology and makes sweat turn into blood.

Heaven and God's presence are going to be so great that we can't even imagine the splendor.

Q. What does it mean in Chapter 1 to break off the porch and head home?

I've got a friend that always asks men, "How's your walk?"

That question is so telling, because it implies care for the person, concern for their well-being, knowledge of what is really important, but also, it implies movement. Lao-tzu is credited with, "A journey of a thousand miles begins with a single step."

Jesus affirmed the holiness of movement with Scripture and in the mechanics of the universe. A pool of stagnate water rots. A home without movement becomes stale. The universe is in constant movement. The story of Jesus' ministry seems a constant parade of activity and motion.

Breaking off the porch means setting into motion a new course.

If the house represents a life of sin that each of us has created, then the first thing to do is to walk away from that sin.

I recognize this is cavalier to say. Some are so broken and wounded by sin—theirs or others'—that they can't imagine living apart from it. Others have nurtured a lizard of sin so large that their lives are consumed just tending to its needs. Even those who count themselves as lightly under the yoke of sin feel that life with a taste of sin here and there is fuller than the alternative.

With the caveat that addiction and self-hatred is serious, and professional help may be necessary, I suggest these four steps to breaking off the porch and beginning a walk home:

Repent. Of all the things Jesus taught us, this is the one that He could not model for us—this was His one prescriptive action. It was so important that it defined the ministry of John the Baptist and was a central theme of the ministry of Jesus Christ.

BUT FROM THERE YOU WILL SEEK THE LORD YOUR GOD, AND YOU WILL FIND HIM IF YOU SEARCH FOR HIM WITH ALL YOUR HEART AND ALL YOUR SOUL. - DEUTERONOMY 4:29	NOW IN THOSE DAYS JOHN THE BAPTIST CAME, PREACHING IN THE WILDERNESS OF JUDEA, SAYING, "REPENT, FOR THE KINGDOM OF HEAVEN IS AT HAND." - MATTHEW 3:1-2

> MY SHIELD IS WITH GOD,
> WHO SAVES THE UPRIGHT IN HEART.
> GOD IS A RIGHTEOUS JUDGE,
> AND A GOD WHO HAS INDIGNATION EVERY DAY.
> IF A MAN DOES NOT REPENT, HE WILL SHARPEN HIS SWORD;
> HE HAS BENT HIS BOW AND MADE IT READY.
>
> - PSALM 7:10-12

> ZION WILL BE REDEEMED WITH JUSTICE AND HER REPENTANT ONES WITH RIGHTEOUSNESS. BUT TRANSGRESSORS AND SINNERS WILL BE CRUSHED TOGETHER, AND THOSE WHO FORSAKE THE LORD WILL COME TO AN END.
>
> - ISAIAH 1: 27-28

> FROM THAT TIME JESUS BEGAN TO PREACH AND SAY, "REPENT, FOR THE KINGDOM OF HEAVEN IS AT HAND."
>
> - MATTHEW 4:17

A perfect life in communion with God was Jesus' greatest achievement and also the reason that the cross was so difficult to bear. In our lives, we walk daily—apart from God—and wonder why we lack peace. I've told of the power that repentance has had in my life, but all revival began with earnest repentance.

> NOW JOSHUA WAS CLOTHED WITH FILTHY GARMENTS AND STANDING BEFORE THE ANGEL. HE SPOKE AND SAID TO THOSE WHO WERE STANDING BEFORE HIM, SAYING, "REMOVE THE FILTHY GARMENTS FROM HIM." AGAIN HE SAID TO HIM, "SEE, I HAVE TAKEN YOUR INIQUITY AWAY FROM YOU AND WILL CLOTHE YOU WITH FESTAL ROBES."
>
> - ZECHARIAH 3:3-4

All of us stand filthy in front of God, but our belief in Jesus makes us clean.

From there, true, genuine repentance for our sin is the straightest path home along a highway called righteousness. Failure to repent is an act of war against God. But wouldn't it be just like Him to put the keys to a kingdom within the reach of a child or a soldier lying wounded on a battlefield or a father searching for a place for his family to sleep?

We are forgiven for our transgressions through the blood of Jesus, but there is something about the humility required to repent for sin that reveals the presence of God. For me, the additional cost of doing it in front of others adds sacrifice, and every time I repent in front of men, God shows regard for my sacrifice.

Repentance—literally meaning to change your mind and go the other way—brings redemption, justice, and rightness within the world. There really isn't a downside, so long as it is true. But don't let that definition throw you. The physical activity of repentance is pleasing to God.

Don't wait.

Immerse yourself in Scripture. It takes five minutes to read a chapter of the Bible, yet setting aside that time is extremely difficult.

There is something bordering on mystical that happens in your life when you commit to reading and studying Scripture. Just like nine ladies cannot have a baby in a month, the steady plodding of reading a little or a lot each and every day begins to work miracles.

In my life, if I read seven chapters all at once each week, I forgo the power that reading a single chapter a day for a week unlocks. I cannot cite specific Scripture about it, but I dare you to produce different results. Ten times out of 10, when my heart gets off track or I'm developing self-centered relationships or I grow unthankful, it's clear that I've not been in the Word lately.

Men died for the Bible. Did you know that? Thou-

> THEREFORE, TAKE UP THE FULL ARMOR OF GOD, SO THAT YOU WILL BE ABLE TO RESIST IN THE EVIL DAY, AND HAVING DONE EVERYTHING, TO STAND FIRM. STAND FIRM THEREFORE, HAVING GIRDED YOUR LOINS WITH TRUTH, AND HAVING PUT ON THE BREASTPLATE OF RIGHTEOUSNESS, AND HAVING SHOD YOUR FEET WITH THE PREPARATION OF THE GOSPEL OF PEACE; IN ADDITION TO ALL, TAKING UP THE SHIELD OF FAITH WITH WHICH YOU WILL BE ABLE TO EXTINGUISH ALL THE FLAMING ARROWS OF THE EVIL ONE. AND TAKE THE HELMET OF SALVATION, AND THE SWORD OF THE SPIRIT, WHICH IS THE WORD OF GOD.
> - EPHESIANS 6:13-17

sands died in pursuit of a reliable, readable translation written in a language that people actually spoke. Other men, who spent their lives studying Scripture, felt its power was too great for you and me to even access. Doesn't that make you want to read it?

With repentance, you've got to want that yourself. You must love God so much that you don't care about embarrassing yourself or digging up forgotten corners of your life.

But this is different. You can will yourself to read for a while, but eventually it will slip. Ask God to change your preferences and to build a thirst for Scripture in you and to increase your curiosity about Him. We sometimes think God won't affect our free will, but if it is our will for it to be affected, He'll do it—if you ask.

> SO DO NOT BE LIKE THEM; FOR YOUR FATHER KNOWS WHAT YOU NEED BEFORE YOU ASK HIM. PRAY, THEN, IN THIS WAY: 'OUR FATHER WHO IS IN HEAVEN, HALLOWED BE YOUR NAME. YOUR KINGDOM COME. YOUR WILL BE DONE, ON EARTH AS IT IS IN HEAVEN. GIVE US THIS DAY OUR DAILY BREAD. AND FORGIVE US OUR DEBTS, AS WE ALSO HAVE FOR-GIVEN OUR DEBTORS. AND DO NOT LEAD US INTO TEMPTATION, BUT DE-LIVER US FROM EVIL. FOR YOURS IS THE KINGDOM AND THE POWER AND THE GLORY FOREVER. AMEN.
>
> FOR IF YOU FORGIVE OTHERS FOR THEIR TRANSGRESSIONS, YOUR HEAVENLY FATHER WILL ALSO FOR-GIVE YOU. BUT IF YOU DO NOT FOR-GIVE OTHERS, THEN YOUR FATHER WILL NOT FORGIVE YOUR TRANS-GRESSIONS.
>
> - MATTHEW 6:8-13

Spend time in Scripture as one seeking its truth and you'll see the world through different eyes—His eyes.

Pray. Mountains have been written on prayer. We teach our children to begin praying when they are young, but what is prayer's purpose?[xiii]

If you view prayer as an opportunity to tap into God's power to serve you, then not only is prayer frustrating, but it's boring. The purpose of prayer is not to conform God to our will, but to submit our hearts to God's will.

Matthew 6 holds the Lord's

---

13 For more listen to Andy Stanley at Buckhead Church, Red-Letter Prayers: Our Father

Prayer and the way that Jesus taught us to pray. Look at each of the verses here and roll them over in your mind. In verse 9, Jesus instructs the listener how to pray and says, "Our Father…"

These two words have moved mountains for me. Not only is Jesus reaffirming His relationship to God, but He is pulling you and me and mankind up into brotherhood with Him and sonship with God. It is incredible.

Does that matter to you?

We've talked about how everlasting life and the Kingdom of God is something that most of the world yearns for out of their oppression. Do you really care whether you wake up tomorrow in your house or within the Kingdom of God?

We've talked about how love can power our obedience to the Law. Do you really care whether you are on the field for God or are you good with nosebleed seats?

We've talked about how God gave us belief. Do you really see God providing your provision, or does your labor feed your family?

We talked about repentance. How much are you willing to give up to move closer to God? Are you willing to make a change today—even a small change—in light of that day when you will stand in front of

> AND HE WAS SAYING TO THEM ALL, "IF ANYONE WISHES TO COME AFTER ME, HE MUST DENY HIMSELF, AND TAKE UP HIS CROSS DAILY AND FOLLOW ME."
> - LUKE 9:23

> JESUS SAID, "REMOVE THE STONE." MARTHA, THE SISTER OF THE DECEASED, SAID TO HIM, "LORD, BY THIS TIME THERE WILL BE A STENCH, FOR HE HAS BEEN DEAD FOUR DAYS." JESUS SAID TO HER, "DID I NOT SAY TO YOU THAT IF YOU BELIEVE, YOU WILL SEE THE GLORY OF GOD?" SO THEY REMOVED THE STONE. THEN JESUS RAISED HIS EYES, AND SAID, "FATHER, I THANK YOU THAT YOU HAVE HEARD ME. I KNEW THAT YOU ALWAYS HEAR ME; BUT BECAUSE OF THE PEOPLE STANDING AROUND I SAID IT, SO THAT THEY MAY BELIEVE THAT YOU SENT ME." WHEN HE HAD SAID THESE THINGS, HE CRIED OUT WITH A LOUD VOICE, "LAZARUS, COME FORTH.
> - JOHN 11:39-43

Christ? Will you drop everything because of the sacrifice that Jesus made? Will you pick up anything?

How long should we pray, anyway? When Jesus raised Lazarus from the dead, He prayed for only a few seconds—and even said He's only praying so that others will know God did it and not Him.

> AND HE TOOK WITH HIM PETER AND THE TWO SONS OF ZEBEDEE, AND BEGAN TO BE GRIEVED AND DISTRESSED. THEN HE SAID TO THEM, "MY SOUL IS DEEPLY GRIEVED, TO THE POINT OF DEATH; REMAIN HERE AND KEEP WATCH WITH ME." AND HE WENT A LITTLE BEYOND THEM, AND FELL ON HIS FACE AND PRAYED, SAYING, "MY FATHER, IF IT IS POSSIBLE, LET THIS CUP PASS FROM ME; YET NOT AS I WILL, BUT AS YOU WILL." ... HE WENT AWAY AGAIN A SECOND TIME AND PRAYED, SAYING, "MY FATHER, IF THIS CANNOT PASS AWAY UNLESS I DRINK IT, YOUR WILL BE DONE."
> - MATTHEW 26:37-40, 42

But in Gethsemane, as we just saw, Jesus prayed through the night and until morning. Read Matthew 26 again, closely. I remembered Him asking for God to take the suffering away, but that's not what He did. He didn't pray like I would have prayed, asking for relief or escape.

He prayed for God's will to be done. He prayed that His will would be conformed to God's will. He *prayed*.

This is harder than it looks. Try praying with someone that is dying or sitting with someone who is jobless or homeless and being OK with God's will being done. God wants to know our requests, but when we can look at our menu of requests and truthfully say, "I'll have what He's having," we receive God's true gift here on earth: Peace.

Andy Stanley, a nationally recognized pastor in Atlanta, said, "The length of your prayers should be determined by how long it takes you to get to the place where you can say, with all your heart and all of your soul and all of your strength, 'Thy will be done,' even if I hate it."

Start there. It may take a lifetime, but *syncing our hearts with God's heart is the purpose of prayer.*

Listen. Have you ever had lunch with a friend who shows up late, talks for the whole hour, telling you exactly what's going on in her life, and then throws twenty dollars on the table midsentence and runs out? You'd say, "No. Wait a minute. Let me tell you what I think. Don't you care what's going on with me? You've got a couple of things wrong about me, and I want to make some plans with you later. Wait."

Often, this is exactly what we do to God.

Starting today, after prayer and in a quiet and private spot, set a timer for a couple of minutes. Just sit silently and listen. Have a pen and paper to jot down anything that comes to mind because, more often than not, God has something that He has died to tell you. Take a moment and just listen for it.

When I do this, I've had things placed in my mind that I hadn't thought of in 15 years. It could be a sin or a person to call or a job left undone. Get quiet with God and give it time. I'll also guarantee that, at first, you'll feel like it's fruitless or that you're doing it wrong.

> AFTER THE EARTHQUAKE CAME A FIRE, BUT THE LORD WAS NOT IN THE FIRE. AND AFTER THE FIRE CAME A GENTLE WHISPER.
> - 1 KINGS 19:12

Try to clear your mind— I concentrate on the color black and when my thoughts wander, I bring back a black screen to clear my head. As you progress, add a minute or two. Don't think about the time, just enjoy it and sink into the quietness of it.

"God whispers to us in our pleasures, speaks in our conscience, but shouts in our pains: it is his megaphone to rouse a deaf world."[49]

If you will give audience to God's whispers, He won't have to shout. And if He does shout, you'll recognize it as a loud and resounding, "*I love you.*"

Lastly, **Curate**.

In a large city, a number of years ago, a curator put on a wonderful show at a prestigious museum. He worked to assemble what he hoped would be the greatest representation of the canon of work by the Dutch Master painter Rembrandt. Over the years, he had amassed a single example of every subject that Rembrandt ever painted.

Before the opening night, the curator invited a major patron to view the collected works. This patron's financial support and connections could push the show into a wider circle throughout the community and increase its visibility.

One night before the opening, the patron showed up 20 minutes late and walked through the gallery, viewing the masterpieces the curator had assembled. For the next two hours, the curator listened as the patron shared his breadth of knowledge on Rembrandt and critiqued the paintings. He said:

> *"We can't include that painting,"* and
> *"I wouldn't put those two together,"* and
> *"Couldn't the artist have lit this one better?"* and
> *"How could he have chosen her to paint?"*

As the evening came to a close, and the major patron had opined on each and every work, he finally said what he'd been practicing saying all week: "Well, old man, I'm in. If you'll make the changes I suggested, then I'll sign on to sponsor the show."

Ever so softly, the curator said, "Thank you for coming tonight. Your sponsorship won't be necessary. This artist's work has been established by all history, and when viewing a masterpiece, it is not the painting that is on trial, sir, but the patron."

> BLESSED ARE THE POOR IN SPIRIT, FOR THEIRS IS THE KINGDOM OF HEAVEN. BLESSED ARE THOSE WHO MOURN, FOR THEY SHALL BE COMFORTED. BLESSED ARE THE GENTLE, FOR THEY SHALL INHERIT THE EARTH. BLESSED ARE THOSE WHO HUNGER AND THIRST FOR RIGHTEOUSNESS, FOR THEY SHALL BE SATISFIED. BLESSED ARE THE MERCIFUL, FOR THEY SHALL RECEIVE MERCY. BLESSED ARE THE PURE IN HEART, FOR THEY SHALL SEE GOD. BLESSED ARE THE PEACEMAKERS, FOR THEY SHALL BE CALLED SONS OF GOD. BLESSED ARE THOSE WHO HAVE BEEN PERSECUTED FOR THE SAKE OF RIGHTEOUSNESS, FOR THEIRS IS THE KINGDOM OF HEAVEN.
>
> - MATTHEW 5:3-10

What you think about and how you view the Gospel is of monumental and eternal importance. There may be no greater decision you make than how you view God's very Word. Do you mold the Bible to fit your life and sensibilities, or do you shape your life, choices, and preferences around its truth? What you think of the masterpiece that is the Gospel in no way changes it. You may disagree with this commentary or the way I've laid out this story, but chalk that up to my shortcomings. It was never the Gospel that was on trial.

There will be a day when how well each of us conformed our lives around the Gospel will be, by far, the most important thing about us. Choose today to become a curator of God's truth. When things look askew, look deeper into the Word to determine how God's truth lives in it. Don't become a patron. Don't assume that your small corner of the world's outlook, built upon a single moment in time, can in any way second-guess a masterpiece that has stood for thousands of years.

In these five—repentance, Scripture, prayer, quiet listening and curation—we find no greater opportunity to leave the porch. Start there.

This list isn't the only way to run home. The entire story of the Gospel and this Gospel Story is packed with wisdom for honoring God. But, again, throughout the Bible, God honors those that take something they should have loved and put it on an altar to Him.

If you don't yet know what that means in your life, then following these disciplines for ten days will tell you. Whether you're OK, drowning in sorrow or feeling pretty good, these disciplines—just 30 minutes a day—will lead you toward eternal life here on earth, while we wait for God's perfection to return.

And so we end where we started.

A rooster once crowed cannot be uncrowed. The first crow of the rooster is familiar. It is the moment you recognize something as true and stop to try and remember how you know it. The first crow of the rooster is the reminder that you're late, but still have time to make it on time. It is the moment of opportunity.

But the second crow is coming. The moment when it is too late to believe, but we will all know. The second crow brings grief and weeping and that empty feeling of opportunity lost.

> BUT HE DENIED IT, SAYING, "I NEI-
> THER KNOW NOR UNDERSTAND WHAT
> YOU ARE TALKING ABOUT." AND HE
> WENT OUT ONTO THE PORCH. THE
> SERVANT-GIRL SAW HIM, AND BE-
> GAN ONCE MORE TO SAY TO THE BY-
> STANDERS, "THIS IS ONE OF THEM!"
> BUT AGAIN HE DENIED IT. AND AF-
> TER A LITTLE WHILE THE BYSTAND-
> ERS WERE AGAIN SAYING TO PETER,
> "SURELY YOU ARE ONE OF THEM,
> FOR YOU ARE A GALILEAN TOO."
> BUT [PETER] BEGAN TO CURSE AND
> SWEAR, "I DO NOT KNOW THIS MAN
> YOU ARE TALKING ABOUT!" IMME-
> DIATELY A ROOSTER CROWED A SEC-
> OND TIME. AND PETER REMEMBERED
> HOW JESUS HAD MADE THE REMARK
> TO HIM, "BEFORE A ROOSTER CROWS
> TWICE, YOU WILL DENY ME THREE
> TIMES." AND HE BEGAN TO WEEP.
>
> - MARK 14:68-72

Right now, we're there with Peter and the girl from Chapter 1, standing on the porch, with a moment of opportunity. We can still change. We can still believe. We an make decisions that are authentic to our beliefs. We can break off that porch and run into the arms of the great Creator. Or we can turn around and walk back into getting things done that same way the world tells us that things get done.

This moment, before the rooster crows twice, is our time. It is the age of the church and a moment of opprotunity to be ready.

Be ready.

Curate one or more of the following:
Matthew Chapters 26 through 28
Mark Chapters 15 & 16
Luke Chapters 21 through 24
John Chapters 18 through 21

Scripture Index

Old Testament

New Testament

Reference Notes

1 Plantinga, Cornelius, "Engaging God's World…" on Amazon Kindle.

2 If I've got to cite this, I'm extremely disappointed…

3 Initially heard in Tim Keller's sermon Watching for the Son

4 Lewis, C.S., Perelandra on Amazon Kindle, Chapter 13

5 Dante, Paradise Lost, The Angelic Orders: http://www.italianstudies.org/comedy/Paradiso28.htm

6 Dickens, Charles. *A Christmas Carol and Other Christmas Stories* (New York: Fall River Press, 2009), 43.

7 Stephen Hawking lecture, "The Beginning of Time" http://www.hawking.org.uk/the-beginning-of-time.html

8 Ross, Dr. Hugh, The Creator and the Cosmos

9 Attributed to Sir Fred Hoyle, Professor of Astronomy and Mathematics, Oxford University

10 Charles Darwin, The Origin of the Species

11 http://www.heritage.org/research/reports/2008/06/revisiting-the-explosive-growth-of-federal-crimes

12 see Lon Solomon's sermon on Genesis "#6 Satan's Strategy Against Eve" available on iTunes

13 From the NET Bible Translation notes

14 Solzhenitsyn, Aleksandr I. *The Gulag Archipelago 1918-1956* (New York: Collins, 1974), 168.

15 Tozer, A.W., *The Pursuit of God*, (Camp Hill, PA: Wingspread Publishers, 1982), 64.

16 Lewis, C.S., *The Problem of Pain*, (New York: Harper Collins, 2001), 34-35.

17 http://en.wikipedia.org/wiki/Roman_roads

18 http://www.artba.org/about/faqs-transportation-general-public/faqs/

19 http://en.wikipedia.org/wiki/Roman_roads

20 http://en.wikipedia.org/wiki/Cilician_pirates

21 Montefiore, Simon Sebag. *Jerusalem, A Biography*, (New York: Alfred A. Knopf, 2011), 60.

22 http://en.wikipedia.org/wiki/Roman_Empire

23 Montefiore, *Jerusalem, A Biography*, 60.

24 ibid, p. 82

25 ibid, p. 112

26 http://profootballtalk.nbcsports.com/2012/03/08/arian-foster-remembers-his-moms-sacrifice/

27 drawn heavily from Tim Keller's Sermon Series, King's Cross: The Gospel of Mark (Part 1-The Coming of the King) and particularly the lesson titled Prayer, Word and Deed.

28 http://redeemercitytocity.com/content/com.redeemer.digitalContent-Archive.LibraryItem/503/Hope_for_Your_Work.pdf

29 prayer by Bryant Cornett, c. 2007, if it happened at all

30 http://agapepartners.org/articles/97/1/The-Parable-of-the-Good-Samaritan-Unveiled--a-True-Story-of-Humankind/Page1.html

31 Tim Keller's Sermon Series Proverbs: True Wisdom for Living from the lesson entitled Strangeness and the Order of God

32 Raising Arizona movie (1987)

33 Hugo, Victor. *Les Misérables* (Boston, MA: T.Y. Crowell & Company, 1887), Book Fourth:143. This chapter, called "Book Fourth.—Javert Derailed." is worth a read at http://goo.gl/Oe3nVH

34 http://en.wikipedia.org/wiki/Pharisees

35 Hugo, *Les Misérables,* Book Fourth:150

36 http://www.stellarhousepublishing.com/Gospel-dates.html#.UOs5v-Q0WSo

37 http://www.cslewisinstitute.org/webfm_send/1390

38 from a Tim Keller sermon on King's Cross

39 O'Connor, Flannery. *A Good Man is Hard to Find* (Apple iBooks)

40 Milosz, Czeslaw. Discrete Charm of Nihilism. 1998 for the New York Review of Books

41 Tim Keller in King's Cross Sermons

42 Tim Keller's sermon series King's Cross sermon in a lesson titled Mocking Jesus

43 Andy Stanley Sermon, When Truthie met Gracie, May 2012

44 Tozer, A. W. *Whatever Happened to Worship?: A Call to True Worship* (Camp Hill, PA: Wingspread Publishers, 2006), 13.

45 http://www.bibleteachingnotes.com/templates/System/details.asp?id=29183&fetch=7872

46 http://en.wikipedia.org/wiki/Hematidrosis

47 Bapetel, Eric. *Supernatural Immunity: Exploring God's Keeping Power from Psalm 91 and More,* (Bloomington, IN: Xlibris, 2012), 142.

48 http://www.saintpolycarp.org/Saint_Polycarp_bio.htm

49 Lewis, *The Problem of Pain,* 91.

ABOUT THE AUTHOR

Bryant Cornett grew up in a Southern Baptist Church in Amarillo, Texas. He graduated the Johns Hopkins University and spent the next two years starting a business in Vietnam. In 2009 Bryant began an earnest pursuit of God and intensive study that led (in a not-so-straight path) to *A Rooster Once Crowed*. Bryant is also a commercial real estate broker in Atlanta living with his wife, a native Mississippian, three kids and a puppy named Cocoa Cola Cornett. Bryant currently attends Peachtree Road United Methodist Church. To connect with this ministry, or see upcoming books or events, contact us at:

Full Porch Press
info@fullporchpress.com
or visit www.fullporchpress.com

Full Porch Press
1266 W Paces Ferry Road
Suite 140
Atlanta, GA 30327-2306

PRAISE FOR DIANE KELLY'S
PAW ENFORCEMENT SERIES

"Kelly's writing is smart and laugh-out-loud funny."
—Kristan Higgins, *New York Times* bestselling author

"Funny and acerbic, the perfect read for lovers of Janet Evanovich." —*Librarian and Reviewer*

"Humor, romance, and surprising LOL moments. What more can you ask for?" —*Romance and Beyond*

"Fabulously fun and funny!" —*Book Babe*

"An engaging read that I could not put down. I look forward to the next adventure of Megan and Brigit!"
—*SOS Aloha* on *Paw Enforcement*

"Sparkling with surprises. Just like a tequila sunrise. You never know which way is up or out!"
—*Romance Junkies* on *Paw and Order*

"A completely satisfying and delightful read. By being neither too 'cute' with its police dog lead, nor too dark with its serious topic, the author delivers a mystery that is a masterful blend of police detective and cozy fiction."
—*Kings River Life* on *Enforcing the Paw*

"Oh, how I love this series! Officer Megan Luz has an LOL dry humor and wit rivaling that of Kinsey Millhone. Her K-9 partner, Officer Brigit, is smarter and more protective than any three men on the force put together.

Add some of the more bizarre cases in the whole Fort Worth Police Department, and handsome firefighter Seth and his bomb-sniffing dog, Blast, and the reader is treated with a deliciously intense novel."

—*Open Book Society* on *Enforcing the Paw*

"Four Paws Up! This is a fabulous series that is sure to win the hearts of mystery fans and dog lovers alike!"

—*Books and Trouble*

THE LONG PAW
OF THE
LAW

Diane Kelly

St. Martin's Paperbacks

This is a work of fiction. All of the characters, organizations, and events portrayed in this novel are either products of the author's imagination or are used fictitiously.

THE LONG PAW OF THE LAW

Copyright © 2018 by Diane Kelly.

All rights reserved.

For information address St. Martin's Press, 175 Fifth Avenue, New York, NY 10010.

ISBN: 978-1-250-19735-1

Our books may be purchased in bulk for promotional, educational, or business use. Please contact your local bookseller or the Macmillan Corporate and Premium Sales Department at 1-800-221-7945, ext. 5442, or by e-mail at MacmillanSpecialMarkets@macmillan.com.

Printed in the United States of America

St. Martin's Paperbacks edition / November 2018

St. Martin's Paperbacks are published by St. Martin's Press, 175 Fifth Avenue, New York, NY 10010.

10 9 8 7 6 5 4 3 2 1

To Holly Ingraham. Thanks for taking a chance on an aspiring novelist and making my dream of becoming a published author come true. Working with you all these years has been a privilege and a pleasure.

ACKNOWLEDGMENTS

Thanks to Colonel (Retired) Patricia A. Mance for suggesting the title of this book. It's perfect!

As always, a big thanks to the talented team at St. Martin's Paperbacks who took this book from the first draft to the bookstore shelves. Oodles of gratitude to my editors, Holly Ingraham and Hannah Braaten, for being so wonderful to work with. Thanks to Jennie Conway, Nettie Finn, Sarah Melnyck, Paul Hochman, Allison Ziegler, Titi Oluwo, Talia Sherer and the rest of the team at St. Martin's for all of your work in getting my books into the hands of readers, reviewers, and librarians. Y'all are the best!

Thanks to Danielle Christopher for creating such fun book covers for this series.

Thanks to my agent, Helen Breitwieser, for all you do to advance my writing career.

Thanks to Liz Bemis and April Reed of Spark Creative for your work on my Web site and newsletters.

Thanks to fellow authors D.D. Ayres, Laura Castoro, Angela Cavener, Christie Craig, Cheryl Hathaway, and

Angela Hicks for your feedback and friendship. It's great to have such a wonderful support system!

And finally, thanks to every one of you wonderful readers who chose this book! Enjoy your time with Megan, Brigit, and the gang.

ONE
HUMAN SACRIFICE

The Father

It was two in the morning on a late September Thursday when the Father waited in the dark parking lot of a former convenience store on Rosedale. Like many of the older buildings on this stretch of the road, it had been razed to make way for new construction. Temporary chain-link fencing had been erected around the rubble until it could be hauled away.

The outdoor temperature was unseasonably cold for north Texas. He'd kept the engine and heater running in his truck, and now the inside of the windshield had fogged. He pulled the end of his flannel coat sleeve over his hand and reached out to wipe the glass with the cloth.

A shadow appeared ahead, moving toward the truck, eventually taking the shape of a man. The man's breaths were visible in the air, hanging about his head like conversation bubbles in comics.

The Father hit the button to unlock the doors and the man climbed inside, quickly closing the door behind him.

"Any problems?" the Father asked.

"None."

Good. The Father gave the man an approving nod and slid the truck into gear.

TWO
BYE-BYE BABY

Fort Worth Police Officer Megan Luz

My K-9 partner Brigit and I were patrolling the Mistletoe Heights neighborhood in the wee hours of the night when my cell phone jiggled to life. I cast a glance at the screen, which indicated it was my boyfriend Seth calling.

I pulled over to the curb, jabbed the button to accept the call, and put the phone to my ear. "Hey."

Brigit raised her furry head off the cushion in her enclosure behind me, her brown eyes watching me closely. My partner wasn't just a large shepherd, she was a smart one, too. She knew that me talking to someone on my phone or radio meant we might be called into action. Brigit lived for action. Me? I'd be happy if everyone obeyed the law, took each other's hands, and sang "Kumbaya." Of course if everyone conducted themselves so perfectly, there'd be no need for police officers or detectives, and I'd have to come up with new career goals. But human nature being what it is, my job was in no danger of becoming obsolete any time soon.

"Can you come to the station?" Seth worked as a

bomb squad technician and firefighter for the Fort
Worth Fire Department. His station was located within
the confines of my beat, only about a mile from my
current location.

"I'm not due for another break yet." As much as I'd
like to see him, I couldn't shirk my duties.

"This is official police business."

Instinctively, I sat up straighter in my seat. "It is?
What's going on?"

He kept his cards close to his vest. "Come see," was
all he said before hanging up.

"Official business," I repeated, looking back at my
partner. She pricked her ears to listen. "What do you
think that means, girl?"

She offered a small wag of her tail, the canine equivalent of a shrug.

I slid the phone back into the cup holder, made a
quick check of the dark street, and pulled out, aiming
directly for the station. When my cruiser pulled into the
front parking lot, I spotted Seth standing in the station's
lighted foyer, his broad back to the glass door. An army
reservist, Seth sported blond hair cut in a short, military
style. His angled head and bent elbows told me he held
something in his arms. Three other firefighters and one
of the paramedics were gathered around, looking down
at whatever he was holding.

Seth glanced over his shoulder as I parked. His yellow Lab, Blast, recognized my cruiser and ventured
closer to the door, his wet nose pressed to the glass, his
tail eagerly whipping back and forth.

I opened the door of my cruiser and stepped out into
the night. The air was unusually cold tonight, a not-
so-subtle reminder of the winter weather to come. It

couldn't come soon enough for me. The summer had been a scorcher. Grassfires fueled by dry, dead vegetation had kept Seth and his fellow firefighters busy the last few weeks.

I opened the back door to let Brigit out of the car. If I was going to get a little time with my boyfriend, she should get some with hers, too, right? Her nails clicked as she hopped down to the pavement and trotted along beside me.

Doug Harrison, a seasoned, dark-skinned paramedic, pushed the door open as I approached. I acknowledged his gracious gesture with a nod and smile.

"All right, Mister Mysterious," I said as Brigit and I stepped inside. "What's the big secret?"

As the door swung shut behind me, Seth turned around. Cradled in his arms was a newborn infant swaddled in a baby-sized quilt. The baby was sound asleep, its chubby face pink against the white trim of the colorful blanket. Atop its head was a knit cap in the same brilliant purplish blue as the accents adorning the quilt.

I stopped in my tracks and looked from Seth to the other men and back again. As far as I knew, none of their wives or girlfriends had been pregnant. Besides, who'd bring their child to the station at this late hour? I took a step closer, noting tufts of shiny black hair peeking out from under the tiny cap. "Whose baby is this?"

Seth shrugged. "I don't know. I was checking the hoses on the truck a few minutes ago, and a guy just walked up and handed the baby to me. Said he was making a safe drop."

My mouth fell open. Though the Texas Safe Haven

Statute, sometimes referred to as the "Baby Moses Law," had been in effect since 1999, it had rarely been utilized. The law allowed parents of a baby up to sixty days old to leave the infant at any designated safe place, which included hospitals, freestanding medical clinics, and fire or emergency medical stations. So long as the baby was handed over to an employee and was unharmed, the parent would not be charged with abandonment or neglect. The statute was enacted after a rash of dangerous abandonments, with the hope that the law would save young lives by giving desperate parents a legal and anonymous way out of difficult, hopeless situations.

As Brigit raised her head to give the baby's blanket a curious and thorough sniff, I reached out to run a finger over the baby's soft cheek. "Is it a boy or a girl?"

Doug chimed in. "Girl. I checked her for signs of trauma. Everything looked okay."

Thank God. Domestic violence was one of the most difficult things police officers faced on the job, and the stakes and emotions increased exponentially when children were involved.

The baby began to stir inside the blanket, her eyes fluttering. "Uh-oh." Being the oldest of five children, I knew newborns had only two modes—fast asleep and feeding frenzy. And if you didn't feed them fast enough, they'd scream loud enough to wake Satan's minions in the deepest circle of hell.

Seth's eyes flashed in alarm and he held the baby out to me. "Here! Take her!"

I scoffed. "You run into burning buildings and defuse explosives for a living, but you're scared of a tiny baby?"

"Yes!" He thrust the baby at me again. "Babies are terrifying."

I rolled my eyes but took the baby from him and settled her in my arms, gazing down at her. "Hi, cutie."

Her body wriggled and her tiny mouth opened in a toothless yawn as she struggled to wake. Looking at her, I couldn't help but have questions. Why did her parents give her up? What circumstances had they faced that forced them to make this heartbreaking choice?

Despite the Texas legislature's attempts to restrict abortion in the state, it was still legal under certain circumstances. The mother of this child would presumably have had the option of terminating her pregnancy if she'd had the means and inclination to do so. But she hadn't. *What does that tell us? Where did you come from, baby girl?* My gut squirmed with that same sense of frustration I felt when it was clear Brigit knew something I didn't and couldn't communicate it to me.

As the other men wandered off to return to their tasks, Harrison said, "One of the guys ran to the store for diapers and formula. He should be back soon."

"Great." Instinctively, I hiked the baby into a more upright position in my arms and began to bounce and sway side to side. She yawned a second time, blinking her eyes against the harsh glare in the bay. When I looked up again, I caught Seth eyeing me, a soft smile on his face.

He lifted his dimpled chin to indicate the baby. "Don't get any ideas."

I rolled my eyes a second time. "Don't you, either." I planned to take the detective exam as soon as I was able. The last thing I needed was a child getting in the way of my career aspirations. That said, I'd want a kid or two later, once I'd had a chance to solve some big cases, prove my mettle. Did I want my children to also be Seth's kids? Maybe. Probably, even. But there'd be time to figure all of that out later. We'd only been dating a little over a year and we were in no rush to settle down and start a family.

The baby began to fuss, emitting little mewling, hi-cuppy cries. "It's okay, baby girl," I told her in my best soothing voice as I cranked my bounces up a notch. "Everything's okay."

Of course that wasn't true. Everything was most definitely *not* okay. If things were okay, she'd be with her mother and father right now. *Only a few hours old and already she's been abandoned by her parents and lied to by a cop.* Not an auspicious start, was it?

I pushed the button on my shoulder-mounted radio to contact dispatch, giving my current location. "A baby girl was dropped off here. Can you notify Child Protective Services so they can send someone over to pick her up?"

The dispatcher's voice came back. "Will do. How's the baby doing? Is she all right?"

I pushed the button to respond, but before I could get the word out the baby mustered up every bit of her strength and let loose a wail. *Waaaaaaaah!*

"My Lord!" the dispatcher cried. "She's got some lungs on her!"

"Sorry." I pulled the baby away from the mic lest she burst the dispatcher's eardrums. "But I guess that's a good sign, huh?" A sick baby wouldn't have been able to muster up such a strong sound.

Thankfully, the firefighter who'd gone for formula

pulled into the lot. Seth met him at his car and took the bag of provisions from him. As Seth carried the bag into the station, I followed with the baby. *Waaaaah!* Brigit and Blast padded along after us. When we reached the kitchen, Seth pulled the items from the bag and set them on the table. He looked from the table to me, raising his voice to be heard over the baby's cry. "What now?"

It had been a long time since I'd been around an infant. None of my friends were mothers yet, and the last time I'd babysat was over a decade ago. But having helped my parents with my four younger siblings, I remembered the basics.

"Rinse the bottle and nipple," I directed. "Then pour a couple of ounces of formula in the bottle and run it under hot water for a few seconds to warm it up just a little."

Seth did as I'd told him and handed the warm bottle to me. I checked the temperature by dabbing a drop on my wrist. As Goldilocks would say, it was just right.

"Dinnertime, little g-girl." Actually, it was more of a midnight snack, but she was too young to know the difference. She was also too young to realize I suffered from what was now only a minor stutter, but which had virtually silenced me during my childhood. Of course my struggles with my speech seemed minor in comparison to what this baby faced.

I slid the nipple between the baby's lips, teasing the roof of her mouth until she clamped down and began to drink. The little thing had darn impressive suction, the bottle pulling against my fingers. I had to tighten my grip lest she suck the bottle right out of my hand. *Suck-suck-suck.*

Her cry having been answered, she blinked to clear the tiny tears she'd mustered along with her wail, the little drops running down her temples to dampen her hair. As I gazed down at her, I couldn't help but wonder who her mother was. Was the baby also wondering if *I* was her mother? My mind recalled the children's book *Are You My Mother?* The bird in the book had an acute lack of self-awareness, inquiring whether various animals of other species and even a piece of construction equipment were its mother. *Sorry, kiddo. Not me.*

I took a seat at the table while she ate. Now that the baby was at dog level, Brigit and Blast took the opportunity to check her out more fully. They sniffed her blanket and her little curved ears, sniffed at the bottle, too. As if to get a complete look at the baby, Brigit grabbed the loose tip of the knit cap and pulled it off the baby's head, releasing a cascade of fluffy black hair that would be right at home on a Muppet.

"Bad dog!" I tucked the bottle under my chin to hold it still for the baby and reached out to grab the cap from Brigit's teeth. "Give me that."

Brigit released her hold on the cap, turning her attention back to the baby. She sniffed the infant's dark hair twice—*sniff-sniff*—then opened her mouth and gave the baby's head a slick lick from back to front. *Slup.* The girl's hair now stuck up in a point above her forehead, like Alfalfa from *The Little Rascals.* Unsanitary, sure, but adorable as heck, too.

I looked up at Seth. "Take a picture." Whoever the baby ended up with long term, they should have a glimpse into her first few hours. Hopefully they wouldn't be disgusted by dog germs. They didn't seem to bother the baby. She continued to drink, undeterred by the dog slime. *Suck-suck-suck.*

Seth pulled out his cell phone and snapped a quick pic of the baby with her canine coif. "She must get that dark hair from her mother."

"What makes you say that?"

"The guy who handed her off was blond. Or at least his beard was."

Hmm. Were blond genes recessive? I wasn't sure. "Was he young?"

"No. I'd put him around my age."

In other words, the guy was around thirty. Again, *hmm.* I'd expected the father of the baby to be younger, maybe even a teenager, but I supposed parents of all ages could find themselves unable to take care of a baby. And while the Baby Moses Law had an age limit for the child, it didn't impose any age restrictions on the parents giving up the baby.

Brigit and Blast gave the little girl one last sniff before losing interest in her and wandering over to the fridge. Brigit nudged the door with her nose, looked over at Seth, and woofed. The dog might not speak English, but she could nonetheless communicate very clearly with us humans when it came to certain things.

"All right, Brigit." Seth stepped over and opened the fridge. "What sounds good?" he asked my furry partner. "Hot dogs? Bologna?"

Brigit stuck her nose into the fridge. She started by sniffing the lower drawer where the fruits and vegetables were kept, but worked her way up to the higher drawer, which contained hot dogs and a variety of lunch meats. She nudged the upper drawer and sat back on her haunches, gazing up at Seth expectantly.

Seth opened the drawer, reached inside, and retrieved the hot dogs, a package of ham, and a package of bologna. Brigit nudged the bologna with her snout.

"Bologna it is." Seth returned the other items to the drawer and finagled a couple slices of the lunch meat from the package. He tore the slices into strips and hand-fed them to Brigit and Blast, who wagged their tails in appreciation.

One of the other firefighters wandered in, grumbled when he found the coffeepot empty, and set about brewing a fresh pot.

The baby's sucking eventually slowed and I removed the bottle from her mouth. "Tummy full now, sweetie?"

She replied with a cute baby toot.

"I'll take that as a 'yes.'" I rounded up a dish towel and draped it over my shoulder. Properly protected now, I put her up to my shoulder and patted her back until she offered up an itty-bitty baby burp. *Burp.* Fortunately, the burp was all that came out of her. Burping my younger brother Joey had always been more akin to an exorcism. You never knew what manner of demon might spew forth.

"Shoot," said Seth's coworker, pulling a coffee mug from the cabinet. "With all the noises that baby's making, she'd have been right at home at my frat house."

I looked down at her and offered her her first piece of advice. "You steer clear of frat houses, hear me?"

The baby now fed, I rounded up a diaper from the grocery bag and carried her across the hall to Seth's bunk to change her. The dogs plopped down on the floor and engaged in a tussle, mouthing each other's necks and limbs and growling playfully. Seth leaned against the door frame while I laid the baby down on the bunk and unwrapped her blanket. The piece was an intricate work of art, featuring quilted bluebonnets, the state flower, which blanketed roadsides and fields each spring. The person who had made the quilt had found the perfect shade of fabric for the flowers, which were a unique mix of royal blue with a hint of purple. The baby wore a soft pink gown and blue crocheted booties that matched her cap. Whoever made the clothing and blanket was skilled with both crochet needles and sewing needles. *Had they been made by the baby's mother?* It must've taken hours and hours to hand-stitch the blanket and crochet the cap and booties. *That says something, doesn't it?*

"What'll happen to her?" Seth asked.

I pulled the tapes on the girl's diaper to loosen it. "CPS will take her to a hospital for a complete exam and to get the shots and other stuff that's normally given to newborns. Once she's released, they'll find a foster home to take her in until she's put up for adoption." She'd have no shortage of takers. Healthy babies were in big demand.

After wiping the baby's teeny, perfectly pink bum, I wrapped it in a fresh diaper and left her in Seth's care while I went to the bathroom to dispose of the old diaper and wash my hands. When I returned, I spread out her quilted blanket and plunked her down in the center of it, pulling each of the points in and tucking the last one in by her chin as if she were a burrito. "There you go, sweetie. Snug as a bug in a rug."

I picked her up and gently placed a kiss on her forehead. When I turned around, I caught Seth eyeing me. He said nothing, but his eyes made it clear there was a lot going through his head at the moment. *What is he thinking?* Whatever it was, he didn't seem intent on sharing it with me, at least not yet. I didn't push him. He tended to clam up when asked about his thoughts and feelings, but I'd learned that if I gave him enough time he'd eventually share the important ones with me.

The baby looked up at me with her glassy, unfocused newborn eyes. At the same time, my heart swelled with some type of maternal instinct and my gut wrenched at the thought that this moment could be critical in the baby's formation of her thoughts of the world. I had no idea what she'd endured so far. Just because she hadn't been bruised or battered didn't mean she'd been cuddled and coddled and welcomed to the world the way every new baby should be. I had to reassure her that the world was a good place, at least for the most part, and that there was a special place in it just for her—even if she hadn't found it yet.

I raised her up until her face was only inches below mine. "Would you like me to sing you a song, baby girl?" Unfortunately, the only lullaby I could remember was "Hush, Little Baby" and, frankly, the song's message didn't sit well with me. The lyrics basically told the baby that if it shut up and didn't complain or question, it would be rewarded with a diamond ring and other gifts. Hell, that was the arrangement many philandering men had with their wives. *Screw that!* Better this little girl forgo jewelry and other material things and instead learn to stand up for herself. *Hmm. What to sing, then?*

When I hesitated, Seth cocked his head. "You don't know any lullabies?"

"Only 'Hush, Little Baby,' and no way am I shushing her. She's got a right to speak her mind."

"How can she speak her mind? She doesn't know any words yet."

"That doesn't matter."

Seth looked up in thought. "Okay, how about this song, then?" A classic rock fan, he launched into Cat Stevens's hit from the seventies, "If You Want to Sing Out."

I gave Seth a smile and a nod, and sang along with what lyrics I knew, rocking back and forth gently on the bed with the baby in my arms. He stepped over and sat down next me, draping an arm around my shoulders and rocking with me.

We were in the last verse of the song, singing to the baby about how there were a million things to be, when Harrison rapped on the open door. We stopped singing and looked up.

"CPS is here," he said. "The caseworker's waiting in the lounge."

"Okay." I looked down at the little baby once again, feeling an odd need to explain myself to her before handing her off forever. "I'm about to turn you over to a social worker. She's going to get you medical treatment and find you a good home. I might never see you again, but I'll be thinking about you and I won't ever forget you, okay?" I pressed my lips to her cheek and whispered in her ear. "Have a wonderful life, little one. Don't let anyone or anything hold you back from chasing your dreams."

My eyes pricked with unshed tears and emotion gripped my throat. *Sheesh.* If I was this choked up, how difficult must it have been for her parents to give her up?

Seth reached out and gave the baby a soft chuck on the chin. "Good luck, squirt." Was it just my imagination, or did he sound a little choked up, too?

We stood and made our way down the hall to the lounge. A woman in her forties who looked like she'd been roused from a deep sleep stood waiting, a well-used infant car seat in her hand.

She set the seat down on the coffee table and turned to me and the baby. She gazed down at her. "What a cutie. We'll find her a family in no time."

The social worker reached out her arms to take the baby. Before I handed her over, I gave the baby one last, tight cuddle and closed my eyes in a quiet prayer. *Goodbye, baby girl.*

As the woman took the baby from me, the corner of the blanket that had been behind the baby's head flopped over, and loose threads on the trim caught my eye.

Wait. That's not just loose thread. There's a word there, too.

I gasped as my mind processed the image before me. *The thread spells "HELP!"*

My palm shot up in a stop motion. "Wait!"

The woman froze. "Something wrong?"

I gestured to the quilt. "I need to take a closer look at the blanket."

She gave me an odd look but shrugged. "Okay." She freed the baby from the blanket and handed it to me.

Seth stepped closer, a puzzled look on his face.

My fingers frantically worked the fabric until I found the word on the trim. I held it up. "Look! This thread spells out 'Help!'"

The word was followed by what appeared to possibly be the remains of a stitched peace sign, a circle with an inverted *Y* inside. It was hard to say for sure given that the thread had pulled loose, a couple inches of it hanging from the fabric. But on close inspection I could see tiny holes in the fabric where the needle had gone through. Oddly, there were two such holes inside the circle, on either side of the vertical line. *What does that mean?* If the stitching was, in fact, a peace sign, the symbol would be at odds with the word "help." Terror and tranquility were polar-opposite concepts.

Seth and the caseworker leaned in, squinting for a moment before making out the word, their eyes popping wide in surprise. The three of us stood in stunned silence for a moment, trying to process things.

Seth eyed me intently. "What does it mean?"

There was no way to know for certain. But I did know one thing. "It means Brigit's about to be put to work."

Before my partner and I stepped away, the caseworker asked, "Is it okay if I take the baby to the hospital now? I don't want to put it off too long."

"Sure," I replied. After all, it wasn't like the baby could provide any testimony, tell us where she'd come from and who'd brought her here. Too bad. It would make things so much easier.

I exchanged business cards with the caseworker so we'd be able to contact each other as necessary. Official matters over with, I reached out to the baby one last time, picking up her tiny hand in mine. Instinctively, her little fist tightened around my index finger, as if she were holding on for dear life. Her eyes opened and seemed to focus on mine, imploring me to do what the word on the blanket asked, to help.

Brigit and I will do our best, little one.

THREE
SMELL YA LATER

Brigit

Megan clipped Brigit's lead onto her collar and directed the dog to put her nose to the ground. Brigit happily obeyed. Tracking was fun, like a game of hide-and-seek. Brigit never lost this game. She had the best nose in the biz. The best part about it was that Megan would give her a treat afterward, an edible paycheck.

Sniff-sniff. Sniff-sniff.

Brigit could smell where the ground had been disturbed, smell one of the same human scents that had been on the baby's blanket. She continued on, following the scent across the parking lot of the fire station and out onto the sidewalk, where it mingled with the scents of discarded chewing gum and cigarette butts and car exhaust and a thousand other scents her sensitive nose could distinguish. She followed the smell to the curb, out into the street, and diagonally across it, picking it up again on the sidewalk on the other side.

She trotted along with Megan jogging by her side. Down the block they went, then down another. She could smell the same scent but slightly more faint, meaning the man who'd gone this way had backtracked over a trail he'd left not long before. Yep, her nose could create a virtual time line of activity, not only picking up scents but discerning how fresh they were.

Sniff-sniff. Sniff-sniff.

Finally, the scent petered out in a dark parking lot. Brigit snuffled around to make sure she couldn't pick it up again. But no. The scent disappeared here.

She sat down and looked up at Megan to let her know the trail stopped here. *Paycheck, please!*

Megan reached into her pocket and removed a liver treat, tossing it to Brigit along with a "Good girl!"

FOUR

SOLITUDE IS GOOD FOR THE SOUL

The Father

Juliette sat bolt upright in the bed as he walked into the infirmary empty-handed. Her dark hair was still matted with sweat from childbirth. "Where is she? Where's my baby?"

The Father looked from the young woman to her parents. Juliette's dad was an average-sized man with plastic-framed eyeglasses and a bald spot on the back of his head where his brown hair was slowly retreating toward his ears and forehead. Her mother had the same petite build and dark, silky hair as Juliette, though a few strands of gray had recently crept in. Both were the human equivalent of church mice. Timid. Quiet. Undemanding of attention. Much like the others in the compound, they'd taken the Father's sermons on humility to heart.

The Father spoke softly and used his most solemn voice as he ducked his head in mock sorrow. "Your baby is with the Lord."

Juliette gasped loud enough to be heard in the heavens, her eyes going so wide it was a wonder they didn't fall out of her skull.

Her mother's face clouded, while her dad reflexively rose from his chair next to the bed, his face pained. "What are you saying, Father?" he asked.

"I'm sorry," he replied softly. "The baby had a bad reaction to the immunizations. The doctors did all they could, but . . ." He raised his palms and looked upward.

Juliette's eyes welled with tears and she put her hands to her face as if she could shut out the news. She spoke through her fingers. "She's . . . *gone*?"

"She is. I'm so sorry."

The young woman dropped her hands and her mouth opened again, but she made only a choking sound, as if she couldn't force any more words past the grief strangling her. Her entire body began to tremble as she broke down in sobs. A moment later, she shrieked, "Nooo!" She threw back the covers, getting tangled in them and falling to her knees on the wood floor as she attempted to stand on legs too weak from childbirth and grief to support her.

It gave the Father no small sense of pleasure to see her so feeble and desperate.

"No! Please, God! No!" She gulped air as she looked up at him through eyes blurred with tears. "Why didn't you let me go with you to the hospital? Why?"

How dare she question his decisions!

"It wouldn't have made a difference," he said. "You couldn't have saved her."

Brushing back her own tears, Juliette's mother attempted to both console her daughter and help her up from the floor. "You'd just given birth. You needed to rest."

"This was God's will," the Father added, his voice still low but firmer now. "We may not always understand His plan, but we must accept it."

If not for her father taking his daughter's arm, the Father had no doubt she'd have found the strength to hurl herself at him, rip him apart. Her parents offered her useless platitudes. They told her that the Father was right, that as unfair as things seemed she must accept God's will. That her baby was in heaven, a perfect place. That she'd see her precious child again someday, that they'd be reunited and her grief would be forgotten.

Juliette sobbed inconsolably as her mother helped her back up onto the bed and stroked her hair. Her mother made another attempt to offer her daughter some solace. "You'll have a chance to have another child one day after you're properly married, a child who will have a willing father and won't know the shame of having been conceived in sin."

That last comment from her mother sent the young woman right over the edge. She glared up at the Father with such hate and rage that for a brief instant terror gripped him. *Would she tell them the truth about who had fathered her child? Would she reveal their secrets?*

She didn't, though. Instead, she pushed her mother away and screamed, "Get out! All of you! Get out now!"

Her parents attempted to placate her with apologies and more talk about the beauty and wonders of heaven, but she only grew more adamant.

She pointed at the door. "Get out! I want to be alone!"

The Father backed out of the door and motioned for

Juliette's parents to join him in the hallway. They emerged, looking grief-stricken and helpless.

He closed the door behind them. "Don't worry," he said. "She'll come around. Right now, though, she needs some time to come to terms with what's happened. You two head over to the church. I'll meet you there in a few minutes to pray."

The ever-obedient couple nodded and walked out. They'd always appreciated his leadership, trusted his guidance. When he'd found them homeless and penniless on the steps of that locked church in Fort Worth over a decade ago, they'd been relieved and more than happy to put control of their lives in his capable hands. *If only their daughter could be so humble and compliant.*

Once they'd gone, he summoned his men from the adjoining room. Jeb and Zeke followed him as he opened the door to Juliette's room.

On seeing the Father in the doorway, she grabbed fistfuls of her white cotton nightgown in her hands and screeched, "This is all your fault! You're not a man of God! You're the devil!"

Snatching the glass lamp from her bedside table, she hurled it at him. Luckily for him, her aim was poor. The lamp struck the door frame and shattered, glass tinkling down onto the wood floor.

She'd pushed him right over his edge, too. He turned his back to the girl, stepped into the hall, and addressed his men, forcing his voice to stay calm even though his blood boiled. "Take her away. She needs solitude to heal."

And isolation to be punished.

"Yes, Father," the two said in unison.

"No!" She fought the men in vain as they grabbed her. "No!"

Her cries intensified as the men dragged her kicking and screaming out of her room. Zeke held her from behind and slapped a hand over her mouth to silence her as he forced her out the back door. Jeb closed the door behind them.

A grin slithered past the Father's lips. In eleven years, he hadn't managed to break that stubborn girl.

But this ought to do it.

FIVE
WHO'S YOUR DADDY?

Megan

Damn!

I'd hoped to catch the man who'd left the baby, question him about the cryptic message sewn into the trim of the blanket. But there was nothing here but the remains of a razed convenience store. Whoever the man was, he'd disappeared into the night.

Brigit and I had done what we could for now. Anything further would require a detective to be brought into the case. I whipped out my cell phone and dialed Detective Audrey Jackson. Jackson was one of the more senior detectives in the Western 1 Division, and she'd graciously taken me under her wing. Someday I hoped to be in her shoes, working investigations and solving complex cases. But I had only a year and nine months on the force under my belt. An aspiring detective had to serve at least four years as a patrol officer before being eligible to take the detective exam. *Two years and three months left to go.* Until then, I had to satisfy myself by helping the detectives with whatever tasks they might entrust to me.

Detective Jackson answered on the fourth ring, her voice raspy from sleep. "What's up, Megan?" Her curt response said she knew my late-hour call meant an emergency was under way.

"A newborn was left at the fire station a little while ago. CPS picked up the baby. She appeared to be unharmed, but when I was handing her over I saw a message sewn into the hem of her blanket. The word 'help' followed by an exclamation point."

"'Help'?" She groaned. "That doesn't sound good. Where are you now?"

"Heading back to the fire station. Brigit trailed the man who dropped off the baby to a construction site on Rosedale, but it looks like he got in a vehicle there and left. We're turning b-back now. I'll make note of the security cameras on the route."

"Good work. I'll throw on some clothes and meet you at the fire station."

We ended the call and I continued on, Brigit walking by my side now. As my partner and I retraced our steps, I made a mental note of each building along the way that had outside security cameras. *Dental office? Yes. Barbershop? No. Dialysis clinic? Yes.* Hopefully one of the cameras had picked up the vehicle driven by the man who'd dropped off the baby, snagged his license plate number. *He has some explaining to do.*

As Brigit and I cut through a dark alley behind a deli, I pulled my flashlight from my belt and clicked it on, shining the beam around the eaves and looking for a camera. As we walked past a Dumpster, Brigit stopped next to it and went stiff, her nose and one paw raised. I knew that telltale pose. *Something is here.* Was the man hiding behind the garbage bin?

I signaled for Brigit to follow me backward a few steps for safety and addressed the Dumpster. "Sir? You back there? Come on out and let's talk."

There was no sound for a few seconds until Brigit began to whine, her body quivering in anticipation. *Yep. Definitely something back there.*

"Sir?" I said again. "Come on out, please."

But no man came out. *Ugh.* My heart thrummed like a bass line at a night club. Given the cry for help stitched into the blanket, this man could be dangerous. I yanked my nightstick from my belt and flicked my wrist. The telescoping baton extended with a sharp *snap!* Having twirled a baton with my high school's marching band, I felt much more comfortable with this particular weapon than I did with my gun.

"I'm going to count to three," I warned the man, "and if you haven't come out I'm sending my dog in." I took a deep breath. "One." No movement or sound came. "Two." Still no movement. *Damn it!*

Next to me, Brigit shook like a paint mixer, ready to launch herself after our target. Still, as handy as Brigit's special skills could be and as much as she enjoyed her work, I didn't like sending her into dangerous situations armed only with her teeth.

"Three." My voice sounded more like a plea than a demand at this point.

Still nothing.

I had no choice. I issued the order for Brigit to flush out the man behind the Dumpster.

Brigit took off around the big metal bin, her claws scrambling on the asphalt. The next thing I knew, something came tearing around the other side of the Dumpster, coming straight at me. But it wasn't a man.

Instead, it was a furry beast that was all fangs and fur and dark rings.

"Aaah!" I cried out in surprise and instinctively jumped back as the enormous raccoon shot past me, followed by my partner. "Brigit!" I hollered as she bolted after the beast. "Get back here!"

She chased the varmint a few more feet, then made a U-turn and headed back my way. She sat at my feet, wagging her tail, her mouth hanging open as she panted gleefully.

I closed my baton, returned it to my belt, and shook my finger at my partner. "We are not out here to police the raccoon population!"

The *woof* she offered in reply told me she disagreed entirely.

My partner and I continued on, eventually making our way back to the fire station. Seth and Blast waited for us out front, their foreheads furrowed in worry.

Seth held the blanket in his hands, his shoulders slumping when he spotted me and Brigit without the man in tow. "Didn't find him?"

"No luck. He's already left the area."

Headlights swept across us as Detective Jackson turned into the parking lot. She was out of her car in a heartbeat, gesturing to the blanket in Seth's hands. "That the blanket you told me about?"

"Yes." I took it from Seth and found the message on the trim. "See? Right here. *'Help!'*"

She held it up to the light and took a look. "That's what it says, all right. But maybe it's just referring to the baby."

"I don't think so," I said. "I think whoever sewed that was referring to herself."

"What makes you think that?" Jackson asked.

Good question. A tough one, too, because I didn't really have a good answer. "Instinct?" I said with a shrug. "Plus it doesn't seem to me that the mother would ask for help for the baby if the mother knew the baby was going to be taken to a fire station. The mother would know her baby would get help."

Jackson cocked her head. "You've assumed the mother was the one who sewed the word into the blanket. Why?"

I gestured to the quilt. "Look at it. It's beautiful. The hand-quilting would have taken a long time. It was a labor of love. Whoever made it must have loved the baby very much."

Jackson stared at the fabric, as if willing it to speak to her, to tell her its secrets.

"See this, too?" I asked, pointing at the additional stitching after the word. "I think it might be a clue of some sort. It looks kind of like a peace sign."

"Hmm." She squinted. "Maybe. Hard to say with the thread hanging loose." She lowered the blanket, glanced around, and pointed to the security camera mounted over the bay, directing her next question to Seth. "Any chance you can show us the footage from the camera?"

"The captain can." Seth motioned for us to follow him.

We went into the building and made our way back to the captain's office. The balding man was at his desk working on his computer, the light from the screen reflecting off his forehead. He glanced up as we stepped into the doorway.

Seth made quick introductions. "Captain Nelson,

this is Detective Audrey Jackson from the Fort Worth PD."

The man stood and extended his arm across his desk to shake hands with the detective.

Jackson got right down to business. "We have some concerns about the baby that was left here. Can you show us the footage from the camera out front? I want to see the man who brought her in."

"Of course." He pulled up a chair for the detective and sat back down in his. Seth and I took up spots on either side of them. Brigit and Blast plopped down on the carpet, engaging in a playful tussle.

It took a couple of minutes for the captain to log into the security system, pinpoint the proper camera feed, and drag the timer back to an hour prior. "Here we go." He clicked his mouse to start the footage.

The screen showed the dim front parking lot, the image ending just past the curb. For a minute or two, the only thing we saw was an occasional elongated human shadow cast by a firefighter working in the lit bay behind the camera. Then a man emerged from the darkness at the edge of the screen. He wore jeans, work boots, and a dark zippered jacket. He had a ball cap on his head and a baby held awkwardly in his arms. The cap cast the upper part of his face in shadow, making it impossible to discern his features. What I could see of his chin and jawline appeared fuzzy. It wasn't clear to me whether the fuzziness was his facial hair or whether it was a result of the poor-quality video.

He stopped a dozen feet from the camera and shifted the baby in his arms. As he moved her, the edge of the blanket caught on the zipper of his jacket. He tugged it free. *Is that how the thread ended up hanging loose?*

The man's mouth opened as if he were calling out to someone inside the bay. A few seconds later, Seth appeared, his back to the camera. He walked up to the man. Though we couldn't see Seth's face, it was clear he'd asked the man a question because the man paused for a second before speaking again.

The detective cast a glance at Seth. "What did you ask the guy?"

"If the baby was his."

"And?"

"He said it was."

As she turned back to the screen, the image showed Seth pulling a radio from his belt and speaking into it. A moment later, Douglas Harrison appeared. While the man continued to hold the baby, Harrison loosened the blanket and pulled up the baby's gown, evidently searching for signs of abuse. He, too, said something to the man.

Anticipating the detective's next question, Seth said, "Harrison asked the guy whether he wanted to provide any family medical history. He said 'no.' That was it."

We continued to watch. When Harrison offered a nod, the man turned and retreated at a brisk pace. Seth and Harrison disappeared from the camera feed as they went into the station.

"As soon as we went inside," Seth told Jackson, "I called Megan."

"Then I called you," I told her.

"And here we are." The detective was silent a few beats before speaking again. "Did the guy say anything about the baby's mother?"

Seth shook his head. "Not a word."

"It was hard to tell much about him from the footage. What did he look like?"

Seth shut his eyes for a moment, as if to better visualize the man, before opening them again. "He had a light beard, maybe a week's growth. Short hair. Couldn't really see his eyes well because of the hat."

The detective and I looked to Harrison, who confirmed Seth's description with a dip of his head.

"Any scars?" I asked. "Moles? Birthmarks?"

"Not that I noticed," Seth said.

"I didn't see any, either," Harrison added.

"What about piercings? Tattoos? Missing teeth?"

Seth raised his palms. "If he had any of those things they didn't catch my eye. My focus was mostly on the baby."

"Mine, too." Harrison lifted his shoulders, indicating he hadn't noticed any piercings, tattoos, or missing teeth, either. With no discernible features, the man who'd left the baby would be difficult to firmly identify, especially if he shaved off the beard.

Jackson and I exchanged glances. Her tight face looked as pensive as I felt. *What now?* She gestured to Brigit. "Show me where she took you."

The detective followed as, once again, Brigit and I retraced the steps taken by the man who'd left the baby. The raccoon watched us from the roof of the deli as we made our way down the alley.

When we reached the demolished convenience store, Jackson looked around. "See anything? Maybe some trash left behind? A discarded cigarette butt?"

We turned on our flashlights and slowly scanned the area, but all we saw was dust and gravel.

"I've got nothing," I told her.

"Me, neither."

As we returned to the station, I opened my notebook and tore out the page listing the sites with security cameras. I handed it to the detective, and pointed them out along the way.

When we reached the parking lot of the fire station, we stopped by our cars. Despite the urgency of the situation, we had nothing to go on at the moment. No car for units to watch out for. No fugitive on foot. No ID on the man, so no home or workplace to visit. My gut twisted in frustration.

"I'll make some calls," Jackson said, "see about taking a look at the security footage on the dentist's office, the dialysis clinic, and the doughnut shop." She thumbed her key fob to open her trunk, retrieved a large evidence bag, and slid the blanket inside for safekeeping. "I'll be in touch if we find anything out. In the meantime, why don't you give the caseworker a call. Tell her not to move forward with any adoption plans until we sort this out."

I lifted my chin in acknowledgment and stepped back to allow her to climb into her car. She cranked the engine and backed out, raising a quick hand in good-bye.

As the detective's cruiser turned out of the lot, Seth stepped out of the bay and came over to stand in front of me. "What a night, huh?"

"You can say that again." I bit my lower lip as my gut twisted even tighter in fear. "You think the baby's mother is okay?"

"I don't know, Megan." Seth took a step closer,

wrapping his arms around me. He leaned down to whisper in my ear. "But I know you'll do everything you can to find out."

He knows me well.

Seth gave me a squeeze, brushed his lips against my temple, and backed away.

I opened the back door of the cruiser and signaled for Brigit to get into the car. Once she'd hopped up to her platform, I rounded the car and climbed into my seat. I pulled the caseworker's business card out of my pocket and dialed her number.

"Hi," I said when she answered. "It's Officer Megan Luz." Through the phone came the sound of an infant crying in the background. "Is the baby okay?"

"She's fine," the woman said. "Not happy about getting her shot and having drops put in her eyes is all."

"Can't say that I blame her." *Poor little thing.* "Detective Jackson asked me to give you a call. She's taken a look at the blanket, too, and we've watched the security-camera video of when the baby was dropped at the station. We have some questions that need to be answered before the baby can be released for adoption. The detective said to let you know so you could put things on hold for now."

"Okay," the woman said. "I've got a wonderful couple looking to adopt who would be willing to foster her in the meantime. I'll place her in their home. That way, if she becomes available, she can stay with them."

"Sounds great." The more stability the baby had in her early life, the better.

We ended the call and I slid my phone into the cup holder for safekeeping. As I exited the lot, dispatch came over the radio. "Got a call from a resident of Fairmount. Someone smashed the window of his car." She rattled off an address on west Jefferson Avenue.

Glad for the distraction, I grabbed the mic. "Officers Luz and Brigit responding."

My foot punched the gas and, a couple minutes later, applied the brake as we approached the victim's house. A fortyish couple stood in their driveway next to their shiny black Lexus. Broken glass littered the concrete at their feet, reflecting the moonlight like a disco ball. All that remained of the passenger window was a few shards sticking up from the door.

I unrolled the windows on the cruiser so Brigit could get some air, but left her in the car for now. No sense risking her cutting her paw. I climbed out, stepped over, and introduced myself, extending my hand. "I'm Officer Megan Luz. Can you tell me what happened?"

"We were fast asleep only a few minutes ago," the woman said, "when the car alarm went off." She hiked a thumb at her husband. "He came out to take a look and found the window smashed."

In cases like this, there were generally three possible explanations for the crime. One, the smashed window could be personal, a vendetta, someone settling a score. Two, the crime could be nothing more than vandalism, a disaffected youth taking out his frustration at the world on an innocent car. Or three, it could be thieves looking for electronics or drugs or gas station credit cards, the types of things people tend to leave in their cars even though common sense tells them they shouldn't. "Is anything missing from the vehicle?" I asked, hoping to rule out one or more of the possibilities.

"My work laptop," the man said.

Bingo. I wasn't surprised it was a theft. Burglaries are a beat cop's bread and butter.

"My Steve Nash bobble-head is gone, too," the man said. "It was on my dash. I got it back when he played for the Mavericks. It's a collector's item now."

Though I wasn't a huge sports fan, during my childhood my father and brothers had watched plenty of games on TV, including basketball. I remembered Steve Nash from years ago. He wore the number 13 jersey, defying superstition and playing like a superstar alongside Dirk Nowitzki. Nash's longish hair seemed to be perpetually wet with sweat.

I took out my flashlight and shined it into the car. The seat, dash, and floorboard were covered with broken glass. A few shards had made it to the driver's seat as well. I shined the light on the visors. No remote control was clipped there. I saw none on the console, either.

I stepped back and returned my attention to the couple. "Do you have a remote for the garage door?"

"Yeah," the man said. "We keep it in the glove box."

Lest I disturb any fingerprints, I slid my right hand into a latex glove, opened the car door, and reached inside to unlatch the glove box. Inside was an owner's manual, the usual insurance and registration paperwork, and a shiny metal tire gauge. Nothing else.

The man peeked in over my shoulder. "The remote's gone, too? Hell!"

"Did you see anyone out here?"

"No," he replied. "I looked up and down the street but there was no one in sight. I turned off the alarm and called 911 from my cell phone." His brows rose in hope. "Do you think you'll be able to find out who took my computer and get it back?"

Honestly? The odds of recovering the laptop were slim to none. This was one of those cases where an ounce of prevention was worth a pound of cure, but this guy would learn that lesson the hard way. Still, I wouldn't throw in the towel before making an honest effort. I closed the door and stepped back. "I'll get my partner. See if she can find a trail to follow."

Returning to my squad car, I opened the back and let Brigit out, clipping her lead to her collar. The broken glass extended out three feet or so. I took her as close to the car as I dared without risking injury to her paws, and issued the command for her to find and track the trail of the thief. She put her nose down and began to snuffle about. A few seconds later, she set off down the driveway.

"We'll be back!" I called over my shoulder as we went.

Brigit led me down to the sidewalk and turned, snuffling her way, pulled along by the scent. For the second time that night, I jogged along behind her. *I'm definitely getting my steps in today.* Unfortunately, our efforts yielded the same result as earlier. A dead end. Brigit stopped a couple of streets over, snuffled in a broad circle and sat down, indicating this is where the trail ended. The thief must have climbed into a car here and taken off.

Again, we retraced our steps. My eyes scanned the surroundings for security cameras. This time, I saw none. *Darn.*

Brigit and I returned to the house, where I showed

my gratitude by giving her another liver treat and another "Good girl!"

The couple turned anxious eyes on me.

"The trail ran cold," I said. "Whoever broke into your vehicle must have climbed into a car a couple of streets over. Unfortunately, there doesn't appear to be security cameras on any of the houses along the way."

The man groaned. "Just my luck."

I pointed to their double garage doors. "Since the thief got your remote, I'd suggest manually locking your garage doors until you can have the system reprogrammed. We've seen this type of thing before. Often the culprit will come back another time and use the remote to sneak into the garage. Sometimes they'll grab a few tools or a lawnmower. Other times they get into the house and go for other items."

The woman's eyes shone with trepidation and she turned to her husband. "That's it. We're getting an alarm system."

I gave her a nod. "Not a bad idea." I left them with my business card and instructions to call me if they had any further problems.

Brigit and I returned to our cruiser and continued our patrol. The rest of the night was quiet. Well, other than Brigit snoring on her comfy cushion in the back of the car.

We returned to the Western 1 station just as the sun was coming up. I hoped today would be a brighter day for the baby girl.

SIX
THE NOSE KNOWS

Brigit

Brigit was dozing in their bed, her head draped over Megan's thigh, when her nose woke her, issuing an urgent all-points bulletin.

Cheese! Someone's got cheese!

Brigit raised her head and pricked her ears. Sure enough, she heard the siren call of plastic wrap crinkling. She leaped off the bed and ran to answer the call, her paws sliding on the flooring as she careened around the corner into the kitchen. Their housemate Frankie stood at the counter, a slice of processed cheese in her hand.

Frankie looked down at Brigit. "Can't get anything past you, can I?"

Brigit wasn't sure what Frankie's words meant, but she knew her odds of getting some cheese were better if she wagged her tail and sat down obediently. Humans were suckers. She plunked her hindquarters down on the floor. *Cheese me! Now!*

Frankie pulled the refrigerator open, reached into the drawer, and snagged another slice of cheese, tearing

it into strips for Brigit and hand-feeding them to
her. When she finished, she gave Brigit's ears a nice
scratch.

Yep. Humans are total suckers.

SEVEN
*SILO*TARY CONFINEMENT

The Father

The three men approached the old concrete silo, which sat in the field adjacent to the compound. The tall stone wall around the compound would obscure any view the church members might have of the farmland outside the refuge. The bottom of the silo was further hidden by the tall and thick red tip photinia bushes the Father had strategically ordered his men to plant around the tower. The structure leaned a degree or two to the left, like a leaning tower of Pisa on the Texas plains. The roof and the attached ladder were rusted, generating copper-colored streaks that ran like veins down the long sides, as if the aging silo were a marble tower. Of course the silo wasn't the only thing around here that bore a deceptive façade.

The Father hadn't seen any value in the edifice when he'd bought the fifty-acre spread over three decades ago. He'd had no intentions of storing mass quantities of grain. But when he'd needed a place to safely and secretly stash someone, a place where sins could be contemplated and cries could be stifled, he'd soon realized the old structure provided the perfect spot. With the addition of a five-gallon water jug, a canvas cot, and a portable camping toilet, a person could be contained there for quite some time. *For as long as it takes . . .*

"Careful, now," he told Zeke and Jeb. "That girl's likely to be unpredictable."

The men nodded. The Father stepped back as Zeke put the key in the padlock and popped it open. Before Zeke removed the lock, he put his mouth to the frame of the heavy metal door. "No funny business. Sit down on the cot and don't get up until Jeb's set your lunch down. Understand?"

A meek voice came from the other side of the door. "I understand."

Zeke removed the lock and pulled the door open, the hinges emitting creaks of protest. As the opening widened, allowing sunlight into the dark space, the Father could make out the girl sitting on the cot inside. Her cheeks were streaked with tears, the front of her dress wet with milk that had leaked from her breasts. She blinked as her pretty blue eyes adjusted to the light.

Jeb stepped forward with the metal bucket that contained her meal. A hard roll. A boiled egg. A small navel orange. Enough to keep her alive, but not enough to keep her strong. The Father knew from experience that her will would be easier to break if she were also feeling physically weak.

As Jeb set the bucket down on the ground just inside the door, the girl sprang from the bed like a rabid jack-in-the-box and emitted a roar worthy of a caged tiger. She rushed the man, knocking him backward into the doorway. She tripped over his body as she attempted to escape, landing with one knee in Jeb's gut, the other in his groin. As Jeb turned his head sideways and retched, the Father fought the urge to laugh. *Good thing that moron hasn't had his lunch yet.*

As Zeke grabbed the girl's left arm, she screeched like a banshee, reached up with her right hand, and raked her nails over his face, leaving four deep, red gouges all the way from his temple to his mouth.

She's got even more fight in her than I thought.

Still, he'd break her eventually. He'd always managed to break the others before, make them see the error of their ways, repent their sins. Well, most of them, anyway. The ones who hadn't broken he'd had to handle in other ways. He hoped it wouldn't come to that. It was too messy.

Blood oozing from the claw marks, Zeke yanked the girl up from the ground and flung her back into the silo like a rag doll. She crashed into the cot, knocking it over, her hand-quilted blanket falling to the dusty floor. As the Father pulled Zeke out of the way, the girl scrambled to get to her feet. Just as the girl launched herself at it again, the Father slammed the door shut. Her body impacted the door with a dull thud.

The Father pulled Jeb to his feet. Jeb put one hand on the silo and cupped the other around his crotch, still coughing and gagging.

The Father gave his best men a simultaneous pat on the back. "The Lord appreciates your sacrifice." As for himself, well, he appreciated both their loyalty and gullibility.

EIGHT
SKETCHY

Megan

I was still in bed when Detective Jackson phoned around two in the afternoon on Friday. I grabbed my phone and jabbed the talk button. "Hello, Detective."

"No luck on the camera footage from the businesses," she said without preamble. "The guy moved quick. Couldn't tell much about him."

"What about the vehicle he was driving? Did any cameras pick up the car?"

"A camera down the block from the construction site picked up several cars shortly after the baby was left at the station. Most of them check out. But there was a dark pickup truck that passed eight minutes after the baby was left at the station. The license plates had been removed. All we could tell is that it's a Ford F-150. Judging from the style of the grill, it's a late nineties model."

The truck had to be the car the baby's father was driving, right? "Which way was it headed?"

"West," Jackson said. "Of course that doesn't tell us much. The truck didn't show up on footage from a gas station west of Henderson or on cameras from a clinic to the south. My guess is they turned north up Henderson and headed to I-30. No telling which way they went once they got to the interstate."

"Where do we go from here?" It was her case, of course, but the fact that she'd called to give me an update told me she planned to involve me, or at least to let me shadow her for the experience.

"I've searched the Fort Worth PD records to see if any of our officers pulled over a truck without plates last night. No luck. But I've put in inquiries with the sheriff's department and some of the surrounding cities to see if any of their people might've pulled the truck over. In the meantime, I'm heading over to the fire station with a sketch artist. We'll see what Seth and Douglas Harrison come up with."

I was already slipping out of my sleepwear and into jeans and a T-shirt. "I'll meet you there."

A good sketch of a suspect could make all the difference. After the horrific bombing in Oklahoma City, investigators tracked the Ryder truck, which had contained the explosive materials, to the rental location in Junction City, Kansas. People who'd interacted with Timothy McVeigh, the perpetrator of the heinous crime, provided descriptions used by the sketch artist to make a composite drawing. The sketch was released and widely publicized as the manhunt was under way. If not for that sketch, the officers who later pulled McVeigh over for traffic violations might not have realized he could be the man wanted for the senseless mass murder.

When I finished dressing, I rounded up Brigit and we headed out to my metallic blue Smart Car. Given all the talk of climate change and in an attempt to reduce both my carbon footprint and my gasoline expenses, I'd bought the tiny two-seater a few years ago. Of course that was before Chief Garelik had partnered me with Brigit who, at nearly a hundred pounds, outweighed every other K-9 on the Fort Worth force and eighty-two percent of all supermodels. When Brigit sat in the seat, the tips of her ears brushed the top of the car, causing her to constantly twitch them as we rode along. Fortunately, our drive and her discomfort would be short.

Jackson's plain sedan was already parked in the fire station's lot when I pulled in a few minutes later. I parked next to her and led Brigit inside. We found Seth, Harrison, and Detective Jackson gathered around a table in the station's kitchen. Blast, who'd been lying at Seth's feet, leaped to his paws and trotted over to greet us at the door.

Seth glanced up and gave me a "hey," while Jackson patted the seat next to her, indicating where she'd like me to sit.

At the end of the table sat the sketch artist, a grizzled man who looked old enough to have once shared paintbrushes with Vincent van Gogh. His gray hair hung in a mass of curls and frizz around his shoulders. He even wore a black beret, though the artsy effect was somewhat offset by his denim shirt, jeans, and scuffed cowboy boots. Perhaps he wore it ironically? Seth and Harrison sat on either side of him. A sketchbook turned to a blank page lay on the table in front of the artist and he held a charcoal pencil aloft, ready to begin. While many departments had replaced their sketch artists with computer software, it would be far more interesting to see this guy go about the procedure old-school style.

Once I'd sat down, Jackson made quick introductions and gestured to the artist. "He's seen the video."

The guy clucked his tongue. "Didn't help much, though. 'Course that's why I'm here, isn't it?" His question needing no answer, the artist launched into a series of questions directed at Seth and Harrison. "Let's start with the feature that most stood out to you. What would you say that was?"

Seth shrugged, his face tight and pensive. "Hard to say. Like you saw in the video, the guy's ball cap made it hard to see his face."

Harrison likewise said, "Other than the fact that he needed a shave, nothing jumps out at me." He shook his head and raised his palms. "Sorry."

"Don't put too much pressure on yourselves," the artist told the men, leaning back casually in his chair. "This sketch doesn't have to be exact. Long as we get a reasonable resemblance, it'll still help."

Seth's shoulders relaxed a little and Harrison exhaled an audible breath of relief.

"How 'bout we try another tack," the artist said. "How'd you describe the shape of the man's face?"

"Long," Harrison said without hesitation.

"Yeah," Seth agreed. "Sort of horsey."

Detective Jackson's brows quirked and she jotted down a note. I pulled my notepad from the breast pocket of my T-shirt and did the same. *Long, horsey face.* As I'd learned in my criminal justice studies at Sam Houston State University, criminal anthropometry, identifying suspects by measurements, began with Alphonse Bertillon, who worked as a records clerk in a Paris police department back in the late 1800s. In addition to maintaining photographs of suspects both from the front and in profile, his identification system included measuring each suspect in five main regards: the length of the head, the width of the head, the length of the foot, the length of the forearm, and the length of the middle finger. My mind pictured long-ago suspects being asked to flip the proverbial bird while a fastidious Frenchman used a ruler to measure their middle digit. No doubt many willingly complied with the request to make the gesture: *8.7 centimètres. Merci beaucoup.*

The system proved quite useful back in those days, helping police catch and accurately identify repeat offenders. In the early 1900s, however, fingerprinting replaced Bertillon's system when the former proved to be a more exact identification technique. Still, when a fingerprint could not be obtained, the fundamentals of anthropometry came into play in attempting to identify a suspect.

The artist put his pencil to the paper, scrawling a loose, long shape. "That it?"

"Not quite," Seth said. "His cheeks were more sunken."

"Gotcha." The guy flipped to a fresh page and made a second attempt, this time adding angular planes on the sides. "That more like it?"

Seth nodded.

The artist asked about the man's mouth next. "Full lips? Thin lips? Wide mouth? Small?"

Harrison said, "Thin and on the small side."

The artist continued to question them as he sketched the suspect's mouth. "Anything distinguishable about his teeth? Straight? Crooked? Caps? Silver fillings? Any of them obviously chipped or missing?"

"Not that I recall," Harrison said.

"Me, neither," Seth concurred.

"All righty," the artist said. "I'm going to add the beard now. You two say 'when.'"

His pencil *scritch-scritch-scritched* on the page as he added whiskers to the man's face. He glanced up occasionally, an eyebrow arched as if to ask, *Are we there yet?*

When the artist had shaded the face to the appropriate degree, Seth said, "When."

Harrison nodded in agreement. "You might want to put some whiskers along his neck, too. His beard wasn't groomed at all."

The artist scratched out a few more strokes along the neck of the suspect. When he was done with the beard, he asked, "How about his nose? Narrow? Wide? Long? Flat?"

"Short," Harrison added. "Seemed a little out of proportion to his face."

"Right," Seth said. "It turned up a little, too."

"A snub nose." The artist angled his head and again put his pencil to the page.

Seth and Harrison leaned in to take a closer look.

"Slightly longer," Harrison said, "but not by much."

The artist added a few more strokes to elongate the nose on the as-yet-eyeless face. When everyone was satisfied, he asked, "What about his eyes? Were they deep set? Bug-eyed, maybe?"

"Neither," Seth said. "They were small and fairly close together."

The artist turned to Harrison. "You remember

anything more? A shape maybe? Almond? Up-turned? Downturned? Hooded?"

"Round and kinda beady," Harrison replied, "like Seth said."

The artist drew a pair of small, circular, close-set eyes before following up with another question. "How about his brows? Were they thick? Thin? Arched? Straight?"

"Couldn't tell 'cause of the cap," Harrison said, to which Seth nodded in accord.

"All right." The artist twiddled his pencil between his fingers. "How about the ears? Were the lobes attached? Did his ears stick out? Did they hang low and wobble to and fro?"

Harrison held a hand to his own ear, as if subconsciously comparing them to the suspect's. "His ears were narrow but extra long. The tops stuck up over the sides of his cap."

"That's right," Seth said. "And his lobes were long, too."

After drawing the ears to the witnesses' satisfaction, the artist looked to them again, his eyes narrowed. "Tell me about the cap. Color, length of the bill, how it sat on his head."

"He wore the hat pulled low." Seth mimicked putting on a cap and tugging it tight.

"Yeah," Harrison concurred. "And it was dark, like you saw on the video. Black or navy blue or deep green. Not sure. Had a long bill. It was dusty, too, like maybe the guy'd been doing some work outside. Or I suppose he could be a contractor. My wife and I had new tile installed at our house a few weeks ago and there was dust everywhere. Drove her crazy."

The detective and I jotted more notes. Mine read: *Dusty hat. Works outside? Or indoors in a dusty environment? Maybe a contractor? Long ears.*

When the artist finished drawing the ball cap on the portrait, he held up the sketch pad. "How's this?"

"Wow." Seth turned to Harrison and the two exchanged wide-eyed glances, as if surprised how well the artist had captured the suspect neither had thought they'd remembered well.

Harrison whistled. "That's as damn close as you could get."

Seth gave the man a pat on the back. "You sure know your stuff."

The man offered a humble lift of his shoulders. "You do something for forty-two years, you learn a few things." The artist ripped the sheet from his sketch pad and handed it to Detective Jackson with a dip of his head. "Always a pleasure, ma'am."

"Likewise," Jackson said. "Can't thank you enough."

The man offered a sly grin. "You know the department's getting a bill, right?"

A few minutes later, Jackson, the sketch artist, and I parted ways in the parking lot. As Brigit and I climbed back into my car, I thought about the baby's blanket, covered in the beautiful bluebonnets that someone had so painstakingly and lovingly stitched. Bluebonnets only bloomed in the spring, but fall flowers could brighten both the flower bed at home and my dark mood. Worrying about the baby girl not only had my gut in a twist, but it had my heart feeling hollow.

I aimed the car for a nursery. There, Brigit and I made our way up and down the rows. My feet came to a stop in front of a display of vivid yellow mums in terra-cotta pots. I knelt down next to my partner. "What do you think of these?"

Brigit wagged her tail. She might be color-blind, but she still had good taste.

I chose two of the biggest mums and put them in my cart. We continued on to the pansies. The nursery offered yellow, white, orange, light purple, and deep purple varieties. *Which would look best?* The bungalow-style house Brigit and I shared with Frankie and her fluffy calico cat Zoe was mauve with ivory trim and a blue door. The deep purple pansies would complement the exterior paint as well as the potted mums, which I planned to set on either side of the front door. "Let's go with these," I said to Brigit, earning me a smile from an elderly woman looking at the snapdragons on the next row. Maybe it was odd for me to talk to Brigit, but even though we didn't speak the same language we found plenty of ways to communicate, me in my way and she in hers. Working and living together 24/7 gave us a strong bond. She was my partner, my roommate, and best friend, and sometimes I nearly forgot she wasn't human.

I loaded a full tray of the purple pansies in my cart and had just begun to step away when I turned back around and wrangled a tray of the yellow pansies into my cart, too. As we waited in line at the checkout, Brigit sniffed the stuffed decorative scarecrows lined up along a row of hay bales. She glanced up at the one directly in front of us and let out a loud bark. *Woof!*

"You want a scarecrow?" I asked her.

Again she wagged her tail and looked up at me expectantly. More than likely she planned to have some fun pulling the stuffed man apart, but how could any-one resist her big, brown eyes?

"Okay, girl," I told her. "He's all yours."

The scarecrow went into my cart, too.

We checked out and returned to my car. The mums took up the floorboard, while the pansies were crammed in what little space there was behind the seats. The scarecrow rode along between us like a redneck crash-test dummy, staring out the windshield, scaring no one with that goofy smile on his face.

Frankie opened the front door as I was unpacking the car in the driveway. My roommate was tall and trim but tough, a roller derby queen who dyed her blond hair bright blue. "Need a hand?" she called.

"Sure."

She came over and relieved me of the flat of pansies in my arms. I turned around to get the scarecrow, but Brigit had already grabbed his arm between her teeth and was dragging him out of the car and along the driveway. She pulled him up the stairs and onto the porch, where she dropped him. I retrieved the mums, took them onto the porch, and positioned one on each side of the door. Picking up the prone scarecrow, I car-ried him to the flower bed and shoved the bottom of the pointed stake on which he was mounted into the ground.

"I'll get a hammer," Frankie said, aiming for the garage.

I followed her and rounded up a trowel. While she hammered the scarecrow's support post deeper into the ground, I dug holes in the soil around his feet. Frankie and I knelt in the flower bed together and planted the pansies. As we worked, we discussed the abandoned baby.

"There was some stitching on the blanket that looked like a symbol of some sort. It looked like a peace sign, but it was hard to be sure."

She looked up from the flowers she'd just planted. "You think it was a wish for the baby? That she would have a peaceful life?"

"Could be. But my gut tells me it's a clue. The blanket was meticulously made, but the word and symbol looked messy. Like they'd been sewn in a hurry."

"Maybe they were sewn by someone else."

"I hadn't considered that." Still, it was possible that whoever had sewn the words in the blanket had purchased it somewhere, maybe in anticipation of keeping the baby. Maybe the decision to give her up had not been planned in advance, but had been a sudden and hasty one, forced upon the baby's parents somehow. My mind reeled. *Ugh*.

When we finished, we stood and stepped back.

Frankie pronounced the fall flowers and scarecrow "Festive."

"We should get some pumpkins, too," I suggested. A few pumpkins situated at the scarecrow's feet would look cute.

"I'll add them to the grocery list," Frankie said.

Frankie used to work at a grocery store and had done the bulk of our grocery shopping there. When Seth had suggested she try firefighting, she'd jumped at the opportunity and given up her job stocking shelves to become a firefighter. Nevertheless, she continued to shop for our groceries, visiting with her former coworkers at the store between loading the cart with her potato chips and sodas and my soy yogurt. In return, I took primary responsibility for maintaining the lawn. Given that the bulk of the yard work involved scooping up Brigit's poop, it was only fair.

Frankie stepped onto the porch to go back inside, but turned around at the door. "We need to buy some Halloween candy, too. What kind should I get?"

"How about little boxes of raisins?"

She scoffed. "You want kids to egg our house?"

She had a point. Kids weren't likely to be happy with dried fruit when they were expecting refined sugar and chocolate and red dye number 3.

Rather than waiting for me to make another suggestion, she made an executive decision. "I'll see what's on sale." With that, she went back inside.

Now that we were finished here, I loaded Brigit back in the car to drive to the house Seth shared with his mother and grandfather. Seth's grandfather, Ollie, could be a royal jackass, but I was able to ignore his barbs, at least for the most part. According to Seth's grandmother, who'd died when Seth was young, Ollie had been a much different, much happier man before serving as a tank mechanic in Vietnam. Seth, too, had served in the army. Ordnance detail. He'd spent several years in Afghanistan disabling improvised explosive devices. The things he'd learned about explosives made him a perfect fit for the city's bomb squad. Other things he'd learned in Afghanistan would be much better forgotten, but it was unlikely he'd ever be able to fully set those hard lessons aside.

I drove under the Interstate 35 overpass and, a few minutes later, pulled up in front of the house in the Morningside neighborhood. The Rutledge place looked like the before picture in a magazine article on home remodeling. The house comprised a mishmash of building materials ranging from gray wood siding to the chipped orange brick that walled in what had once been the garage. The shingles on the roof were likewise mismatched, some gray, some black. Seth performed the required maintenance, but little else. Not because he was lazy, but because he lacked inspiration. It had been a long time since the house had felt like a home, and the place could really benefit from some TLC.

That's where I came in.

How many years had it been since flowers had graced the small bed underneath the living room window? My guess was no flowers had bloomed there since Seth's grandmother had passed. "It's about time, isn't it?" I asked Brigit.

She wagged her tail in agreement.

I climbed out of my car. After letting Brigit out into the yard, I retrieved the flowers and the trowel and aimed for the flower bed. I knelt down, slid my hands into my cotton gardening gloves, and aimed my trowel at the dirt to dig my first hole. The blade ricocheted off the hard-packed soil, giving me a painful zing in the wrist.

"Sheesh!" I told my partner, who was sniffing around the bed. "The ground is hard as concrete."

I jabbed the pointed end of the trowel at the dirt several more times, but barely managed to loosen a dust speck. This wasn't going to work. Luckily for me, Brigit enjoyed digging. In fact, she was already pawing at the bare dirt. While I normally chastised her for digging up the grass, in this case her skills could prove useful. "Go to it, girl."

Brigit scratched and scratched at the dirt, eventually breaking through the dry surface and unearthing the darker, moister ground underneath. Once she'd dug deep enough, I gently nudged her aside and began planting the pansies while she tore up a fresh spot a foot or so over. "Good girl!"

We were nearly done when the screen door banged open. Ollie stepped out onto the porch. "What in the Sam Hill are you doing out here?"

I used the trowel to gesture to the flowers. "Surprising you."

"I don't like surprises!" he snapped. "Got more than enough of them in 'Nam."

"But this is a *good* surprise."

He harrumphed. "You should've asked my permission before you come trespassing all over my property."

Ornery old coot. "I didn't ask because you would have said no."

"Damn right I would have! Those flowers are going to need water and fertilizer. Who's got time for that?"

Ollie spent all day in front of the television. He had plenty of time to water and feed the flowers. But no sense pointing that out to him, he'd only get angrier. Instead, I stuck the last of the flowers in the ground, tamped the dirt down around them, and stood. I stepped back to admire them. "They look nice, don't they?"

Ollie grunted and waved a dismissive hand, stepping back inside and letting the screen door swing closed behind him with a loud *SLAP!*

What a party pooper. Would he ever come around?

I wondered what, if anything, could reach him, bring him out of the sour mood he'd been in for decades. I looked down at Brigit and it hit me. *Friends.* Ollie had recently mentioned some old army buddies he hadn't seen in years.

Maybe it was time for a reunion.

NINE
GETTING GRUBBY

Brigit

Digging in the dirt was so much fun!

Brigit loved the feel of the moist soil between her paws, the aroma of raw earth. And when she'd uncovered that wriggling grub, he was a delicious bonus. Why Megan had made that high-pitched squeal and said "Ew!" was beyond her. Brigit guessed maybe Megan had never eaten a grub. She should try one sometime. She'd probably like it.

TEN
FATHER KNOWS BEST

The Father

Sunday evenings were quiet at the compound. Good thing his house in the back corner was set apart from the communal bunkhouses and the small love shack he allowed the married couples to use for their scheduled weekly conjugal visits. He didn't want anyone to hear the moaning and groaning and squeals of pleasure emanating from the fifty-five-inch television mounted on his bedroom wall. Peace, love, and harmony were the primary tenets of their sect. But of the three, it was the "love" that the Father liked best. Sure, it was a sin for others to watch people fornicate on TV. But how could he preach about the sins of the flesh if he didn't see what all the fuss was about? For him, watching this show wasn't debauchery. It was research.

Even though he realized the actresses on his screen were embellishing things for their audience, it made no difference. Real or not, his cock was hard as a rock.

Knock-knock-knock.

He muttered some choice words to himself. *Who the hell can that be?*

He grabbed the remote and turned off the TV. Standing, he pushed down on his groin, willing his erection to disappear. The last thing he needed was one of his flock noting the tent in his robe. The people who lived here believed he was pure at heart, above all earthly desires. *What a bunch of idiots.*

But they were *his* idiots.

He walked out of his bedroom, making sure to close the door behind him. Though the rest of the compound had no access to the Internet or television, it was only right that their leader kept a pulse on the outside world, right? And keep a pulse he did. Hell, his dick throbbed so hard it was a wonder it didn't explode.

"Coming!" he called. Or at least he would have been if whoever was at the door hadn't interrupted his evening's entertainment.

He passed through his small kitchen and into his living room, stopping at the door to peek out the peephole. Standing on the porch of his modest frame home was a lanky woman with stringy gray hair, a beaklike nose, and dark peach fuzz at each corner of her upper lips, forming furry quotation marks around her mouth.

Margaret.

Ugh.

At least he didn't have to worry about his boner any longer. If anyone could make a man soft in an instant, it was her. Ironic, because she was most certainly a virgin, and virgins generally had a special sort of sexual appeal. Doubly ironic because she served as the compound's midwife, delivering the babies other women had conceived, though Margaret would likely never bear a child herself. None of the men in the compound had expressed any interest in marrying and bedding her whatsoever.

The Father took a breath, worked up a smile, and opened the door. "Hello, Sister Margaret. What takes you away from your time of rest and personal reflection, and brings you to my door this evening?"

Her expression sheepish, she performed a curtsy in her loose-fitting, homemade dress before looking up at him. "So sorry to bother you, Father Emmanuel. I was wondering about Sister Juliette. She wasn't at the service this morning. I stopped by the infirmary to check on her, but she wasn't there. Is she all right?"

"So kind of you to think of others, as always." *You damn busybody.* He offered a placating smile. "Sister Juliette asked to have some time alone in a private place. She needs a chance to grieve and to seek God's forgiveness for her sins. You understand, of course."

She bowed her head. "Yes, Father."

Good thing he'd had some time to think things through on the drive home from the fire station Friday night, come up with some reasonable explanations. Dropping off the baby had been an impulsive move, something quite unusual for him. But when Juliette had refused to let him touch the newborn child, she'd pushed him too far. He reigned over this dominion, and it was high time the obstinate little bitch accepted that fact.

Margaret's mouth began to open again, but the Father was already tired of her and her questions. He raised a palm to stop her. "No need to worry, Sister Margaret. Sister Juliette will be back with the flock very soon."

She nodded, but tears rimmed her eyes. "It's just so heartbreaking about the baby."

"Heartbreaking, indeed. But Sister Juliette is barely twenty and unmarried. The father did not step up to claim the child as his own or offer any type of support—"

"A sin in itself!" she cried. "Perhaps he should be called to account."

It took everything in him not to shove the woman backward down the steps to his door. He stared at her intently. "Surely you are not forgetting that God calls upon us to forgive, Sister Margaret."

He let his words hang in the air for a moment, and she responded by hanging her head.

"You speak the truth," she said in a voice barely louder than a whisper.

"My point," the Father said, "is that the circumstances would have been less than ideal. The baby's father might have insisted on visitation, or even sued for custody. What might it have done to Juliette's child if she were taken outside our walls? The last thing any of us need is someone from the outside meddling in the life we've worked so hard to build here. We must trust that God knows best. We must respect His will. To do otherwise would be prideful."

This ugly bitch can't argue with that, can she?

Before she had a chance to try, he said, "Thank you for coming by, Sister Margaret. Please tell Sister Abigail that I have some time for her now. She mentioned she'd like me to join her in prayer."

They'd join all right, but it wouldn't be in prayer. Unlike Margaret, Abigail was one sister he enjoyed seeing down on her knees.

ELEVEN
UNPLANNED GARAGE SALE

Megan

I was back on the day shift the following Monday. Before heading out in the cruiser, I spent a few minutes searching the Web at the station, looking to see if anyone in the area had put a Steve Nash bobble-head up for sale on eBay or another site. Nothing came up. No listings for the brand and model of computer that had been stolen from the Lexus, either. *Dang.* I'd known it was a long shot. Still, it would be nice to actually solve a burglary case now and then.

"C'mon, girl," I said to Brigit, who'd flopped down at my feet to take a nap. "Time to get to work."

She lumbered to her feet and followed me out the door to our cruiser so we could set out on patrol.

Though the calendar had turned to October, it seemed someone forgot to tell Mother Nature. By nine in the morning the temperature was already in the upper seventies and was forecast to climb into the nineties by midday. Though the air conditioner was turned up, Brigit panted softly in her enclosure behind me as we cruised up and down the streets of our division.

Dispatch came over the radio. "Got a report of a burglary at a residence on Eighth Avenue near Berry. Who can respond?"

I snatched my microphone from the dash and pushed the button. "This is Officer Luz. Brigit and I can take it."

The dispatcher gave me the address and I aimed the cruiser south. In minutes, we pulled up to the older residence. The place was a single-story ranch with dark brown wood siding, a narrow porch, and a single-car garage. A Kia Soul in a vivid lime green sat in the driveway. The front door appeared intact and none of the windows were broken, giving no obvious signs of forced entry. But perhaps the thief had entered through the back. Brigit and I had recently handled a stalking case that started with a broken bedroom window and ended in horrific violence. *The things people do to each other.* My body shuddered at the recollection. I shook my head to shake away the thought.

As I rolled down the windows for Brigit, the front door of the house swung open and a thin, thirtyish woman stepped out. She wore sandals, skinny jeans, and a loose bohemian blouse, along with impeccably applied makeup. Her lips were somehow both glossy and natural, her cheeks had a dewy glow, and her lashes appeared to be at least two inches long. Her blondish hair was swept back and held in place by a trio of small claw clips.

She came down the steps. "Thanks for coming!" she called.

We met halfway on the path that led to her entry. She

held out a French-tipped hand and introduced herself. "I'm Felicia Bloomquist."

"Officer Megan Luz." After we shook hands, I said, "I understand you were robbed?"

She nodded. "I went into the garage this morning and found everything of value gone."

"Not a fun way to start a day, huh?"

"You can say that again!"

My gaze shifted to the garage door. There were no dents, no scratches, and no keyless entry pad that could have been decoded. "Does your garage have a service door?"

"No," she said. "The only way into the garage is through the garage door or the door from the kitchen. Nothing from the house was taken."

"Let's take a look around."

The woman waved me inside. I followed her into the living room, which was bright with both light and color. The walls were painted in a vivid teal hue, while her contemporary sofa sported flamingo-pink fabric. We made our way across the wood floor and into the small kitchen, where colorful pottery adorned the open shelves. A stackable washer and dryer towered in a small alcove off the kitchen. At the back of the alcove was the door that led to the garage. Felicia opened it, stepped through, and flipped on the light switch.

As I passed through the doorway after her, I reached out and tapped my knuckles on the door to test it. The door was solid, reinforced steel. A glance at the knob told me it bore a heavy-duty dead bolt. The trim bore telltale gouges and scratch marks, indicating someone had tried to gain access to the interior of the house, but had lacked either the tools or the time. The only things left in the garage were a large rolling garbage can, a broom, and a plastic recycling bin. No lawnmower, rakes, or other gardening tools.

I turned to Felicia. "Did they take your lawn equipment?"

"No," she said. "I keep all the stuff for the yard in a locked shed out back. But they took my bicycle, some lawn chairs, and my entire inventory."

"Inventory? What kind of inventory?"

"I sell several lines of products. Nouveau Toi cosmetics. Manhattan Metals and Baubles brands of jewelry. Vestments and Eleanor Neely clothing and accessories. Sunflower Power energy and weight-loss snacks. Most direct sellers only sell one type of product, but I'm a complete-style consultant. I make people over from head-to-toe, inside and out."

"Sounds like a clever sales strategy."

"I try to think outside the box. It's served me well so far. My first year doing direct sales I doubled what I earned managing a cosmetics counter at the mall."

"Impressive."

"Thank you." She smiled and lifted her shoulders to her ears in a coy gesture. Back to the matter at hand, she said, "I keep the heat-sensitive products in the house, but I had over six thousand dollars in inventory in here."

Whoa. "That's a lot of inventory."

Was she telling me the truth? Or was this an attempt at insurance fraud? People sometimes claimed to have had very expensive things stolen when, in fact, they'd never owned any such things in the first place.

To feel her out, I asked, "Don't most people order online and get direct shipment from the companies?"

"They do," she agreed. "But that's after they make their first purchase. My first sales are normally made in person. You know, at in-home parties where I do facials and makeup for the customers, help them choose flattering clothing and jewelry. That's why I keep a lot of the products on hand."

The bike and lawn chairs were likely to end up in a garage sale across town or sold on the streets for next to nothing. The skin-care products, makeup, jewelry, and clothing were a different story. They could be sold at market rates and yield the burglar a pretty penny.

I told her as much. "My guess is whoever took your stuff probably intends to sell it at a flea market or online."

There was a dozen or more places throughout the Dallas-Fort Worth metroplex where vendors rented booths for a fee and sold products ranging from furniture and kitchenware to jewelry and cosmetics. More than one vendor had been busted for selling black-market goods at such places. I made a mental note to take a look at them in my spare time.

"Anybody you know who might have been involved?" I asked. "A neighbor? A friend? A customer who asked a lot of questions about your inventory?"

She raised her palms. "I can't think of anyone."

I gestured at the door frame. "It looks like they tried to get into your house."

Now it was she who shuddered. "Oh my God. I don't even want to think about that."

Who could blame her? Robbers sometimes used

deadly force when surprised by a resident who'd unexpectedly come home and stumbled upon them. Other
times, home invaders hid inside to await the residents,
further evil in their hearts.

Establishing a potential time line was critical. To
that end, I asked, "When was the last time you were in
your garage before you found it empty this morning?"

"Hmm." She looked up in thought before returning
her gaze to me. "It was yesterday evening. I got an
order from one of my customers. Lipstick emergency.
She'd dropped hers on the curb and it rolled into the
sewer."

"Did you take the delivery to her?"

"Yes, I did," Felicia said. "I left around eight o'clock.
I ran a couple of errands on the way back. It was about
ten when I got home. The news was just starting."

"Whoever robbed you must have hit while you were
gone," I told her. "They might have been watching your
house, waiting for you to leave."

She shuddered again. "That totally creeps me out."

"I know how you feel." I'd once found pictures on a
suspect's laptop of me and Frankie in our bathing suits
washing our cars in our driveway. We'd had no idea
he'd been watching and photographing us. Talk about
feeling violated. "Any chance that customer might have
called you about the lipstick to lure you away from
home?"

"I doubt it," she said. "She's been a customer a long
time and she offered to come here to get the new tube
of lipstick. I told her I'd be out and about anyway and
would be happy to bring it to her."

Given those facts, the customer didn't seem likely
to be involved in the theft.

I continued my questions. "I didn't see a keypad outside or any damage to your garage door. Does anyone other than you have a remote control?"

"No," she said. "Just me."

"Where do you k-keep your remote?"

"In my car."

"Show me." If my sneaking suspicions were right, her device would be missing.

She led me back through the house and out the front door. On seeing us come back outside, Brigit stood in her enclosure, wagged her tail, and issued a soft *woof.*

I gestured to the squad car. "Mind if I give my partner a potty break?"

"No problem."

I walked over to the cruiser, let Brigit out of her enclosure, and clipped her lead onto her collar. After she took a quick tinkle on the grass, she stood and looked up at me, wagging her tail, ready to help if needed. My partner had a darn good work ethic for a cop who wasn't paid even minimum wage.

By this time, Felicia had the door open on her Soul and was rummaging around in the front. She opened the center console and the glove compartment, and even knelt down on the driveway to feel under the seats.

Looked like my sneaking suspicions were right. "The remote's not there, is it?"

She stood and backed up, her perfectly made-up face scrunched in confusion. "No. I always tuck it in the change holder, but it's missing."

"You're not the first person I've spoken to recently who's had their remote taken," I told her. "Burglars realize that people don't think of them the same way they think of their keys, but remotes are essentially a free pass into someone's place."

The woman bit her lip and groaned. "Sometimes I leave the windows rolled down a little on my car. You know, so it's not so hot when I get in?"

Though it was an unsafe practice, I completely understood. As dang hot as it got in Texas, a windshield screen sometimes wasn't enough to keep a car cool. Still, a human hand could easily slide though a narrow opening and snag a remote. I gestured to the dashboard. "Any chance you had a bobble-head on your dash?"

"No," she said. "Why?"

"Just trying to determine if there's any pattern to the thefts." So far, there didn't appear to be. This burglar seemed to be simply an opportunist, taking whatever might be easy to grab rather than targeting specific items to steal.

I raised Brigit's leash. "My partner can sniff around, see if she can trail the suspects."

She looked down at Brigit, as if addressing my partner. "That would be great."

I led Brigit over to the garage door and issued the command for her to seek a trail. She sniffed around the edge and bottom of the garage door, her nose a natural tool that no form of modern technology had yet to match. *Snuffle-snuffle-snuffle.* After a few seconds, she turned and headed back down the driveway at a slow pace, which told me the trail she'd sniffed out was weak. It was no surprise given that it had been around twelve hours since the burglary had taken place. As I followed, she trotted slowly along, cutting through the grass and going over the curb, into the street. The woman stood in her driveway watching us work as Brigit snuffled her way halfway down the block. There she sniffed around in a broad circle and eventually sat, giving me the signal that the trail petered out here.

"Good girl!" She'd earned herself a liver treat and a smooch on the forehead. While kissing your partner was generally against department policy, I didn't have to worry about Brigit reporting me to internal affairs.

The two of us headed back to the woman's house. No security cameras appeared on any of the houses along the way. *Darn.*

As I returned to the driveway, I pointed back to where Brigit had stopped. "The trail ended there, just a few houses down. I'll talk to your neighbors, see if any of them might have noticed a suspicious car out here last night. I'll also get a crime-scene tech out here to dust for prints, but it's possible whoever robbed you didn't leave any." After all, the only thing they'd had to touch to get into the garage was the remote, which hadn't been found and was presumably still in the burglar's possession. "In the meantime, I'd suggest you manually lock your g-garage door, get a new remote, and have your system reprogrammed. From now on, lock your remote in your glove box."

"I will," she said. "Lesson learned."

"Do you have invoices for the products?" I asked. "They'll be needed to prosecute the thief if they're found. You'll also need them for your insurance claim. It would be helpful if I could get brochures for the products, too. That would help me recognize them if I come across them somewhere."

"Of course," she said. "Come on in and I'll round them up."

We went inside. While I waited in her foyer, she stepped into her home office off the living room. She emerged a couple of minutes later with the paperwork and a small silver bag with NOUVEAU TOI printed in black ink on the side. She handed me the brochures, along with still warm, freshly made copies of invoices showing she had indeed made product purchases adding up to thousands of dollars.

"Thanks." I handed her my business card. "If anything comes up, don't hesitate to call me."

She thanked me and handed me a business card of her own. The card gave her name—followed by her title—Personal Style Consultant. She also handed me the gift bag. "There's some Sunflower Power energy snacks in the bag. Skin-care samples, too. Give the cream a try. It'll help with those problem areas on your face."

My face has problem areas?

Before I could ask where, exactly, the problem areas were, she proceeded to look me up and down, her lip quirking. "I offer private consultations. You should definitely give me a call. I can help you choose clothing that works for your body type. That outfit you're wearing isn't exactly flattering."

Sheesh. It's not like I chose to wear these godawful polyester pants and a utility belt that made my hips look as wide as a barn. It's a uniform!

Despite her insults, I'd give this investigation my best, as always. My face might have problem areas and my uniform might be unfashionable, but my work ethic was beyond reproach.

I headed down the block in the direction Brigit had trailed. I tried four different houses along the route, but nobody was home. I left my business card tucked into the mailbox at each house, scrawling "please call me" across the top of them. An elderly woman was home at a fifth house, but she hadn't noticed any unusual cars parked out front the evening before. She wagged her brows. "I was entertaining a gentleman caller."

"Thanks, anyway," I said with a smile. "Stay out of trouble."

She gave me a wink. "No promises."

I fished a square Sunflower Power snack out of the bag as Brigit and I headed back to our cruiser. My eyes scanned the nutritional information on the back of the package. According to the data, the snack was packed with all sorts of vitamins and iron, as well as 24 percent of the recommended daily allowance of protein and 35 percent for fiber. The ingredients list was short. Sunflower seeds, agave nectar, and dried apricots. No preservatives or artificial coloring. *Hmm.* This little treat could both taste good and be good for me, too.

I tore through the crinkly wrap, the sound garnering Brigit's attention. She kept a bead on me as I removed the round, cookielike snack and took a bite.

The instant the bite hit my taste buds my throat responded with a gag reflex. This snack might be healthy, but it tasted like sugar-coated Styrofoam and felt like the same on my tongue. *No, thanks.*

I forced the bite down and held what remained of the snack out for Brigit to sample. She snatched the cookie out of my hand. After chewing just once, she crinkled her nose in a recoil reaction. She opened her mouth and let the wet remains fall from her tongue to the grass. Once the snack was on the ground, she flopped over onto her back and rolled on it.

I looked down at my partner. "I take it you're not a fan of Sunflower Power Snacks, either, huh, girl?"

Leaving the remains behind for the earth or ants to claim, we climbed back into the squad car and set out on patrol. We'd only made it to the corner when my cell phone chirped. I pulled to the curb and checked the screen. Detective Jackson was calling. With any luck, she'd have learned something about the pickup we'd seen on the security-camera videos. Maybe it would lead us to the man who'd dropped off the baby.

I jabbed the button to accept the call. "Good Morning, Detective. Any word on the truck with the missing license plates?"

"None," she said. "Seems nobody spotted them."

Darn.

"Swing by the station," she said. "I need your help." With nothing further, she hung up.

Detective Jackson needs me? My chest swelled with pride. Or perhaps my sports bra was just riding up. Either way, off Brigit and I went.

Minutes later, the two of us were at the station, heading down the hall to Jackson's office. Brigit's claws clicked and clacked along the tile, catching the attention of my rusty-haired former partner Derek the "Big Dick" Mackey, who sat at a desk in the shared open office space. He cast his eyes my way and raised his middle finger to scratch his nose in a not-so-subtle *F you* gesture. Such professionalism, no? He'd never quite forgiven me for Tasering him in the family jewels. Of course I hadn't quite forgiven him, either, for pissing me off to the point that I totally lost my cool and nearly lost my job. But that unfortunate incident had led to me being partnered with Brigit, so it was hard in hindsight to see it as a mistake. Brigit was a far better partner than Derek had ever been. She was smarter, smelled better, and worked harder.

Ignoring Derek's rude gesture, we continued on to Jackson's office. She sat in her high-backed rolling chair, the baby blanket on the desktop in front of her. Detective Hector Bustamente, my other mentor, sat in one of the chairs facing her desk. Bustamente was a portly man with thick lips and little regard for his appearance. But while there wasn't much going for him on the outside, he had a nimble brain on the inside. He was a clever, intuitive investigator and basic all-around nice guy.

"Good morning, Detectives," I addressed them, and slid into the empty chair.

"Officer Luz." Bustamente gave me a nod and reached down his hand to give Brigit a scratch behind the ears. "Sergeant Brigit. You're looking in good form today."

She responded by wagging her tail and licking his hand.

Jackson tapped an index finger on the trim of the blanket. "Remember the symbol you noticed on the blanket Thursday night?"

"The peace sign?"

"Yeah. I didn't think much of it at the time, but you've got good instincts, Megan. I decided to look more into it, and ran it by Hector. We think it might be this." She swiveled her monitor to face my direction.

On the screen was a peace sign with a slight modification. The vertical line was bisected by a horizontal one about a quarter of the way from the top, making it look like a small letter *t* or a cross.

After eyeing the screen, I stood and hunkered over the blanket. She handed me a magnifying glass to take a closer look. I felt like a younger, female version of Sherlock Holmes as I used it to examine the symbol. Sure enough, the two needle holes on either side of the vertical line indicated the symbol might have included a crosshatch before the thread caught on the man's jacket. As I retook my seat, I gestured to the symbol on her screen and asked, "What does the symbol mean?"

Bustamente responded. "It's the symbol for the People of Peace."

"The People of Peace? Who are they?"

"They claim they're a church group," Bustamente said solemnly, "but they've got all the earmarks of a cult. The members believe they are the chosen, exalted ones and the rest of us are unholy and condemned to hell. They're led by a man who calls himself Emmanuel. Nobody seems to know where he came from or who he really is. They live in a secluded compound on the eastern edge of Benbrook Lake."

Benbrook Lake sat to the southwest at the far reaches of the Fort Worth city limits, well outside my patrol division. Because the initial crime—*if* there even was a crime—took place in our precinct, Jackson would retain control over the investigation, no matter where in the city it might lead.

I'd grown up in Fort Worth and lived here all my life, other than my time at Sam Houston State University in Huntsville. Still, the People of Peace rang no bells for me. "I've never heard of them. How long has the group been out there?"

"At least three decades," Jackson said. "Their place

was in the boonies when they bought it way back then. They keep a very low profile. Hector and I spoke with detectives from their precinct. They said they've had no trouble from the group. A couple asked for help getting their son out of the church several years ago, but their son met with them and said he didn't want to leave. The couple filed a court motion to force their son to undergo a psychological evaluation, but the People of Peace hired the Dallas law firm of Gertz, Gertz, and Schwartz and successfully fought it. The group claims that anyone living there is free to go at any time."

"Do you believe it? That they're free to go?"

Jackson issued a derisive snort. "Not for a minute. If they aren't kept there by actual force, they're intimidated into staying. That's how these so-called churches operate. On fear and threats and manipulation."

One glance at Bustamente and it was clear he felt the same way. For good reason, too. Cults had a long, sordid, and often violent history in the state of Texas. We'd discussed them in my criminal psychology class in college.

While there were cults going back to the early 1900s in Texas, the more notorious ones came later. The Children of God began as a Christian movement in the late 1960s but, with the influence of hippie "Jesus Freaks," devolved into something else entirely. Members turned over all their worldly possessions to the group, and took on new biblical names. To draw in male members, females engaged in what was called "Flirty Fishing," essentially an evangelical form of religious prostitution. The group's leader, David Berg, allegedly led the group in orgies at its 425-acre home near Thurber.

In 1992, Austin became home to the Buddhafield cult, which had been run out of Los Angeles. The group's leader, a former actor and self-proclaimed guru, went by various names, including Michel, Andreas, and the Teacher. The group lived cooperatively and in seclusion. However, given the leader's theater and dance training, he led the group in productions at the One World Theatre he'd established in the city. The group imploded in 2007 due to sexual manipulation and mistrust. The leader relocated to Hawaii and founded a new group there. The theater still operated in Austin, under new ownership.

Ninety miles to the south of Fort Worth sat Waco, the site of the deadly 1993 battle between Branch Davidians cult members and agents from the Bureau of Alcohol, Tobacco, and Firearms. Members who'd left the group's compound told of illegal weapon stockpiles, polygamy, and the cult's leader, David Koresh, forcing himself on young female residents. The cult had amassed a veritable armory of weapons, preparing for Armageddon. Their preparations launched a self-fulfilling prophecy. When law enforcement attempted to serve a search warrant, a shootout ensued. Four ATF agents lost their lives. Fifteen more were wounded. Several cult members were killed in the initial confrontation. A seven-week siege ensued. During that time, the FBI negotiated the release of a number of children. After fifty-one days, the standoff came to an end when government agents employed tanks and tear gas to force their way into the compound. Fires erupted, their source later debated. Some said the tear gas ignited the fires. Others claimed they were started by the cult members themselves. In the end, dozens more Branch

Davidians had died, including many children and Koresh himself. More debate ensued over whether the cult members had made a suicide pact.

In 2008 came similar allegations of teenaged girls being forced into marriages with much older men. As a result, fifty-two children were removed from the Yearning for Zion Ranch in Eldorado, a small town in a remote area of west Texas. The ranch had been founded by polygamist Warren Jeffs. Because the ranch had been used in criminal activity, it was forfeited to the state.

Texas was also the birthplace and longtime home of Marshall Applewhite, leader of the Heaven's Gate cult, which believed in an odd mix of astrology, mysticism, and metaphysics. After Applewhite convinced his followers that a UFO following the Hale-Bopp comet would gather their souls, the group committed mass ritual suicide in San Diego, California, in 1997 when the comet passed the earth. They were found covered in purple shrouds, all wearing black Nike sneakers, as if they intended to run a 10K on the gold-paved streets of heaven when they arrived. It would be laughable if it weren't so damn tragic.

Another polygamist cult with ties to Texas was the Church of the First Born of the Lamb of God. It was founded by Ervil LeBaron, after a split from another church formed by his brother, and subsequently moved to Mexico. Though he was convicted of murder and sentenced to prison, Ervil proceeded to reign from jail, ordering followers to kill rival church leaders. He died in prison in 1981, but six remaining family members later orchestrated the "4 O'Clock Murders," in which three former church members and a child were shot dead within minutes of each other in various locations in Texas in 1988.

A more contemporary, puritanical cult was the Church of Wells, named after the east Texas town where it sits. Run by two former street preachers in their late twenties, the group focused on asceticism— living simply with a focus on spiritual goals, prayer, and fasting, while rejecting entertainment and sensual pleasures. *Hey, at least one of the cults had to try something new and avoid sexual deviancy, am I right?* The elders encouraged members to reject anyone not in the group, including their families. The members, most of whom were in their twenties or were children, cut all ties with the outside, interacting only with those who were part of the church, a process known as "shunning." When parents attempted to communicate with their daughter, who'd disappeared inside the cult, members accused the parents of attempting to kidnap her. Members of the cult also routinely attended the services of other churches in the area, accusing congregants of a lack of morals. Not exactly the way to win friends and influence people, but the leaders reveled in the rejection, as if being eschewed by the evil, immoral world proved their righteousness and superiority. So much for pride being a sin, huh?

"So how c-can we help?" I asked.

"You and Brigit can be another pair of eyes and ears," Jackson said. "Protection, too. We're going out to the People of Peace compound to see what we can learn."

A visit to a cult? *Holy guacamole!*

TWELVE
RAWHIDE

Brigit

Brigit wasn't sure exactly where Megan had driven her and the lady whose clothes smelled faintly of the sausage she'd had for breakfast. But the dog knew from the unusual scents and sounds coming through the open window that wherever they'd come was beyond their normal patrol area.

"Need a potty break, girl?" Megan asked.

Brigit wagged her tail. She knew what "potty" meant, and even though she didn't need to potty, she always liked getting out of the car and stretching her legs and sniffing around a new place. Besides, there was a big cow with long horns at the fence nearby, and she wanted to check him out.

She hopped down onto the dried grass that lined the road. Megan clipped the leash onto Brigit's collar, but there was enough give for Brigit to take the few steps over to the fence. The cow standing inside noisily chewed his cud as he stared at her.

Brigit stared back. She pitied the creature. He was inside a fence, trapped, his life limited to a few acres of land and whoever might happen to venture onto it. Brigit, on the other hand, had far more freedom. She was always meeting someone she'd never met before, going somewhere she'd never been. She couldn't imagine leading such a restricted existence.

Still, despite their differences, there was no reason the two couldn't be friends, right? Given that she couldn't get through the barbed wire to sniff the steer's rump, she whipped out her tongue and licked the cow on the snout by way of greeting. He responded with a snort and stomped his foot. Guess he didn't like the dog interrupting his lunch.

"Come on, girl," Megan said, pulling Brigit back. "He's still a bull, not a burger."

THIRTEEN

MANNA FROM HEAVEN

The Father

He watched discreetly from a bench at the reflecting pond as Jeb ascended the silo at the far side of the adjacent acreage, a bucket in one hand. It probably wasn't safe to climb so high single-handed on a rusty old ladder, but it was the only way to get food and water into the silo without opening the lower door. The last time they'd done that, Zeke had come away with a face striped in blood. Of course, the Father wasn't about to take on such a potentially risky task himself. If the Father fell to his death, what would become of his people? Jeb, on the other hand . . . Well, Jeb was expendable. He followed orders without question, but if he perished there were half a dozen others who stood ready to take his exalted place as the Father's right hand.

Jeb reached the top of the ladder. He propped the bucket on a rung and untied the length of rope attached to the top of the ladder. After tying it to the handle of the bucket, he slid open the rusty panel on the curved steel dome that topped the silo. At this distance, the

Father couldn't hear the anguished wail of the woman inside, but he was certain she'd be putting up some sort of fuss. *Stupid bitch.* All she'd had to do was follow his simple instructions, do as she'd been told, and she could've avoided this whole mess. This was all her fault, really.

As Jeb began to lower the bucket into the silo, the Father noticed a few of the women look up from where they were gathering cantaloupes in the compound's garden not far from where he sat. Among them was Juliette's mother.

"Hello, sisters!" he called, raising a hand and standing from the bench. "Looks like your hard work paid off. Never in my life have I seen so many cantaloupes!" Fortunately, the women turned his way, his attempts to distract them successful. *But damn it, could Jeb move any slower and be any more obvious?*

He needn't have worried. The women sent smiles back his way and returned his wave.

"We've got them coming out our ears!" Sister Elisabeth called back as she placed another cantaloupe in her wheelbarrow.

Sister Amy chimed in. "They'll be a nice treat at dinner tonight."

"They most certainly will. I can hardly wait." By that time, Jeb had descended out of sight. *This is almost too easy.*

FOURTEEN
COMPOUND QUESTIONS

Megan

At Detective Jackson's direction, I had pulled the car over on a small rise on Old Granbury Road, about a quarter mile from the property owned by the People of Peace. She wanted to get the lay of the land before we went in.

Out here on the plains, the land was covered primarily by grass and scrubby mesquite trees. Mesquites weren't much to look at and provided scant shade, but their beans had served as a major food source for settlers and pioneers. In the mid 1800s, those on the Texan Santa Fe Expedition, whose mission was to secure trade routes with New Mexico, even boiled mesquite beans as a substitute for coffee. As for me, I'd stick with my freshly ground French roast, thank you very much.

While this area was about as far as you could get from downtown and still be in the city limits, the suburbs had begun to encroach, new housing developments popping up within a mile or two of the compound. A few more years and the People of Peace could find themselves adjacent to a big box store, car dealership, or fast-food franchise.

I'd let Brigit out for a potty break on the side of the road, but she had yet to tinkle. So far all she'd done was engage in a staring contest with an enormous longhorn munching on grass inside the fence. When she whipped out her tongue and licked his face, he issued a snort and stomped a big hoof. No sense upsetting the bull. If he got angry enough, the barbed wire might not be enough to stop him.

"Come on, girl. He's still a bull, not a burger." I gave a gentle tug on Brigit's leash. "Back in the car."

My partner turned her head and gave me a sour look, but obeyed.

When I returned to the driver's seat, Detective Jackson lowered the small pair of binoculars she'd been using to survey the compound. "I see a Dodge Ram pickup, a Chevy Silverado, and a Toyota Tacoma. No Ford F-150."

Did that mean we were off base coming here? That the peace sign on the blanket was just a peace sign and not the symbol of this group? Or did it just mean the truck was elsewhere at the moment, or maybe parked somewhere out of sight?

Jackson handed me the binoculars. "Take a look. Tell me if you see anything of note."

According to the quick research Jackson had performed online back at the station, the waterfront property on Lake Benbrook had been purchased by the People of Peace in 1987. It included eighteen acres that had previously served as a summer camp for kids, as well as an adjacent thirty-seven acres zoned for agricultural use.

I put the glasses to my eyes and scanned the property. "Whoa!"

I'd expected the place to look like an austere military outpost, but it was nothing of the sort. Rather, the place was beautiful, a virtual paradise on the Texas prairie, colorful, lush, and inviting.

In the center of the compound was a tall wood building with a pointed roof and bell tower. The building had been painted a crisp white. Rows of narrow stained-glass windows ran along each side. The combination cross-and-peace-sign symbol was painted in bright green paint on the double doors. That particular building, which I'd pegged as the group's church, was flanked with vibrant red knockout roses. The bushes were still in full bloom thanks to the fact that Texas summers ignored the calendar and generally overlapped well into the fall.

To one side of the church was a long brick building with a wide porch and a metal triangle hanging from the eaves. My guess was that the building had once served as the children's camp dining hall and now served as the communal eating place for the compound's residents. The bricks had been painted robin's egg blue with white trim. Several wooden picnic tables were arranged outside the doors in the shade of a large live oak so that the residents could enjoy their meals outside in nice weather.

There were a number of other large buildings scattered around the property. Most of these were also built of brick, and sported similar cheerful paint in bright hues. The two long structures on either side of the dining hall appeared to be bunkhouses. One was painted lavender, the other a sage green, respectively the women's and men's quarters would be my guess. On the other side of the church was a square building with yellow paint, flanked by an expansive playground complete with monkey bars, five swings, a jungle gym, and both a straight and swirly slide. The yellow building must be the school.

Two large wooden barns sat side by side, both painted the traditional bright red. The doors to both of them were open. One revealed a handful of men moving about the heavy equipment inside. Another man sauntered out of the barn with a fishing pole over his shoulder, evidently headed to Lake Benbrook, which sat at their doorstep. Poofs of gray smoke wafted from a black stovepipe emerging from the barn's roof. Women moved about inside the other barn, evidently working too, though from this distance I couldn't discern exactly what they were doing. Just outside the door of the women's barn was a wooden pen in which one might expect to find pigs or goats. Instead, several toddlers teetered about safely inside, overseen by a grandmotherly woman who sat in a rocking chair, a chubby baby on her lap. Another older woman pushed a baby in a swing that hung from an overhead beam. Despite the church's relatively primitive ways, on-site day care for working mothers was a progressive idea.

Closer to the gates stood a wide aluminum prefab building with four extra-tall garage-style doors. A green John Deere tractor sat on the gravel in front of the building. The building probably stored other lawn and farming equipment. *Could the pickup be parked inside, too?*

At the far end of the property was a small house, probably the leader's residence. An even smaller structure, hardly bigger than a child's playhouse, was situated between the house and the rest of the property. The purpose of that particular structure was unclear.

In addition to the buildings, the compound included a rectangular swimming pool enclosed in safety fence, a basketball court, a tennis court, a baseball diamond, and a sand volleyball court. Soccer goals sat at either end of a long, grassy area. A croquet court had been set up on a stretch of grass, too, as had a badminton net. If I didn't know better, I'd think the place was a family-friendly lakeside resort.

A chicken coop had been erected along the western edge of the compound, the hens pecking around in the sunshine in the outdoor part of their enclosure. Two older girls emerged from the henhouse, carrying baskets filled with enough eggs to host the biggest Easter egg hunt or make the world's biggest frittata. Women worked in a vegetable garden nearby gathering cantaloupes, while a trio of frisky dogs frolicked up and down the rows, not a care in the world. Next to the vegetable garden was a gorgeous flower garden with a reflecting pond covered in water lilies. A man with a white beard sat on a bench, seemingly enjoying the beauty around him.

A stone wall covered in honeysuckle, morning glories, and trumpet vine formed a perimeter around the compound, separating the People of Peace from the rest of the world. The compound appeared to be the ultimate gated community, offering all kinds of amenities right on your doorstep.

Interestingly, while there were many trees scattered about the compound, all of them were well within the interior, leaving a clear perimeter inside the wall. There was a similar perimeter around the outside, all foliage near the wall removed. It reminded me of the perimeter around the state prison in Hunstville, the city in which I'd attended college. The perimeter reduced the risk that inmates could escape, and allowed guards a clear shot at them if they did. I supposed the same general idea applied to these grounds. The owners of the children's camp had likely cleared trees from along the walls to discourage naughty adolescents from climbing the trees to sneak off or onto the camp property. Of course, the People of Peace could have planted trees in the open spaces if they'd chosen to, but they hadn't. Were the leaders of the church also trying to keep their people from escaping?

With the binoculars still at my eyes, I said, "The place looks idyllic."

Jackson harrumphed. "Looks can be deceiving."

She could say that again. In my police work I'd encountered person after person who wasn't at all what they appeared to be. A peeping Tom, a corrupt politician, and, most recently, a stalker. All of them had seemed like nice enough folks at first glance. But when the truth eventually came out, I'd learned that there was evil hiding behind their harmless façades.

At the far end of the property sat an array of solar panels to provide power to the compound. Being this far out and built so long ago, the camp likely utilized well water and a septic system. With eggs from the chicken coop, crops from the vegetable garden and adjacent farmland, and fish from the lake, one could live their entire life on the property and want for nothing. It wasn't a surprise the group would aim to be self-sustaining. They seemed to want no part of the world outside their walls. This compound was their refuge, their bit of heaven on earth. Besides, if they were self-sustaining, it would mean that the authorities couldn't turn off their electricity or cut off their food supplies in an attempt to force them out, as the federal government had done with the Branch Davidians in Waco. It was a clever strategy. I made a mental note to head for the compound in the event of a zombie apocalypse. The People of Peace would probably be the last to succumb to the undead.

My mind went from contemplating the compound as a zombie refuge to wondering why such a factional, faith-based group would not keep the baby among them. Why send one of their own, an innocent, defenseless baby no less, out into the evil outside world? Why not raise her in their faith and their fold?

Movement at the edge of my field of vision caught my attention and I shifted my focus to an old, slightly cockeyed silo on the adjacent farmland. As I watched, a man climbed down a ladder affixed to the silo. Brave guy. As rusty as the ladder looked, it could give way at any moment and send him plummeting to his death on the dirt below. Rather than risk seeing that happen, I returned the binoculars to Detective Jackson. "Nothing's jumping out at me."

"All right," she said. "Let's roll."

I cranked the engine, slid the cruiser into gear, and drove down the small hill. At the bottom, I turned onto the gravel road that led to the compound's gate, which was set back a hundred yards or so from the main road. Two signs in the same red color and shape of stop signs sat on either side of the road. Rather than STOP, however, they read, respectively, PRIVATE PROPERTY and

NO TRESPASSING. The signs didn't stop me and the detective. We were on a mission.

Dust clouded up in our wake as the gravel *ping-ping-pinged* against the bottom and sides of the squad car. As we pulled up to the gate, we were greeted by another improvised stop sign mounted on the metal bars. This one was at least four feet across and read PRIVATE—NO ENTRY. TRESPASSERS WILL BE PROSECUTED.

Jackson eyed the sign and turned to me. "Not exactly welcoming, are they?"

"Not at all."

Up close like this, I realized the stone walls were even higher than I'd estimated, ten or maybe even twelve feet tall. I briefly flashed back to my days in the police academy, where we recruits had to scale a six-foot chain-link fence. It wasn't easy by any stretch of the imagination, but at least you could get a toehold in the links, wrap your fingers around the top of the fence for leverage. As smooth as these stones were, only a skilled rock climber would be able to get a grip or toehold and scale this towering wall without a rope.

I pulled the squad car to a stop in front of the wide iron gate situated in the northeast corner of the property. Inside, a wooden privacy fence formed a wall to the right, with a second gate at the end. The setup reminded me of the two-gate installations at many dog parks, designed to prevent dogs from escaping the enclosure. Was this double-gate design intended to prevent residents from escaping? Could be. It seemed that the tall bushes planted behind the second gate were also designed to obscure the view if anyone tried to get a peek into the place.

We waited for a moment or two, but no one came to

the gate. I glanced over at the keypad for the security system mounted on a pole to my left. Without a code, the keypad was useless to us. Then again, at the bottom of the pad was a circle of small holes. A speaker. Maybe we could rouse someone. I was about to ask Detective Jackson what we should do when she reached over and flipped on my siren. *WOO-WOO!*

When I reflexively jumped in my seat, she cut me a glance. "Sorry. I'm not feeling patient this morning." She flipped the siren on again, twice in quick succession. *WOO-WOO! WOO-WOO!*

We watched the gates and, half a minute later, a man appeared behind the second one. He held a leash in his hand. A furry, fanged mutt that looked more monster than dog was at the other end of it, a shiny choke collar encircling his neck. The man was dressed in thick cargo pants and an untucked khaki shirt that likewise had a lot of pockets. Unfortunately, he looked nothing like the man the sketch artist had drawn. Though he was Caucasian and appeared to be around the same age as the suspect—thirty or so—this guy had dark hair, a round and clean-shaven face, and a wide nose. His build was wrong, too. The guy who'd left the baby was tall and lean, while this guy was of average height and stocky.

Both the detective and I raised a hand in greeting. Rather than return the gesture, he stared at us for a long moment.

Jackson muttered, "Come on, guy. We haven't got all day." She turned her hand the other way and waved him forward.

He pulled a key chain out of his pocket, thumbed through the set until he found the right one, and inserted it into a heavy-duty padlock holding the second gate closed.

Jackson and I exchanged a glance. The fact that the second gate had a different type of locking mechanism, one controlled by a key, told us that whoever was in charge here strictly controlled the comings and goings of the People of Peace. They also controlled access by anyone from the outside world. Nobody would get on—or off—this property without permission.

As Jackson climbed out of the car, I unrolled the windows so Brigit could get air. She raised her nose to the mesh and sniffed, her nostrils twitching as she took in the scents carried on the breeze. I exited the car and together Jackson and I approached the first gate.

"Good morning!" Detective Jackson called cheerfully.

The man stopped halfway between the gates. "'Mornin'." His speech might be casual, but there was nothing relaxed about his stiff posture and the wary look in his eyes. The dog, too, was stiff and wary. "Somethin' I can do for y'all?" the man asked.

"There sure is." Jackson stepped right up to the gate and thrust her hand through the bars. "I'm Audrey Jackson, a detective with the Fort Worth Police Department." She angled her head to indicate me. "That's Officer Luz."

I stepped up and put my hand out, too, briefly wondering if the man would grab it and yank on it until my head slammed into the metal bars. In my time on the force, I'd learned anything was possible. Luckily for us, he made no such move. Instead, the man dropped the dog's leash and came forward. He tentatively shook our hands, but failed to identify himself.

Nonplussed, Jackson said, "How would you like me to refer to you, sir?"

He hesitated a moment, then said, "I'm Jebediah."

A biblical name if ever there was one. Now that we were face-to-face, I gave him a closer look. Nothing struck me as unusual until my eyes reached his boots. *They're dusty.* Seth had mentioned that the man who dropped off the baby had dust on his hat. Was it nothing more than coincidence? Dusty boots would be expected in a place that lacked pavement. But this dust wasn't the whitish-gray type that came from gravel. It was light brown and seemed thicker and coarser than the usual dirt particles a person would pick up from the ground. My eyes made a second sweep, moving upward. Dust had settled on his shoulders and in his hair, too. The pockets of his shirt were lumpy, the head of what appeared to be a screw sticking out of the pocket on his right.

"I'm hoping you can help us," Jackson said. "A frantic mother and father came by the station this morning. They said their daughter has seemed upset and unhappy lately. The girl left the house yesterday evening and hasn't been back since."

Police were not required to tell the truth when interrogating suspects or fishing for information. A certain amount of trickery was permitted in the interests of justice. To that end, Jackson reached into her pocket and pulled out a photo of a smiling teenaged girl with milk-chocolate skin and loose curls that played about her face. I recognized the photo as one of her niece that she normally displayed on the bookshelf in her office. She held up the photo so Jebediah could take a look.

He cut his eyes to the picture before turning them back on Jackson.

She tucked the picture back into her pocket. "The mother says her daughter's been going through some spiritual turmoil, been trying different churches, looking for answers. They don't live too far down the road. We thought she might have come here."

"She didn't," Jebediah said.

"How can you be sure?" Jackson asked.

"Because I'd have been told if she had," he said plainly. "Nobody's come by."

Jackson nodded. "I understand, and I've got no reason to doubt you. Still, the girl's only seventeen, a minor. It would be best for everyone, you and your group included, if Officer Luz and I came in and took a look for ourselves. You know, just so's we can assure her parents we made an honest effort and that nobody's hiding her." She gestured at the gate. "Open this thing on up and we'll be in and out before you know it."

"Sorry," Jebediah said. "I can't do that."

"Why not?"

"I'm not authorized to let outsiders in," he said. "It's not my decision to make."

Jackson's smile didn't falter. "Okay. Then get me someone who *can* make that decision."

The man hesitated for a brief moment before giving a quick nod, stepping back, and turning to retreat through the second gate, locking it behind him.

Though the detective and I shared furtive glances, we said nothing as we waited for him to return. For all we knew, someone was listening through the speaker on the keypad.

A full ten minutes later, Jebediah returned and once again unlocked the interior gate. Though he appeared to be alone, it was clear from the glance he cast to his side that someone else waited out of view. After he slid the gate open, he stepped back, interlocked his fingers over his belly, and bowed his head deferentially.

From around the corner came a man in his fifties with a white beard, a dark brown robe belted at the waist, and lace-up work boots. He resembled Obi-Wan Kenobi or an age-progression of Jesus, had the carpenter/messiah not been nailed to a cross in his early thirties. The Jedi Jesus carried himself with the confidence of someone who was used to getting his way, who ruled his kingdom, who knew the force was with him.

He strode up to the gate, and looked me and Jackson over before eyeing the cruiser. The man's gaze seemed to narrow slightly when he spotted Brigit standing in the back, her tail wagging. He returned his attention to me and the detective. "Good morning, ladies."

Jackson returned his greeting, while I responded only with a dip of my head.

"Are you the guy in charge?" Jackson asked.

"No." The man chuckled and pointed a finger up to the sky. "*He* is the guy in charge."

"Of course." Jackson played along, offering the man a chuckle in return. "But He's got you on duty down here, right?"

"Yes, He most certainly does." The man's gray eyes went from one of us to the other. "I understand you're looking for a young woman?"

"We are," Jackson said. She pulled out the photo again and showed it to the man. "We think she may have come this way. We just need to come inside, verify that she's not here, and we'll be on our way. Nobody's in any trouble here, so there's no need for concern. We'd just like to get her found and back home so we can get about our day."

The man extended his arms to his sides in the quintessential holy statue stance. "I'm sorry, ladies, but that is not possible."

"Why not?" Jackson asked.

He lowered his hands. "Because my people do not wish for their peace to be intruded upon. We've created a life of safety and solace here, sheltered from the evils of the outside world. As I am sure you can surmise, allowing armed police officers into our home would disturb the peace my people have sought and found here."

A vein pulsed in Jackson's jaw. "What's your name, sir?"

"I'm Father Emmanuel," he replied.

"I meant your given name."

His mouth spread in a patronizing grin while his arms spread again. "That's the name the good Lord gave me when I answered his call."

So he'd answer God's call, but not our questions, huh?

Jackson's vein pulsed a second time, but she didn't push him to more clearly identify himself. "Father Emmanuel," she said in her most calm, polite voice. "I respect what you've built here. But Officer Luz and I can be quick and discreet. Your people will hardly know we're here. Surely you and your people would not want someone to unduly suffer."

"Romans chapter five says we must glory in our sufferings," he replied, refusing to budge. "Suffering produces perseverance, character, and hope. But if you would like to leave your contact information, we would be happy to ask the young woman to get in touch with you if she does happen to come by our refuge."

"We'd appreciate that." Jackson retrieved a business card and handed it to him. I did the same.

Father Emmanuel read over our cards before tucking them into a pouch on his belt. "Good day, Detective Jackson." He gave her a nod before turning to me and doing the same. "Officer Luz." With that, he turned and strode back through the second gate and out of sight.

With one last baleful look in our direction, Jebediah locked the gate and likewise disappeared.

The detective and I returned to the cruiser. Brigit flopped down on her platform and issued a sigh, seemingly disappointed she hadn't been asked to chase or trail a suspect or search for drugs. Despite sometimes sleeping on the job, the dog had a good work ethic.

I maneuvered the cruiser in a tight three-point turn to head back down the gravel road. "What now?" I asked Jackson.

"We try to get a search warrant. They might be God's chosen people, but even they can't say no to a search warrant."

FIFTEEN
BLOWING THEIR COVER

Brigit

Brigit glanced back over her furry shoulder as Megan drove their car away from the place with the stone walls. Brigit wasn't sure why Megan had come out here, but she was sure of what she smelled. The breeze that blew by had carried the familiar scents of the two people she had smelled on the blanket of the baby that had been at the fire station. The dog knew from experience that when she repeatedly smelled a person at places they went to, it often meant they would end up chasing that person. Maybe not today. Maybe not tomorrow. *But soon.*

SIXTEEN
SHOPPING LIST

The Father

He thought things over as he and Jeb walked along the path. The Father wasn't sure what to make of the detective and officer who had come to the compound. *Were they on the up and up, merely looking for the teenaged girl in the photo?* Could be. More than once someone had come unbidden to their gate, seeking to join them. Then again, the alleged missing girl could be nothing more than a ruse, a veiled attempt to gain access to the compound to get information about the baby.

He was probably being paranoid. Dropping a baby at a fire station wasn't illegal. In fact, there was a state statute allowing for babies to be left in such places, no questions asked. Any attempt by law enforcement to follow up on a safe drop would be totally at odds with the purpose of the law.

Even so, paranoid or not, it couldn't hurt to take some precautions. Today's visit had caught him totally unawares. If law enforcement returned, he'd like to have some warning, some time to prepare.

He turned to Jeb. "Round up one of the men. I need you to make a run to Tractor Supply. Take the Chevy." Until he determined whether there was something going on, it was best to keep the Ford out of sight.

SEVENTEEN
UNWARRANTED

Megan

As we drove to the magistrate's office, Brigit happily gnawed on a nylon bone in the back of the car.

Jackson stared out the window. "Father Emmanuel is quite a character, isn't he?"

I cut her a look before returning my gaze to the road. "You think he's for real? That he really thinks he's doing God's work? Or is he just a shyster?"

Jackson shrugged. "Hard to say. I can't imagine he thinks he looks attractive in that godawful burlap bathrobe. Either way, he's not made me happy this morning. I've got a million and one investigations to work on and I don't appreciate him wasting my time."

Time was always in short supply for law enforcement.

I checked my side mirror and signaled to change lanes. "Did you notice how he referred to the group as 'my people,' like he owns them?"

Jackson grunted. "Slavery comes in many different forms these days."

Twenty minutes later, we stood before the magistrate, a balding man with a shiny scalp and a semicircle of curls rounding the back of his head, connecting one of his ears to the other.

Jackson gave the man a quick review of the events from the preceding Thursday night. "A baby was dropped off late that night at a local fire station by a man who appeared to be around thirty." She hiked a thumb to indicate me. "Officer Luz responded to the call from the station. She summoned Child Services. When she went to hand the infant over to the caseworker, she noticed something strange about the stitching in the baby's blanket."

"Strange?" asked the magistrate, looking from the detective to me and back again. "What do you mean 'strange'?"

Jackson laid the bluebonnet baby blankie on the bench before him. She pointed to the word sewn into the blanket. "See that? The word 'help' is sewn into the trim. We believe it could be a cry for help from the baby's mother."

The man slid on a pair of cheap plastic reading glasses and leaned in to take a look. "Well, the thread does spell 'help.' That's clear. But how do you know that whoever sewed that word wasn't just asking for help for the baby?"

Jackson cut me a discreet glance. She'd asked me the same thing earlier and I'd been the one to convince her I thought something was up.

The detective returned her focus to the magistrate. "We believe the mother wants our help because she gave us a clue to finding her. We suspect she's a member of the People of Peace. It's a religious group that lives in a walled-in property near Benbrook Lake."

"People of Peace?" said the judge. "Never heard of 'em."

"I'm not surprised," Jackson said. "They work very hard to keep a low profile. At any rate, their symbol is a combination cross and peace sign." She pointed to the loose threads. "It looks like whoever stitched the message in the blanket also stitched their symbol. Some of the threads have pulled loose, but if you look closely at the needle holes, it's like a dot-to-dot puzzle of their mark."

He leaned in again, even closer this time, and blinked twice. "Not seeing it. Could be just a regular peace sign. Might even be something else entirely. Heck, if you ask me, it looks like a star." He looked back up at the detective. "You been out to the property yet? Talk to anybody?"

"Officer Luz and I went out to the church compound earlier to see if they'd let us in voluntarily, but their leader refused to give us access. We made up a ruse about looking for a runaway teenager."

The magistrate issued a disapproving grunt. "I'm not sure that was such a good idea."

Guilt gripped me. *Am I wrong about all of this?* It was one thing for me to screw up. It was another thing for me to drag Detective Jackson down with me. But even more worrisome was the thought that I was right. If this judge didn't give us a search warrant, there was no telling what types of bad things could result. It wasn't my place to say anything, but in my panic words blurted from my mouth before I could stop them. "We can't know for sure what the person who sewed the word meant. But don't we owe it to her to find out?"

The magistrate slid his glasses off and pointed the earpiece at me. "I think you owe it to her *not* to find out. The safe drop law was intended to protect the privacy of mothers and fathers who surrender their babies. If law enforcement goes hunting down the parents, it would defeat the intent of the statute, discourage them from making safe drops, and we'd be back where we were years ago, with babies being left all over town and some of them not found until it was too late." He shook his head. "Any link to that church is highly speculative, at best. Even if you convinced me the baby came from the group, it's not clear a crime has been committed and the downsides are substantial."

One of those downsides was that the judge could get potential flack from the religious community if he allowed us to force our way into a church compound. Groups were sometimes permitted to hide dirty secrets behind their religious identities, knowing the potential for public outcry about the separation of church and state and religious sovereignty would keep law enforcement at bay. Child-abuse scandals, adultery, and financial foul play had been swept under many a prayer rug.

"Sorry, you two," the judge concluded. "I know you mean well, but no can do."

Frustration gripped my innards. *Ugh! Just let me do my damn job!* I was tempted to order Brigit to take the man down and refuse to call her off until he issued a warrant. Of course I'd be out of a job, then.

While I grappled internally with my emotions, Jackson, on the other hand, took the judge's ruling in stride. "Thank you, sir."

We left the building and returned to the cruiser, loading Brigit in her pen, taking our seats, and belting ourselves in.

I put my hands on the wheel, but didn't start the car. "What do we do now?"

Detective Jackson exhaled a long breath. "We do nothing."

"Nothing?" My hands involuntarily squeezed the steering wheel. "How can we do nothing?"

She angled her head and gave me a pointed look. "You've got good instincts, Officer Luz, but sometimes you've got to learn when to call it quits. The law isn't on our side here. Like the judge said, we don't have clear evidence of a crime."

"But what if there's someone who needs our help?" The thought of leaving a woman in a hopeless, helpless situation made me feel sick inside.

Jackson gave me a sad smile. "There will always be someone who needs our help, Megan. We won't even know who some of them are and, even if we did, we'd never be able to help them all. We've just got to help the ones we can and hope fate or God takes care of the others. You've got to accept that fact or this job will eat you alive."

I knew she was telling me the truth, but I didn't like the truth at that moment. Call me naïve or overly optimistic or even stupid, but I wanted to change the truth . . . or at least change it in this one case, if I could.

"Would it be all right if I kept an eye on the compound?" I asked. "Maybe drive by every so often just to see if the Ford pickup shows up?"

Jackson sighed and closed her eyes. "You really don't know when to give up, do you?"

She might be admonishing me, but she wasn't telling me no, either. "So I can drive by?"

She opened her eyes and cut me a look. "Use discretion and be careful. I don't want my ass getting chewed out if you screw up."

Woo-hoo! "Thanks, Detective."

I dropped her at the station and headed back out on patrol. As much as I wanted to go back to the hill and spy on the compound, they were likely on alert now. Better to give them a little time to let down their guard.

Did they suspect why we'd really come to the compound? Or did they buy our story? There was no way to be sure. I hoped we hadn't tipped them off, but what if we had? What might they do? And what if I was totally off base here? What if there was nothing going on at the People of Peace compound? What if the symbol really was just some loose ends of thread and I was harassing a bunch of lost souls whose only crime was to want to be left alone? Or what if the baby's mother had only wanted help for her baby, and my actions could cause her more emotional trauma? The last thing I would want to do was make things harder on a mother who'd been unable to care for her child. *Ugh . . .*

The remainder of my shift involved handling standard traffic offenses. Speeding. Reckless driving. A broken taillight. Not exactly the type of work that challenged the mind. But I had to handle these kinds of ho-hum tasks in order to achieve my goal and become a detective.

I'd just issued a speeding ticket to a businessman in a silver Lexus when my mother texted me on my cell. *Can you help me study tonight?*

Mom had been a college student when she'd met my

father. The two married young and, as young people
are wont to do, fornicated recklessly. They'd also fornicated without contraception, as the Catholic church
would have them do. The results of the careless copu-
lation included both yours truly and Mom putting her
plans, vague as they were, on hold for the next two and
a half decades. With the youngest of my four siblings,
Gabby, now in her mid-teens, my mother had some free
time on her hands and decided it was high time to pursue her dreams. She still hadn't quite figured out exactly what her dreams were yet, but decided it couldn't
hurt to get some of the basic courses out of the way
while trying to decide what she wanted to do with the
rest of her life.

I texted her back. *Sure. I'd be happy to help.*

She responded with, *Great! I'll make dinner.*

More *ugh* . . . The word "great" simply did not apply to my mother's dinners. My father and we kids had
managed to choke her meals down all these years
because the alternative, cooking for ourselves, sounded
like a lot of trouble. Still, even if the food would be
substandard, it would be nice to see my family. My irregular work schedule meant I didn't get by their house
as often as I'd like.

When our shift was up, Brigit and I drove to
Walmart, where I picked up a pair of binoculars in the
sporting goods department. Brigit herded me over
to the pet aisle, where she nosed through the toy selections.

"You're spoiled rotten," I told her, as if it were her
fault. It wasn't, of course. It was *mine.* But you try saying no to that sweet face of hers. It's impossible.

After looking over all the options, she plucked a squeaky rubber pig from a peg. *Oink-oink.*

That high-pitched noise would get old fast. "Any chance I can talk you into a quiet toy? Something plush?" I retrieved a stuffed mallard. "This one looks fun." I waved it around in front of her. "See?"

Brigit let me know in no uncertain terms that it was the pig or else. She looked up at me and emitted a soft growl. *Grrrrr.*

"All right," I conceded. "You can have the noisy pig."

I returned the duck to the shelf. Brigit carried the pig in her teeth to the checkout, where she reared up on her hind legs and dropped it on the belt for the cashier to ring up.

Our shopping trip complete, we headed over to my parents' house in the Arlington Heights neighborhood, which sat to the west of downtown, near the arts district. My parents' house was a three-bedroom, two-bath, one-story frame structure, with peeling yellow paint. Not exactly the kind of place you'd see gracing the cover of *Better Homes & Gardens.* But my family had managed to eke out a relatively stable and happy life here over the years.

I parked at the curb, unloaded Brigit, and gave her a few seconds to relieve herself on the grass before heading up the walk.

When I opened the door, my mother's voice came from the kitchen. "In here, Megan!"

Brigit trotted in ahead of me, heading right past my mother's three identical orange tabby cats. Mom claimed she could tell them apart, but I had my doubts.

Upon seeing Brigit, the ginger-haired trio stood up on the back of the couch, arched their identical backs, and issued identical hisses. *Hissss!*

My partner ignored the cats and aimed straight for their bowl of kibble in the kitchen, treating herself to a crunchy treat. I, on the other hand, admonished the felines with an eye roll. "Drama queens."

I found my mother and my brother Joey at the kitchen table. My mother had red hair and freckles, the quintessential Irish look. While she'd passed some of those freckles along to me, my darker skin and dark hair were courtesy of my father, who was of Mexican descent. Yep, my siblings and I were typical American mutts, a little of this, a little of that. Joey had earbuds in his ears and was bopping his head in time to music while doing homework on his laptop. My mother, on the other hand, was doing her homework old-school style, poring over a thick American history textbook.

I ruffled Joey's hair and gave a "hey" in hello to my mom. "Where's Gabby and Dad?"

"Gabby stayed after school to work on the yearbook," Mom said. "Your father's picking her up."

I reached for the handle of the refrigerator. "How're the classes c-coming along?"

"Great!" She closed the book and hugged it to her chest. "My American history class is so interesting."

Joey issued a derisive grunt. Apparently his music hadn't entirely drowned out our conversation and, also apparently, he did not share my mother's enthusiasm for history.

I retrieved the bottle of cranberry juice and poured myself a glass before taking a seat at the table.

My mother held out a stack of index cards on which she'd written questions and answers. "Here. Quiz me."

"Okay." I took the homemade flash cards from her and mixed them up before selecting one to read from. "What was the Stamp Act?" I was pretty sure I'd once known the answer myself, but for the life of me I couldn't recall it at the moment. That piece of knowledge had probably been lost while I'd attended the police academy, its place in my memory banks superseded by a section of the Texas Penal Code.

"I know that one." My mother raised an index finger. "The Stamp Act imposed taxes on printed paper such as newspapers and legal documents. It was enacted in 1765 to raise money to support the colonies."

"Your answer is correct!" I announced in my best game-show-host voice. Moving on to the next card, I asked, "Where did the First Continental Congress meet and when?"

"They met in the fall of 1774," Mom replied, "in . . ." She snapped her fingers three times, as if the gesture would jog her memory. Evidently, it did. "Philadelphia!" she cried. "In a building called Carpenter's Hall."

"You are correct!" I placed the card at the back of the stack.

Having downed the kitty kibble and sniffed her way around the house to see what might be new or interesting, Brigit returned to the kitchen. She made her way over to me, sat on her haunches, and draped her chin over my thigh. I ran my hand over her head as I asked my mother the next question. "Who was Thomas Paine?"

Before Mom could answer, Brigit raised her nose in

the air and twitched her nostrils. But it didn't take a canine's superior senses to scent the burning smell, though. My nose detected it now, too. "It smells like something's burning."

My mother glanced at the stove. "Oh, no! I forgot to set the timer!" She leaped from her seat and ran over to open the oven. Dark smoke wafted out. She jabbed the button to turn the oven off, retrieved two pot holders from the counter, and pulled out a cookie sheet bearing a charred veggie pizza. Mom hadn't so much cooked our dinner as she had cremated it.

She waved the pot holder over the pizza in a desperate attempt to cool the food and dissipate the smoke. "Thomas Paine wrote *Common Sense,* which is famous for the quote 'These are the times that try men's souls.'"

The homework question now answered, she grabbed a knife from the drawer and rubbed the serrated edge back and forth across the blackened bits. "Good news. It's still edible if I scrape the top and edges off."

The front door banged open and my sister Gabby's voice preceded her into the kitchen. "Hey, Megan!"

I stood in anticipation of my sisterly hug, delivering it promptly and lovingly when she flounced into the room. "Hey, Gabs. What's new?"

"Homecoming's this weekend," she said. "T.J.'s taking me to the dance. He's being very secretive. I think he might be getting me a triple mum!" She covered her mouth with both hands to stifle her squeal of excitement.

A triple mum would set her boyfriend back some serious bucks. Spending so much money on flowers that would dry up and die in a day or two seemed imprudent to me, but if a triple mum made my sister feel special, who was I to judge?

Dad came in the front door, Gabby's backpack in his hands. "Did you forget something, Gabby?"

She turned, saw her backpack, and gave herself a head slap. "Oh, right. My homework."

Dad came over and gave me a peck on the cheek. "Hey, Megan. How's everything going?"

"There's been some burglaries in the area," I warned him. "Be sure to lock your garage-door remotes in your glove compartments. The thieves are stealing the controllers from the victims' cars, and using them to get inside their houses and rob them."

Dad raised a brow. "That's actually a clever strategy."

"Thieves can be crafty." Too bad they didn't use their smarts for good instead of evil.

As I stood to help my mother serve what passed for dinner in the Luz household, my dad yanked the earbuds from my brother's ears. "Go wash up."

Soon we were all seated at the table, forcing down dry, crunchy slices of pizza. The food might not taste great, but if dog biscuits were any indication, it was probably cleaning our teeth.

Over dinner, I told my family about the baby that had been abandoned at the fire station. "She was adorable. Had a full head of black hair."

"She did?" Mom said. "You don't often see a newborn with much hair. Of course all of you had a full head, too."

"Like a bunch of little monkeys," my father added.

Joey curved his arms to scratch his armpits and issued his best chimpanzee imitation. "Ooh-ooh, ah-ah."

"That reminds me," Mom said, "I need to add bananas to the shopping list."

When we finished eating, I took care of the dishes so my mother could have a few extra minutes to prepare for her midterm. When the last dish had been dried and put away, I bade everyone good-bye. "Good luck tomorrow, Mom. If you get an A, I'll take you out for ice cream."

"Ooh!" She grinned. "That's an incentive if ever there was one."

Brigit and I arrived for duty an hour early Tuesday morning. While I wanted to keep an eye on the People of Peace compound, I didn't want to leave my beat understaffed during my shift. I figured I could swing by the compound before my shift started, again on my lunch hour, and a third time at the end of my shift. Maybe I'd see something that would give me a clue.

My partner and I headed southwest. Brigit played with her new pig as we rode. *Oink-oink. Oink-oink.*

I eyed the dog in the rearview mirror. "That toy is getting on my nerves. I have half a mind to toss it out the window."

Brigit didn't give one dog biscuit about my frayed nerves. *Oink-oink.*

As we neared the small rise above the compound, I slowed down to give myself more time to scope things out. The cruiser peaked the hill and my eyes spotted something new down below. An elevated deer blind had been erected just inside the wall by the gates, where someone inside could keep an eye on things outside the gate. Three others had been erected, too, one in each of the other corners of the property. *Hmm . . .*

The improvised lookout towers told me that despite his tranquil countenance yesterday, Father Emmanuel had not been happy about me and Detective Jackson showing up at the place without advance notice. But did the precaution mean he knew we'd actually come about the baby, not the alleged missing teen? Did the watchtower mean he was trying to hide something? Or was it simply a tactic to prevent another intrusion on his people? Was he a sinner or a saint?

We rolled down the hill and past the secluded grounds. In my peripheral vision, I spotted movement in the tower, someone keeping watch, possibly reporting to Emmanuel that a police cruiser had just gone by.

My partner and I continued on down the road and drove into the lakeside park. Here, we were well out of sight of anyone in the deer stands. I pulled the cruiser into a spot in the small lot closest to the People of Peace spread and opened Brigit's enclosure. "C'mon, girl. Let's go for a hike."

My partner might not understand exactly what a hike was, but she could tell by the tone of my voice that she was in for some fun. She turned to grab her pig, but I was quicker than her. I snatched it up and held it over my head. "Porky stays in the car."

She gave me a dirty look, but hopped down to the pavement. I tossed the pig back into her cage and closed the door. After consulting the trail map posted at the kiosk at the edge of the lot, I found the trailhead for a path that ran reasonably close to the western wall of the property. Brigit and I took off down the dirt path. While I strode straight ahead, Brigit took the opportunity to stop and sniff the various scents other animals had left behind, sometimes lagging behind me, sometimes bolting ahead, but always staying within view.

My eyes caught an occasional glimpse of the stone wall through the scrubby foliage to my left. The People of Peace made it clear that the property, though adjacent to the public park, was off limits. Every twenty feet or so, the words PRIVATE PROPERTY were painted in bright orange lettering that stood out in stark contrast to the wall.

When we were about halfway down the trail, Brigit stopped on the trail ahead of me and pricked her ears. I came up beside her and listened. *Nothing.* I wouldn't want to give up my opposable thumbs and ability to walk upright in order to become a dog, but having a canine's superior auditory capabilities sure would come in handy. We proceeded on and twenty seconds later, I could finally detect what Brigit had heard.

Cluck-cluck. Cluck. Cluck-cluck-cluck.

Chickens. We must be near the chicken coop I'd spotted from the hill the day before.

The trail veered away from the church's acreage and headed back toward the shoreline, circling to the parking lot where it had begun. As I loaded Brigit back into her enclosure, my ears picked up another faint sound that seemed to be coming from the compound. *Ding-dong, ding-dong, ding-dong.* The church bells were ringing.

I climbed into the cruiser and drove back up the hill, pulling to the side to take a final look down into the property below. The two hundred or so residents of the property were gathered in a circle in front of the church, their hands linked, like Dr. Seuss's Whos in

Whoville when they sang their Christmas song. *Must be morning prayers.*

We drove back to our usual beat and spent the morning patrolling. I was waiting at a red light on a cross street at University Drive when I spotted Derek Mackey in his cruiser directly across the street. After he'd lost some evidence in a drug case, Captain Leone hadn't let him patrol alone for a few weeks, assigning him another officer to serve as his babysitter and make sure he didn't screw up again. Derek had managed to keep his nose clean and the captain had eventually let him go solo again.

As the two of us ignored each other and waited for our respective lights to turn green, a kid in a Corvette came up University on my side of the street. He was doing ninety-to-nothing, weaving in and out of traffic as if trying to win a race at Texas Motor Speedway. He nearly rear-ended a Hyundai Accent—*screech!*— before swerving around it and punching the gas, his tires squealing as he accelerated.

What a dumb butt. Didn't he see the two squad cars on either side of the road? Maybe he'd been going too fast to see us. That or by the time he'd spotted us it was too late. Either way, it was time to put a stop to his reckless driving.

"Hang on, girl!" I called back to Brigit as I switched on my lights and siren. As soon as the cross traffic stopped to let me out, I turned out onto the street after the guy. Derek, likewise, turned onto the street, siren wailing and lights blazing. *Woo-woo-woo!* The Big Dick pulled up next to me and cut me a glare.

Glaring back at him, I grabbed the mic for my

radio. "He's mine, Derek. Back off." After all, the kid had been speeding down the side of the road closer to me. Proximity should count for something.

"Aren't you too good to patrol?" Derek shot back, taking a quick look at the road ahead of him before cutting his eyes back to me. "I thought you were a junior detective now."

The guy couldn't stand that my hard work and dedication had gained me favor with the detectives. Ironic, given that he was buddy-buddy with the chief of police.

Rather than argue the point, or unnecessarily endanger civilians and my partner, I slowed down. "He's all yours."

"Damn right he is!" Derek snapped, muttering "asskisser" before hanging up his mic.

When I slowed down, Brigit flopped back down on her cushion and issued a sigh. She knew high speeds meant she might get to chase someone, and she was disappointed this pursuit hadn't ended in a takedown. "Sorry, girl." Though she hadn't actually earned a liver treat, I finagled one out of my pocket and gave it to her anyway, dropping it over the top bar of her enclosure. *Yep, spoiled rotten and all my fault.*

EIGHTEEN

THIS LITTLE SWINE OF MINE

Brigit

She wolfed down the liver treat and set back to work on the pig, squeezing the little pink porker with her teeth. *Oink-oink. Oink-oink.* Playing with the rubber prey appealed to Brigit's inner wolf, and she was having a heck of a time. *Must kill pig!* She picked the little pig up in her mouth and shook him back and forth. *Oink-oink! Oink-oink! Oink-oink!*

So fun! *Die, piggie, die!*

Oi— The pig went silent as one of Brigit's fangs broke through the rubber. She shook him again, but nothing happened. Looked liked she'd succeeded. Darn. She hadn't really wanted to kill the thing. She'd only been playing.

She dropped the pig to the platform of her enclosure and put her head down on her paws. *Stupid cheap toy.*

NINETEEN
BABY FROM BABYLON

The Father

"Please!" she begged, on her knees with her hands clasped in front of her as if in prayer. "Please let me out of here! I promise I'll obey from now on."

The Father felt a smug satisfaction slither inside him. "Why should I believe you, you Whore of Babylon? You vowed to remained chaste until marriage. You made a promise to God. You didn't keep that promise, did you?"

Maybe he was being overly harsh, but he wasn't in a good mood and it was likely her fault. Police officers had come to the property yesterday, and he couldn't be sure whether the story they'd given him was true. A lookout in the new tower he'd had erected had radioed earlier to tell him a cruiser had gone by. It wasn't necessarily unusual for the police to patrol out here given that people sometimes got a little rowdy when camping or fishing in the adjacent park. Still, it made him edgy to have law enforcement about.

"No." She gulped as tears poured down her cheeks. "I didn't keep my promise to God to remain chaste. But

I'm sorry! I've repented! God has already punished me by taking my baby from me. Why must you do more?"

She was wearing down, but the fact that she'd dared to question him said she wasn't completely broken yet. She wasn't as stupid as the rest of his flock, as willing to swallow whatever warped, self-serving logic he decided to feed them. When her parents had joined the People of Peace years ago, she'd been a mere ten years old. But even then she'd looked at him not with adoration and awe, but with skepticism and distrust.

He should have banished Juliette and Luke from the compound the moment he'd caught the two in the chicken coop seven months ago. Eggs weren't the only thing getting laid in the structure that night. He'd already refused them permission to marry, told them he would reconsider if and when he sensed they'd grown enough spiritually. Yet they'd blatantly defied him, gone behind his back and snuck around to be together in the most biblical of ways. He'd never felt such fury! If the other members of the People of Peace found out he'd allowed Juliette and Luke to disobey him, to sin right there within the sacred walls of the compound, his hold on the others could begin to loosen.

"Out, you sinners!" he'd hissed like a serpent when he'd found them, inadvertently scaring the hens, who'd clucked and fluttered their wings where they sat on their nests. As Juliette yanked the hem of her dress down and Luke pulled up his pants, Father Emmanuel pointed across the wide compound in the direction of the gate. "You two are banished! You don't deserve to remain inside these walls!"

Juliette had burst into tears. "May I speak with my parents before I go? Tell them good-bye?"

He'd taken a deep breath to regain his composure. "No. I will talk to your parents and Luke's mother in the morning and tell them what you've done. They will understand why you could not be allowed to remain."

It gave Father Emmanuel no small sense of pleasure to see the look of helplessness on Luke's face. The young man might be strong and smart and handsome, but he was powerless to help the woman he loved.

Luke had fallen to his knees in front of Father Emmanuel, his hands clasped in desperation. "Please don't do this! We don't want to lose our families!"

Juliette fell to her knees, too. "Please, Father! We're sorry! Please allow us to redeem ourselves! We'll serve any penance!"

He'd mulled things over. Though he'd banished the occasional member from the compound as a reminder to the others that they lived there at his pleasure, he always chose members whose absence would not be deeply felt. But if he banished Juliette and Luke, he ran the risk that Juliette's parents and Luke's mother would want to leave as well. Though he'd found their parents quite easy to convince and control in many aspects, despite his best efforts he hadn't been able to successfully sever the strong family bonds they'd arrived with. If the three of them left in search of their banished children, if they rejected the earthly paradise he had provided them, Emmanuel would appear weak and not in control of his flock. Moreover, Juliette and Luke were well liked by the other members of the church, and had many friends within these walls. Their banishment would cut deep across the compound, raise questions and, quite possibly, resentments. The life

Father Emmanuel built here could begin to erode, disintegrate.

"I'll let you stay on one condition," he'd told Juliette and Luke.

"Anything, Father!" Luke had cried.

Tears wetting her cheeks, Juliette had nodded her head frantically. "Yes, anything!"

He looked from one of them to the other. "You two must stay away from each other. No sitting together in the manna hall or at services. No joining hands in the prayer circle. And certainly no lying with each other!" Of course he knew that he also had to dangle a carrot in front of them to encourage them to keep their mouths shut. "You have soiled yourselves for anyone but each other. If you obey me for a year, stay clear of each other for four seasons, I will reconsider your request to marry. But you must not tell anyone of this bargain I have made with you. If you tell a soul, I will put you outside the walls in an instant."

"Thank you, Father Emmanuel!" Luke cried up at him. "Thank you for showing us God's mercy!"

Juliette had bowed her head. Father Emmanuel had thought it a sign of submission at first, but when she upchucked the vegetable stew they'd had for dinner, he realized he might have another problem on his hands. *A little problem with hands of its own.*

"Juliette," he'd asked, "are you with child?"

She'd pulled a lace-edged handkerchief from her pocket to wipe her mouth and nodded, a fresh round of tears welling up in her eyes. "I believe I am, Father."

It took all his strength to fight the urge to slap the disobedient little slut across the face.

That Jezebel could ruin everything!

"You must go, after all, then," he'd told them. "A child will be proof that you two have sinned here, that you have willingly defied the word of God." Worse yet, they'd defied Father Emmanuel, which chapped his ass far worse than any biblical breach. "Were it a small transgression, it could be forgiven. But lust is one of the seven deadly sins. I would be no man of God were I to allow you to disrespect the Lord here on His hallowed ground."

"Please, no!" Still on her knees, Juliette looked up at him. "Please!"

"I see no other solution," he said, though he was racking his mind for one. Sending the two of them away could lead to a dangerous domino effect. An idea crept into his mind then, and he worked through it, thinking out loud, making them believe the idea was theirs. "Of course, you could tell the others that you made a mistake, Juliette. You could say that you met a boy somewhere . . ." He trailed off, leaving her to fill in the blanks.

She promptly did. No one could ever accuse Juliette of being stupid. "I could say I met a young man when I was selling eggs at the farmer's market."

Given that the only time she left the compound was to sell the eggs, it was the only place she could have met someone who wasn't a member of the People of Peace.

She continued. "I'll say that the devil got into me and I sinned with the man."

Luke looked pained at the mere thought of the woman he loved being with another man, but he didn't stop her.

Though it might be bearing false witness against the fictitious father of the child, it wasn't an unfathomable story. Father Emmanuel had attended the farmer's market on various occasions. He knew that a young man who sold honey in the adjacent booth often traded a jar of his sweet honey for a dozen of Juliette's farm-fresh eggs. She'd brought the honey back to the compound and shared it with the others, even mentioned the yellow-and-black-striped shirts and funny, fuzzy antennae the boy wore to get the attention of potential customers.

Juliette reached up and grabbed Father Emmanuel's hands, holding them in tight desperation. "I will let the others know that I begged you for forgiveness and permission to raise my child among the People of Peace. That you, in your mercy, allowed me and my child to stay."

It was less than an ideal solution, but there was no ideal solution to be had. Either he banished the young couple and risked their parents' departure, allowed them to remain while openly acknowledging their mutual sin committed within the compound walls and in direct defiance of his leadership, or he used Juliette as a precautionary tale for others about the risks and dangers of the sinful and scary outside world. He'd decided to go with the latter.

In retrospect, maybe he should have banished Juliette and Luke, after all, allowed their parents to leave as well. Juliette posed a challenge, that was for sure. Regardless, he'd break her . . . even if it was the last thing he did.

TWENTY
WHAT'S IN STORE

Megan

When it neared noon, I turned my cruiser to the southwest once again. I'd packed a sandwich and planned to eat my lunch on the road, put in some unofficial overtime to spy on the People of Peace.

When we ascended the hilltop this time, my eyes spotted people from all over the compound heading toward the dining hall, including the children from the school, some of whom ran ahead of their friends. I passed the compound, circled through the park, and drove back up the road. Unfortunately, the visit had told me nothing new. My bladder, however, told me I better find a ladies' room.

I pulled over and consulted my maps app. The image showed a place called Benbrook Burgers, Beer, and Bait a half mile down another road, and I headed back out. Shortly thereafter, we pulled into the lot. The place, which looked like a rustic log cabin, turned out to be a combination gas station, convenience store, bait and tackle shop, diner, and gift boutique. The building was decked out for Halloween, with colorful pumpkins and gourds piled near the doors and a skeleton and witch seated in a pair of rustic outdoor rocking chairs as if engaged in conversation.

I retrieved my partner from the back, clipped her lead onto her collar, and brought her inside with me. After using the facilities, I decided to take a look in the gift shop. After all, I was still officially on my lunch hour and sometimes these out-of-the-way places offered unusual and interesting items.

We wandered through the doorway that separated the convenience store from the gift shop and meandered past a wooden barrel filled with clear bags of candied pecans, their label pronouncing them *Proudly Made in Pecan Crossing, Texas, Just for You!* An adjacent bin offered classic wooden children's toys, handcrafted locally according to the sign. A yo-yo. A truck. A boat. A pop gun. Carving in each of the toys noted the name of the toymaker—Craig's Classic Toys. Several beautiful pottery pieces were displayed on a shelf nearby. A placard identified the potter as someone doing business as Kiln Me Now.

The scent of seasonal pumpkin spice led me to a shelf along the back wall. There I found an assortment of taper candles. The slight imperfections told me they'd been dipped by hand. On the shelf below were metal candleholders that looked like they'd also been forged by hand. Next to them was a unique set of rustic silverware in a sun motif with matching napkin rings. Unlike the other items, the candles and metal pieces had no sign identifying the person who'd crafted them.

A saleslady stepped up next to me. "Can I help you with something?"

"Just browsing." I held a pumpkin candle up to my nose and inhaled its beautiful scent.

The woman gave me a smile. "Smells great, doesn't it?"

"They caught my nose the minute I stepped into the store." I tucked the pumpkin spice candle under my arm and picked up one in a deep green color.

"That's the piñon pine," the woman said. "It's one of our most popular for Christmas."

I decided to get one of the pine-scented candles for Detective Jackson, a thank-you for trusting me and my instincts. I chose two candleholders, as well, one for me and one for the detective.

As the woman moved on to straighten a display of country-themed cookbooks, Brigit wandered down the aisle and pulled the leash taut. She sniffed the air and looked back at me over her shoulder in her "follow me" expression.

"What is it, girl?" I walked toward her and she hustled ahead, pulling the slack taut again. Whatever she'd scented, she seemed in a hurry to get to it.

She led me to a table at the back. Handmade quilted items in all colors and sizes were stacked on the table. Pot holders. Place mats. Blankets. Brigit proceeded to stick her nose into one of the piles of blankets, as if fixated on one in particular. She nudged the blanket and, when that didn't free it from the pile, grabbed the white trim with her teeth.

"No!" I put the candles and holders down and gently wrestled the fabric from her fangs. Luckily, the quilt was undamaged. Good thing, because the handwritten price tag attached to the trim read $250. Not exactly the type of thing a person could afford on a cop's salary.

Brigit sat on her haunches and looked up at me, issuing the passive alert she was trained to give when she detected drugs. But I hadn't ordered her to search. Surely there weren't drugs hidden among these quilts. Or was there? Had a customer seen us come in, panicked, and ditched some weed among the blankets?

I turned back to the stack of quilted blankets, examining each one before setting them aside. A red, white, and blue blanket covered in Texas flags. A dark blue blanket adorned with stars and moons. A third in pastel patchwork. One with a magnolia blossom motif and another featuring a prickly-pear cactus complete with the hot-pink fruit. Finally, I reached the one Brigit had tried to pull out.

Oh my gosh! Though this quilt was big enough for a queen-sized bed, it bore beautiful bluebonnets, just like the baby's blanket.

I looked down at Brigit. Had she smelled familiar scents on the quilt? Is that why she'd alerted on it? I had no idea why she'd dragged me over here to show me the blanket. But I was darn glad she had.

I reached into my pocket and pulled out a liver treat. "Good job, Brigit!" I fed her the treat with one hand, while stroking her head with the other. "Good job!"

I pulled up the photo of the baby on my phone and compared the handiwork to the blanket in front of me. *It's identical.* Could it be a crazy coincidence? Or had the person who'd crafted this quilt simply used the same pattern as the person who'd made the baby's blanket? Maybe the person who'd sewn the cry for help into the trim wasn't the baby's mother as I'd thought. Maybe the baby's mother or father had simply bought a quilt here for their child, and the cry for help stitched into it was unrelated to the baby. Still, that would mean someone inside the compound needed help.

I picked up the blanket and thoroughly checked the trim. No words. No symbols. Nothing was stitched into the fabric. I examined a couple of the other quilts. Their trim bore no symbols or words, either.

I carried it over to the sales clerk. "I didn't see a sign on these quilts. Do you know who made this?"

"I don't know exactly who made that quilt," she said, "but I get them from a church group down the road. The women there make the quilts and I sell them on consignment."

My heart bump-bump-bumped in my chest. "A church?" I repeated. "Are you talking about the People of Peace?"

"If that's the one by the lake, then yes."

It took everything in me not to throw a victorious fist in the air and yell "Woo-hoo!" *I was right! The symbol hastily stitched on the blanket was a clue!*

She continued. "They're not Amish, but they're something like that. Quakers, maybe?" She shrugged.

"So you've met the women who make the quilts?"

"Only one of them," she replied. "Older woman, seventy or so."

Despite the Bible story about Sarah giving birth to Isaac when she was ninety, miracles were rare. Barring a modern-day immaculate conception, there was no chance the woman was the baby's mother. But could she be her grandmother?

"The woman comes by first thing every Monday morning with a younger man to collect their percentage and drops off new quilts and whatnot."

"Whatnot?" I repeated. "What's the whatnot?"

She pointed to the candle display. "The same group makes the candles. The men from the church make the candleholders and the rocking chairs that are on display out front. You might've noticed them on your way in. Everything they make is very well crafted." She looked up, leaned toward me across the counter, and whispered as if to keep God from overhearing her next words. "That church group has made me a small fortune, I tell you what." She stood up straight again, speaking at normal volume. "They make jams and jellies, too, but I can't sell those."

"Why not?"

"Because of the Texas Cottage Food Law. It allows sales of edible, small-batch food products, but only at farm stands, farmer's markets, or county fairs, that type of thing. To be sold retail, food items have to comply with FDA labeling requirements and other regulations."

Food regulation was generally handled by the health inspectors rather than the police department, so I wasn't familiar with the law. But she'd given me some interesting information to ponder. Of course I wanted to know more. "The people who bring you the stuff," I said, "do you happen to know their names?"

"I'm sure they told me at some point." She looked up in thought. "I can't remember the woman's name, but the guy could be Elijah or Ezra. Or maybe it was Zachariah or Zebediah? All I know for sure is that it was something old-fashioned and biblical sounding like that. But, like I said, the man's not exactly a talker. Neither is the woman. They're all business."

There could be a Zachariah or Zebediah at the

property, but I had a sneaking suspicion it might be Jebediah, the guy who'd come to the gate when we'd visited the property yesterday.

The woman cocked her head, her eyes narrowed. "Why are you asking? You're not going to try to buy direct from them, are you?"

"And cut out your profit? I wouldn't dream of it." I offered her a smile. "I'm on the PTA at my kid's school." Suddenly I had a child. Looked like there'd been an immaculate conception, after all. Or at least an immaculate *de*ception. "We've got a fall festival coming up and we're looking for vendors. I thought maybe the church would want to buy a booth." Actually, I'd landed an overtime gig next month working security at a fall festival, but the event made a convenient and easy excuse for my questions.

"I'd give you their contact information if I had it," the woman said. "But they've never given me a phone number or e-mail address. I'm not sure they even have a telephone or computer at their place. They seem to live simply from what I can tell."

Simple life or not, it was impossible to get by without some source of income. I now knew how the People of Peace earned money to pay for the things they couldn't produce themselves, like their vehicles and gasoline. Unfortunately, the information didn't seem to lead anywhere.

"At any rate," the woman said, "if you want that quilt, you better buy it now. Those bluebonnet ones always sell fast."

"As much as I like it," I told her, "I can't afford it right now. Maybe next payday."

"Sure." She took it from me. "I'll put it back for you."

I purchased the two candles and candleholders, thanked the woman, and led Brigit back to the cruiser.

"Good girl!" I ruffled her head and gave her three more liver treats for her exceptional performance. Of course I realized that she'd probably alerted on the familiar smell precisely because she'd hoped to earn the treats, and that a K-9 who gave false alerts could become problematic. But at the moment, I was thrilled she'd led me to what could be a very valuable clue.

Once I was seated, I phoned Detective Jackson and told her about the bluebonnet blanket I'd found at the store. "The salesperson confirmed that the blanket was made by a woman belonging to the People of Peace."

"Nice work, Megan," she said. "That's good evidence linking the baby to the church. Unfortunately, it's not enough. The magistrate won't issue a search warrant until we have some evidence indicating a crime has been committed."

"But we can't get evidence a crime has been committed unless we get into the compound!" If only we could get into the compound, we could talk to the baby's mother and find out if she'd been abused or threatened, if the cry of help was for herself.

Jackson sighed. "Yep. It's a vicious circle."

Vicious circle indeed.

On the drive back to the precinct, I made a stop at one of the flea markets on my route. Figured I might as well check things out. A few of Felicia Bloomquist's neighbors had found the business cards I'd left at their doors and since given me a call, but none of them had seen anything suspicious. If I was going to find the burglar, it looked like I'd have to be a little more proactive.

Brigit and I strode up and down the rows of vendor

booths, looking for any that sold the same makeup, jewelry, and clothing lines pedaled by Felicia Bloomquist.

As we made our way up the third aisle, my eyes spotted a table bearing silver and copper jewelry from the Manhattan Metals line. A woman wearing a half-dozen pieces from the catalog sat behind the table. She treated me and Brigit to a smile. "Hi, there."

I returned the greeting. "Thought my partner and I would do a little shopping on our lunch hour."

She stood from her seat. "See something you like?"

"This one's nice." I picked up a copper cuff bracelet and slid it onto my wrist.

"That looks great on you!" she gushed. "And it comes with a matching necklace and earrings."

She didn't know it, but I was much more interested in her than I was the jewelry.

I returned the bracelet to the table and feigned nonchalance as I picked through several pairs of earrings displayed on a swatch of black velvet. "Been selling jewelry long?"

"Couple of years," she said. "Got tired of working for the man and decided to be my own boss."

I picked up a pair of silver earrings engraved with hearts. "These are cute. I have twin sisters who would love them. Got another pair?"

She shook her head. "Not on hand, but I can order you a second set. It only takes two to three days for them to arrive."

"Darn," I replied. "Their birthday is tomorrow. I don't want to be late with a gift."

The look of disappointment on her face gave me a twinge of guilt.

"I'll think about them for Christmas. Do you have a card or brochure I can take with me?"

If she had no such cards or brochures, she could be the thief. If she did, she was probably innocent.

She bent down and reached under her table. When she pulled her hand back, it contained a sales catalog with her business card stapled to it. She handed it to me. "You can order online if you like. My link is listed on my card."

"Thanks."

Brigit and I ventured up and down the remaining aisles, but saw no one else selling any of Felicia's brands. We returned to our beat for the remainder of the afternoon. Though we cruised by the People of Peace property again at the end of our shift, nothing unusual caught my eye. Was the baby's mother inside, missing her child? Was she inside, but relieved that she'd been able to surrender her baby to someone who would be better able to care for it? Or was I off base here and the mother somewhere else entirely?

Would I ever have some answers?

TWENTY-ONE
TRICK OR TREAT

Brigit

It had been a long shot. But it had paid off.

Megan hadn't asked her to trail anyone today. But when Brigit's nose picked up the smell of the same man she'd scented when her partner had ordered her to trail from the fire station a few days earlier, the dog thought she might earn a treat by pointing out that his smell was on a blanket in the store. Megan hadn't given her just one treat, but four. *Score!*

Brigit had caught whiffs of him as they'd driven near the lake, too. He smelled of cedar and sweat and his own unique human odor. But that was then and this was now. Now they were home and Megan was opening a can of dog food in the kitchen for Brigit's dinner. She put her paws on the counter and wagged her tail in encouragement. *Hurry up! I'm hungry!*

Megan dumped the contents of the can into her bowl and placed it on the floor. "Chow time."

Yum!

TWENTY-TWO
THE WAGES OF SIN

The Father

When morning prayer circle concluded Wednesday morning, he proceeded to his office at the church to look over the paperwork Jeb had left for him. He took a seat at his desk and ran his eyes over the bank statement and the records from their sales at the farmer's market and the country store down the road. They'd taken in two thousand dollars less this quarter, and the preceding one had been down a grand from the one before that.

That whore's sins have cost me.

Sister Juliette's pregnancy had not been an easy one. After the third time she hadn't made it to the door and heaved her half-digested breakfast in the dining hall garbage can, he'd ordered her to take her meals alone in the sisters' quarters. Her headaches and exhaustion had slowed her down, too. She'd produced only a fraction of her usual output of quilts and it was reflected in the bank balance. Those bluebonnet blankets were her specialty, and they always sold quickly. Hell, if he'd thought about it, he should have kept the one she'd made for her baby. They could've gotten a hundred bucks for it.

It wasn't just her labor he'd lost, either. Having the men keep watch in the deer blinds kept them away from their woodworking and the metal forge.

Bitch cops and their bitch dog. The blanket of deception he'd so carefully weaved all these years now had a loose thread, and could unravel if he didn't handle things the right way. There was nothing illegal about dropping a baby at a fire station. So why did they keep driving by? Were they still looking for that girl in the photo? He'd looked online but hadn't found anything about a missing girl. Of course the police department treated runaways differently than kids who'd been abducted. They didn't issue alerts and put their photos on the news.

Maybe he was overreacting. He wasn't slipping, was he?

He sat up straight. *Of course not.*

He turned back to the numbers on the page before him. That whore had cost him enough. It was time to get her out of the silo and put her back to work.

TWENTY-THREE
CREATIVE PURSUITS

Megan

The magistrate judge hadn't budged on the search warrant. No surprise there, but nonetheless I was disappointed and disheartened. If someone needed help, I wanted to provide it.

As Brigit and I patrolled our beat Wednesday morning, my mind worked overtime, trying to find a creative way to get into the church compound to search for the baby's mother. Only if we found her could we learn her true intention when she stitched the cry for help into the baby blanket. Had she been abused or threatened? Was she being held against her will? Or had she simply wanted someone else to help the baby she was unable to care for? Not knowing was like having a team of hungry rats gnawing their way through my gut.

I stopped at a red light. An H&R Block location sat in the small strip center to my left, taking my mind back to a case at the Shoppes at Chisholm Trail mall. A special agent with the Internal Revenue Service Criminal Investigations had worked undercover at one of the stores, hoping to nab one of the owners for tax evasion. She'd let me know she was there in case the poop hit the fan and things got out of hand. I remembered her telling me that other law enforcement agencies often pulled the IRS into their investigations, because when someone committed a crime that resulted in financial gain, the culprit very often failed to report their ill-gotten income on their tax forms. The agent, Tara Holloway, had also been involved in a high-profile tax fraud case against a well-known televangelist from Dallas. I didn't know much about tax law, especially how it applied—or *didn't* apply—to churches, but if the People of Peace wasn't properly reporting, maybe a tax investigation could give us a back door into the compound.

I pulled into the strip center, parked, and phoned Detective Jackson and told her my idea. "What do you think?"

"I think it's worth a quick phone call to the IRS," she said. "Can't hurt."

When we hung up, I found Agent Holloway in my contacts list and tapped the screen to place the call. She answered on the second ring. "Hello, Officer Luz. How are you?"

"At a dead end. I'm hoping you might be able to help me, Agent Holloway."

"Actually, it's Pratt now," she said. "I got married."

"Congratulations!" I told her the reason for my call. "We need some grounds for getting into the compound and taking a look around. I realize I'm probably grasping at straws here, but figured it was worth a shot." If treasury agents gained legal access to the compound, local police could go in with them for protection. I'd be able to take a look around for clues.

"I'll take a look at their tax records," she said. "If there appears to be a basis for launching an investigation, I'll let you know."

"Much appreciated. Let me know if I can ever return the favor."

My partner and I had been patrolling another half hour when a man wearing khakis and a button-down flagged me down from his driveway in the Ryan Place neighborhood.

I pulled over and rolled down my window. "Can I help you, sir?"

"I hope so," he said. "Someone tried to break into my car last night."

A Ford Flex sat in his driveway, but the vehicle showed no obvious signs of damage, at least not from this distance. I rolled down the cruiser's back windows for Brigit, cut the engine, and climbed out of the car. "Show me what you've got."

A small dog in the yard next door peeked through a knothole on the fence, spotted me, and began barking up a storm. *Yip-yip-yip!*

Brigit talked back to loudmouth. *Woof!*

The man led me over to the driver's window. Now that I was closer, I could see the window bore a crack near the top. There was also a small notch in the rubber trim near the top of the crack.

Yip-yip-yip!

"See that crack?" the man said. "It wasn't there when I left the car in the driveway last night. There's fingerprints all over the glass, too."

Yip-yip!

I bent over to inspect the glass. Sure enough, the morning sun showed a number of prints near the top of the glass. The evidence pointed to someone using a tool to try to force the window down. Why the thief hadn't finished the job was unclear. Maybe he feared he'd been spotted and aborted his malevolent mission.

Yip! Yip-yip!

I angled my head toward the neighbor's fence to indicate the dog. "You've got a good watchdog over there. Any chance something set him off last night?"

"Yes," the man said. "'Round two in the morning he started barking up a storm. I switched on my lights and was about to come outside when he got quiet. I guess my neighbor brought him inside."

"The dog was probably trying to warn you that someone was out here," I said. "He probably scared the burglar off."

As if to confirm my conclusion, the dog issued another *Yip!*

My focus shifted to the vehicle's interior. A garage door remote hung from the visor in clear view.

I stood up. "We've had multiple reports of garage-door remotes being stolen from cars. In at least one of the cases, the thief returned and used the remote to get into the garage and steal property. It would be a good idea to start locking your opener in your glove box."

I pulled out my pen and pad of paper, and jotted down the salient information. Victim's name. Address. The date. "I'll see about getting a crime scene tech out here to lift a print. Maybe it will match someone in the system." I tucked the pad back into my pocket and handed him my business card.

"Thanks." The man turned and headed back into his house.

My cell phone wriggled in my pocket. I retrieved it to find a one-word text from Seth. *Lunch?*

I texted him back. *Noon? Spiral Diner?*

He replied with *See you then* and the kissy-face emoji.

When twelve o'clock drew near, I dropped Brigit at home and drove on to the restaurant, which was only a short drive away. Seth's Nova was already in the parking lot. I joined him in the foyer. A few minutes later, we were seated at a booth, perusing our menus.

After we placed our orders with the waiter, Seth eyed me across the table. "I took your suggestion about inviting my grandfather's army buddies to visit. Harry and Leonard. They were tank mechanics with him. They're flying in Friday night."

"Fantastic!" Maybe a visit with his old buddies would take Ollie back to better times, before the weight of the war crushed his spirit.

While I was jubilant, Seth was less enthusiastic. "My mom and I aren't sure it won't backfire. You never know with that old coot."

"If things go south," I told him, "feel free to tell your grandfather it was my idea. I'll take the blame."

"That was already our plan." He shot me a wink to let me know he was joking.

We were halfway through our meal when my phone bleeped. The readout indicated it was IRS Special Agent Tara Pratt calling me back.

I accepted the call. "Hi, Tara. Any luck?"

"Sorry," she said, "but no. I can't share detailed information about the People of Peace account, but their tax records appear complete and correct. In fact, the church was audited last year and came through with flying colors. They've paid all of the unrelated business income tax due on their sales. They use a reputable CPA firm to prepare their tax reports. Nothing raised any red flags."

"Darn." I'd been hoping there'd be some reason to suspect tax fraud. A tax investigation could allow law enforcement to sneak in the back door at the compound, so to speak. Unfortunately, a little thing called the U.S. Constitution prevented law enforcement from faking charges without grounds. I thanked Tara. "I appreciate you looking into things for me."

"No problem. Take care."

I ended the call and groaned. "Sometimes I think the abandoned-baby case is a lost cause. Maybe I'll never know if the mother is okay."

"First responders can't save everyone," he said, solemnly. "I know that as well as anyone."

"Detective Jackson told me the same thing." I had to accept that I couldn't help everybody, I had to learn to let things go. But how could I let this go when a woman, a mother no less, might be in trouble?

We finished our meal in quiet contemplation and parted with a quick kiss in the parking lot.

"Be careful out there," Seth called as he unlocked the door on his Nova.

"Right back at ya."

I rounded up Brigit from the house and we resumed our patrol. The rest of day was as futile as the morning had been. *Ugh.*

We were meandering our way back to the station

near the end of our shift when a call came in about a car accident a few blocks away. When none of my fellow officers took the call, I reluctantly retrieved my mic. "Officer Luz and Brigit responding."

Auto accidents were no fun to work. They could be quite time-consuming. The drivers often got into arguments over whose fault the accident was, and if someone had been injured there could be blood and gore. *Eek.*

As I drew near the accident scene, I saw plenty of gore. *Or should I say gourds?* The intersection was covered in the carnage of what would have become dozens of jack-o'-lanterns had they not lost their lives here today. Chunks of orange-colored rind lay everywhere among gooey guts of stringy, seedy pulp. Humpty Dumpty might have taken a great fall, but he wasn't alone when it came to farm products.

From the positions of the vehicles, I surmised that the large SUV had run a red light and T-boned the vegetable truck, which had been loaded with pumpkins on their way to a grocery store or another location. Adding insult to injury, the driver behind the truck had then rear-ended it.

As I turned on my lights and pulled up to the scene, a Ford Fiesta entered the intersection and slid on the goop, spinning out and popping up over the curb on the other side.

Now I've seen everything.

I pressed the button on my shoulder-mounted radio. "I need backup and a street cleaning crew," I informed dispatch. "We're going to have to close this intersection down."

An hour later, and forty-five minutes after our shift was supposed to have ended, Brigit and I finished up at the crash site and headed home for the day.

Thursday morning, I set out for the property bright and early. As I crested the rise, I saw three men down below exiting the gate. One carried fishing poles and a tackle box. The other two were at either end of a lightweight aluminum rowboat. Looked like they planned to do some early-morning fishing.

I rolled on past them and circled through the park, passing them again on my way back out. The trio cast glances in my direction. I raised a hand in a friendly greeting and forced a smile. Though they waved back, their gestures were halfhearted at best. They didn't seem to have much interest in interacting with those of us in the real world, least of all someone who represented the worst it had to offer—crime and violence.

We returned to our patrol. Later that morning, a call came in from the crime scene tech who'd lifted prints from the vehicle in Ryan Place. I pulled to the curb to take the call.

"We didn't get a match," she said. "Whoever tried to force their way into the car doesn't have a record."

Perhaps I could change that. "Thanks for checking."

I called the victim to share the news. "The prints on your car's window didn't match anyone in the database. Sorry."

"Damn," he muttered. "It cost me two hundred dollars to replace the window and fix the rubber trim. Would've liked to stick that to him."

"Don't blame ya. If anything changes, I'll let you know."

I ended the call and sat back in my seat. Every investigation I was working seemed to be at a dead end. I eyed Brigit in the rearview mirror. "Are you as frustrated as I am?"

Apparently not. While she glanced up from the chew toy she was cleaning her teeth on, she didn't stop gnawing or express a scintilla of angst. *Oh, to be a dog. Living in the moment, so carefree.*

Friday brought my first break.

The man whose car window had been smashed and laptop stolen in Fairmount phoned me around ten in the morning. "This could be nothing," he said, "but a guy just came to the door claiming to be a magazine salesman. I had an early dentist appointment and took the day off. I parked my car in the garage so the driveway was empty. It probably looked like nobody was home. Anyway, I told him I wasn't interested, but if he wanted to leave a brochure I'd ask my wife and get back to him. He claimed he didn't have any brochures. I asked for his contact information, but he was evasive, just said he'd come back another time. He gave me a creepy feeling, like maybe he was checking to see if someone was home before he tried to get in with the remote. Of course he wouldn't have gotten far. We did what you said and manually locked the garage door."

The situation definitely sounded suspicious. "How long ago was this?"

"Just now," he said. "I'm upstairs watching out the window. The guy's headed south down the block. He's almost to the corner. He hasn't stopped at any other houses."

"What's he look like?"

"Skinny white guy with light brown hair. He's wearing a solid red shirt and jeans."

"Got it. My partner and I are on our way."

I switched on my flashers, but kept the siren off. No sense in warning the guy that I was coming. As I approached their street from the south, I kept my eyes peeled for someone on foot. All I saw was a female jogger clad in pink spandex. Just before the turn, my cruiser was passed by an older-model silver Suburban with rust around the edges. The passenger seat appeared empty, and a Latino man with brown skin and black hair sat at the wheel. *Not our guy.*

I took the corner and turned onto the street, but instead of stopping I made the block to see if I could spot the guy somewhere nearby. No such luck. He seemed to have disappeared.

I returned to the house, where I let Brigit out to stretch her legs. While she sniffed around at the end of her leash, I asked the man for more details.

"How tall would you say he was?"

"About my height," the man said. "Around five foot ten."

"Any distinguishing characteristics?" I asked.

"Is ugly a distinguishing characteristic?"

"It could be." I whipped out my pad and pen. "How, exactly, was he ugly?"

"Greasy hair and skin. Nose like raw meat. He had dingy teeth, like he hadn't brushed in a while. The whites of his eyes weren't white, either. They were yellow."

All of these signs told me he was likely a drug addict. Not unusual at all for a burglar. They tended to be unable to keep a steady job and resorted to stealing from others to pay their living expenses and fund their habits.

"I drove around a little before stopping here. I'd hoped to spot him but didn't notice anyone fitting his description. I'll cruise around a little more, see if he turns up. If so, I'll be back in touch."

"Thanks."

Brigit and I returned to the car and drove up and down the streets in a six-block radius. *Nothing.*

I pulled to the curb, fished Felicia Bloomquist's business card out of the pouch on my belt, and gave her a call.

"Hi, Miss Bloomquist," I said when she answered. "It's Officer Luz."

"Ready for that style consultation?"

Sheesh. "No. Just have some questions for you. Any chance you're home?"

"I am."

"Great. I'll be there shortly."

In just a few minutes, the cruiser rolled to a stop in front of Felicia's house. Brigit and I went to her door and spoke with her there.

"I just talked to one of the other victims," I told her. "He said a guy came to his house trying to sell him magazines. It's possible he was casing the place to break in. Did a magazine salesman come to your place before you were robbed?"

Her eyes popped wide. "Yes! A guy with a Spanish accent came by right when I was leaving to take the lipstick to my customer."

The other victim hadn't mentioned an accent. Was Felicia talking about a different person?

She continued. "I told the guy I might be interested

but didn't have time to talk because I was on my way
out. He said he could come back later, but I told him it
would be late by the time I got back." She gave herself
a slap to the head with her palm. "I'm such an idiot!"

"Don't be too hard on yourself," I said. "People do
things like that all the time. Honest folks don't think the
way criminals do." I took out my pad. "You mentioned
the guy who came to your door had a Spanish accent.
What did he look like?"

"He had brown skin and thick black hair," she said.
"His hair really needed a trim. It looked super sloppy."

"Was he tall? Short? Skinny? Heavy?"

She lifted one shoulder. "I'd say he was average-
sized all around."

"Clothing?"

"He was wearing a solid white polo shirt tucked into
his jeans. No belt. Brown heavy-duty work shoes with
yellow laces and thick soles. His shoes were scuffed
pretty badly. There wasn't much leather left on the tops
of the toes."

Leave it to a style consultant to notice the minute
details.

"Was anyone with him?" Her description didn't
match the one the man had given me. It was possible
the two suspects were in cahoots, taking turns approaching potential victims to make identifying them
more difficult.

"I didn't see anyone else," she said.

"What about a vehicle?"

She shook her head. "Didn't see a car, either. Seemed
like he was on foot. Of course I assumed he'd parked
somewhere on the street and was making his way up
and down the block, hitting up all my neighbors, too."

On a hunch, I asked, "Did you notice a silver Suburban parked nearby?"

"Not that I remember. But I was in a hurry and didn't pay much attention to anything."

I closed my pad and slid it back into my pocket. "Thanks for the information. If this leads anywhere, I'll let you know."

Friday evening, I rode with Seth and his mother out to the Dallas-Fort Worth airport to pick up Harry and Leonard. Harry was flying in from Florida, Leonard from Illinois. Luckily, their flights were scheduled to arrive only twenty minutes apart.

We had no idea what the two men looked like, so I'd written their names on opposite sides of a piece of paper we could hold up to catch their attention. As the passengers on the plane from Florida drifted into the baggage claim area, it was clear the sign had been unnecessary, at least where Harry was concerned. The tall, trim black man spotted Seth and aimed directly for us, calling out, "Holy Moses! You look just like your grandpa from back in the day."

He greeted all three of us with warm hugs before stepping back. "So Ollie's turned into an old grump, huh? That explains why I never heard from the so-and-so after I came back Stateside. I wrote him some letters, even tried to call him long-distance once back when it cost an arm and a leg. Nothing."

Lisa bit her lip. "My mother told me my father wasn't the same man when he came back from the war."

Harry snorted, though his voice was soft when he spoke. "Hell, honey. None of us were."

We stood in an awkward yet solemn silence for a

moment before he clapped his hands once and said, "Let's get my bag and round up Leonard."

He retrieved his suitcase from the belt and we moved en masse to the baggage claim carousel for Leonard's flight. Harry spotted him the second he came through the door and hollered, "Leonard! You look as stupid as ever!"

Leonard was a white man with a bald head, a gray beard, and a round belly that hung over the waistband of his pants. "Takes one idiot to know another!" His face broke into a grin as he rushed forward and grabbed Leonard in a warm embrace that turned into a jovial wrestling match, ending when Harry took Leonard down in a headlock.

When Harry released him, Leonard stood and asked, "How's Mabel? She still putting up with you?"

"Hoo." Harry shook his head. "My old lady got *old*."

The smile on his face said he didn't mind it one bit, that he'd enjoyed growing old with her. Too bad Ollie hadn't had the chance to grow old with Ruth, Seth's grandmother and Lisa's mother. If she'd lived longer, maybe he would have eventually come back around.

"What about Sheila?" Harry asked Leonard.

"She got old, too!" he said.

Harry cocked his head. "Think we did?"

Leonard waved a dismissive hand. "Hell, no. We're still kids."

The five of us made our way out to the parking garage and piled into Seth's Nova.

Harry looked around at the interior of the car. "Bench seats. The smell of vinyl. This car takes me back. I bought an Impala right after I got home from the war that was a lot like this. Should've hung on to it."

"You could buy one and rebuild it," Seth suggested.

"That's a thought."

We aimed for Fort Worth and pulled into the driveway at the Rutledge house a half hour later.

Lisa cast a nervous glance at me and Seth. "How should we handle this?"

Before either of us could respond, Leonard said, "Me and Harry will go to the door. Let's see if Ollie recognizes us."

All of us exited the car. While the two older men headed to the front door, Seth, Lisa, and I hung back by the car.

Both Harry and Leonard put their knuckles to the door and rapped loudly. When nobody answered, they knocked again, louder and more insistently. Shortly thereafter, Ollie yanked the door open, his other hand on his rolling oxygen tank, the tubes hanging from his nose.

"Stop that damn bang—!" He stopped shouting midword and his mouth fell open. He looked from Leonard to Harry, speechless. A small panic had just begun to well up in me when Ollie threw up his arms and clasped both men firmly by the shoulders. "You sons of bitches!" he cried with glee, an openmouthed smile lighting up his face. "What the hell are you doing here?"

They gestured in our direction.

"Your grandson invited us for a visit," Leonard said. "Paid for our plane tickets and everything."

"That's right," Harry added. "He said you could use a good time." He raised his palms to his sides. "Who better to provide a good time than yours truly?"

"I know that's right!" Ollie let loose with a heartfelt chuckle.

Before we knew what was happening, the men had disappeared inside, the screen door slamming shut behind them with a loud *whap!*

Lisa and Seth exchanged looks.

Seth's brows rose in disbelief. "I don't think I've ever seen him smile before."

Lisa shook her head slowly, similarly incredulous. "And I've definitely never heard him laugh."

"Well," I said, "there's a first time for everything."

I only hoped the smile and laugh Ollie offered tonight would be the first of many.

TWENTY-FOUR
DOUBLE DATE

Brigit

While Megan and Seth sat together on the couch, watching a movie on TV, Brigit and Blast tangled on the rug. She grabbed one of his back legs in her mouth and flipped him over onto his back.

She had him now.

Before he could get out of the vulnerable position, she jumped on top of him and took his throat in her teeth. Had this been a real fight, she would've ripped his throat out right then and there. But since they were only playing, she mouthed him gently while he wriggled underneath her, trying to get free. Though she knew she could keep Blast pinned to the rug, it was more fun when there was some give and take. She released her hold and allowed him to get up, then let him take her down this time.

On her back now, Brigit looked up at the couch. She saw that Seth and Megan were play-fighting, too. Seth had his mouth on Megan's neck. But instead of fighting back like she was supposed to, Megan was just letting him bite her. She didn't know how to play right, how to defend herself. Good thing Megan had Brigit around to keep her safe.

TWENTY-FIVE
MERCIFUL ME

The Father

It was near midnight and full dark when Zeke opened the silo door and Emmanuel shone his flashlight inside. The beam revealed Juliette lying on her cot. She put up a hand to block the glare and sat up, but made no move to rush the door and escape. *Good. Maybe the slut had learned a thing or two in here.*

Keeping the beam locked on her, Emmanuel stepped to the doorway. "Can you behave as God would have you?"

Lit up like a Broadway actress in a tragedy, she nodded and softly said, "Yes. I can."

He lowered the flashlight so that it shined on the ground at her feet. "Then you may return to the flock."

She slowly stood and stiffly shuffled toward him. He stepped back to allow her outside. As she passed him, he thrust a small ceramic urn at her.

She looked down at it, hesitating. "What is that?"

"Your child," he said. "Ashes to ashes, dust to dust."

Staring down at the vessel, she burst into silent,

shoulder-shaking sobs. After a few seconds, she took the urn, clutching it to her chest.

"You may spread her ashes in the garden if you like," he said. *Or you can shove 'em where the sun don't shine for all I care.* Fortunately, the ash didn't smell too much like the cedar and mesquite logs he'd burned in the dining hall's fireplace to produce them. Tossing some lighter fluid on them had been a good idea, ensured the wood had burned completely.

Juliette nodded and sniffled loudly.

"Everyone has missed you," Emmanuel said, "especially the sisters. They'd love to have you join them in the sewing circle again after breakfast tomorrow. I'm sure you're eager to get things back to normal."

As for himself, he was eager to get his bank balance back up where it should be. He turned to Zeke. "Take her to the infirmary. She can sleep there tonight and go back to the women's quarters tomorrow evening."

As the two headed off, he felt a smug satisfaction. *I'm back in control.*

He remembered the first time he'd felt that heady rush of power. It was over thirty years ago, when he'd been only a few years older, but so much wiser, than Juliette.

Emmanuel had been the seventh of thirteen children, the fourth boy, born Philip Peter Swafford in central Mississippi to Southern Baptist parents who had heeded God's command in Genesis 1:28. *Be fruitful and multiply.* Given that his parents didn't drink, dance, or play cards—such activities were the devil's doing—Emmanuel supposed there'd been nothing else for his parents to do come Saturday nights but work on their multiplication.

Having no formal training but being handy with a hammer, Philip Peter's father took what work he could find as a handyman. His earnings kept the family fed—barely—but left nothing for luxuries or even some of the basic necessities. Young Philip Peter was small for his age, a condition emphasized by the fact that he had to wear his older brothers' well-worn and ill-fitting hand-me-down clothes, earning him the scorn of his only slightly better dressed classmates, who not-so-affectionately dubbed him "Pee-Pee."

When he wasn't in school, Philip Peter had been forced to go along on jobs with his father. Helping his father repair drywall, replace rotten boards, and install toilets had taught the young boy a lot, primarily that he did not enjoy manual labor. *He'd go to hell before he'd follow in his father's footsteps.* No, he planned to go to trade school, maybe even college, and land a job that paid enough that he could finally afford all the material things that had been denied to him in his childhood. A color television. A car. Shoes that nobody else had worn before him.

He'd experienced a growth spurt during his junior year of high school, shooting up five inches seemingly overnight, his once-bare face now sprouting dark, manly hair he'd had to shave every other day. The angelic redhead he'd had a crush on since kindergarten finally noticed him, sending a shy smile his way as they sat in English class. With Philip Peter's new stature came just enough confidence to return the smile. The girl passed him a note, invited him to come to a jubilee at the Church of the Holy Star, an independent, nondenominational church where her father preached. He'd been thrilled that she'd wanted to spend time in his company. He hadn't realized at the time that that one note, that invitation, would change his life forever.

At that jubilee, he'd heard the girl's father preach. To his surprise, it wasn't all hellfire and brimstone, the fare of fear offered at the Southern Baptist church his parents dragged him and his siblings to. On the contrary, Pastor Ray acknowledged that, while God was an all-powerful being with high expectations of his people, God could also be loving and accepting and provide a refuge from a cruel world where children were forced to work as soon as they were old enough to hold a hammer, to go to bed with a half-empty belly in a cramped and cold room with seven siblings, and be called "Pee-Pee" by their peers.

Finally, Philip Peter had found a warm, welcoming home.

He'd found a second, and much more attentive, father, too. Pastor Ray took a shine to the eager young man, and taught him everything he knew about God, theology, and the Bible, assigning him tasks around the church, preparing him to serve as an assistant pastor. Little did Pastor Ray know that the young man he was mentoring was watching his every move, learning how to be even more charismatic, how to seduce people with words and promises of better things to come.

Philip Peter had not only learned some new things about religion under Pastor Ray's tutelage, but he'd also learned some things about himself during that time. He'd learned that, while he could make a decent living as the plumber he'd become after completing the community college program, the material things he'd once longed for and now owned failed to provide the satisfaction he'd expected. He'd learned that the respect and adulation of the fellow congregants felt far more gratifying.

The others were impressed by his ability to quote the perfect scripture for every occasion, from happy to solemn to tragic. They sought his guidance on everything from child-raising to marital matters, as if he were some sort of guru. For the first time in his life, he was in control, not only of his own life, but of other people's as well.

And he reveled in it.

When Pastor Ray took his family and a portion of the church on a mission trip to Mexico for a month in the summer of 1987, Philip Peter stayed behind and seized the occasion to separate the most devoted and needy from among the flock. He combined the disparate but equally effective styles of the Southern Baptist preacher and Pastor Ray, offering his own unique blend of spirituality. He preached increasingly factious sermons over the four weeks, insisting that those who truly loved the Lord had been called, along with him, to live in a newer, better, purer way.

By the time Pastor Ray returned, his congregation had been torn apart, plundered by the young man he'd trusted to tend to his flock while he was away.

Philip Peter, under his newly assumed name Father Emmanuel, led his followers to a new life in Texas, one funded by the donations of their cash and sale of their property. He left behind what remained of the Church of the Holy Star, as well as the preacher's daughter he'd deflowered after making empty promises of marriage and children he had no intention of fathering. His younger siblings had been nothing but pains in the ass to him, more competitors for what little food was on the table, more brats his parents expected him to look after on occasion. Why would he want to tie himself to one woman and bring children into his life when he could live free on his own terms?

Twenty-eight people had come with him from Mississippi to Texas at the end of that summer, and dubbed themselves the People of Peace. Over the years, they'd fixed up the old camp they'd purchased and taken in more folks on a trial basis. Father Emmanuel carefully chose whom he allowed permanently into the fold, turning out those who didn't pass his tests of devotion and deference. They numbered just over a hundred and fifty souls now, a strong yet manageable number.

And he reigned over them all.

TWENTY-SIX
IN A JAM

Megan

I wasn't on the work schedule for the police department on Saturday, but I wasn't going to let a little thing like not being on official duty and earning no pay keep me from doing my job. The abandoned baby had become an obsession for me. It had been over a week since the cute little thing had been left at the fire station. In the meantime, what might have happened to the person who'd stitched the cry for help into the baby's quilt? I was almost afraid to think about it. Then again, thinking about it motivated me to keep going until I had some definitive answers. If there was any chance a woman was in jeopardy, I was going to save her. To hell with those fairy tales in which the damsels in distress waited for a prince to save them. We women would work together to save ourselves.

I planned to leave Brigit at home today. She'd earned a day off. Besides, I wanted to spy incognito today. As many times as Brigit and I had cruised by the compound in my squad car, we could be raising suspicions within the People of Peace. Better for them not to know I was keeping a close watch.

Frankie was already awake, sitting in her pajamas at the table and drinking coffee, when I wandered into the kitchen at just a few minutes after seven. I wasn't surprised she was up. Working rotating shifts as we both did screws with your biorhythms.

She ran her eyes over me, taking in the fact that I was already dressed in jeans and a light sweater. "Going somewhere?"

"I'm going to spy on the cult compound," I told her as I pulled the canister of oats from the cabinet to make a quick bowl of oatmeal. "Thought I'd try to be less conspicuous today." I pulled out a pot and filled it with water. "What's on your agenda for the day? Got some time you can spare?"

"I've got derby practice at four," she said. "I'm free until then."

"Want to come with me?" I asked. It couldn't hurt to have another set of eyes check out the place. Maybe she'd notice something I didn't. Besides, it would be nice to have human company. Brigit was a great partner and a good companion, but our conversations tended to be very one-sided.

Frankie shrugged. "Sure. Why not?"

We ate breakfast and soon we were heading to the compound in Frankie's Nissan Juke. Though her car was red, it was still less conspicuous than my two-seater Smart Car. She'd generously allowed me to drive.

As we were going up the hill that overlooked the church property, a white Chevy pickup hauling a flatbed trailer crested it, coming from the opposite direction. *There'd been a white Chevy pickup in the compound, hadn't there?* At this distance, all I could tell was that there were two people in the cab. But as it drove past, I caught a glimpse of the man at the wheel. He had a long face, a snub nose, and sunken cheeks, just like the man in the police sketch.

Oh my God. Is it him? The man who abandoned the baby?

I hooked a U-turn as soon as we were over the hill where he wouldn't be able to see us in his rearview mirror.

"Whoa!" With her right hand Frankie held on to the dash for dear life, her left hand bracing against the ceiling. "Give a girl some warning next time!"

"Sorry!" I cried as I careened across the gravel shoulder and back onto the asphalt. "The guy who dropped the baby just drove by in that truck. At least I think it's him."

"So we're going to follow him?"

"Yes. I want to see where he goes." I reached into my purse, retrieved my binoculars, and handed them to Frankie. "Keep an eye on him with these. I can't get too close or he'll be on to us."

"Gotcha." She took the binoculars from me, removed them from the case, and put them to her eyes.

I slowed for a few seconds to put some space between our car and the truck before driving up the backside of the hill. The truck had about a quarter-mile lead on us by that point, far enough that they might not spot us behind them, yet close enough that we could follow their movements.

"What's on the trailer?" I asked.

"A couple of wooden benches and rocking chairs,"

she said. "There's some wooden crates, too, but I can't tell what's in them."

We tracked them for several turns before they headed onto Highway 377 toward Granbury. Fortunately, this road was more heavily traveled, and we could blend in more easily.

Frankie lowered the binoculars. "How far are we going to follow them?"

Theoretically, they could drive as far as the southern tip of Argentina from here, but I doubted that was their plan. "They sell their furniture to the public," I told Frankie. "They're probably taking it to a store in Granbury."

Granbury was a quaint town, with an old-timey square and a half-dozen bed-and-breakfasts that brought weekend tourists in from around the metroplex. It would be the perfect place to sell handmade furniture.

We trailed them until they took an exit down Fall Creek Highway. Just before entering town, they pulled off onto a smaller paved road where dozens of people were setting up tables and canopies to sell their wares. A sign near the road announced FARMERS MARKET TODAY 8 TO NOON.

"Let's give them time to set up," I said, "then we'll go check things out."

I drove past and continued on into town, where we parked and waited for half an hour, chatting and catching up. Despite the fact that we lived together, the two of us were often like ships that passed in the night, rarely home together and, even if we were, rarely both awake at the same time. I told her about Ollie's old army buddies coming to visit, and she told me about a new recruit on the Fort Worth Whoop-Ass derby team.

"She puts me to shame," Frankie said.

"I doubt that." I'd seen Frankie play multiple times. She was incredibly fast and agile, the star of her team.

"It's true," Frankie insisted. "She skates at the speed of sound. At our last bout, she made a sonic boom."

"Well," I said, "there's nothing wrong with being second-best."

"Says the woman who's bound and determined to make detective in the shortest time possible." She rolled her eyes and cut me a knowing look.

"Okay," I acquiesced. "There's nothing wrong with *you* being second-best."

We shared a chuckle.

Once we thought we'd given it long enough, we drove back to the farmer's market. Cars streamed into the parking lot, shoppers eager to get there early for the best selection of fruits, vegetables, and other merchandise. We parked and headed toward the booths. I had never been face-to-face with the man who'd left the baby, but I realized that Jebediah or Father Emmanuel might have described the cop who'd come to the gate to him. Still, I was probably unrecognizable. My long hair was down today, rather than up in the tight bun I wore while on duty. I also had much more makeup on, and had purposely avoided wearing anything in dark blue. My jeans were faded and my sweater was a soft lavender color that coordinated with my tennis shoes. Perhaps Personal Style Consultant Felicia Bloomquist would approve of this outfit?

There was a mere hint of fall in the air this morning

as Frankie and I passed bin after bin of sweet potatoes, okra, onions, peppers, and zucchini. I stopped at a booth and selected four large sweet potatoes to purchase. They'd make a good side dish. Frankie, in turn, bought a loaf of fresh banana bread. I also stopped at a booth selling homemade dog biscuits and bought three of the largest size for Brigit.

"There they are," I whispered to Frankie as I spotted the man from the truck. He stood under a portable vinyl canopy, speaking with an older couple who were examining one of the wooden rockers. As the men spoke, the woman plunked her sizable butt down in the chair and tested the thing out, going so far as to swing her legs upward to see just how far the thing would go. I half expected her to cry "Wheee!" Though he was turned sideways and I could only see his profile, it was clear the man selling the furniture was the same man in the police sketch, the same one from the fire station video.

As we approached the booth, I noticed a thirtyish woman in what appeared to be a handmade dress sitting at a table on the other side of the furniture display. A knit shawl was draped about her shoulders. Though a ribbon tied at the back of her neck attempted to tame her coarse hair, it bushed out around her makeup-free face. She must have been the second person in the truck. On the tabletop in front of her were mason jars filled with jams, jellies, and fruit preserves in shades ranging from orange to red to blue. The hand-dipped candles and candleholders were displayed, as well, along with silverware and napkin holders similar to the ones I'd seen in the bait shop. Folded quilts hung on two wooden racks behind her.

Could she be the baby's mother? Hard to say with her belly hidden behind the table.

Frankie and I ventured up to her display in what I hoped was a nonchalant manner. Difficult to feel inconspicuous when your heart is beating a thousand times a minutes and your body temperature is up ten degrees.

I eyed the labels on the jellies. After speaking with the woman at the country store, I'd researched the Texas Cottage Food law and learned that the products required a label including the common name of the product, the name and address of the food operation, a statement that the kitchen was not inspected by government health inspectors, and a statement disclosing whether the product contained any common allergens such as nuts, milk, or eggs. Interestingly, while the labels on these blueberry, raspberry, and peach products reflected the address of the church compound, they did not identify the People of Peace as the name of the food operation. Rather, the label identified the producer as Mary Seeger. It seemed that the People of Peace were trying to remain under the radar, to draw as little attention to themselves as possible.

I gave the woman a smile. "Are you Mary?"

She smiled back and nodded.

"I'm having a hard time deciding," I told her. "They all look good."

She stood from the folding chair she'd been sitting on and I surreptitiously glanced at her abdomen. Though the dress she wore wasn't tight, it was fitted enough for me to see she had no telltale baby bump. Having four younger siblings, I remembered it took two to three months for my mother's belly to return to normal after she had each of them. This woman hadn't given birth recently. She wasn't the baby's mother.

Then who is? And is she all right?

"The raspberry jelly is my favorite," Mary suggested. "Would you like to try them?"

"Heck, yeah!"

"Me, too," Frankie added.

She shook several crackers from a box onto a napkin and spooned a small dollop of the various jellies onto each of them. Frankie and I tried each of the samples. They tasted fruity and fresh.

"They're all so good." I shrugged. "I still can't make up my mind."

"You could get a jar of each," Mary suggested. "Then you wouldn't have to decide. They're normally six dollars apiece, but I'll give you all three for fifteen dollars if you'd like."

I laughed. "You're a good salesperson, Mary. I'll do it."

While she placed the jars of jelly in a small paper sack, I gestured to the quilts. "Those blankets are beautiful. Did you make them all yourself?"

"No," she said. "I'm not that handy with a needle and thread. I stick to canning."

I stepped over to take a closer look. "Who made them, then?"

"My sisters," she said.

I wasn't sure if she meant actual blood-relative siblings, or if she'd used the term "sister" to refer to her fellow female members of the church. To get clarification, I said, "That's a lot of quilts. How many sisters do you have?"

She offered another smile. "I'm blessed with many."

So much for clarification, huh?

I lifted each of the quilts on the racks to take a look at those underneath. Just like the quilts at the Benbrook Burgers, Beer, and Bait shop, these quilts included a range of designs, many of which were the same as the ones for sale at the store. It made sense that the quilters would duplicate their designs. By repeating the same patterns, they could complete the quilts faster and thus earn the church more money. There was the same red, white, and blue blanket covered in Texas flags. The dark blue blanket with stars and moons. The pastel patchwork. Another featured the flowering magnolia tree I'd seen on a quilt at the store, while another included the prickly-pear cactus design. But none featured the bluebonnets I'd seen on the baby's blanket or on the quilt at the shop.

I looked back at the woman, hoping my questions would seem merely curious rather than an attempt at interrogation. "Do your sisters work together on these blankets? Or do they work on them separately?"

"We have a sewing circle," she said, "but each of the sisters works on her own unique design."

Her words told me two things. The fact that she'd said "the" sisters instead of "my" sisters meant the women she referred to were not biological relatives. The fact that the quilts were not a group effort and that each woman had her own special design told me the bluebonnet blanket could indeed be a clue as to the identity of the baby's mother, just as I'd suspected.

"These are very pretty," I said. "Do you have any others I could look at?"

"Sorry," she said. "That's everything we made this week."

What did it say that there was no bluebonnet blanket here? Did it mean the baby's mother hadn't made a quilt this week? If so, why not? Was she recovering from the birth of her child? Could be. Then again, my mother was always back to near full speed after a few days of rest. Could the fact that there was no bluebonnet quilt here mean that the baby's mother was hurt . . . *or worse*?

Next to us, the couple decided on the rocker, and I heard the man who'd abandoned the baby offer to carry it to their car. He turned around and, for the first time, I got a good look at him head-on.

Oh my God.

Beginning above his brow and running down across his left eye and cheek were four distinct pink lines. Someone had clawed this man's face, hard. But was it an offensive move or a defensive one? And who had done it? Could it have been the baby's mother? Or maybe it had been Mary. Were Mary and this man husband and wife? Had she found out he'd fathered a child with another woman and attacked him in a resentful rage? This was the stuff of soap operas. Was it also the stuff of the People of Peace?

My eyes moved to the man's arms and hands. While wounds to the face tended to be offensive, meaning the person with the wounds was the victim, scratch marks on the arms and hands were defensive injuries, indicating the wounded person had been the primary aggressor and the victim had tried to fight them off. Unfortunately, the man wore not only long sleeves that completely covered his arms, but he wore work gloves as well. His arms and hands were completely hidden.

If there were defensive wounds on his arms and hands, there was no way of knowing.

I knew it might seem rude to ask about the scratch marks but I also knew the chances of me getting another opportunity to do so were slim to none. I had to take a chance. Besides, when he'd glanced my way, there'd been no flicker of recognition or even suspicion. He had no idea I was the cop who'd come to the gates of the People of Peace, hoping to get inside.

I gestured to his face. "Ouch. That had to hurt."

He glanced my way and hesitated just a brief second. "A little," he mumbled as he turned his attention back to the chair and picked it up.

"What happened?" I asked.

He cut a sideways glance at me, and it wasn't a happy one. "I tripped. Got scratched by a saw."

The man was likely lying. The scratches seemed too wide and long to have been made by a saw. Plus, there were four of them, equal to the number of fingers (not counting the thumb) on a human hand. What were the odds of that? My instincts told me they'd been made by a human. But who? The baby's mother? Had he gotten into a fight with her?

"I'm a nurse," I told him. Hey, if he could lie, so could I. It was only fair. And purportedly being a nurse would explain my interest in his injury. "You should put some cream on that to prevent infection and scarring. You should get a tetanus shot, too, if you're not current."

"Good advice. Thanks." Turning his back to me, he addressed the couple. "Where to?"

The woman motioned back toward the north parking lot. "We're parked that-a-way."

With that, they headed off.

I turned back to Mary. "The furniture is really well made. It must be nice to have a husband who's so handy."

"Zeke?" She shook her head slightly. "He's not my husband."

I made a mental note of the man's name. *Zeke*. Possibly short for Ezekiel. "He's not?"

"No."

She didn't elaborate and it seemed like it would be awkward and obvious I was fishing for information if I asked more questions. Instead, I handed her three fives and accepted my bag of jellies.

I bade her good-bye as Frankie and I walked off.

"We'll be back here in two weeks if you want more!" she called after me.

I mentally filed that information away. It might come in handy.

TWENTY-SEVEN
CRUNCH TIME

Brigit

She heard Frankie's Juke pull into the driveway and stood up on the couch where she'd been snoozing to look out the window and bark a greeting. *Arf-arf!* Zoe, Frankie's cat, didn't bother to get up to greet their roommates. Cats had really bad manners. They were useless, too. They didn't perform watch duty, and they couldn't defend their human if someone broke in. They couldn't go for walks with their person, either. Why any human would want one of the beasts Brigit would never understand.

Megan climbed out of the car with two bags in her hand. Brigit wondered what was in them. Bags could mean good things, like toys or treats. Then again, sometimes bags only contained boring stuff a dog would have no interest in, like shampoo and cleaning spray. Dare she hope there was something fun for her inside?

A moment later, Megan and Frankie came in the door. Brigit met them there, her tail wagging in welcome.

Megan looked down at Brigit, held up one of the bags, and shook it. "Got a surprise for you, girl!"

A surprise? For me?

Megan pulled a big dog biscuit out of the bag and held it out to her. Brigit gave it a quick sniff. *This biscuit smells yummy!* She took it in her teeth and trotted over to the rug, where she flopped down and attacked it. *Crunch-crunch-crunch.*

Zoe hopped down from the couch and ventured over to sniff at the crumbs.

Oh, no you don't! Brigit warned her off with a growl. *Grrrr. This biscuit is mine!*

TWENTY-EIGHT
LOAVES AND FISHES

The Father

On Sunday evening, Father Emmanuel lay back on his bed and exhaled a long, relieved breath. The worship service had gone well this morning. They had a full load of furniture and quilts ready to ship to the store in the morning. None of the men in the watch towers had seen a police car all weekend. Things seemed to be settling down, getting back to normal.

Unfortunately, normal around here sometimes meant *dull*. Billy Joel got it right when he said sinners had much more fun than saints. The occasional private "prayer session" with a female member aside, reigning over a kingdom on the north Texas prairie offered little excitement.

He should plan an event, something to celebrate the official start of fall that was coming up. The men had been having a bit of luck on the lake recently. Why not a fish fry? The women could bake homemade bread to go with it. He'd call the event Loaves and Fishes. Of course Jesus probably hadn't served those two fishes fried, but Jesus was from the Middle East, not the southern U.S.

Father Emmanuel stretched his legs and congratulated himself on his cleverness.

TWENTY-NINE
SOMETHING FISHY
GOING ON

Megan

I'd spent two full hours Saturday afternoon on the police databases and online, trying to find information on Mary Seeger. Her name was the first full name we had of anyone in the compound, and I hoped it could lead to more information.

I'd found birth certificates for several Mary Seegers. I suspected she was the one who'd been born in Sherman, Texas, forty-three years ago. I also found a driver's license that expired eight years ago. She was much younger in the photo, of course, but she'd also been wearing a full face of makeup and a bright red top that revealed just a smidgen of cleavage. What had happened to this woman that had made her join the People of Peace and give up her life on the outside, including her driving privileges? I found no marriage license, no divorce proceedings. Her Facebook page, which had been dormant for nine years, included a few photos of her with fellow members of a Baptist church in Dallas, where she evidently lived at the time. Her posts hinted at her dissatisfaction with her spiritual journey, at her disgust with the hypocrisy she'd encountered within her faith community, at her desire to reach a new level of enlightenment. Her final post bade her Facebook friends good-bye and said she was moving to a new place where she could better glorify God and live in accordance with his teachings and with others who shared her beliefs. Her cryptic message paraphrased Matthew 7:7. *I asked and it was given to me, I sought and I found, I knocked and the door was opened to me.*

That door must have been the gates to the People of Peace.

While her Facebook friends included another person with the last name Seeger who appeared to be a cousin, no other family members seemed to be among them. My search showed her mother had died relatively young, in her late fifties, of cancer. Her father was still alive and living in Sherman, ninety miles to the northeast, just shy of the Oklahoma border. I wondered if Mary was still in contact with him.

Unfortunately, none of the information helped me figure out anything about the People of Peace. The members of the church certainly seemed intent on keeping their secrets.

Sunday brought some much-needed respite from work. Seth and I planned to go watch Frankie's derby bout.

A couple minutes before two o'clock, Brigit announced the arrival of Seth and Blast by standing on the front windowsill, looking outside, and barking her head off, her tail wagging so fast it was a furry blur. *Woof! Woof-woof-woof!*

When I walked into the living room, she left the

window and went with me to the door, she looked up at me and issued another *woof,* telling me to *hurry up!* I opened the door to find Seth and Blast on the porch. While Seth greeted me with a quick kiss, Blast trotted inside. After exchanging butt sniffs, Brigit and Blast began to wrangle in play on the rug.

I grabbed my purse, stepped onto the porch, and locked the door. As I turned to follow Seth to the car, my mouth fell open and I stopped in my tracks. Ollie was sitting in the front seat of the car, his friends in the back. "You got your grandfather out of the house?"

According to what Seth had told me before, Ollie hadn't left the house in years, spending his days in his chair with his oxygen tank as his primary companion. His activities consisted of watching television and griping about everything and everyone like an old grump.

"*I* didn't get him out," Seth said. "Harry and Leonard did. They've forced him to get out of his chair and dragged him all over town to see the sights. He keeps protesting, but they won't take no for an answer. When I told them you and I were going to watch roller derby, they said it sounded like fun, so I invited them to come with us."

Though I felt an urge to gloat, to remind Seth that inviting his grandfather's old army buddies out for a visit had been my idea, I restrained myself and settled for giving myself an imaginary pat on the back. *Way to go, Megan!* During my relatively short time as a cop, I'd learned that anger was often a manifestation of hurt and pain. I'd suspected that Ollie's crankiness was a result of both the PTSD and the heartbreak of living without his beloved wife, who'd died before her time. Looked like I'd been right.

"Hi, guys," I called, giving the men a wave as we approached the open door of the car. They returned the greeting in kind.

Seth leaned the bench seat forward and I crammed into the back with Leonard and Harry, sitting between the two. Seth took his place in the driver's seat and we headed out.

As we drove to the skating rink, Ollie and his buddies sang along to a classic rock station playing songs from the late sixties and early seventies, the era in which they'd been young men serving in Vietnam.

When the first few notes of Creedence Clearwater Revival's "Down on the Corner" played, Ollie turned back to look at his friends, the clear tubes from his oxygen tank bisecting his wrinkled face. "I can't hear this song without tasting *bun bo nam bo.*"

"That sure was good stuff," Leonard agreed. "I miss it."

"Me, too," Harry agreed. "But that's the only thing I miss about Vietnam."

Leonard leaned forward to look past me and cut his buddy a knowing grin. "What about Mai Linh? I bet you miss her, too, don't you?"

Harry heaved a dramatic sigh. "Every minute of every day. That woman stole my heart."

Ollie issued a grunt. "Along with your wallet."

Harry shrugged. "There was only three dollars in it and a photo of President Johnson."

"Johnson?" Leonard said. "Shoot. I thought that was a picture of your girl from back home."

The three shared a jovial chuckle.

We arrived at the rink a few minutes later and ventured inside, Ollie rolling his oxygen tank along beside him. Frankie's boyfriend, Zach, looked up from the front row of bleachers and waved us over. One of Seth's army buddies, Zach was hardworking, dark-headed, and tall, a good match for my roommate. *Who says blind dates don't work out?*

As a fellow veteran, Zach warmed up to the three old codgers right away and vice versa. Before we knew it, the five were trading stories of what it was like to serve in Vietnam versus Afghanistan, and as tank mechanics versus explosive ordnance disposal specialists.

Today, the Fort Worth Whoop-Ass was playing the Conquistadorables from San Antonio. Both teams had good track records, so the bout would be a competitive one. It would also be a loud one. A large, raucous crowd had amassed, their encouraging shouts echoing inside the metal building.

Geared up in skates, pads, and helmet, Frankie skated over to greet us. She pulled her rubber teeth protector from her mouth and gave the group a welcoming smile. "Hey, y'all."

I held out an arm to indicate Ollie, Leonard, and Harry. "We brought some new fans."

I introduced the men to Frankie, who shook their hands as well as she could with her wrist guards in place. "Thanks for coming out," she said.

Leonard held up his hand for a high five. "Knock 'em dead."

Frankie gave him a smile, a solid slap, and a salute. "I'll do my best, sir." She slid her mouth guard back into place and skated off.

A few minutes later, the teams finished their warm-up laps and the bout began. As usual, Frankie skated like a woman on fire, a blue-haired blur on the track.

Though her new teammate was barely over five feet tall, her smaller stature made her nimbler, and she zipped in and out of the other skaters with ease and precision, not once tripping or falling. The noise rose to a nearly deafening level as one team scored, then the other, the fans whooping and hollering in support.

Harry eyed the women with awe. "These broads are tough!"

"You ain't kidding," Ollie replied. "They make the Vietcong look like a bunch of pantywaists."

We cheered and hollered and pumped our fists throughout the bout, leaping to our feet when the final score was 141 to 127 in favor of the Fort Worth Whoop-Ass. Frankie skated over for a round of congratulatory back pats and high fives.

"Great job!" I told my roommate.

"One of these days," she told me, "I'm getting you out on this rink."

I had to admit, it looked like fun. But my skating skills were beyond rusty. I'd probably break my tailbone in the first five seconds.

As we returned to the car, Seth turned to his grandfather. "Why don't we grab a bite to eat? There's not much in the fridge at home. You and your buddies cleaned it out."

"What can we say?" Harry replied. "We're growing boys."

It had been decades since the three men had been boys, but their visit was clearly making them feel young again. I was glad to see it.

Their earlier discussion gave me an idea. "How about we go for Vietnamese food?" I suggested. "There's a good *pho* place not far from here that also serves noodle and rice dishes."

"Groovy," Harry replied.

"Far out," added Leonard.

Ollie sealed the deal with, "I dig it."

We drove to the restaurant and were greeted by the enticing, savory smell of Vietnamese cuisine. The five of us enjoyed a delicious meal together before returning home. Seth left me with another kiss at my door. As wonderful as that kiss was, and as fun as the day had been, my thoughts turned immediately back to the abandoned baby once the door closed and I was left alone with my thoughts.

How is she doing?

Is she thriving?

Is someone missing her?

On the following Tuesday morning, those questions were still fresh in my mind. I phoned the caseworker who had picked up the baby at the fire station. After identifying myself, I said, "I know this is probably an odd request, but is there any chance I could see the baby again? I've been worried about her."

"She's in good hands," the woman assured me. "The O'Neills are wonderful people. But I know how you feel. I get attached to these kids, too. It's an occupational hazard."

She gave me the couple's phone number and I dialed it as soon as the caseworker and I had wrapped up our call.

Mrs. O'Neill answered on the fourth ring. After identifying myself, I said, "I don't want to intrude, but

I can't stop thinking about the baby. Any chance I could come see her sometime?"

"Of course," the woman said. "And if you're free now, it's a good time. She's awake and alert."

I jotted down the address, plugged it into my GPS, and we were on our way to the South Hills neighborhood. In minutes, Brigit and I pulled up in front of a single-story gray brick home with white trim and bright yellow shutters. The place looked clean and homey.

As Brigit and I headed up to the porch, a full-figured woman with strawberry-blond curls met us at the door, pushing open the glass storm door while expertly cradling the baby in the other arm. She gave me a bright smile. "Good morning."

"'Morning." Though I was speaking to the woman, my gaze had already moved to the baby. The baby had the same silky dark hair, I remembered, but her skin color had normalized and her eyes could now focus. She wore the bluebonnet-blue hat she'd had on the night she'd been left at the station. The yarn brought out the color of her eyes. She moved her arms and shadow-boxed with chubby little baby fists.

"My gosh!" I said, taking in her full, round cheeks. "Is that really the same baby?"

The woman laughed. "Believe it or not. She's growing like a weed. Seems she's always hungry."

The baby looked right at me and cooed. *Ooo.* My heart melted into my shoes.

"Would you like to come inside and hold her for a bit?" Mrs. O'Neill asked.

"I'd love to."

She stepped back to allow me and my four-legged partner into the foyer, and we followed her to the living room. Baby equipment crowded what would have otherwise been a spacious room. A swing sat in one corner, a playpen in another. A bouncy seat sat on a soft blanket that had been spread across the rug in the center of the room. A glider with a matching ottoman sat opposite the sofa, burp cloths draped over the arm.

The woman gestured to the glider. "Why don't you sit there? She loves to be rocked."

I ordered Brigit to sit on the floor as I slid into the glider chair and stretched my hands out to take the baby from the woman. Once I had a good hold on the infant, I set the chair in motion, gliding back and forth with the baby in my arms. She looked up at me and her mouth opened, as if she had questions she wanted to ask if only she knew how to make her vocal chords form them.

I took her itty-bitty baby hand in mine. It was soft and warm and perfect. *This is pure heaven. Too bad her mother is missing out on this.*

Mrs. O'Neill perched on the edge of the sofa. "We were told that we'll get her if she's made available for adoption. I'm trying not to get my hopes up, but I can't help myself. Any idea when y'all might know something?"

At the rate things were going, we might never know the real story about this baby. But at some point, if we couldn't get answers, the adoption would be allowed to proceed. Still, I couldn't foresee when we might get to that point. It could take days, or it could take weeks.

"I'm sorry," I said on a sigh. "I wish I could give you a definitive answer. We're doing our best to sort things out."

She nodded and offered a patient smile. "I'll just

have to trust that things will work out the way they're supposed to."

I looked back down at the baby. "Hey, little girl. You sure are a cutie."

She replied with a blink.

Mrs. O'Neill cocked her head. "Do you think she looks more like a Harper or a Piper?"

Uh-oh. This woman is already picking out names. "That's a tough one," I said. "Harper, maybe?"

When the baby began to wriggle and fuss, the woman handed me a bottle. I put it to the baby's lips and she latched on tight, sucking with gusto.

Mrs. O'Neill laughed. "Told you she's always hungry."

A few minutes later, she'd polished off the bottle and I decided to hand her back to her foster mother for burping. Mrs. O'Neill draped a cloth diaper over her shoulder and clutched the baby to her chest, patting the little one's back. The baby emitted an adorable little *"bup."*

"Thanks for letting me see the baby," I said.

"Anytime you want to come by," Mrs. O'Neill said, "you're more than welcome."

She walked me and Brigit to the door, where I gave the baby a little wave good-bye. The baby was too young to offer a sincere smile, but when her lips turned up in another eruption of gas I chose to believe it was a divine sign of encouragement.

Brigit and I returned to our cruiser and set back out on patrol.

It was a slow morning, very few calls coming in on the radio. After getting nowhere in the People of Peace case, I decided to put some more effort into the burglaries, see if I could find Felicia Bloomquist's stolen inventory. If I could find the person or persons responsible, maybe I could also find the stolen laptop and the Steve Nash bobble-head that belonged to the man who drove the Lexus. Of course, chances were the computer and doll had already been sold on the black market.

I drove to the Sell 'N Swap, another location that offered sales space for rent in an old warehouse. I led Brigit inside with me but wrapped her leash around my hand to shorten it, keeping her close to my side. She had a strong tail and I didn't want to risk her accidentally knocking over something expensive.

The vast majority of the vendors here dealt in antiques of one kind or another. One booth offered only vintage glassware. Another offered grandfather clocks in a variety of sizes, their *dings* and *dongs* not quite in synch as they struck the quarter hour. Yet another vendor specialized in old lunch boxes and offered one in a Pac-Man design, another with a Peanuts comic-strip theme, and a third featuring the Incredible Hulk in an earlier incarnation.

I strolled on until I reached a booth selling sports memorabilia. The operator of the booth was a tall man who appeared to be in his late thirties or early forties. A San Francisco 49ers ball cap sat atop his bald head, while a jersey from the now-defunct Houston Oilers football team stretched across his broad shoulders and chest. The vendor stood behind his table, a man in a Dallas Stars T-shirt on the other, the two haggling over an autographed Vancouver Canucks official hockey puck.

"Will you take fifty?" asked the customer.

The vendor crossed his arms over his chest. "Fifty-five. That's my final offer."

The customer reached back for his wallet. "You've got yourself a deal."

While they finished their exchange, I took a quick look around. The booth comprised three tall, wide metal shelving units, the kind normally found in garages or outdoor storage sheds. The vendor appeared to have economized on presentation to maximize his profits. Crowding the shelves were plastic boxes protecting the treasures inside, everything from vintage baseball cards featuring Ken Griffey Jr. and Pete Rose, to golf balls autographed by Jack Nicklaus and Arnold Palmer. Three contained bobble-heads. LeBron James in a Cleveland Cavaliers jersey. A shirtless Muhammad Ali in red boxing gloves and white shorts. Another featuring an unidentified Chicago White Sox player. The latter was marked "1968 Nodder." A bin sitting on the table in front of me held autographed photos in plastic sleeves, everyone from Nascar legend Dale Earnhardt to tennis star Serena Williams. I flipped through it until the two men finished their transaction.

After sliding the cash into a zippered fanny pack at his waist, the vendor turned to me. He took in my uniform and glanced down at Brigit, but his countenance remained calm, no sign of alarm upon seeing law enforcement at his booth. "Something I can help you with, Officer?"

"There is," I replied. "My father was a huge fan of Steve Nash when he played for the Mavs. Dad had a bobble-head doll but my dog here chewed it up." I angled my head to indicate Brigit. Okay, so I was bearing false witness against my partner, which was a sin. But

I was doing it to catch someone who'd broken another commandment, *thou shall not steal.* If my made-up story about the damaged doll could lead me to finding the burglar, two wrongs could make a right in this instance. "Any chance you've got a Nash bobble-head?"

"I don't have one on hand," he said, "but we dealers have a network. If you can give me a few days to ask around, I might be able to hook you up."

"That would be great." This man wasn't the thief, but maybe he could lead me to the lawbreaker.

I reached into my pocket, retrieved one of my business cards, and handed it to him. He whipped out a pen, turned the card over, and scribbled *Steve Nash Mavs bobble-head* on the back. I thanked him and moved on.

As I circled around to the second row of booths, I came across a man in a rolling chair with his feet propped up on the end of the long table in front of him. He stared down at a tablet that streamed a James Bond movie. On his table were a wide variety of products sold in multilevel marketing platforms, including a number of cosmetic and skin-care lines. Avon. Mary Kay. Nouveau Toi, the same brand sold by Felicia Bloomquist, whose inventory had been swiped from her garage.

Aha! Or maybe aha. This guy was neither Latino nor sporting a hamburger nose, like the two magazine salesmen the victims had described. But maybe the sales calls were a coincidence, unrelated to the thefts. After all, they'd described totally different men, and there were a lot of guys going door-to-door selling magazines, home-security systems, or soliciting lawn care or painting gigs.

I stopped in front of the table to examine the

merchandise. Brigit examined it, too. But while I used my eyes and hands, she used her nose, sniff-sniff-sniffing at the boxes and tubes and jars. A peacock-blue eyeliner caught my attention. I'd seen the product listed for $21 in Felicia's catalog. This man had put a sticker on the package offering it for $8. Other items seemed to be similarly priced, offered at much less than usual. Given the typical markups for direct-sales products, this guy would be making a minuscule profit on the products, if any, had he paid wholesale for them. Of course if he'd stolen the products, any price, no matter how small, would put him in the black.

A trio of brass coat trees sat to the side of the table. Hanging from the hooks were a number of clothing pieces, including dresses, tops, pants, skirts, and leggings in fun prints. The brands were identified by hand-lettered index cards taped to the rod. Cabi. Agnes & Dora. Du North Designs. Vestments, another brand Felicia sold.

Could this man be the burglar who'd stolen her inventory? Only one way to find out, and that was to ask him questions and see if he came up with reasonable answers.

I picked up a boxed jar of Nouveau Toi skin cream bearing a $12 price tag. If I recalled correctly, Felicia's catalog listed this item for $36. The cream claimed to be organic and made from all-natural ingredients, including shea butter, cocoa butter, and jojoba oil. Heck, if it didn't make my skin look better, I could spread it on a cracker. "Will this cream help with my problem areas?"

The man looked up at me. "What problem areas?"

"These." I waved a hand in front of my face. "They're pretty bad." *Or so I'd been told.*

He lifted an unconcerned shoulder. "I don't know. Read the box." He went back to his movie, customer service be damned.

Frankly, I felt more than a little miffed. "Aren't you going to help me? Isn't that part of your duties as a brand representative? Don't they train you on this stuff?"

He didn't even bother to look up this time. "I don't rep these brands. I just sell 'em. I sell 'em cheap, too. If you want information, you'll have to call someone else and pay them full price."

"How can you sell these products if you aren't an official rep? Isn't that a violation of the companies' policies?"

"Maybe," he said. "But if that's the case, that's between the company and the person who signed a contract with them. I didn't sign anything, so I'm not bound. You're a cop. You should know that."

I didn't bother explaining that contracts were a civil law matter, and police handled only criminal matters. "If you don't buy from the companies," I asked, "then how do you get this stuff?"

His eyes were still on his screen as he explained. "I buy out people who are looking to get out of direct sales and want to get out from under their inventories. There's a lot. People lose interest or find they're having to work too hard to make a buck."

His explanation made sense, but was it the truth? "Can you prove it?" I asked.

He looked up now, his expression wary. "Say what?"

"Can you prove you bought this inventory?"

He pulled his feet off the table and put them on the floor, sitting up straight. "Why would I need to do that?"

"Because you're selling some products here that are identical to ones that were stolen from a home in the area just a few days ago."

His face clouded. "I didn't steal a damn thing and I don't appreciate the insinuation."

That makes us even, because I didn't appreciate your tone and inattentiveness, either.

He reached under the table and retrieved a plastic bin. After prying off the lid, he pulled out a large yellow envelope and handed it to me. "Here. See for yourself."

Inside were printouts relating to inventory he'd purportedly bought on eBay, as well as handwritten receipts for cash purchases he'd evidently made in person. Still, these documents could be fakes. "Willing to show me your PayPal and bank accounts?"

"If it'll put an end to your baseless accusations, hell yeah, I will."

As I watched, he laid the tablet on the table and logged into his PayPal account. There, he showed me several transactions and the name of the recipients of his payments. I ran a search on my phone with the recipient's name and the name of the brand they sold, verifying via Web sites or past-dated social media promotions that they'd been involved in selling the brands. We ran through the same routine with his bank account.

"Satisfied?" he demanded.

I held up the jar of skin cream. "If this gets rid of

my problem areas I will be." I pulled $12 cash from my wallet and handed it to him. "Thanks for clearing things up."

Though he was still scowling slightly, he dipped his head in acknowledgment and resumed the Bond flick.

Having struck out on the burglary case, yet again, I aimed for the People of Peace compound. As usual, I stopped at the top of the hill and pulled out my binoculars to take a peek. Nothing struck me as unusual, just people going about their business. I set the glasses aside and cruised on down the hill.

On my way into the park, I passed two men on foot with fishing poles. Both were clean-shaven and wore tan fishing hats, the strings hanging down in front of their chests. One of them carried a tackle box. Their plain shirts told me they'd been sewn by hand. These guys had to be from the People of Peace compound.

I drove slowly around the park road, stopping at a lot near the shore. Texas weather tends to change on a dime, and doesn't always follow the seasons. It was as if Mother Nature liked to toy with us, and had a spinner she used to determine what the weather would be on any given day. Today, that spinner had landed on warm and windy.

I parked the cruiser, climbed out, and let my partner out, too. She trotted onto the grass and popped a squat. I whipped a doo-doo bag from my pocket and promptly cleaned up the mess, tossing it into a metal trash bin with a *klunk*. Even though I had to deal with Brigit's poops, she was still less disgusting a partner than Derek had been.

A breeze blew in, parting Brigit's fur down the center of her back as she trotted toward the shoreline. She watched as three pairs of ducks soared in and landed on the water. Bounding into the water, she began to swim out to them. I made no move to stop her. She was having fun, getting a little exercise, and there was zero chance she'd actually harm the birds. They'd fly or paddle off before she got too close.

I wandered along the shore, picking up any flat rock I saw, and skipping it across the surface of the water, keeping track of my best score. Four skips. Then five. A flat rock the size of a half dollar skipped a whopping seven times.

Out on the water, the ducks spotted Brigit and took to flight. Disappointed, she swam in a semicircle and headed back to shore. I stepped away to give her a wide berth as she emerged from the water. She stopped once all four paws were on dry land and gave herself a thorough shake, sending up a shower. Fortunately, I'd learned to stay well out of range when she was wet.

Her ears pricked and she turned her head to the side. She raised her snout in the air now, scenting.

"Smell something, girl?"

She turned and began to trot in the direction she'd looked. I could have called her back, but I was curious to know where she was going. Just like Detective Jackson had learned to trust my instincts, I'd learned to trust Brigit's.

I followed her as she entered a small copse of trees, ducking my way under low-hanging branches, and sweeping away spiderwebs with my hand. Eventually we emerged on the other side. The two men I'd seen earlier were standing on the shore, poles in hand, fishing line running from the poles to spots in the water a dozen yards out.

My first instinct was to retreat or at least stop, to keep my distance for fear of frightening them off. But then I realized they were not forest animals and that this situation posed a unique opportunity for me to learn more about these men.

"Having any luck?" I called, continuing in their direction.

They turned, looked at me, then looked at each other.

"Not yet," said the closer one after a brief hesitation.

Brigit reached them and sniffed around their tackle box. I didn't stop her. One of the men cast her an annoyed look, but said nothing.

I walked up to them. "What are you hoping to catch?"

There was another hesitation before the man who'd spoken earlier said, "Catfish."

On hearing the word "cat," Brigit looked up and around, scenting the air again. When she neither saw nor smelled a cat, she continued sniffing the tackle box.

I knew squat about fishing, but I had to engage these guys if I wanted to learn anything. "You fishing for fun? Catch and release?"

"No," the man said. "Fishing for food."

"My dad likes catfish, too," I said. "The spicier the seasonings, the better."

Like the fish, these men didn't bite. Instead of picking up the conversation with a reply, they let my words just hang in the air. *So that's how you're going to play this, huh?* Given that my attempts to engage them in friendly banter hadn't worked, I took a different tack. "You two have fishing licenses?"

"Yes." The closer man put a hand to the reel and

turned it quickly to retract the string. "They're in the tackle box."

When his lure popped up out of the water, he finished reeling it in, leaned his pole against the tree, and began walking toward the tackle box.

I stepped between him and the box and stopped him by raising a hand. "Hold on just a minute." For all I knew, there could be a handgun in the box. Out here, there'd be nobody to witness him shooting me or Brigit. It couldn't hurt to take precautions. "Mind if I open it myself?"

"If that's what you prefer."

Keeping one eye on him, I stepped over to the box and knelt down to open the latches. *Snap-snap.* As I lifted the lid, a tray attached to the hinges swung forward. Lying right on top were two fishing licenses. One was issued in the name of Glenn T. Clarke, the other in the name of Joshua A. Purcell. Both had expired on August 31.

I looked up from the box. Because the fishing licenses contained no personal photograph, it was impossible to tell which one of these men was Glenn and which was Joshua. "Which one of you is Mr. Clarke?"

The one closer to me reflexively raised a hand. "That's me. But I go by Elijah."

Did nobody at the People of Peace compound use their given name? *Sheesh.* I eyed the other. "I suppose that makes you Mr. Purcell."

He nodded.

"I hate to tell you two," I said, though I didn't hate it at all, "but these licenses are expired." Call me immature, but after their leader had refused to let me and

Detective Jackson into their compound—or *refuge*—
it felt good to push back a little, flex a little muscle.

"Expired?" Glenn/Elijah repeated, looked genuinely
surprised.

Joshua did, too, his brows lifted to the bottom of his
fishing hat. "I thought they were good until the end of
the year."

I shook my head. "Nope. That's a common miscon-
ception. Texas fishing licenses run from September first
of one year to August thirty-first of the next."

The men exchanged glances. I debated what to do.
Normally, wardens from the Texas Parks and Wildlife
Department handled hunting and fishing violations.
Calling the TPWD out was one option. Another option
was to simply give them a warning. My gut told me to
go with the latter. As much as I would enjoy giving
them a little hassle, antagonizing members of the
church wouldn't serve my purpose, which was to get
into that compound and search for the baby's mother.
Better to try to build some rapport, if I could.

I closed the tackle box, snapped the latches closed,
and stood. "No worries," I told them. "I don't want to
ruin your good time. I suspect the fish would be of a
different mind, though." I forced a chuckle and was
glad to see both men break a small smile, too. "Just be
sure to get current licenses before you come out again.
The guys from Parks and Wildlife might not be so for-
giving."

The men nodded. Glenn said, "Thanks, Officer."

Now that I'd hopefully earned their trust, I wandered
a little closer. "Are you two from that place next door?
The church camp?"

"Refuge," Joshua corrected me. "It's a refuge."

I dipped my head in acknowledgment. "I love patrolling out here by the lake. It's so pretty. It's a good place for my partner to stretch her legs, too. I was glad when we were asked to fill in at this division." I hoped they'd take this tidbit back to the guards in the watchtowers. Maybe they'd assume my regular drive-bys weren't so much an attempt to keep an eye on the People of Peace as to enjoy the scenery. "Seems like it would be nice to live out here, so close to the water. How long have you two been living in the refuge?"

They hesitated again. Clearly they weren't happy to give me any information, even if it was something as simple and useless as the length of their residence. Nevertheless, they gave me answers, however reluctant.

"About two years," Glenn said quietly, as if afraid someone might overhear. Father Emmanuel, perhaps?

"Four," said Joshua in an equally soft voice.

"Looks like a big place. How many people live there?" I'd seen over a hundred at the prayer circle, by my quick estimate. But I had no way of knowing if all of the members had been in the circle at the time.

Glenn's evasive answer would have earned him an F on any math test. "A good number," he said.

Sheesh. How many was "a good number"?

"My dad used to take me fishing when I was little," I said, lying again. "I didn't much like baiting a hook, but I liked having that special time with my father. You guys ever bring your kids out here?"

"We don't have any," Glenn said.

Both men were reasonably attractive and at the age when the majority of men had settled down, married, and reproduced. These men could be gay, I supposed, but it seemed the more likely explanation was that Father Emmanuel, like many cult leaders, devalued families and encouraged more communal ties. The family bond was seen as a threat to the members' loyalty to the larger church, and romantic relationships were touted as sinful and selfish.

Brigit had wandered to the edge of the water and pawed at something, pulling it up onto the dry land. The breeze carried its odor my way. *Dead fish. Ick.* She sniffed it, licked it once, then proceeded to flop down on top of it, belly up, and roll.

I scurried over. "No, girl!"

Brigit's wet dog smell would already stink up the cruiser. No sense adding the aroma of festering fish to it.

Brigit stopped wriggling and looked up at me, defiance in her eyes. She protested with a soft growl. *Grrrr.*

I pointed a finger at her. "Don't you talk back to me."

She rolled off the fish, stood, and heaved a sigh worthy of any rebellious teenager.

While I wanted to ask the men more questions, I decided not to push my luck. "It's been nice talking with y'all. It gets a little lonely on patrol. My conversations with my partner tend to be one-sided." I forced another chuckle, clipped Brigit's leash to her collar, and raised a hand in good-bye. "We're heading out now. Have a good day."

They mumbled good-byes in return, and we turned to go.

I repeated the men's names in my mind as I led Brigit back to the cruiser. *Glenn T. Clarke. Joshua A. Purcell. Glenn T. Clarke. Joshua A. Purcell.* At the car, I loaded Brigit into the back, took my seat, and turned my dash-mounted laptop in my direction. I ran a quick search on both of the men and determined Glenn's middle name was Thomas, while Joshua's was Alan. Neither appeared to have a criminal record. No marriage license was issued in either name. While I found their birth certificates, I found none listing them as the father of any children. Like Mary Seeger, these men had let their driver's licenses lapse, though only in the last year. Neither showed up on social media. It was as if they were fading, leading only a partial existence.

It dawned on me then that the children born in the compound might not even have been issued birth certificates. If they didn't have birth certificates, they wouldn't have social security numbers, either. They'd be totally off the grid. The government wouldn't know they existed. The concept was strange and more than a little eerie, as if we had ghosts living among us.

That night, I washed my face and examined it closely in the mirror. Unable to determine exactly where my problem areas were, I applied the Nouveau Toi cream liberally all over. Couldn't hurt, right? I'd be curious to see what I looked like in the morning, whether the jojoba oil and shea and coconut butters would transform my skin.

Smelling like a piña colada, I flopped down on my bed to do a little reading. Brigit hopped up next to me, sniffed my cheek, and whipped out her tongue to swipe me from jaw to brow. "Ew!" I pushed her face away. "Stop that!"

The warm, wet tongue was gross enough, but the fact that her breath smelled like liver treats made it even more disgusting. My protestations only seemed to make her try harder. She went for my face again, putting a paw up on my shoulder for leverage.

"No!" I pushed her back again.

She came after me with just as much determination and before I knew what was happening, we were engaged in an all-out wrestling match on my bed, with her trying to lick the cream off my face and me trying to fend her off.

My cell phone chirped from the bedside table. I grabbed it and checked the screen. *Mom.* Yanking the sheet over my head and cowering under it, I accepted the call.

"I got a 96 on my exam!" my mother cried happily. "Can you believe it?"

"That's great, Mom!" I said. "Congratulations."

"I've got all As so far," she said. "If I can keep my grades up, I could make the dean's list."

"I'm proud of you," I told her.

"I'm proud of me, too. Now I just need to pick a major. I never knew it was so hard to figure out what you want to be when you grow up."

I supposed it was difficult for some people to decide on a career, but for me it had been a no-brainer. I'd loved mysteries, even as a kid, loved to examine the clues and see if I could figure out whodunit. With my stutter, I'd developed a habit of keeping my mouth shut and observing. You can learn a lot that way.

My mother reminded me of the incentive I'd offered her. "Don't forget you promised to take me out for ice cream."

"I'd love to." We agreed to go on my next free evening.

When we ended the call, I sneaked my hand out

from under the covers to return the phone to the table. I reached up and turned off the lamp.

"Good night, Briggie," I said through the sheet, hoping I wouldn't suffocate under here. I had two big cases to solve.

Luckily, the dog seemed to have given up on licking my face. She flopped down next me and settled in for the night.

THIRTY
I CAN LICK ANYONE

Brigit

Her partner sure could be a party pooper. First Megan scolded Brigit for rolling on that wonderfully stinky dead fish, then Megan scolded Brigit again for licking the cream off her face. Why had she put something so yummy-smelling on her face if she didn't want Brigit to lick it?

Megan considered herself the alpha of their two-member pack. Brigit, on the other hand, knew she was the one who was really in charge. She was smart enough to keep Megan in the dark about that fact, and obeyed—*mostly*—while they were on duty. But off duty? Brigit would find a way to get what she wanted.

She lay still and quiet next to Megan until she heard Megan's breaths become slow and shallow. Brigit knew that meant her partner was asleep now. Taking the edge of the sheet in her teeth, Brigit carefully eased it back until Megan's face was exposed. She gently put the end of her tongue on her partner's forehead and waited to see if Megan would react.

She didn't.
Good.

Slowly and gently, Brigit licked the cream from Megan's face. She had no idea what was in the stuff, but it tasted greasy and good.

At one point Megan stirred and Brigit quickly put her head down and closed her eyes. When her partner stopped moving, Brigit opened her eyes just a little bit. Megan's were closed. The coast was clear again. She continued to gingerly swipe the goo with her tongue.

When Megan's face was completely clean, Brigit licked her lips and put her head down on the pillow next to Megan's. *Yep, I'm the boss here.*

THIRTY-ONE
PRIVILEGES

The Father

Thursday afternoon, he sat in his office in the church building, writing Sunday's sermon. He'd decided to speak about loss, how pain and grief were essential to appreciating life's joys, how suffering was an integral part of God's master plan.

He had assumed things would move on quickly, that the women would avoid talking about Juliette's baby in an effort to put it all behind them.

He'd been wrong.

Those cackling hens wouldn't shut up.

The hidden microphones he'd had installed in their work barn and bunkhouse brought him no end of discussion about how the "poor little thing" had been "taken much too soon." No matter how many times he reminded the women that death takes a person to God's holy realm and was something to celebrate rather than mourn, the death of Juliette's baby hung like a dark shroud over the refuge.

Ecclesiastes 3:1–8 was the go-to verse for times like these.

*To every thing there is a season, and a time to
    every purpose under the heaven:
A time to be born, and a time to die;
A time to plant, and a time to pluck up that
    which is planted;
A time to kill, and a time to heal;
A time to break down, and a time to build up;
A time to weep, and a time to laugh;
A time to mourn, and a time to dance;
A time to cast away stones, and a time to gather
    stones together;
A time to embrace, and a time to refrain from
    embracing;
A time to seek, and a time to lose;
A time to keep, and a time to cast away;
A time to rend, and a time to sew;
A time to keep silence, and a time to speak;
A time to love, and a time to hate;
A time for war, and a time for peace.*

His sermon would make it clear that the time for mourning and weeping and speaking about the tragic loss of Juliette's child was over. It was now time to heal, laugh, and shut the fuck up.

His radio crackled and Jebediah's voice came over the airwaves. "Father, that female police officer is on the ridge again."

Damn it to hell! "What's she doing?"

"She has a biker pulled over. It looks like she's giving the rider a ticket."

Two of his men had encountered the cop and her dog when they'd been fishing earlier in the week. They'd told him she'd asked some questions. How long they'd lived in the refuge, how many people belonged to the People of Peace. Her questions could have been simple small talk, idle curiosity on her part. After all, she hadn't issued them a citation for the expired fishing licenses, and she'd told them she and her partner enjoyed the lake. The park was the perfect place to let a K-9 out to do its business. Still, she sure seemed to drive by the church on a regular basis. None of the other officers in their area had taken such an interest in them. And the fact that she and that detective had tried to gain entry to the grounds, well, that didn't sit well with him. He had a feeling something more was going on here, and that the "something more" involved the baby.

He pressed the button to respond to Jeb. "Find Juliette," he said. "Get her back in the silo out of sight. Take her through the woods so you won't be spotted."

"Yes, Father."

He whipped out his cell phone and placed a call. He hated spending money on lawyers, but he didn't see another way. Just like there was clergy-penitent privilege, there was an attorney-client privilege. Good thing. He didn't want law enforcement to find out the truth. Not that he was going to tell the attorney the *exact* truth, of course. Just something close enough to the truth to get a useful legal opinion.

THIRTY-TWO
MOTHER GOOSE,
MOTHER GUESS

Megan

Like the two men with the expired fishing licenses, the biker would get off easy, with just a warning. He'd been going fifteen miles over the speed limit, but his infraction gave me the opportunity to do some extra spying from the hilltop without being obvious. While the biker sat on his ride ahead of me and awaited his fate, I sat in my squad car, focused my high-powered binoculars, and took a quick peek at the compound. I also scratched my cheek. The Nouveau Toi night cream hadn't done anything for my skin. In fact, when I woke up this morning, my skin felt sticky and raw, like my entire face had become a problem area.

Down below, the People of Peace went about their daily business. The men worked inside their barn, making their furniture and forging their candleholders, napkin rings, and silverware. Meanwhile, inside their own barn, the women set about dipping candles, quilting, and making jams, jellies, and preserves. The younger children played on the school's playground, while the older ones were presumably inside, attending classes.

Movement at the women's barn drew my eyes back to the building. As I watched a young woman emerged from the barn with a small ceramic jar cradled in the curve of her arm.

Holy guacamole!

The woman wore a knit cap in the same bluebonnet-blue color the baby had been wearing the night it was dropped at the fire station. Her long hair was the same shiny, dark shade as the baby's. She wore a knit sweater that was too loose for me to tell if she had a postpartum bump on her belly.

An older woman followed the younger one out of the barn and joined her. The older woman was gray-haired, with a pear-shaped body, her wide hips causing her to waddle like a goose. The older woman walked with the younger one as she made her way across the compound. The two disappeared under a canopy of trees before reappearing on the other side twenty seconds or so later.

The one I'd pegged as the baby's mother carried the small jar to the garden, opened it, and held it out to sprinkle the contents over a spread of pink lantana. Was it fertilizer of some sort? Seemed a waste to feed lantana this time of year. Though the native, drought-resistant plant had a long blooming season, it was definitely nearing the end.

She's the baby's mother, isn't she? Though I couldn't know for certain, both the evidence and my gut told me she was. *Her* gut told me, too. As the young woman shook the jar with her right hand, she put her left hand to the top of her abdomen and ran it downward. The motion caused the sweater to draw tighter over her still-rounded stomach.

I now knew without a doubt that this woman had given birth to the baby.

I barely had time to process this fact before her head jerked up and turned back toward the barns. A young man had run out of the men's barn and was sprinting toward the garden like his life depended on it. His arm went up in a waving motion and his mouth opened as he appeared to be calling to the women. *Wait. Does he have a black eye?* It was hard to tell given that he was moving.

Before he could make it to the garden, he was overtaken by two other men, one of whom tackled him to the ground as effectively as the best of the Dallas Cowboys' offensive linemen. He wrangled the younger man, eventually pinning him to the earth by sitting on his chest and holding his arms down by the wrists. The other man held his legs down by the ankles. I squinted to get a better look at their faces. The man who'd done the tackling was the man from the farmer's market, the one who'd appeared in the fire station video and police sketch, the one who'd abandoned the baby. The one I now knew as Zeke.

What in the world is going on down there?

"See something?" the biker called back to me.

Crap! He'd turned around and caught me spying.

I leaned to my left to call to him through the open cruiser door. "We've had a rash of people fishing without licenses lately," I told him. "Exceeding the daily limit, too. I thought I saw a boat I recognized on the water."

Liar, liar, pants on fire.

He seemed to accept my explanation. By the time I put the binoculars back to my eyes, the two older men were dragging the younger one back into their barn. He tried to look back over his shoulder once, but Zeke grabbed the boy's chin in his hand and forcibly turned his head back to face forward. The baby's mother and her chaperone stood over the flowers, the older woman's arm draped over the younger's shoulders, which were heaving. I wasn't sure exactly how to interpret what I'd seen, but it was highly suspicious.

Was the younger man the baby's father? I'd assumed it was either Zeke or Father Emmanuel, that one of them, like many cult leaders before them, had engaged in deviant sexual behavior and had abandoned the baby to get rid of the evidence. But maybe I'd been wrong. Maybe the baby hadn't just been taken from her mother, maybe she had been taken from her father, too.

I set the binoculars aside, whipped out my pad, and wrote up a warning for the biker, ripping it from my sheet and climbing out of the car to hand it to him. "I'm sure it's fun to drive fast along these country roads," I told him, "but I'd hate to see you get hurt. Stay within the speed limit, okay?"

He made no promises, nor did he express proper appreciation for the fact that I'd cut him quite a bit of slack. Policing is often a thankless job. "We done here?"

"Yep. You're free to go."

He folded up the citation and tucked it into a pocket on his leather vest. He started the engine on his Kawasaki, revved it in defiance, and motored off with a loud putter.

I returned to my cruiser and raised the binoculars to my eyes again. Both the young man and the baby's mother were out of sight now. I laid the glasses on the passenger seat and retrieved my cell phone, pulling up Detective Jackson on my contacts list and placing a call to her. "I just saw something disturbing in the compound."

"What was it?"

"A young woman, around twenty I'd guess, came out of the barn. She has dark hair, just like the baby, and was wearing a knit hat that looked just like the one the baby had on. Same color and everything. She had a baby bump, too."

"The baby's mother, then," Jackson said.

"That's my thinking, too. An older woman walked with her to the garden. While they were there, a young man came running out of the men's work barn and was waving to try to get their attention. I can't be certain, but it looked like he might have had a black eye. Zeke ran after him and tackled him before he got very far. Another guy helped hold the young man down. It seemed like they were trying to keep him away from the girl. They forcibly escorted him back to the barn. I was in the middle of a traffic stop so I missed what happened next, but when I looked again everyone was out of sight."

"You think the young man could be the baby's father?" she asked.

"Sure seems that w-way. If he's not, he's someone who seems concerned about the baby's mother, at least. And it looks like he's being controlled by the others, kept away from her."

"We've got to get in there," she said. "Lives could be in danger. But we need some protection and a warrant first. We can't risk going in alone or without legal safeguards in place. I'm at a crime scene now, but let's meet at the magistrate's office in an hour. In the meantime, get some backup."

"Will do," I replied. "See you then."

I started my engine and drove down the road to the lakeside park. I parked, let Brigit out of her enclosure, and headed quickly down the path that ran alongside the settlement's walls. When we reached the wall, I stopped and cupped a hand around my ear to listen, see if I could hear any noises coming from inside. There was a faint buzz of a table saw, followed by the *clang-clang-clang* of hot metal being beat into submission, just as the young man had apparently been. I heard no wails, though, no shouting, no cries for help.

Brigit and I scurried back to the cruiser. I jumped on the radio. "Detective Jackson and I will need backup in an hour. We're going into a cult compound. Who can help out?"

Derek's voice came over the radio. "Count me in."

It figured the Big Dick would respond. Any time a situation called for muscle, he threw himself into the thick of it. Derek was the kind of cop you wanted to have your back when things could get violent, but he was also the kind of cop who could give the police a bad name. Simply put, he was not only capable of kicking ass, but he also enjoyed doing it.

"I'm available," said Officer Spalding.

Good. While Derek often didn't know when to keep his mouth shut, Spalding was the strong, silent type. Suspects often found his quiet demeanor unnerving and intimidating. That could come in handy today.

The voice of Summer, one of my fellow female officers, came over the airwaves, too. "I can help, too."

"Great. Thanks." I told them where the compound was located, and suggested they wait for me and the detective at Benbrook Burgers, Beer, and Bait.

I started my car and drove out of the park, past the compound, and headed up the hill. At the top, I met a Mercedes going in the other direction. The driver was speeding, but I didn't have time to worry about that right now. I needed to get that darn warrant and get into the compound.

I'd driven a quarter mile when the Mercedes zipped up behind me, the driver flashing his headlights and honking his horn to get my attention. He must've turned around on the other side of the hill. Was he having some kind of emergency?

I applied the brakes and eased over, momentarily pondering the irony of a police officer being pulled over by a civilian. The situation seemed a little off, so I was extra careful when I exited my vehicle, keeping my body turned to provide the smallest target should he pull a gun.

The driver must have sensed my concern, because he raised his hands where I could see them and stuck his head out his open window. "I'm a lawyer for the People of Peace!" he called. "I need to talk to you."

Ugh. One of the men in the watchtower must have seen me on the hill. Hard to miss a cruiser with flashing lights.

I retrieved Brigit from her enclosure, not because I thought her skills might be needed, but because she, like Derek and Spalding, intimidated people. A little intimidation might come in handy right now.

Together we stepped over to the lawyer's car. He climbed out and met us on the shoulder of the road. He wore a suit in a dark gray that matched his hair, a starched white dress shirt, and a stylish tie that probably cost more than I made in a month.

Brigit stuck her nose in his crotch by way of greeting. *Hello, boys!* I didn't stop her.

The attorney scowled down at my partner and took a step back. Undeterred, she lowered her nose to sniff at his expensive tassel loafers. She gave one a swipe with her tongue. Given her history of chewing up my shoes, I half expected her to take the man's loafer in her mouth and yank it off his foot.

"How can I help you?" I asked.

He jerked his foot back, away from Brigit's prying mouth, and stood on one leg like a well-dressed flamingo. "My client tells me that you and a detective attempted to gain entry to the compound and that you've driven by their grounds repeatedly over the last week or two."

I arched a brow that said *And?* Nothing we'd done was remotely illegal. We were just doing our jobs.

When he began to wobble, he put his foot back down to balance himself. "My client also tells me you've interrogated church members in the park by the lake."

I fought the urge to roll my eyes. "Asking to see a fishing license is hardly an interrogation, sir."

He frowned. Evidently he'd expected me to be a little more conciliatory. He didn't know me.

"Your behavior constitutes harassment," he insisted. "Abuse of power."

Abuse of power? Seriously? I lost the fight with the eye roll, giving him the full Anderson Cooper treatment. "If I'd intended to harass those men, I would've issued them citations. Both of their licenses had expired weeks ago." I pointed back to the hill. "That rise up there? It's impossible to see over, yet people don't even bother to slow down. Speeders could be putting themselves or others at risk. It's my duty to keep the people out here safe."

He gave me an eye roll right back, his pupils traveling the full socket. The only thing missing was an accompanying slide whistle sound. "Let's cut the crap, Officer. You're out here because of the baby, aren't you?"

My head jerked back reflexively. *Well, that admission was unexpected.*

"Look," the attorney said. "It's perfectly legal to leave a baby at a fire station. There's been no crime. The purpose of the safe-haven law is to protect children by allowing their parents to turn them over anonymously. What you're doing here? Spying on the baby's father? That type of behavior will put infants' lives at risk."

He sounded just like the judge and, truth be told, I agreed with the theory of his argument. It was the facts of this particular safe drop that were problematic. In that vein, I noticed he'd said only "father," not "parents." Hmm.

"When babies are left at safe places," I said, "it's almost always the mother who leaves them." Heck, it was a reasonable assumption in most instances that the father wasn't in the picture. "Why did the father surrender the baby? Why didn't he and the mother do it together?"

"Because the mother ran off right after the baby was born," the attorney said without hesitation. "She hadn't wanted a baby, didn't see it as a blessing. The baby's father knew he'd have a hard time raising a child on his own, and that their baby would have a better life with both a mother and a father."

The explanation seemed highly questionable. With everyone living communally in the People of Peace settlement, the baby's father would have had plenty of women willing to help him care for the child. Plus, if their particular brand of religion was so important to these folks, how could one of them send their child away, where it would not have the benefit of the teachings and lifestyle they embraced so wholeheartedly? I also doubted whether anyone could "run off" from the compound. With the high walls and locked gates, only someone highly skilled in pole vaulting or a human spider could escape.

No, I didn't think this man was telling me the truth. Oddly, though, I believed he thought he was.

"Who gave you this information?" I asked. "The baby's father?"

"It's not important who told me."

"It is to me." When he said nothing further, I decided to hazard a guess. "It was Father Emmanuel, wasn't it? Did he tell you he was the baby's father?"

The man replied only by handing me his business card. It wasn't a cheap, run-of-the-mill card with white stock and black print. Nope, this card was ivory, embossed with raised gold leaf that spelled out the firm's name in a fancy font. I ran my finger over it, but said nothing. There didn't seem to be much point. It would only lead to a time-consuming argument and I was eager to get out of there and over to the magistrate's office. Of course I had no intention of giving him a heads-up that we planned to seek a search warrant.

He gave me his best stern look. "If this harassment

doesn't stop, we'll be forced to take legal action. That won't be good for either the Fort Worth Police Department or your career."

My Irish temper flared, but despite the heat inside me I managed to stay cool on the outside. "Understood." I tucked his card into my pocket, signaled Brigit to heel, and returned to my cruiser.

He drove past me as I was loading Brigit in the back of my cruiser. "What's that in your mouth, girl?" Something brown hung from her teeth. *A leaf?* I reached out and wriggled the thing out of her mouth. It was a brown leather tassel. If I hadn't worried she might choke on the thing, I would've let her keep her little souvenir. But since I didn't want to take the risk, I exchanged the tassel for a liver treat. "Here you go, girl."

Half an hour later, I stood before the magistrate judge again, giving him the same information I'd given Jackson. "Zeke tackled the young man, sat on his chest, and pinned his arms down," I said as I wrapped things up. "Another man held his legs. When they let him up, they each grabbed one of his arms and led him back to the barn. He looked back over his shoulder at the young woman, but Zeke grabbed his chin and forced his face forward. I'm fairly certain the young man had a black eye, too." I went on to tell the magistrate that Zeke had deep claw marks across his face. "I saw him at a farmer's market. When I asked him about it, he claimed he tripped and fell on a saw. But the spacing of the marks and the fact that there were four of them tells me the wound was inflicted by a human hand." I held up my hand and hooked my four fingers to demonstrate. "I can't say who he'd fought with, maybe the same young man he tackled today, or maybe the baby's mother. Regardless, it's clear there's violence going on in that compound." The People of Peace seemed to be anything but.

"We need some answers," Jackson said, putting the icing on the cake of our plea. "Before it's too late."

The magistrate chewed the earpiece of his reading glasses as he mulled things over. The deep lines on his brow told me he didn't like the possibility of being responsible for a death or serious injury he could have prevented. Finally, he pointed the earpiece at me and Jackson. "I'm going to issue the warrant," he said, "but I hope you two realize the seriousness of this situation and the potential ramifications. There's no telling what the baby's parents might have told the other members of the church about the baby's whereabouts. The members likely know who the baby's mother is, but the father's identity might not have been revealed to them. I strongly caution you on disclosing that she was left at the fire station and who left her there. Hold your cards close to your vest."

For the second time in an hour, the word "understood" left my lips.

The man signed the warrant and handed it to the detective. We thanked him and left the building. As the door swung shut behind us, Jackson said, "Let's go get some answers."

THIRTY-THREE
TASSEL HASSLE

Brigit

She'd been disappointed when Megan took the leather tassel from her, but it had tasted a little funny anyway and smelled of polish. The liver treat had been an acceptable substitute.

Megan pulled the cruiser to a stop at the store they'd gone to earlier. Brigit put her nose to the cruiser's window and scented. She smelled body odor coming from the big male cop Megan didn't like. The other male cop smelled like the pizza he'd had for lunch. A floral scent came from the other female officer. Brigit also scented gasoline, bait fish, and hamburgers cooking. *Mmm.* Her mouth hung open, a drop of drool falling from her lips. She barked an order to Megan. *Woof! Woof-woof!* Translation: *Get me a burger! Now!*

Megan didn't speak dog, and often didn't understand what Brigit was telling her. Instead of getting her a hamburger, Megan returned to the cruiser and started the engine.

"Sorry, girl," Megan said. "No time for a burger right now. If all goes well, I'll get you one later."

Brigit cocked her head. Megan had said the word "burger." *Maybe she understands me, after all.*

THIRTY-FOUR
OPEN AND SHUT CASE

Father Emmanuel

He couldn't be sure what all the cop had seen from the ridge. The trees would have blocked some of her view into the grounds, but had she seen the scuffle between Zeke and Luke? Just in case, he'd ordered Jeb and Zeke to toss Luke into the silo, too. He didn't like the idea of putting Juliette and Luke in there together. Hell, he'd managed to keep the two apart for months. But he'd had no choice.

The lawyer had called him back after speaking with the cop, told him that being open with the officer about the baby had seemed to surprise her. He could only hope it would also appease her. He was damn tired of her and her K-9 sniffing around his kingdom. He wanted things back under control—*his* control.

THIRTY-FIVE
SEEK AND YE SHALL FIND

Megan

Armed with the search warrant, as well as her gun, pepper spray, and Taser, Detective Jackson led the way to the gate of the People of Peace compound. We four officers followed shoulder to shoulder, Brigit at my knee. There was no need to turn on a siren to get the attention of the inhabitants this time. Joshua Purcell was working guard duty in the deer blind. He'd already spotted us and jumped on his radio to announce our arrival.

"Hello, up there!" Jackson called to the man as we approached.

I raised a hand in greeting. "How are you today, Mr. Purcell?"

He didn't respond to my question. Instead, he said, "What's going on?"

Jackson raised the document. "Serving a search warrant. Come on down and let us in."

"I can't," he said. "I don't have a key. But Father Emmanuel is on his way."

"Okeydoke," she said nonchalantly. "Any chance you've got a gun up there with you?"

"No," the man said. "The People of Peace abhor weapons."

"Good to know." She gave the rest of us a look that said *Don't trust him. He could be full of BS.*

A moment later, Father Emmanuel appeared behind the second gate, dressed in his long brown robe. Today, he had the hood raised over his head.

Derek snorted. "What the fuck is that?" he muttered under his breath. "An Ewok?"

Jackson silenced him with a cutting glance.

Emmanuel gave us a nod in acknowledgment. "I see you've returned," he called, offering a mirthless smile. "With friends."

Jackson raised her hand. "We've got a warrant. You've got no choice but to let us in. No need to make this any more difficult than it has to be."

He made no move to unlock the gate, but stared her down for a long moment before saying, "What is it that you seek, Detective?"

"Still looking for the girl," she said. "She hasn't been found."

We'd strategized in the parking lot of the store and decided to stick with our earlier ruse, at least until we could get Zeke alone and question him about the baby. It would serve both our purposes and the purpose of the Baby Moses law. Zeke obviously knew the baby had been surrendered at a fire station, because he'd been the one to do it. Presumably Father Emmanuel knew of the baby's surrender, too, though it was possible he did not. It could have been Zeke who called the lawyer. We'd be careful not to raise the issue with anyone but Zeke.

Father Emmanuel heaved a long-suffering sigh before pulling a key chain from his pocket, picking through the keys, and inserting one in the lock. He opened the gate and stepped through, walking up to a number pad mounted inside the gate where we waited. Before typing in the code he eyed us pointedly and said, "You'll see that the People of Peace are just simple people with a simple way of living. I daresay you'll be disappointed. We have absolutely nothing to hide."

A paraphrase of the Shakespearean quote popped into my head. *The man doth protest too much, methinks.*

He punched in a code and the gate began to slide open.

Jackson waited only until it was wide enough for her to slip through sideways before proceeding. "Round up all your people," she told Emmanuel. "Have them meet in the church."

Though his jaw flexed, he said, "As you wish." He looked up at Joshua in the deer blind and motioned for him to come down. "Come, brother. Let's gather the flock."

We officers waited near the open double doors of the church as the members streamed in, bewildered looks on their faces, some of them casting worried or irritated looks our way as they took in Brigit, us uniformed officers, and the weapons mounted on our belts. Jackson, Summer, and I offered warm smiles and greetings, doing our best to reassure the congregants that they had nothing to fear. Derek's cocky smirk didn't help,

however. And while several of the women cast appre-
ciative glances at Spalding's muscular form, just as
many men sent grudging glares his way. Evidently they
didn't like their captive brood realizing what they
might be missing.

Eventually, purportedly everyone who lived in the
compound was seated in the church, Father Emmanuel presiding over them from an ornate, high-backed
throne to the side of the altar. Though Zeke sat in the
front row, the claw marks on his face having faded
somewhat, neither the young woman with the blue hat
nor the young man who'd been tackled were in the room.

Jackson looked to me for verification of whether the
two were present. I pretended to scratch my chafed
cheek again, while discreetly shaking my head. *They're
not here.*

Jackson didn't call Emmanuel's bluff, though. Instead, she stepped up next to the altar. "Good afternoon, folks. We are very sorry to interrupt your busy
day, but when I explain I am sure you will understand
why we had to take this measure." She pulled out the
photograph of her niece and held it up. "This girl has
been missing for several days now. Her name is Kendra.
She ran away from her parents' home not too far from
here. Her mother has told me that Kendra had been
going through a difficult and emotional time. Her
friends had begun dabbling in drugs and alcohol and
drifted away when she refused to participate. Her parents were having some marital problems, too. Kendra
was in a very bad place emotionally and spiritually.
We've been searching the area for her, and we simply
need to confirm whether she came to your group looking for help."

One of the toddlers who was sitting on his mother's knee in the front row waved at Brigit. "Hi, doggie!" he cried happily.

While a few of the congregants chuckled or smiled, most remained stoic. These might be the People of Peace, but they looked like a bunch of party poopers.

Jackson gestured to the male officers. "Officers Spalding and Mackey will stay here with you, while the rest of us take a look around. We respect that this is your home, and we will be very careful not to disturb your personal property any more than necessary. When we return, we will release each of you one by one, and ask you some questions. Please know this type of thing is routine and there is nothing at all to be alarmed about. We hope that if any of you has some information about Kendra, you will share it with us. We're not interested in prosecuting anyone here who might have helped her out, and we will gladly sign legal documents giving you immunity if you provide information. Our only goal here today is to find the young lady and return her to her parents." Her spiel complete, she added, "I'd be happy to answer questions if you have any."

She ran her eyes over the crowd, but not a single hand was raised. "Okay, then. We'll get moving so that we can get you out of here as soon as possible. Thank you for your cooperation."

With that, she signaled me, Brigit, and Summer to follow her out of the church. As the four of us made our way to the yellow schoolhouse, the unattended dogs trotted up to meet Brigit. While most exchanged friendly butt sniffs, the wolflike one Jebediah had brought to the gate the first time we'd come to the compound held back, watching warily from twenty feet away. At least he did until I tossed a liver treat his way. "Lighten up, buddy!"

He sniffed the treat where it fell on the ground, gobbled it up, then raised his head, wagging his tail now.

Jackson, Summer, Brigit, and I went into the schoolhouse. Forty or so desks and chairs in various heights were lined up in rows, the shorter ones on one side of the room, the taller ones on the other. Books lay open on the older students' desks. A chalkboard bore the 8 times multiplication table.

Summer pointed to the blackboard. "That right there? That's why I decided to become a cop. No math required."

Actually, cops often had to add up significant sums of drug money or determine just how many grams of crystal meth a dealer had in his backpack. But I knew she was joking so no sense in pointing it out.

We opened the supply cabinet at the front of the classroom, but found no young man or woman hidden inside, only glue sticks, notebook paper, crayons, and colored pencils.

When we'd searched the building thoroughly, we headed back down the steps.

"You know what they didn't have in there?" I said. "A geography textbook or a map." No doubt they hoped to convince the children that the compound should be their whole world. That type of insular education was a disservice to the students.

We continued on to the next building, which was the garage. I reached down and grabbed the handle of one of the rolling doors. As it went up, it revealed several trucks, including the Chevy, the Dodge, and the Toyota.

It also revealed the nineties-era Ford F-150, the truck Zeke had taken to the fire station.

"That's it," Jackson said. "That's the truck the security cameras picked up."

We proceeded methodically through the rest of the compound, looking under every bed in both bunkhouses, checking behind the curtains in the communal showers and the doors to the toilet stalls. Jackson even bent down to look up the wide chimney in the dining hall. There was no one hiding in the big pantry in the kitchen, nobody hiding between the sheets hanging from the clothesline. Inside the barns, we found the vats where the women dipped the candles, the tables where they worked on their quilts. We also found Proverbs 16:27 painted on the side wall—*Idle hands are the devil's workshop.* The same quote appeared in the men's barn, above a table saw.

While I stood back with Brigit securely leashed, Summer and the detective checked the chicken coop. The birds clucked and squawked and fluttered about inside the enclosure, clearly perturbed by the unexpected intrusion. One spread its wings and charged Summer, who slammed the door shut just in time to avoid being pecked. *Bam!*

"Those birds are crazy!" she cried.

When we reached the small structure I'd wondered about, I pulled the door open and looked inside. The only thing there was a queen-sized bed and a night table. As it dawned on me what this building was for, an "Ew!" leaped from my lips. I whispered to Jackson and Summer. "I think this is where the married couples go to have sex."

Summer whispered back. "It's no less disgusting in a whisper than at full volume."

"I know," I whispered back. "It just seems like the kind of thing you're supposed to whisper about."

Jackson's lip curled. "This is a strange, strange place." She whipped out a pair of latex gloves and put them on before lifting the covers to see if anyone was hiding under the bed and opening the drawer on the bedside table. She pulled out a strip of wrapped condoms. "You nailed it, Megan."

I grimaced. I didn't want to nail anything in this room.

Father Emmanuel's house was spare and tidy. Though his furnishings were modest, his electronics were not. He had an expensive laptop computer on his kitchen table, along with a tablet. An enormous television, the only one we'd seen in the entire compound, was mounted to his bedroom wall.

Jackson retrieved his remote from the bedside table and turned the TV on, flipping through the channels. "He's got the premium cable package. Figured as much." She clicked the TV off and returned the remote to the table.

As we aimed for the church, we discussed what we had—and hadn't—found.

"The only books other than the Bible were the textbooks in the school," I said. How could people get by without mysteries and romances and thrillers to entertain them? I knew I couldn't. The lack of books was another indicator that Father Emmanuel was keeping his people isolated from the outside world.

Summer added, "None of them seemed to have family photos. All of the pictures were of groups."

"That's all part of breaking down the family unit," Jackson said. "Typical MO for these types of cults. They try to sever any bonds that aren't connected to the leader or the group as a whole."

That thought pained my heart. My family could drive me up the wall sometimes, but they meant the world to me. We shared not only DNA, but also a special bond forged by shared experiences and concerns. Could people here forge these intimate connections? Or had Father Emmanuel made it impossible?

We returned to the church, where we made a quick round of the restrooms in the foyer. *Nothing.*

Jackson led us back into the church, where she raised a conciliatory hand to the people inside. "Almost done, folks. Just need to check out the back of the church."

Summer and I followed her through a door at the back that led directly from the pulpit to a large office. Bookcases filled with every Bible translation imaginable and a multitude of religious texts lined the walls. The Quran, sacred to those of the Muslim faith. The Hindus' Bhagavad Gita. The Sikhs' Guru Granth Sahib. The Buddhist Tripitaka. Judaism's Talmud and Tanakh. The Tao Te Jing, the primary Taoist text. He even had a copy of the Wicca Book of Shadows. I still wasn't sure whether Father Emmanuel was simply an odd duck or a total fraud, but if he'd read all of these books he must have an enormous knowledge of the world's religions. Maybe I was lazy to simply follow the Catholic traditions of both my Irish and Mexican ancestors, but the Catholic faith seemed as good as any, and I found the familiar rituals comforting. Plus, I thought the stained-glass windows were pretty and I liked the smell of incense.

I wandered over to his desk. On the surface was a Bible tabbed with sticky notes. Next to it were notes he'd made, and what appeared to be the outline for a sermon that began with the well-known verse from Ecclesiastes:

To every thing there is a season, and a time to every purpose under the heaven:
A time to be born, and a time to die;
A time to plant, and a time to pluck up that which is planted;
A time to kill, and a time to heal;
A time to break down, and a time to build up;
A time to weep, and a time to laugh;
A time to mourn, and a time to dance;
A time to cast away stones, and a time to gather stones together;
A time to embrace, and a time to refrain from embracing;
A time to seek, and a time to lose;
A time to keep, and a time to cast away;
A time to rend, and a time to sew;
A time to keep silence, and a time to speak;
A time to love, and a time to hate;
A time for war, and a time for peace.

That verse covered just about every eventuality, didn't it? Unfortunately, our time to seek was over, and we'd lost. We hadn't found the dark-haired young woman in the blue knit cap, or the young man with the black eye.

Jackson exhaled sharply and glanced at her watch. "That was forty-seven minutes of our lives we'll never get back." She motioned for Summer and me to follow her. "The only thing left to do is talk to these folks."

I whispered again. "I thought we weren't supposed to mention the baby."

"We won't," she whispered back. "Not directly, anyway."

We went back into the church.

Jackson addressed the crowd from the pulpit. "Obviously, we didn't find the girl here. Officer Spalding will dismiss you one by one. We'd like to speak with each of you individually. If there's anything any of you know and would like to tell us, we will keep your identity secret. We won't even ask your name. Okay?"

Emmanuel rose from his throne. A blue vein stood out on his neck. Good thing vampires didn't really exist or they'd come straight for this guy and enjoy a feast.

Despite the throbbing artery, he managed to maintain his composure. "I mean no offense to you, Detective, but this is utter nonsense. My people are honest and law-abiding. If they know anything, they'd tell you, right here in front of everyone." He paused for a millisecond before adding, "And God."

"I'm certain they would," the detective said. "But there are specific protocols we are required to follow, regardless of the circumstances." With that, she stepped down from the pulpit and headed down the aisle. Summer, Brigit, and I headed after her.

Jackson addressed the man sitting on the aisle of the back row. "Please step outside with us, sir." As he rose, she turned back to Summer. "Come stand at the door. When I raise my hand, you can call the next person out."

The man walked out ahead of us, and Summer

stopped at the door behind us, propping it open a few inches with her steel-toed shoe.

The man stopped at the bottom of the steps, but Jackson continued past him, motioning for him to follow us to a spot under a tree thirty yards away. "If you have seen the girl," Jackson said, "even outside the refuge, please tell us."

"I haven't seen her," he said. "I'm sorry I can't help you."

"All right," she said. "Thank you, sir. You are free to go."

With a nod, he headed off toward the barns.

Jackson lifted her hand and made a "come-here" gesture with her index finger. Summer opened the church door a little wider, and waved the next person in the pew outside. A middle-aged, auburn-haired woman ventured forth tentatively, walking as if she wasn't sure her feet were worthy of touching the earth. Funny, because as meek as she was, she'd inherit it one day.

Jackson asked her the same question. "Have you seen the girl?"

"No." The woman shook her head, her reddish locks swinging about her face. "I don't know anything about her. I do hope she finds her way home, though. The world can be a scary place when you're all alone."

She seemed to be speaking from experience, but most of all, she was speaking. Maybe she'd tell us something we could use.

Jackson seemed to have had the same thought as I. "Indeed it can," she agreed. She eyed the woman closely, lowering her voice. "Is there anything else that you'd like to talk about? Anything that's caused you concern?"

"Like what?" the woman asked.

Jackson shrugged. "Anything at all."

The woman didn't bite. "No, ma'am. There's nothing else."

"Okay, then. You have a good day."

We continued on, running through the same routine with person after person. Nobody seemed to want to tell us anything. Did that mean they had nothing to tell us, that they were in the dark? Or did that mean they were all in cahoots, keeping a dark secret? We had no way of knowing for sure, but my gut told me these people were being sincere.

The church door opened and one of the few remaining members stepped out, a petite woman in her forties. She had dark, silky hair, similar to the baby's, with a few gray hairs sneaking into the mix. She resembled the young woman I'd seen in the garden. *Could she be the baby's grandmother?*

Detective Jackson asked her the same questions she'd asked the others before her. "Do you know anything about the missing girl?"

"No," the woman said. "I haven't seen or heard anything about her."

"Is there anything you would like to talk about while we're here?" Jackson asked. "If there's anything we can do to help you or your fellow church members, we'd be happy to help."

The woman shook her head.

Before Jackson could dismiss her, I spoke up. "Do you have children or grandchildren, ma'am?"

The woman cut me a wary look. "Why do you ask?"

Jackson sent me a warning with her eyes. *Be careful, Megan.*

I chose my words cautiously. "It's just that the mother and grandmother of the missing girl are heartbroken. I thought if you had children of your own, you might understand how it would feel to lose a child or grandchild. Maybe we could count on you to let us know if the girl shows up here later on."

The woman looked into my eyes with a heavy gaze. My mind willed her to tell me whether she knew the pain of losing a grandchild, one that had been taken from their family. If this woman raised the subject, the magistrate couldn't fault us for crossing the line, right?

Unfortunately, she revealed nothing, saying only, "If the girl comes here, surely Father Emmanuel will let you know."

Jackson and I exchanged a look. Neither of us was sure of anything where the group's leader was concerned.

The woman looked from me to the detective. "Am I free to go now?"

"Yes," Jackson said. "Thanks for your time."

Jebediah was the second-to-last congregant to exit the church and step over to speak with us. "How can I help you?"

"Still looking for the missing girl," Jackson said.

He shook his head sympathetically. "Her parents must be beside themselves." His demeanor today seemed very different than it had when we'd come by before. Then he'd been guarded. Today he seemed open. Ironically, I trusted him more when he seemed to trust us less.

"You know anything?" Jackson asked.

"About the girl?" he replied.

She cocked her head. "Something else you know about?"

Pink blotches blossomed on his cheeks. "No." He rubbed his nose with a finger. Between the blush and the reflexive attempt to hide behind his hand, it was obvious he was lying to us. Jackson didn't let on, though.

"Okay," she said. "If the girl shows up, please give us a call."

"I sure will."

Finally, Zeke emerged from the church and came down the steps. He walked over and stopped in front of us, saying nothing.

"Hello, Zeke," Jackson said.

His eyes narrowed on either side of his snub nose. "How do you know my name?"

Jackson didn't flat-out lie to the man, but she did mislead him. "The church's attorney spoke with Officer Luz." She gestured to me. "He admitted what we already knew about the baby. That you left it at the fire station."

His pupils flashed in alarm now and he turned instinctively to look back at the church, where Father Emmanuel sat inside and out of sight, waiting his turn to be called.

She raised a palm to calm him. "Please don't worry," she said. "You've done nothing illegal and we haven't told anyone else that you surrendered the child."

He said nothing, his expression still wary.

"We've come here only to find out who the baby's mother is," Jackson told him. "The foster parents want to adopt her, but the rights of the biological parents have to be terminated first. Since you are the one who surrendered the baby, there will be no issues where you're concerned. But we need to find the mother so she can sign the paperwork to relinquish her parental rights, release the baby for adoption."

Zeke opened his mouth as if to say something, closed it, and glanced back at the church again, as if unsure how to proceed. Finally, he said, "The baby's mother left the refuge. She didn't want the baby and I wouldn't have been able to raise it on my own."

The baby is a *she,* I thought. Not an *it.*

Jackson said, "It's perfectly understandable why you'd surrender a baby under those circumstances. We just need to know the mother's name and how to get in touch with her so we can get the documentation taken care of."

"You promise you aren't going to tell anyone?" he asked. "I've told everyone that Eve left with the baby. I don't want them to know I gave it up myself."

"We won't tell a soul," Jackson said.

When he looked my way, I nodded in agreement.

"So the mother's name is Eve?" the detective asked.

"Yes," he said. "At least that was her chosen name. Most of us picked new names when we arrived here, to symbolize that we were starting a new life. I don't even know what Eve's name was before."

Jackson's expression turned sour. "Just Eve? That's all you can tell me? No last name?"

"No. Not even Father Emmanuel has that information. I don't know where Eve came from, or anything about her family. But our lawyer told us that it wouldn't be a problem, that when a parent can't be located the government can post notifications about the custody proceedings in the newspaper and that's enough for things to move ahead."

"That's true," Jackson acknowledged. "If the mother can't be found it will have to be done that way. But it takes a lot longer. There's a waiting period. The couple is anxious to get the adoption finalized, to know that the baby is officially theirs. I'm sure you can understand."

"I get what you're saying," he said, "but I've told you everything I know. There's no way to track the mother down. I have no idea where she came from or where she might have gone. She said she came here to forget the past and get a fresh start. She never talked about the life she had before joining us here."

The needle on my bullshit meter was at one hundred percent. This story seemed so cut-and-dried, too neat and tidy to be true. Family-law matters were never so clean-cut. They were dirty and messy and ugly and complicated.

"I guess that's that, then," Jackson said. "Thanks for clearing things up. We'll move ahead without the mother's signature."

He nodded and turned to leave.

Wait. What? The detective was going to let this liar go without confronting him? I knew she must have a strategy, but what was it? The young man and woman could be in danger. We couldn't leave here without getting answers, could we? I doubted Zeke was the baby's actual biological father. The baby was cute and dark-haired, while Zeke was unattractive and blond. And there was no way on God's green earth that this so-called Eve was the baby's mother. We'd come here to get answers, and I wasn't leaving without getting at least one.

Before he could take a step, I blurted, "That birthmark sure was cute."

He turned around.

"The heart-shaped one," I said. "On your baby's behind. I was the officer who responded when the guys at the fire station called to report the surrender. I saw the birthmark when I changed her diaper."

Zeke stared at me a moment before saying only, "I hope she'll have a happy life." With that, he turned and walked away.

THIRTY-SIX
ALPHA AND OMEGA

Brigit

As they left the compound, Brigit bade her new friends good-bye. Most of them were beta dogs, happy to follow the alpha, who was even bigger and furrier than Brigit. One of the dogs was an omega. When she'd gone to sniff his rear earlier, he'd rolled over onto his back in total submission. He did the same thing now, when she passed him to go out the gate. *Have a little pride, would you?*

As promised, Megan drove by the place where Brigit had smelled the burgers earlier and bought her one. Brigit hadn't done anything to earn it. She hadn't trailed, or scented for drugs, or chased anyone down. These bonus treats, doled out for no reason at all, told Brigit she was loved. She returned the sentiment by licking the grease from Megan's fingers when Megan held her hands out after tearing the burger into bites. They took care of each other, her and Megan. That's the way a pack operated, and she and Megan made the best pack ever.

THIRTY-SEVEN
MARK OF THE BEAST

The Father

It was full dark when Father Emmanuel, Jeb, and Zeke approached the silo. Jeb had locked Juliette and Luke in the silo earlier, and managed to climb back over the wall and stash the ladder just in time to avoid being seen by the cops. They'd wasted no time getting that warrant. Maybe calling the attorney had been a mistake, made the cops more suspicious and determined to get into the refuge. Despite the lawyer's assurance that he'd scared off the police officer, Father Emmanuel thought the guy might have overestimated his ability to intimidate the cop. After all, she was a K-9 handler. It had to take some balls to work side by side with a beast who could rip your throat out. Of course Emmanuel had been proven right. The cop hadn't been scared away. Fortunately, she and the detective seemed satisfied after speaking with Zeke. They'd bought the story hook, line, and sinker. The original Eve might have brought about mankind's downfall, but the Eve he'd fabricated had saved their asses today.

Jebediah unlocked the silo. Juliette and Luke leaned against the opposite walls, their mouths, hands, and feet bound by duct tape. They blinked against the harsh glare of the lantern.

Emmanuel looked from Luke to Juliette. "Does your baby have a heart-shaped birthmark on her bottom?"

Juliette's brow quirked, but then her eyes seemed to brighten. *Must be the flickering of the lantern.* She nodded, unable to respond verbally with the tape still across her mouth.

Father Emmanuel turned from her back to Luke. "You understand this was for your own good, don't you? You two have dishonored yourselves and your Lord and Savior with your lust. The rest of us must save you from yourselves. We only want what's best for you."

As his gaze went between them, the two nodded slowly, Juliette closing her eyes as she did so.

"All right, then," Emmanuel said. "You may rejoin the flock."

Jeb yanked the tape off their mouths and cut the strips to release their limbs.

When they were fully freed and had stood, Emmanuel said, "You must stay away from each other from now on, or next time the consequences will be much harsher. You will obey my word now, won't you?"

It gave him no small sense of satisfaction to hear them both say, "Yes, Father."

THIRTY-EIGHT
DIVINE INSPIRATION

Megan

As we'd driven back to the station, I'd asked Detective Jackson why she'd chosen not to confront Father Emmanuel about the girl in the blue hat and the guy with the black eye.

"Because my gut told me not to," she said. "Given that they weren't in the compound, he's got them hidden somewhere we might never find them. Confronting him could be worse for them than if we wait it out, lie low, and do some clandestine surveillance, follow their vehicles."

I knew Detective Jackson had years more experience than me and a better-honed gut, but my gut told me to keep trying. The only problem was, there seemed to be nothing left to do other than what Jackson had suggested. Lie low. Watch from afar. Follow their cars and see where they go. *Ugh*. Detective work certainly wasn't for the impatient.

That evening, I swung by my parents' place to pick up my mother and take her out for ice cream as promised.

While she indulged in a huge scoop of mocha almond fudge, I opted for a fruity raspberry sorbet.

As we sat in the booth, enjoying our treats, she asked me how work was going.

I glanced around to make sure we couldn't be overheard before filling her in on some of the more recent details of the cult case. "I'm so frustrated," I told her, "but I can't figure out what else to do."

"I have faith in you," my mother said. "You'll figure something out."

She might believe in me, but I didn't believe in myself at the moment. Still, there was so much at stake that I couldn't give up. I supposed I could only hope that God might give me an answer.

When I dropped my mother back at the house, she gave me a tight hug through the car window. "I'm not sure I say it enough, but I'm really proud of you, Megan. You've turned out to be a smart, determined, and caring woman. I'd like to take credit for all of that, but I was so busy with your brothers and sister that you basically raised yourself."

What she said was true. Even so, she'd set a good example for me. Not with her cooking or organizational skills, but she'd always been compassionate and hardworking, if a little scatterbrained.

"You were a good mom," I told her. "Still are."

She gave me a soft smile and patted my arm before standing. "Keep the faith, Megan."

I fought a sigh. "I'll do my best."

Saturday afternoon, Seth and I planned to go to a classic car show at Texas Motor Speedway, which sat a few miles north of Fort Worth. He knocked on the door at a few minutes before one, his arrival foretold by Brigit via a series of happy barks. I grabbed my purse, gave Brigit a kiss on the snout, and told her to "Be a good girl while I'm gone. Okay?"

I opened the door to find Seth standing on the porch. His Nova sat at the curb. In the front passenger seat sat Ollie. Looked like he'd decided to come with us.

We walked out to the car and Seth opened the door for me. I squeezed into the backseat and greeted his grandfather with a squeeze on the shoulder. "Nice to see you again, Ollie."

He replied with a grunt, but it sounded like a relatively happy grunt, if there was such a thing.

We headed up Interstate 35 until we reached the speedway. The event was popular, and the parking lot was packed. I feared that Ollie might have a hard time pulling his oxygen tank along behind him, but we walked slow and he seemed to manage fine.

After buying tickets at the counter, we went inside. Parked all along the racetrack were vintage cars arranged by the year of production. At the beginning was a 1908 Model T. It had none of today's safety features. No airbags. No seat belts. No warning lights on the dashboard. Amazing how far things had come in a hundred and ten years.

Ollie leaned in to take a look at the motor. "Would you look at that?" he said to Seth. "That's about as simple as an engine can get."

We moved on, eventually making our way to models released in the 1940s and 1950s. Ollie quickened his pace when he spotted a turquoise and white 1956 Bel Air, moving so fast he nearly ran over a man's foot with his oxygen tank.

Seth and I followed him. He stared at the car, dazed, as if seeing something none of the rest of us could see. "My father had a car just like this," he said softly. "I took Ruthie out in it on our first date."

I stepped up beside him. "Where'd you take her?"

"Drive-in movies. I wanted to see *Thunderball,* but she wanted to see *Doctor Zhivago.* I told her I'd flip a coin to decide. We went to *Doctor Zhivago.*"

"So she won the coin toss," I said.

"Nope," he replied. "It came up heads. I flipped it five more times. Got heads every time. I finally told her we could go see her movie if she promised to kiss me good night. Best kiss I ever got."

My "aww" was nearly drowned out by Seth's "eww." I guess nobody likes to think of their grandparents feeling romantic.

After marveling at the early automobiles and buying soft pretzels and drinks, we moved on to Seth's favorites, the muscle cars of the 1960s and 1970s. We passed a pristine blue Shelby Mustang. A Dodge Daytona in bright red. A gold Pontiac GTO. The image spread across the hood of a black 1978 Firebird reminded me of the army-eagle tattoo spread across Seth's back. It had been a while since I'd seen it. With the unofficial overtime I'd been putting it, I hadn't had a lot of free time lately. Our irregular work schedules also didn't help matters much. Of course I knew I wouldn't be working nine to five once I made detective, either. But one thing to be said for our situation was that we didn't get sick of each other. I supposed that was a plus.

We eased on to a 1978 AMC Pacer.

"I remember when these first came out." Ollie leaned

in to peek inside. "I thought they looked like a fishbowl on wheels. Ugliest car ever made."

"Worse than the Gremlin or Yugo?" Seth asked.

"Hands down."

We moved on to a shiny, burgundy-on-ice Cadillac Coupe DeVille.

"Wow," I said. "This car's nearly as long as a bus."

Eventually we wound our way around to the spec cars of the future, which included a solar-powered model.

"Wonder how long until we'll be driving that," I said. "Sure would be nice n-not to have to stop for gas all the time."

After the car show, we stopped for Mexican food at Joe T. Garcia's in the northside neighborhood. Like many of the cars we'd seen earlier, the restaurant had been around a long time, over eighty years. That's a whole lotta enchiladas.

It was reasonably early, and we were lucky enough to get a table on the extensive patio.

Over margaritas, I asked Seth if he remembered the first time we'd come to the restaurant together.

"Yep," he said. "It was right after that bomb exploded in the mall."

It had been a harrowing experience and left me shaken, but had it not happened I wouldn't have met Seth. *Funny how things turn out, isn't it?* "I definitely needed a margarita then." Heck, I'd needed a dozen.

We continued to chat throughout the meal. Occasionally Ollie slipped back into grump mode, but for the most part he was content and tolerable. I only hoped this new, happier him wasn't just a phase. It sure would

be nice if Seth's family could start putting their dys-
function behind them.

When they drove me home, Ollie waited in the car
while Seth walked me to the door and gave me a good-
night kiss.

"Eww!" Ollie hollered through the open window of
the car. When we turned his way, he called, "Two can
play that game, Seth."

"That's fair," Seth called back before giving me
another kiss. He put his forehead to mine. "See you
later. And stop worrying about the baby's mother. You'll
find her."

He'd read my subtle signals. Though I'd tried to be
as attentive as possible at the car show, my mind kept
going back to the young woman in the blue hat and the
young man who'd tried to reach her. Where were they?
Were they okay? Were they even still alive?

Sunday morning found me online, once again searching eBay and other online sites to see if Felicia
Bloomquist's inventory showed up for sale from a seller
in north Texas. Though I found several people selling
Nouveau Toi, Manhattan Metals, Baubles, Vestments,
and Eleanor Neely products, I found no single seller offering products from more than one of the lines.

Given that I was already up, I decided to meet up
with my family and attend mass. It had been a while.

As I sat in the pew between my sister Gabby and my
brother Joey, I contemplated the predicament. I needed
to get to the young man and woman, but how? If only
we could communicate, they could tell me what to
do, how I could help. But short of smoke signals,

skywriting, carrier pigeon, or drone, I had no way of getting a message into the compound—assuming they even were in the compound. I closed my eyes and silently prayed for God's guidance in helping the baby's mother and the young man.

Unfortunately, no booming voice came from the heavens, telling me what to do. *Darn.* I opened my eyes, finding them aimed at the Bible in the rack in front of me. *Hmm.*

My mind went back to the draft of the sermon I'd seen on Father Emmanuel's desk in the church office at the People of Peace compound. Where did that quote about a time for everything come from again? Ecclesiastes?

I reached out and snagged the Bible, laying it on my lap. I scanned until I found the verses I'd been searching for at the beginning of chapter three. *To every thing there is a season, and a time to every purpose under the heaven.* Basically, the rest of the verse dealt in opposites. Birth and death. Planting and reaping. Killing and healing. Breaking down and building up. Weeping and laughing. Mourning and dancing. Rending and sewing. Staying silent and speaking. Love and hate. War and peace.

Wait. A time to rend, and a time to sew.

And then it hit me, as certainly as God's voice from above.

The baby's mother had sewn her message into the bluebonnet quilt, and the message had reached me. If I wanted to reach her, maybe all I had to do was the same—sew a message in the trim of one of her quilts. I could buy one at the store in Benbrook, rend it, sew a message into it, and return the blanket to the store with a request that it be repaired. The blanket would be taken back to the baby's mother and, with any luck, she'd discover my message and respond, telling me where she was.

The idea was a smart one, and must have come from divine inspiration. I raised my head, looked up at Jesus on the cross, and gave Him a discreet thumbs-up. Was it just my imagination, or had He winked at me?

Gabby glanced my way, a confused look on her face. I pretended to be scratching my belly with my thumb. No sense telling her God had just spoken to me directly through His book. She might think I'd gone crazy. Heck, maybe I had.

As soon as mass concluded, I bade a quick good-bye to my family. I was eager to get out to the store, to buy a bluebonnet blanket so that I could get it back before the man from the People of Peace came by in the morning to collect their earnings and drop off new inventory. Otherwise, I'd have to wait another week. I wasn't sure the young woman—or I—could wait that long.

My mother frowned. "You're not coming home for lunch?"

"Sorry," I said. "I can't. I've got a work emergency."

As I scurried off, I heard her ask my father, "Work emergency? Did she get a phone call or something?"

I was out of earshot before he could respond, already dialing Detective Jackson to share my idea with her. I was only a beat cop, not a detective. My plan could only proceed with her go-ahead.

"I have an idea," I said when she answered. "A way we can get a message to the baby's mom, figure out where she is."

"How in the world would we do that?"

I told her my idea. "She sent a message by stitching it on the blanket, and it went unnoticed." By everyone but me, at least. "If I use the same color thread as the trim, I think I can send her a secret message, too."

"It's worth a shot," Jackson said. "It's also very clever. Good job, Megan."

If I'd been a K-9, my plan would've earned me a liver treat.

Minutes later, I was speeding down the road in my little Smart Car. I whipped into the bank and zipped into the drive-up ATM, withdrawing three hundred dollars and shoving them into my purse before taking off again. Not long thereafter, I turned into the parking lot of the Benbrook Burgers, Beer, and Bait shop.

I hurried inside, rushed past the day's cashier, and aimed straight for the quilts. I dug through the stack, which was much smaller than it had been earlier in the week. The one with the Texas flags had sold. The one with the moon and stars was still here. There was a cactus-themed one I hadn't seen before. But not a single quilt with bluebonnets. *Darn it!*

The clerk, a platinum blonde in her thirties, came over. "Can I help you with something?"

"I saw a quilt here earlier in the week," I said. "A real pretty one with bluebonnets on it."

"The bluebonnet quilt is our best seller," she said, echoing what the other saleslady had told me. "We don't have one in stock right now, but we get shipments on Monday mornings. I'm expecting another one tomorrow."

Ugh! I was already frustrated, and now there would be a chance someone could get to it before me.

"Can you set it aside for me?" I asked. "I really, really want one. Bad."

"It's normally first come, first served," she said.

"What if I pay you for it now?" I pleaded.

She raised a shoulder. "If you're willing to pay in advance, I don't see why we can't hold it for you."

"Fantastic!" I took her by the shoulders. "Thank you so much!"

She smiled and gave me an odd look, probably wondering why a blanket would mean so much to anyone.

I followed her to the cash register, where I paid her in cash. She wrote "Prepayment for bluebonnet quilt" on the receipt and handed it to me.

"What's your name? I'll need to leave a note for the woman who works during the week."

I gave her a combination of my sister's and my roommate's. "Gabby Kerrigan." No sense using my real name. Everyone from the People of Peace had had a chance to read my name tag when we spoke with them last Thursday. If they happened to hear the name Luz, or see it written down somewhere, they might get suspicious and blow my plan.

She jotted the fictitious name down before looking back up at me. "The quilts are usually here by ten at the latest."

"Great," I said. "I'll come by then."

THIRTY-NINE

ON THE SEVENTH DAY, HE RESTED

Brigit

The dog had no real concept of weeks or months or years. She only knew that occasionally Megan left the house and came back smelling vaguely of incense. On those days, Brigit got to be lazy. The dog loved her job, but she loved being lazy, too. Sleeping in. Napping on the couch. Taking a snooze on the rug. Was there anything better than lying on her back in a sunny spot and soaking up the rays?

When Megan returned, Brigit could sense her excitement. She wasn't sure what Megan was all worked up about, but whatever it was seemed big. Brigit could only hope that it would lead to a lot of liver treats.

FORTY
HOUSE ARREST

Father Emmanuel

It was Monday morning now, and the men in the watch towers hadn't seen the cop and her dog at all since they'd left with the detective last Thursday. Zeke said the women seemed to accept his explanation, that the baby's mother had fled to parts unknown and he had no way of tracking her down. The ordeal seemed to finally be over for good.

Still, just in case someone was somehow watching them surreptitiously, he'd had the men string tarps between the trees, essentially creating a canopy over the compound, making it impossible to see inside. If only he'd thought of that sooner. Maybe he could have prevented the detective and her beat cop minions from invading the compound at all. He hadn't appreciated them asserting their authority in his kingdom, making him look weak in front of his people.

He wouldn't let it happen again.

Of course he'd told the flock that the tarps had been put up for next week's fish fry. A lot of planning had gone into the event, and they needed to be ready in case

the weather didn't cooperate. They'd bought the expla
nation, just as they bought everything he told then
These people had no interest in thinking for them
selves. It was easier for them to simply be told what t
do and believe.

In addition to having the tarps installed, he'd als
kept both Juliette and Luke on house arrest in their re
spective bunkhouses. Luke could sand the furnitur
there, and Juliette could still work on her blankets. Em
manuel would be damned if those two would cost hir
another dime.

FORTY-ONE
A TIME TO REND

egan

was scheduled for the swing shift Monday, so I was
le to run by the Benbrook Burgers, Bait, and Beer
ound eleven in civilian clothes. I'd curled my long
ir and layered on the makeup, hoping the saleslady
ouldn't recognize me as the cop who'd been in be-
re and asked about the quilts.

I needn't have worried. The woman I'd spoken to the
y I'd discovered the quilts was busy setting up a dis-
ay of pottery in the far corner and another clerk was
nning the register.

"Hi," I told the woman. "I'm Gabby Kerrigan. I paid
r a quilt yesterday." I laid the receipt I'd been given
a the counter so she could take a look. "The quilt was
pposed to be delivered this morning."

The woman reached down under the counter. "Got
right here." She pulled out a bluebonnet quilt and laid
on the counter.

I fought the urge to squeal. "Thanks!"

She bagged the blanket in an oversized gift bag and
nded it to me. "Enjoy."

I drove back home and took the quilt inside, spreading it out across my bed. "It's beautiful, isn't it?" I asked Brigit.

She responded with a wag of her tail.

A twinge of guilt puckered my gut when I thought about what I was about to do to the quilt. The young woman had put a lot of time and skill and care in crafting the quilt, and here I was, about to rip the thing up. It was a shame things had come to this, but I had no choice. It was the only way I could think of to get in contact with the baby's mother.

I picked up a corner of the blanket, grabbed the front in one hand, the back in the other, and pulled. The fabric didn't budget. *This is solid craftsmanship.* It was going to take something more than my bare hands to tear the blanket apart. I laid the quilt down and ventured into the kitchen to retrieve a pair of scissors from the junk drawer. Just as I was about to cut into it, Brigit looked up at me, cocked her head, and issued a canine question. *Arrur?* Translation: What the heck are you doing?

It dawned on me that a clean cut with scissors might look intentional and raise suspicions. But a ragged tear made by dog teeth? That kind of thing happened by accident.

"Okay, girl," I told her, as I lowered the corner of the blanket in front of her. "I want you to be naughty. Take this blanket in your teeth and rip it."

Brigit cocked her head in the other direction. *She doesn't get it.*

Her mouth hung open slightly as she panted, so I slipped the corner of the blanket inside. She pulled her head back and crinkled her nose. *Still not getting it.*

Leaving the blanket there, I returned to the kitchen and snatched a slice of American cheese from the drawer in the fridge. I went back to the bedroom, used the scissors to cut a small slit in one of the bluebonnets, and rolled up the cheese, stuffing it inside. Done, I dropped the blanket to the floor.

Brigit put her nose down, sniffing the blanket. She looked up at me, her furry forehead furrowed. "It's okay, girl," I told her. "Get the cheese."

Still, she seemed hesitant.

"Where was this good behavior back when you were chewing up my shoes?" I asked her.

I picked up the quilt and started roughhousing with it. I wrapped it around her midsection and pulled, dragging her across the floor. "Come on, Brigit!" I whipped it around as if I were a matador and she were a bull. "Toro! Toro, Brigit! Tear this thing up!"

She reached out with her teeth and grabbed it, looking up at me to gauge my response.

"Good girl!" I said. "Get it! Get it good!"

I pulled back on the blanket and she and I played tug-of-war until the fabric making up the bluebonnet tore with a *rrrriiiippp!*

"Okay, girl," I said. "That's enough."

But I'd unleashed a monster. Now that Brigit had experienced the perverse joy of destruction, she wasn't about to stop. She attacked the quilt with a vengeance, tufts of cotton flying through the air.

"Stop!" I shouted. Besides the fact that I'd paid $250 for the thing and had hoped it could truly be repaired, if she tore it beyond repair my plan would be foiled. The store clerk would suggest I buy a new one. "Stop!" I yelled again.

Brigit was like a shark in a feeding frenzy, whipping her head back and forth. I had no idea how to stop her.

Wait. Maybe I do.

"Squirrel!" I hollered.

Brigit immediately stopped fighting the quilt and dropped it from her teeth. She looked at me, spun on her paws, and ran ninety to nothing for the back door. I tossed the blanket back into the shopping bag and ran after her. She was scratching at the back door like she'd tear through it if I couldn't get it open fast enough.

I turned the dead bolt and threw the door open.

She bolted into the center of the yard, stopped, and looked around, lifting her nose to scent the air. When she smelled no squirrel in the vicinity, she looked back at me with an expression of absolute disgust.

FORTY-TWO
CHEAP TRICKS

Brigit

Crying squirrel? That was a cheap trick. She had half a mind to pounce on Megan, take her to the ground and show her who was boss. What had gotten into her partner today? First she encourages Brigit to tear up a blanket after all that scolding she'd given the dog for chewing up her shoes, then she goes for the false squirrel ploy. Brigit felt tricked and cheated. Her first owner had pulled pranks like this on her all the time, but he'd been an asshole. Why Megan had done it, she didn't know.

At least Megan seemed sorry. She gave Brigit another slice of cheese and scratched her behind the ears. Still, Brigit was mad at her partner. She trotted off in a huff, plopped down on the couch, and lowered her head.

FORTY-THREE
WIRED

Father Emmanuel

He called Jebediah to his office and handed him a wad of cash.

"I need you to buy razor wire," Emmanuel said. "Lots of it. Enough to run the entire perimeter of the refuge."

Jebediah said, "Okay," asking no questions.

If only everyone were so obedient.

FORTY-FOUR
REMOTE POSSIBILITIES

Megan

Tuesday morning, I was ready to return to the store with the damaged quilt. But first, I had to sew my message into it. The night before, I had taken the quilt with me to a fabric store, where I carefully selected the shade of thread that most closely matched the trim. I'd bought a package of the thinnest needles they sold to minimize the marks the needle would make on the fabric. I had also purchased a quarter yard of cotton fabric similar to that used to make the blanket. Other than patching the occasional small hole in my clothes, I'd never sewn much of anything. I'd need to practice on the sample before sewing the message into the blanket trim.

Now that I had all of the necessary supplies, there was the matter of the message. *What, exactly, should it say?* I sat down on my bed, holding the needle and thread aloft, and placed a call to Detective Jackson. "What should I write on the quilt?"

"The message needs to be cryptic," she said. "Something that only the woman who stitched the cry for help would recognize as a response to her earlier message."

I pondered things for another moment. "What if I write 'how, when, and where'?" After all, we'd need to know how to help her, when to do it, and where she'd be when we executed the plan. "You think she'd get it?"

"I think she will. After all, she was sharp enough to think of sewing the message in the blanket in the first place. She seems to be a smart cookie."

We ended the call and I readied the swatch of cotton. *What font should I use?* With its straight lines, block lettering would be easier to sew and probably take fewer stiches, but it was also more likely to stand out among the curved lines on the trim of the quilt. A script style would blend in better. I spent fifteen minutes sewing the words "how, when, where" in different sizes, comparing them to the quilting pattern on the blanket. Though shorter stitches made more needle marks, they also held the thread tight to the fabric, unlike the loose stitches the baby's mother had been forced to sew in haste. Once my technique was perfected, I stitched the message along the trim near the damaged section.

When I finished, I laid the blanket down on my bed to take a look. Knowing the words were there, they seemed obvious to me, like flashing beacons. Better to get an unbiased opinion.

"Frankie!" I called to my roommate. "Can you come here a second?"

She'd been working a double shift to cover for someone on vacation, so I hadn't yet had a chance to tell her of my ingenious plan. If she didn't notice the words, maybe nobody else—other than the baby's mother—would, either.

Frankie stepped into my doorway, still in her pajamas. I waved her in. "Look at this quilt and tell me what you see."

She walked over and looked down. "I see Brigit got a hold of it, if that's what you mean."

"Notice anything else?"

She turned from me back to the quilt, leaning over it. She ran her eyes back and forth for a moment or two before standing back up. "Nothing's catching my eye. What am I supposed to be seeing?"

I pointed out the tiny words I'd stitched along the trim.

"Wow," she said. "I never would have spotted the words if you hadn't pointed them out."

Ugh. Now I was worried I'd made them too inconspicuous, that the baby's mother wouldn't notice them, either. But I had to take a chance and get things moving along.

An hour later, I was back at the country store. The clerk I'd spoken to originally was at the counter, but there was no flicker of recognition when I showed her the blanket. Being out of uniform and without my K-9 partner, I likely made a very different impression.

"What happened?" she asked. "Did a dog get a hold of this?"

I decided it was best to leave the dog out of things, lest she put two and two together, remember me as the K-9 officer who'd come by previously, and inadvertently out me to the People of Peace. "No," I said. "It was the bedsprings. I've got the old-fashioned kind.

The quilt got caught in them and when I tugged it out it tore the corner to pieces."

She looked over the rest of the quilt, which remained intact. "I assume they can fix this," she said. "I'm not sure how long it will take, and I have no idea what they'll charge, though."

"It doesn't matter," I told her. "I'm sure whatever it costs, it will be less than buying a new one."

I left her my cell number to call once she had some information.

"I won't know anything until next Monday," she said. "That's the day the guy from the church brings the stuff in each week."

"No problem," I said, though to be honest, I was screaming inside. *Why does this case have to move so freaking slow?!?*

As I was out on patrol Tuesday afternoon, a request for assistance came in from the Fairmount neighborhood. "We've got another stolen remote," the dispatcher said. "Who can respond?"

I grabbed my mic and squeezed the talk button. "Officers Luz and Brigit responding."

I aimed for the address the dispatcher had provided, keeping an eye out for a Suburban along the way. I saw none. I saw no ugly guy with a nose like raw meat, nor a Latino guy in need of a haircut, either.

As I drew near the house, my eyes spotted a late-model white Chrysler 300 in the drive. *Nice.* The car, as well as the professional landscaping, told me whoever lived here wasn't hurting for money. Unfortunately, it would tell the thieves the same thing.

I pulled up to the curb. The curtains on the front

window parted an inch or two as someone peered out. The drapes closed as I climbed out of the car. I let Brigit out of her enclosure and took her to the door with me.

I'd just raised my hand to knock when the door swung open.

Looking up at me was a woman sporting an abundance of gold jewelry and well-coiffed, champagne-hued hair. It was no wonder she'd peeked out through the curtains. She was probably too short to reach the peephole. She looked to be in her late sixties or early seventies, around Ollie's age.

Her eyes moved down from me to Brigit, who was nearly as big as she was. I'd even say the dog might outweigh her. "My goodness!" she cried. "You're a big pup, aren't you?"

Brigit wagged her tail.

"May I pet her?" the woman asked.

"She'd love it."

The woman reached out a hand and stroked Brigit's head for a moment. When she returned her attention to me, I held out a hand. "Officer Megan Luz." I angled my head to indicate my partner. "The big girl is Brigit."

The woman took my hand. "I'm Beverly Rubin-stein."

Introductions complete, I said, "I understand someone stole the remote for your garage door?"

"Yes. It happened just a few minutes ago," Beverly said. "It was the strangest thing. I was bringing in my groceries from the car." She gestured back to the kitchen, where several bags stood on the countertop. "I'd left the back door open on my car so I could get the bags out. After I carried the first load inside, I was coming back through the living room when I spotted someone through the front window. A young man's heinie was sticking out of my car. He was halfway in the backseat, reaching over to the front. I had no idea what he was doing, and I was so surprised I couldn't move or even speak! He backed out and hurried off. I don't think he even realized I'd seen him. When I went out to my car and looked things over, I found the remote was gone."

It was broad daylight and the car had been left open, the driver certain to return. In other words, the thieves were getting more brazen. That wasn't a good sign. "There's been a rash of these thefts in the area. The burglars steal the remotes with the hopes of using them to get into the houses and steal valuables."

Beverly frowned. "What will they think of next?"

"No telling." *Unfortunately.* Seemed that criminals often stayed a step ahead of law enforcement, figuring out new and crafty ways to rip off other people.

I glanced around the space. There were dozens of pictures of what I presumed to be Beverly's children and grandchildren on the walls and shelves. Given that they all resembled each other fairly closely, it was difficult to tell how many she had. The photos might have chronicled the lives of only two or three kids over the course of decades, or they might be recent photos of twelve different children. At any rate, there didn't seem to be much of value in the living room where we stood. The adjacent dining room, though, was a whole other story. The china cabinet was laden with silver pieces, everything from chafing dishes to platters to a tea service for twelve. She had an extensive collection of crystal, too, and it didn't look like the cheap stuff.

In fact, when I stepped over to take a closer look, I noticed most of it bore the Waterford mark.

I gestured to the cabinet. "I see you have a lot of valuable pieces here."

"My husband and I were both the youngest in our families. Everything got passed down to us, eventually."

"Is your husband home?" I asked.

She walked over to the mantel and put a loving hand on a large urn. "He's right here."

He wouldn't be much help if a burglar broke in. Not unless she used his urn to konk the thief over the head. "So you live alone, then?"

"At the moment, yes. This is actually my son's house. I've lived here with him and his wife and their three kids going on five years now. He's a political science professor at Texas Wesleyan University. He's on a sabbatical in Spain until the end of the spring semester. Took the family with him. They invited me to go along, but I decided to stay put. Someone would need to keep an eye on the house. Besides, I've got a dressmaking business here."

She held out an arm to indicate the study through the open French doors to her right. The room apparently doubled as her sewing room. Four rolling garment racks lined the walls. Hanging from them were dozens of colorful costumes in various sizes, ranging from child-sized to adult. Judging from the sequins, netting, and ruffles, they appeared to be dance costumes. Some seemed to have already been altered, while others still bore the telltale pins indicating where the material still needed to be taken in. At the end of one of the racks hung what looked to be the bodice of a yet-to-be-finished wedding dress. A sewing machine sat on a sewing table in the back corner. The broad cherrywood desk was covered with ivory satin, tiny cloth-covered buttons, shiny sequins, and pearlescent beads.

"You make wedding dresses?" I asked.

"I sure do," she said. "Sometimes brides come in with a pattern. Other times I work with a custom design of my own. I do alterations for several of the dance studios in town, too. Sometimes I even make costumes for theater productions or the Renaissance fairs. My daughter-in-law used to help me while the kids were at school, but now that she's gone I've got more work than I can handle." She gave me a hopeful look. "You don't happen to sew, do you?"

The only thing I'd sewn recently was the message in the quilt. "Sorry. Never learned. Maybe you can put an ad online for a helper."

"That's not a bad idea."

Returning to the matter at hand, which was Beverly's safety, I asked, "Do you have other children in the area? Someone else who can come stay with you for a few days to make sure you'll be safe?"

"Not really," she said. "My son is my only child. All my friends are my age. Not sure they'd be much help. I'm in better shape than most of them."

"What about a neighbor?"

"You know how it is these days," she said with a sigh. "Nobody stays put for very long. They move in and out so quickly I hardly learn their names before the houses go up for sale again."

I cut a glance at her front door but saw no keypad

mounted beside it. "Does the house have a security system?"

"No," she said. "My son tried to talk me into getting one installed before they left, but I didn't want to fool with it. I'm not good with all those high-tech gadgets."

If the house didn't have a high-tech security system, maybe it had a low-tech one.

"What about a dog?" I hadn't heard one bark, but maybe she had an outdoor dog in the backyard. If so, I'd suggest she let it inside.

"I've got Pumpernickel." She gestured toward the corner of the room.

I followed her arm to see a chubby Chihuahua asleep in a round fleece doggie bed. He hadn't stirred when Brigit and I came in, and had continued to lie there in total oblivion since. Brigit wandered over and gave the dog a thorough sniff. Still he didn't stir. Disappointed, or perhaps insulted, Brigit stared at him and issued an insistent *Arf!* When he still failed to respond, she looked up at me, her expression saying, *This dog has really bad manners.*

"He can't hear, can he?" I asked.

"Not well," Beverly said. "He's seventeen years old."

Darn. He'd be useless as a watchdog. He'd make a good doorstop, though. Or maybe we could drag his bed out into the middle of the floor. The thieves might trip over him.

So no family, no security system, and a potential victim who'd be unable to defend herself. All of this information worried me. Any thief who set his sights on this woman's house would have a jackpot waiting for him. I wondered if the thief had seen the woman, realized she'd be easy to overpower. I feared what could happen if the thieves surprised her, or vice versa. Sometimes, what began as a simple burglary ended up as a homicide when a homeowner unexpectedly got in the way.

I whipped out my pad and took some notes. When I finished, I gave Beverly the usual warnings. "Keep your doors and windows locked," I told her, "and manually lock your garage door so that they won't be able to get it open."

"How do I do that?" she asked.

"I'll show you."

We went into her garage from the kitchen. She flipped on the lights. Inside the garage were the usual implements. A lawnmower. Leaf blower. Yard tools. A large plastic cooler and folding lawn chairs. A white baby crib had been disassembled and leaned against the wall next to a padded high chair. Perhaps Beverly's son and his wife planned to go for a fourth child at some point. There was also an ancient dress form, the expandable kind with a hand crank to make it expand or contract, as well as wheels so it could be moved around. Beverly must have used it in her dressmaking business at some point. Someone, probably one of her grandkids, had improvised a head by placing an orange plastic pumpkin on top of it, the type with a handle and a jack-o'-lantern face that kids used for trick-or-treating. They'd also strapped a bright red nylon water vest on the form and draped a hula hoop slantways across the shoulders. The look was simultaneously creepy and amusing.

While Brigit sniffed the storage boxes and garbage

cans, I walked over to the garage door and slid the metal bar to the side. It locked into place with a *click*. "There," I said. "Now the thieves can't get in, even with the remote. Call a garage door company as soon as possible. They can come out and reprogram your unit, give you a new device."

"Okay," she said. "I'll do that right away."

"If anybody comes to your door selling magazines," I told her, "call 911 immediately. We suspect the burglars have been going to the victims' doors posing as magazine salesmen to see if anyone's home before they break in."

"Oh, I don't open my door for anybody I don't know."

"That's a good policy," I told her, "but if they think nobody's home, they might try to get inside. Since they won't be able get in through the garage now, it's possible they might decide to smash a window."

"Oh, my!" Beverly clutched her hand to her chest, her diamond rings glinting in the light from the overhead bulb. "I hope they don't do that!"

"That why it's best to speak to them through the door, tell them you're not interested in whatever they're selling. That way they'll know someone's home and hopefully they won't take a chance on trying to get inside."

The woman looked pensive. "You think they'll come back? Really?"

I hated to tell her the truth, but I knew I had to. "Yes," I said. "I think the chances are good. I'll be sure to swing by as often as I can, okay?"

"Thank you, Officer Luz. That would be right nice of you."

Guilt cramped my gut as Brigit and I left the

woman's house. Beverly would be a sitting duck here, alone and defenseless. I could only hope that if the thieves came back and found the garage door manually locked, they'd give up and move on.

After taking Brigit on another fruitless tracking expedition through Beverly's neighborhood, I returned my partner to her enclosure in the back of the cruiser. Sliding into my seat up front, I grabbed the mic and got on my radio, giving the woman's address to my fellow officers. "Please increase patrols by her house," I said. "The victim is an older woman who lives alone, and I'm afraid what might happen if the thieves try to get in."

My fellow officers replied over the airwaves, promising to keep a close eye on the residence. But would it be enough? Burglars could be in and out of a house in mere minutes. Even if a squad car rolled by every twenty minutes or so, we could miss the thieves entirely. My heart wrenched at the thought of something happening to Beverly, of having to explain to her son and her grandchildren at her funeral why we'd been unable to keep her safe. Hopefully it wouldn't come to that.

Still, I spent the rest of my shift worrying. First I'd worry about the young woman in the blue knit hat. *Where is she? Is she okay? Is she hurt? Is she scared?* Then my mind would shift to the older woman. *Did the burglars try to break in? Is she okay? Is she hurt? Is she scared?* It was one of those days when I wished my job only required me to ask, *Do you want fries with that?*

As I patrolled, a call came in on my personal cell phone. I didn't recognize the number, but it was local so

I pulled into a parking lot to take it. It was the man who ran the sports memorabilia booth at the flea market.

"Bad news," he said. "I've put out feelers everywhere, but nobody can get their hands on a Steve Nash bobble-head from when he played for the Mavericks. Any chance you'd be interested in one with him in a Phoenix Suns jersey?"

"Sorry, but no," I said. "I appreciate you taking the time to look into it, though."

"No problem," he replied. "If you come across anybody else looking for sports memorabilia, send them my way."

"I certainly will."

So much for tracking the burglars through the bobble-head.

When my shift was officially over, the worry I'd been fighting all day overtook me. I couldn't go home. Instead, I drove back to Beverly's house and knocked on her door, Brigit by my side. The curtains spread just an inch or two, but then she opened them wide and gave me a smile and a wave through the window. After closing the drapes again, she came over to open the door.

"If you don't have plans this evening," I told her, "I thought my partner and I could keep you and Pumpernickel company." Not that Pumpernickel would even know he had company. He was still asleep in his bed. Heck, he'd hadn't even changed positions from earlier. I squinted. *He is still breathing, isn't he?* Yep. His bloated belly went slowly up and down, letting me know he was with us, if barely.

"I'd love company!" Beverly said. "Come on in."

I led Brigit into the house. "Something sure smells good."

"It's butternut squash," the woman said. "I've got one baking in the oven. I'd planned to make some squash soup tonight. It's one of my favorite fall recipes. Maybe you and I can make it together."

"I'd like that. But first, I'm thinking we should turn out the lights and put both your car and my cruiser in your garage. That way, if the burglars come by, Brigit and I might be able to catch them." I was more than ready to get the guy or guys off the street.

Beverly's eyes brightened and her mouth gaped. "You're going to run a sting operation? Right here in the house?"

"I'd like to," I said, "if you're game."

"I sure am!" she cried, her lips spreading in the broad smile. "Wait until the gals at the beauty parlor hear about this!"

I went out to her garage and stacked her storage boxes along the back wall. I moved the garbage cans and recycle bins aside, and rolled the heavy dress form into the back corner. Once the floor was clear, I unlocked the manual lock and Beverly and I moved our cars inside, out of sight.

The vehicles dispensed with, we went back into the house, leaving the manual door lock unlocked. While I left the outside porch light on, I extinguished the others inside, lighting my way back to the kitchen with the flashlight app on my phone. Brigit padded along behind me.

Beverly had turned on a small night-light next to the coffeepot. Though the illumination seemed insufficient at first, as my eyes adjusted I was able to see reasonably well.

Beverly poured us each a glass of iced tea, and we

took seats at the kitchen table. She asked about my career history, how I'd become a cop and K-9 handler. Of course I glossed over the part where I'd Tasered my former partner Derek Mackey in the crotch, saying only that we'd been "reassigned" when it became clear we weren't a good match. In return, I asked about her grandchildren.

"Don't get me started on them," she said with a grin. "I'll never stop!" She proceeded to tell me that the two older ones were girls, the youngest a boy. "The oldest is as girlie as they come. She likes to play dolls and dress-up. Her younger sister is a total tomboy. She's into sports and loves to spend time outdoors, camping and such. My grandson turned two right before they left for Spain. I hope he'll remember me when they come back at the semester break."

"I bet he will," I said. "He's probably missing you right now."

Her face looked wistful. "I hope so."

The timer went off on the oven. *Beep-beep.* Beverly stood to turn it off and donned two oven mitts, the things looking as large as boxing gloves on her small hands. She opened the oven and pulled out the squash. The enticing aroma wafted through the kitchen, making my stomach growl in anticipation.

She removed the mitts, retrieved a large pot from the lower cabinet, and placed it on the stove. Pulling the silverware drawer open, she rounded up a spoon and held it up. "Mind scooping out the squash? It's a little hard on my wrists."

"I'd be happy to." I took the spoon and proceeded to scoop up chunks of baked squash, dropping them in the pot. Brigit stepped over to see if I might offer her a taste of whatever I was cooking. "Sorry, girl," I told her. "This is too hot. It would burn your mouth."

Brigit cast me a disappointed look and padded back over to lie under the kitchen table.

Beverly went to her pantry and retrieved a carton of vegetable stock, pouring it into the pot. Next she went for the ginger and nutmeg, tapping the jars over the soup and eyeballing the spices rather than meticulously measuring them. She added a dash of salt before pulling a container of heavy cream from the fridge and pouring some into the pot. "Now we're ready to rumble." She turned on the burner under the pot.

I stirred the soup as it simmered. Pumpernickel finally woke from his nap and waddled, bow-legged and bug-eyed, into the kitchen. He looked up at me with eyes cloudy with cataracts. I wondered what I looked like to him. Probably like a magic genie emerging from a poof of smoke.

Brigit waltzed over and put her nose to his in greeting. His tail began to move back and forth. Awkwardly, he sniffed along Brigit's side, making his way to her back end to get to know her better. He had to raise his head as high as he could to sniff her hindquarters. After doing so, he attempted to wrap his front paws around her back leg and began to hunch. Brigit looked back at him and then up at me, her expression one of surprise and distress.

"Stop that!" Beverly scolded, gently pushing Pumpernickel away with her foot. She shook her head. "What can I say? He's a lover, not a fighter."

She turned off the burner and, when the soup had cooled sufficiently a few minutes later, had me pour it into her blender.

I held up a hand to stop her before she pushed the buttons. "Let me take a look outside first. If the burglars hear the blender, they'll know someone's here."

I walked through the dark living room to the front door and put my eye to the peephole. *Nope. Nobody in my field of vision.*

I returned to the kitchen. "Let 'er rip."

She jabbed the puree button on the blender and let it run until the soup was smooth. She poured two generous bowls, one for herself and one for me, before pouring a couple of ounces of the soup into Pumpernickel's bowl and stirring in an ice cube to cool it down. She set it on the floor and called him to dinner. "Come here, boy! Suppertime!"

Before the slow-moving Chihuahua could get to it, Brigit scurried over and lapped it all up.

"Brigit!" I scolded her. "That was rude."

"Let's get her a bowl, too," Beverly said. After refilling Pumpernickel's bowl, she retrieved another metal dog bowl from under the sink and poured some soup into it for Brigit, once again adding an ice cube. She set it on the floor in front of my partner. Brigit scarfed it up in seconds. *Slup-slup-slup.*

Beverly and I continued to make small talk over our delicious dinner. I learned that while she'd been a homemaker and Girl Scout leader, her husband had been an executive at the Radio Shack headquarters here in Fort Worth back in the company's heyday. "We were very fortunate," she said. "We lived quite comfortably."

In return, I told her about Seth.

"He's on the bomb squad?" she said. "He must be a very brave guy."

"He is. Handsome, too." I decided not to mention his

broad, muscular shoulders and the sexy army-eagle tattoo on his back. Unlike Pumpernickel, Seth was both a lover and a fighter. But no sense giving the woman a visual image that might send her blood pressure over the edge. "He works with an explosives detection dog named Blast. Sometimes Brigit and I go on double dates with them."

Beverly smiled. "Sounds like an ideal relationship. Maybe I'll be sewing you a wedding dress someday."

"Maybe," I said. "But not anytime soon. I want to make detective before I settle down."

"Detective, huh?" Beverly replied. "Well, if you need anyone to vouch for how dedicated you are to your job, tell them to give me a call. I'll put in a good word."

"Thanks."

When we finished our soup, I helped her clear and rinse the dishes. We'd just put the last bowl in the dishwasher when the doorbell rang. *Ding-dong.*

She clasped her hands over her mouth to stifle her squeal of excitement.

I raised a finger to let her know I'd be right back and gave Brigit the hand signal to stay where she was. Her nails would be loud on the wood floors, and if it was the burglars at the door, I didn't want to give them a heads-up that a dog was on the premises.

I tiptoed across the dark living room and put my eye to the peephole. There, directly in front of the hole, was a nose that indeed appeared to be made of raw meat, the result of drug addiction and slapdash skin care. It was no question where his problem area was—right in the middle of his face. I wondered if he'd tried the stolen Nouveau Toi cream on himself.

As I spied through the peephole, he tried the door-bell again, following it up with a knock. *Ding-dong. Rap-rap-rap.*

I tiptoed back into the kitchen. "It's him," I whispered to Beverly. "Go into your bedroom and lock the door. Keep the light off. Brigit and I are going to the garage to intercept them."

Beverly made the "OK" sign with her thumb and forefinger before scooping up Pumpernickel, scampering down the hall, and closing her bedroom door behind them.

I motioned for Brigit to follow me out to the garage, and closed the door behind us. It was pitch-black with the doors shut and the light off. I pulled my flashlight from my tool belt and turned it on. After ordering Brigit to lie down so she'd be hidden by the cruiser, I hunkered down behind the dress form in the back, next to the wall-mounted door control. My heart pulsed like a blender on high power. Sensing my anxiety, and probably smelling my adrenaline, Brigit quivered as she crouched, ready for action. I turned my flashlight off and, once again, we were in complete darkness. My fingers felt around on my belt for the loop, and I slid my flashlight back into it.

Whirrrrr. The remote device was activated and the garage door began to rise. The bare bulb in the center of the ceiling turned on, providing dim light in the large space. The vehicles cast shadows around the edges, where Brigit and I hid. I yanked my baton from my belt and extended it, the *snap* drowned out by the *ruh-ruh-ruh* rumble of the motor and chains lifting the door. I leaned the baton against the wall in easy reach.

Two pairs of legs appeared as the door rolled up. One

belonged to the guy who'd rung the bell. The other pair belonged to someone with scuffed shoes tied with yellow laces. *It has to be the Latino man Felicia Bloomquist mentioned.*

When the door was halfway up, the two men ducked under it, stopping for a brief moment to get their bearings. Sure enough, it was Meat-nose and the Latino-in-need-of-a-trim.

Before they could realize there was a police cruiser in the garage, I pressed the button on the wall next to me to stop the door's ascent. Putting my hands to the back of the dress form, I shoved it with all the force I could muster. The two froze as they stared wide-eyed at the limbless, pumpkin-headed apparition streaming toward them.

"What the—?" Hamburger nose didn't have time to finish his sentence before he took a full frontal hit from the pumpkin-headed dress form, folded in two, and fell back on his butt on the concrete. The hula hoop slid down the dress form and over his head like a plastic snare.

I gave Brigit the order to follow me. Together, we rushed the men. Their mouths fell open and they stared at us for a split second, frozen in place. Then, the reality of the situation kicked in.

"Run!" yelled the Latino. He turned and bolted. Unfortunately, his feet were quicker than his mind, and by the time he processed the fact that the garage door was not fully up, it was too late to stop his momentum. His body kept moving while his forehead smacked the bottom of the door with a resounding *clang!* Dazed by the impact, he rocked on his feet and put his hand to the bloody gash on his forehead. When he pulled his hand back and saw the blood, he crumpled to the ground, inadvertently pushing the button on the remote in his hand.

Meat-nose, who hadn't yet made it up from the floor, seemed to realize his only chance for escape was to scramble under the descending door. He pushed the hula hoop off his shoulders, turned over onto his belly, and attempted to soldier-crawl through the narrowing space. Unfortunately for him, but luckily for me, the garage door moved faster than the thief. He screamed bloody murder as it came down on his back, probably afraid he'd be crushed. The door held him in place for a couple of seconds before the safety mechanism activated and it headed back up.

I grabbed at his legs, but he kicked my hands away and pulled his legs through before the door was fully up again. By the time the door rose enough for me to duck under it, he was already halfway down the block, heading for the silver Suburban parked there.

"Stop!" I hollered. "Police!"

Despite my order, he didn't stop. If anything, he picked up speed now that he knew a cop was on his tail. There was no way I'd be able to catch him before he reached the vehicle. My partner, on the other hand, could have him facedown on the asphalt in six seconds flat.

I gave Brigit the signal and off she went, her nails scrabbling on the concrete. Lest he awake and attempt to escape, I quickly cuffed the unconscious, bleeding man at my feet. Oddly, when I pulled his right hand back, I noticed it was still holding Beverly's remote.

Once he was cuffed, I reached out and plucked the remote from his hand. It would soon be going in an evidence bag.

One down, one to go. I took off after my partner, feeling every bit her inferior sidekick.

On hearing the pounding footsteps gaining on him, the burglar twisted around to look behind him. Not a smart thing to do. The move put him off balance and he got tangled up in his own feet. As Brigit leaped up to take him to the asphalt, he went down on his own. She ended up sailing through the air over him, performing an improvised K-9 long jump, landing several feet past him. She scrabbled on the street, turned around, and charged back in his direction. By that point, I was on him, too, and she and I met over the guy's back.

He started to push himself to a stand, but I put a foot to his back and forced him down. "Don't move!" I shouted. "Or you'll get the baton!"

I pushed the button on my shoulder-mounted radio and called for backup. With help on its way, I bent down to cuff the guy. He wasn't cooperating. No matter how many times I shoved him down, he tried to get up again, making it impossible for me to get the handcuffs on him. Brigit danced on her feet next to us, wanting a piece of the action, her expression reading, *Let me at 'im! Let me at 'im!*

Trying to keep this guy down was wearing me out, and very soon I was nearly out of steam. I stepped back to let Brigit take a shot. "Do your thing, girl."

As the guy pushed his torso up, Brigit leaped onto his back. With nearly a hundred pounds of dog on him, he collapsed to the ground again. Brigit grabbed the back of his shirt in her teeth and sprawled across his shoulders, pinning him down.

Now that my partner had disabled the guy, I could grab his wrists and get the cuffs on him.

Woo-woo-woo! The sound of the siren grew louder as my backup approached. A few seconds later, a cruiser careened around the corner, its tires squealing and headlights playing about as the car pinballed off the curb. The cruiser swerved too far in the other direction before straightening out.

The burglar, Brigit, and I were in the middle of the road, the cruiser coming right at us at warp speed. There was no time to get Meat-nose out of the way and, frankly, he was the least of my priorities. I shoved Brigit off the thief's back and in front of the parked Suburban, then dived after her, my face and hands skidding across the pavement.

SCREEEEECH!

The stench of burning rubber met my nostrils, but no sound came from the burglar behind me.

Uh-oh.

Had my backup run him over? *Oh, God, I hope not.* We'd both be in deep doo-doo for sure.

I mustered every bit of courage I had and forced myself to look back at the street, expecting to see a hundred and sixty pounds of roadkill. Instead, the burglar lay there intact, his left cheek flat on the asphalt as he stared bug-eyed at the tire that had stopped a mere three inches from his face. His mouth flapped, but no noise came out. His eyes rolled back in his head and he went limp, passing out.

The passenger window came down on the cruiser as I leveraged myself to a stand, my scraped-up palms looking as much like raw meat as the burglar's nose.

"Is he dead?" Derek called through the window.

I picked a pebble from my bleeding palm. "Get out here and see for yourself." *You dumb-ass Dale Earnhardt Jr. wannabe.*

Derek shoved the gearshift into park and climbed out. He circled around his open door and looked down at the guy. He nudged the man with his toe. "Hey, buddy. You dead?"

When there was no response, he knelt down, grabbed the guy by the shoulder and turned him over. The man's entire face looked like uncooked hamburger now, and the crotch of his jeans was soaked. He might not have died in actuality, but he'd probably die of embarrassment when he came around.

I bent down and checked Brigit. "You okay, girl?"

She wagged her tail happily. She had no idea how close we'd just come to being mowed down in the street by my former partner.

The man on the ground began to moan. As he came to, I helped him to a sitting position, then assisted Derek in getting him into the back of the squad car.

I pointed down the street. "There's another one back at the house."

While Brigit and I jogged back down the street to Beverly's home, Derek climbed back into his cruiser and headed down the road, stopping at the end of her driveway. As my partner and I ran up, we found the old woman repeatedly poking the prone suspect with the business end of a push broom. Pumpernickel stood stiffly next to her, looking off in a random direction, probably unsure where he was and having no idea what was going on.

"I peeked out my bedroom window," Beverly called as we approached. "I saw this guy trying to get away while you were dealing with the other one. He was wobbling all over the place like a drunk, so I thought I could take him. Turns out I was right." She gave him one last, solid, bristly jab and stood the broom up proudly next to her. It was taller than she was.

I gave the woman a pointed look. "You know I have to give you the lecture about how dangerous it was for you to confront a suspect, how you should leave the policing up to the professionals, right?"

"Of course," she said. "Consider me lectured." She broke into a big grin. "It was worth it. I was excited before, but just wait until the girls at the salon hear I beat the guy with my broom!"

I called an ambulance for the suspect with the head injury, asking dispatch to send another officer to accompany him to the hospital to be checked out. Derek took off for the station with the other suspect, and I jotted down notes for my report.

When we finished, I bade both Beverly and Pumpernickel good-bye. "Take care!" I called from the cruiser, my raised hand waving out the open window.

"Come back for a visit anytime!" Beverly called.

Though I wasn't technically on duty, and hadn't been in hours, I wasn't about to go home. Instead, I went with a team to the apartments of the two men we'd arrested. Meat-nose's place was filled with stolen electronics, including a laptop with the logo of the company the first victim had worked for. I hoped the computer was still operational. The shaggy Latino's apartment was filled from floor to ceiling with silver items, jewelry, and box after box of Nouveau Toi products. The Vestments and Eleanor Neely garments were draped over his dinette. The Steve Nash bobble-head stood proudly atop his refrigerator.

Though they'd likely sold some of the stolen property, with thousands of dollars in stolen items still in their possession, these two idiots would be going away for a long time. I was glad I could finally put one in the "win" column. And with this case out of the way now, I could focus fully on the People of Peace investigation. I was more determined than ever to find the baby's mother and get some answers.

FORTY-FIVE
LOVER AND LIVER

Brigit

Brigit had felt sorry for the old dog who'd tried to romance her. He might once have been a little Latin lover, barking *ay-yi-yi* and having his pick of the pound, but those days were well behind him now. And while she hadn't been interested in his overtures, she was nonetheless flattered he'd found her attractive.

When Megan had tossed her a second liver treat after they'd returned to the house, Brigit caught it mid-air and carried it over to the dog, dropping it in front of him. He didn't seem to notice, just stared blindly ahead, his mouth hanging open slightly as he exhaled a wheezy breath.

He's going to need a little help, isn't he?

She'd put a paw on top of his head and gently pushed down until his nose was close enough to the treat that he could smell it. Unassisted, he reached his head the rest of the way down, picked up the treat with the two teeth he had left, and gobbled it down. He lifted his head and wagged his tail to thank Brigit for sharing.

She'd wagged hers in return. *Anytime, little guy.*

FORTY-SIX
A STITCH IN TIME

Father Emmanuel

In the middle of the morning the following Monday, Jeb stepped into the doorway of Father Emmanuel's office at the church. Emmanuel looked up at him. "How'd we do?"

Jeb held out the manila envelope that contained the consignment sales proceeds. "We had a good week."

"Glad to hear it." As Emmanuel took the envelope, he noticed Jeb had one of Juliette's signature bluebonnet blankets draped over his arm.

He gestured to the quilt. "What're you doing with that?"

"It was returned to the store. It got torn and whoever bought it wants it repaired. I'm going to take it to Juliette and see if she can fix it."

A situation like this had never happened before. He waved the man closer. "Let me take a look."

Jeb laid the quilt on the desk and pulled back a corner to reveal one of the bluebonnet squares. The fabric looked like it had been shredded by a pack of rabid wolves. He looked back up at Jeb. "Any idea what happened here?"

"The salesclerk said it got caught in a bedspring."

Could a bedspring really cause this much damage? He supposed it was possible. He remembered being pinched by a rusty old bedspring once when he was young. It hurt like hell and left a purple bruise on the back of his thigh that didn't go away for weeks. He looked up at Jeb. "What did you say we'd charge for the repair?" If fixing this blanket would take up time Juliette could otherwise be spending to make a new quilt, it had better be worth it.

"Fifty dollars," Jeb said.

Emmanuel mentally calculated. "Sounds fair." Especially since this blanket didn't appear to be Juliette's best work. The stitching along the trim looked uneven, the curved, quilted pattern off a bit.

As he leaned in to take a closer look at the odd stitching, Jeb said, "The fish aren't biting again today."

Emmanuel looked back up. "How many fish we got in the freezer?" he asked. "Enough for Friday's fish fry?" The last thing he needed was for the loaves-and-fishes event to be a bust. The mood around the compound had been somber and subdued since news of the death of Juliette's baby had spread. These people needed a pick-me-up.

"We're getting there," Jeb said. "Elijah and Joshua have been out at the lake every day since they got their new fishing licenses, but there's been a couple days when they came back empty-handed. I saw them on my way over here. They said the fish were nowhere to be found this morning."

Emmanuel felt his ire rise. Those two men were his least productive in the woodshop and forge. That's why he'd assigned them to fishing in the first place. Now it turned out they weren't much good at catching fish, either. He was barely breaking even on those two, if that. They'd better get on the stick and learn to carry their own weight or he might have to start making some alternative plans for the two of them.

"Thanks, Jebediah," Emmanuel said, folding the corner of the fabric back over as he dismissed the man. He pushed the blanket toward him across his desk. "Don't forget to take this quilt with you."

FORTY-SEVEN
COOPED UP

Megan

Saturday morning, I made the rounds of the burglary victims to let them know we'd recovered their stolen property.

I went first to the home of the man with the Lexus. He came to the door decked out in workout gear.

"We found your laptop," I told him. "Your bobble-head, too."

"Fantastic!" he said to me before turning his head to call back into the house. "Hey, honey! The cops found Steve Nash!"

I gave him instructions on how to reclaim his property. I repeated the instructions to Felicia Bloomquist, whom I visited next.

"Thanks so much!" she said. "I didn't think I'd ever see my stuff again."

Neither did I.

"Here." She pushed a box of Sunflower Power snacks into my hands. "Take these as a thank-you."

I wasn't sure whether she was actually trying to express her appreciation or simply attempting to unload an unpopular product on me. In case it was the former, I accepted the box and offered a "thanks" in return.

"You know what," she said, looking me up and down. "Some new inventory just arrived and there's a coral dress that would be gorgeous on you." She waved me in. "Why don't you come try it on?"

What could it hurt? I hadn't bought myself anything new in a while.

She went back into her office and rummaged through a large cardboard box before returning to the foyer with a dress in a soft shade of orange akin to a Creamsicle. It was long-sleeved, with a peplum waist and a fitted skirt.

I reached out to touch the shiny knit fabric. "It's so soft."

"Doesn't wrinkle, either." She held it out to me. "Try it on. If you like it, I'll sell it to you for my cost."

Brigit came with me as I changed out of my uniform and into the dress in the spare bedroom. When I emerged, Felicia had a full-length mirror out and ready.

"Wow!" she said. "That dress was made for you."

I had to agree. I liked what I saw as I turned side to side to check myself out from various angles in the mirror. The fit of the dress was perfect and it flattered my figure. "It's a little dressy," I told her. "I don't know where I'd wear it."

The consummate salesperson, she convinced me there'd be an occasion in my future that the dress would be just right for. "New Year's Eve," she suggested, "or maybe a wedding or bridal shower. If you don't buy it, you'll be kicking yourself then."

Before I could say anything more, she reached into a jewelry case and pulled out an amethyst-colored pendant, dangly earrings, and a coordinating bracelet. "This set would be perfect with the dress."

I put on the pendant and bracelet, and held the earrings up to my ear. She was right. They were perfect.

By the time I was back in my uniform and out of her house, I'd spent $132 on a dress and jewelry that I wasn't sure I'd ever have occasion to wear. Then again, I carried a gun. If I didn't find a chance to wear the outfit soon, I could force Seth to take me somewhere fancy.

I headed off in my cruiser. While I planned to take my new dress and accessories home with me, I drove back to the station and stuck the box of Sunflower Power snacks in the cabinet in the break room. Just because I didn't like the snacks didn't mean someone else wouldn't, right? Call me petty, but I secretly hoped Derek Mackey might wolf one down and gag on it.

Late the following Monday morning, I got a call from the clerk at the Benbrook Burgers, Beer, and Bait store.

"The man from the church took the blanket back with him this morning," she said. "He said it'll be fifty dollars to repair it. He's not sure how long it will take. A couple of days, probably. He said he'd drop it by when it's done."

Woo-hoo! After weeks of hoping for a break in the case, we might finally get one. We'd been lying low, trying to watch the compound from a distance, and it had been getting us nowhere. I tried not to think of the possibility that the young woman might overlook my message. If that happened, we'd be back to square one.

Two days later, on Wednesday afternoon, the clerk called me again. "Your blanket's ready," she said.

"Great! I'll come get it after work."

The instant my shift was over, I zipped home, jumped out of my police uniform, and hightailed it out to the country store. I ran inside, fifty dollars in cash at the ready. The woman was on a stepstool, decorating the higher shelves with garlands of fake autumn leaves. She glanced over as I rushed in. "Hi, there. I'll be with you in just a minute."

My mind screamed what my mouth could not. *Get your butt down here and get me my blanket!* I wanted to see if the baby's mother had replied to my message. And I wanted to see *now*.

Unfortunately, the clerk didn't share my sense of urgency. What seemed like hours later, the woman finally climbed down from the stepstool and went behind the counter to retrieve my quilt. When she laid it on the counter, I handed her the fifty dollars, grabbed the quilt, and tucked it under my arm, heading for the door.

"Don't you want a receipt?" she called after me.

"No, I'm good!" I called back.

I sprinted to my car, closed the door, and unfolded the blanket, looking for the square that had been mended. It was in one of the four corners. To my amazement, the quilt had been repaired so well that I couldn't immediately tell which corner was the right one. I had to examine the trim around each one carefully, searching for words stitched into the fabric.

I looked at the first corner. *No.*

The second. *No.*

Third. *No.*

It's got to be the fourth, then. *Bingo!*

In response to my questions of *how?*, *when?*, and

where?, the young woman had sewn *bring rope, Friday 8 P.M.,* and *wall by chicken coop.*

Though her sentences were not complete, the message was clear. She wanted me to help her climb out of the compound by supplying a rope she could use to climb over the wall.

Given what I'd observed when spying on the compound, I knew the women collected eggs from the henhouse twice a day, once in the morning and once in the evening. She must be on duty for egg collection this coming Friday. But my observations had also told me that nobody in the compound ever did anything alone. No doubt someone would be with the young woman that night. Would that someone run back to the church leaders to tell them the young woman was attempting an escape? Or would that someone have mercy, let the baby's mother climb over the wall unimpeded?

I had no idea how things would play out, but I had to be ready for any eventuality.

I whipped out my phone and dialed Detective Jackson. "I've got the blanket back. She responded."

I read Jackson the words that had been sewn in response to my questions, and expressed my concerns about how the rescue might go down.

"We might buy ourselves and the young woman some additional time if we create a distraction," she said.

We racked our brains. *How do you distract people who live inside an enclosed compound?* It was the same conundrum I'd had with getting a message inside. Short of hovering over the compound in a helicopter or shooting off fireworks that could be seen from within, the options for distracting the inhabitants were extremely limited.

Wait . . . Fireworks . . .

Why was the idea of fireworks stuck in my head? My subconscious mind seemed to be working on something. I only wished it would tell my conscious mind exactly what it was.

Boom. The idea broke free. It dawned on me that while fireworks on a random night in October might be too suspicious, a fire might not be. After all, with the grass on the sides of the roadways brown and dry this time of year, fires along the shoulders were fairly common, often caused when smokers tossed a burning cigarette butt out of their car windows as they drove along. If the fire started on the rise above the compound, it would be visible from within the walls. Moreover, the noise from the trucks and hoses could help cover any noise the young woman and I might make during her rescue. After all, we might have to raise our voices to communicate over the wall.

I ran the idea by Jackson. "What do you think?"

"I think you're brilliant," she said.

Brilliant? Me? Aww, stop.

"Call Seth," she said. "See what they'd need in the way of approval to get this done. In the meantime, I'll put out a call for officers willing to put in some overtime Friday night. You'll need some backup who can shuttle the girl out of there as quickly as possible, and I want to have other officers in the area in case any poop hits the fan. You never know with these groups. These guys claim to be pacifists, but when they're backed into a corner there's no telling what could happen."

As soon as we ended our call, I phoned Seth. "We need help from the fire department." I explained the plan Jackson and I had come up with. "It doesn't need to be a big fire. Something small should work fine. Just enough to cause a distraction."

"I'll run this by the captain," Seth said, "but I'm certain we can make arrangements for a controlled burn. Sure you don't want us to blow something up, though? An exploding propane tank would be a lot of fun on a Friday night."

"Only to *you*." My Friday nights could stay explosion-free, thank you very much. One bomb in a lifetime had been plenty for me.

Late Friday afternoon, Brigit and I drove to the fire station to get prepared for the rescue planned for later that evening.

Seth loaded the things he'd need to start the roadside fire into the back of a pickup. Newspapers. A red plastic can with a spout. A small box. Blast sniffed the items as they passed by and sat, his nose pointing into the truck bed, issuing the passive alert he'd been trained to give.

Seth chuckled and ruffled the dog's ears. "It's okay, buddy. I've got it under control."

When he was finished, we signaled Brigit and Blast to follow us over to the grass. We didn't have to ask Brigit twice. She flopped down on her back and wriggled, letting the grass scratch her back.

I went to the cruiser and returned with a coil of thick rope. Brigit and Blast romped and tussled on the lawn, flirting in doggie fashion, while Seth and I spread the long rope across the grass.

Seth and I met in the center of the rope and turned our backs to each other. We moved slowly away from each other, tying knots every foot or so to create footholds. Curious, Brigit and Blast trotted over.

Brigit picked up my end of the rope in her mouth, wagged her tail, and looked up at me with an expression that said, *Let's play tug-of-war!*

Hey, I was game. I grabbed the rope and tried to pull it out of her mouth. "Gimme-gimme!"

Brigit wasn't about to give me the rope. She clamped down harder and lowered her chest for better balance. I yanked the rope side to side, but all I managed to do was make Brigit's head turn to and fro.

Seth whistled to Blast, who ran to his pack leader. The two of them picked up the other end of the rope, Seth with his hands, Blast with his teeth.

"Battle of the sexes!" Seth hollered.

I turned around. "You're on! Prepare to be humiliated."

While Seth and Blast pulled their end of the rope, Brigit and I pulled ours, leaning backward and using our legs as leverage. Brigit outweighed Blast, but Seth had at least forty pounds on me. Inch by inch, they pulled Brigit and me toward them.

The firefighters who'd been working the bay came out to cheer us on, choosing respective teams to root for. Some chose by department, fire versus police. Others chose by sex, males versus females.

Frankie was among them. Her allegiance was to her roommates. She stood on the sidelines, pumping a fist in the air and shouting, "Me-gan! Bri-git! Me-gan! Bri-git!"

Brigit dug her claws even deeper into the grass and

dirt and bent lower. Following her lead, I bent my knees further, lowering my center of gravity. When the guys pulled us two more inches in their direction, Frankie ran over and joined our all-female team. She grabbed a hold of the rope in front of me and pulled back with all her might. In short order, we'd made up all the ground we'd lost and then some.

"How do you like us now?" I hollered.

Not to be outdone, one of the male firefighters ran over to join Seth and Blast's team. Soon, everyone had picked one side or the other and was pulling as hard as they could.

EEERT-EERT-EERT!

On hearing the alarm, the firefighters immediately dropped the rope and ran into the station. The game ended in a draw as suddenly I fell backward onto my butt.

FORTY-EIGHT
TRAILBLAZERS

Brigit

Brigit bounced around in her enclosure in the back of the cruiser. She wasn't sure why Megan had left the lights off on their car, or why she was driving across the bumpy field to get to the park when they could have just taken the road. But she could smell adrenaline on Megan. She knew that smell meant they might be in for some more fun. She could smell something else, too. Fried fish. Seth had fed her some once and she'd liked it. Then again, other than that icky cookie Megan had offered her a while back, there wasn't much food she didn't like.

The ride smoothed out when the cruiser rolled onto the asphalt. Megan parked the cruiser and let Brigit out of the back, giving her the order to remain silent. She motioned for Brigit to follow her down one of the park's trails, the same one they'd gone down before.

Brigit scented the surroundings as they quietly made their way down the trail in the dark. *Raccoon. Possum. Skunk.* She smelled a snake, too, but the scent grew fainter as it slithered away.

Soon they were walking next to the tall wall. Brigit heard clucking noises, smelled the chickens and their eggs and their poop. But she smelled something else, too. She smelled a woman, the same one she'd smelled on the blankets and in the garden.

She raised her snout and flexed her nostrils. *She's on the other side of this wall.*

FORTY-NINE
HELLFIRE

The Father

The loaves-and-fishes event was a hit. People were eating and laughing together, chatting and playing games. Sometimes this place really did feel like paradise.

He took in a deep breath of the cool fall air. As he did, his nose detected a hint of smoke. Had someone left a fire going in the forge? Lit the fireplace in the manna hall? It didn't seem likely. The men were careful and everyone was outside tonight.

That's when he saw it.

At the top of the hill outside the compound, orange flames flickered. The grass on the side of the road was on fire.

Damn!

The last thing he needed was the fire coming close to the compound and his people being forced to evacuate. Being off-site might provide Juliette and Luke a chance to run away. It might also mean that Officer Luz would return and spot Juliette and Luke among the throng, realize the two hadn't been in the church the day she and the detective had questioned the members.

Zeke hurried over and pointed up the hill. "You see that? The brush caught fire."

By then, several other members of the group had spotted the flames, too. They'd forgotten their meals and stood, watching the flames and murmuring.

Jeb rushed over, too. "Should we do something? Maybe get the hoses ready?"

Emmanuel stood, ready to rush to the church office and call 911 from the only phone in the refuge. But before he could move or respond to his men, he heard the wail of distant sirens. The fire department sure had responded quickly. *Good.* They should have the fire extinguished in minutes and the People of Peace could return to their meal.

"No need to worry!" he called, motioning for the group to retake their seats. "It's just a small grass fire and, as you can hear, firefighters are on their way. We're safe here. Let's not let it spoil our good time."

The murmurs ceased and everyone took their seats again like the dutiful flock they were. He wondered how many of them would have gone up the hill and run through the flames if he'd told them to do it, that it would purify their souls. Hell, he was half tempted to find out.

FIFTY

WHERE THERE'S SMOKE...

Megan

The wail of the sirens on the fire truck carried through the night. The smell of the smoke wafted over, too. I hoped that the fire would prove to be enough of a distraction to allow the baby's mother to escape. The breeze carried another smell, too. *What is that? Fried fish?*

With my fellow officer Summer in place nearby, Brigit and I hurried down the park trail that ran alongside the compound's wall, our footsteps pounding on the dirt. When I heard the sound of chickens clucking, I knew I was near the coop. I rushed to the wall. "Are you there?" I called as loud as I dared.

"I'm here!" came a faint female voice. "I'm coming!"

There was a bang that sounded like a door slamming, followed by louder clucking, the flap of multiple sets of wings, and a second female voice calling out, "Juliette! What are you doing?"

Juliette? That must be the name of the baby's mother.

"I'm sorry, Naomi!" Juliette cried. "I'm getting out

of here and I know you'll run back and tell the others if I don't tie you in the coop!"

The door banged again, but softer, as if it could only open an inch or two. "Juliette!" Naomi shrieked, her cry punctuated with a *squawk*. "You can't trap me in here with these hens! They'll peck me! Come back here!"

But Juliette didn't go back. Instead, she ran to the wall and cried, "Whoever you are, I'm ready! What do I do?"

It hit me how horribly sad it was that this desperate young woman's only hope was to put her trust not in her family or fellow church members, but in total strangers. She'd done it when she'd sewn the message in the quilt, and she'd done it again now. Or perhaps she'd put her trust in God.

I cupped my hands around my mouth to direct my voice. "I'm going to throw a rope over so you can climb out!" I whipped out the rope I'd brought, ready to toss an end over the top of the wall. I'd tie the other around a tree to give her some leverage.

"What about the razor wire?" she called back.

Razor wire? I looked up. *Holy crap.* At some point in the last couple of days, razor wire had been attached to the top of the wall. If the young woman tried to climb over it, she'd be sliced to pieces, like a ham in a deli.

The *bang-bang-bang* continued, and Naomi shrieked again, "Let me out! Now!"

Following her cry were more fluttering wings, more *cluck-cluck-clucking,* and several insistent *squawk*s. Naomi wasn't happy about being trapped with the birds, and they seemed equally unhappy to have her trapped in their home with them. As bad as I felt for

Naomi, though, she would have to fend for herself. I'd come for the baby's mother.

But what now?

Without a pair of wire cutters, the young mother couldn't go *over* the wall. I didn't have a sledgehammer or battering ram to break *through* the wall. If she couldn't go over it and she couldn't go through it, that left just one option. *She'll have to go under it.*

"Dig!" I called. "It's the only way!" Though she couldn't use the rope to escape, I nonetheless tossed an end over so she'd know exactly where I was and could dig from the other side. "Look for the rope! It'll show you where I am. Dig there!"

"I see it!" she cried.

There was a cacophony of cackles and clucks and squawks and Naomi cried out again. "These birds are attacking me!"

"I'm sorry!" Juliette called. "Get in the corner and turn your back to them! You'll be all right!"

I fell to my knees and clawed at the earth. The top layer was packed hard and my fingernails tore as I raked at the ground with all my might.

This isn't working!

I have to dig faster!

I whipped out my flashlight, shined it around, and spotted a stick that was around an inch in diameter. I snatched up the stick and jabbed the end at the solid soil in an attempt to loosen it. *Jab-jab-jab.* My elbow protested in pain, but the earth began to loosen so I didn't stop. I could ice my arm later.

Once I was through the top layer, the moister lower layer was easier to get through. Still, my fingers were hardly an efficient tool. *My kingdom for a shovel!*

I shone the light around again and found a bagel-sized rock with a sharp edge. I grabbed it and used it like a scraper, plunging it into the soil and pulling it toward me to tear up inch after inch of soil, layer after layer, dirt clod after dirt clod.

Brigit watched me with interest. When she realized I was digging a hole, she joined in next to me, clawing at the dirt with her paws. Her longer, tougher nails gave her a huge advantage. In just a minute or two of digging, she reached the bottom of the wall. It would've taken me five times as long to accomplish the task.

"Keep going, girl!" I encouraged as I struggled alongside her. "Good girl!"

Brigit dug and dug and dug, kicking up dirt, some of it ending up in my hair and eyes and ears. But she could bury me in dirt as long as she got the baby's mother out.

"Good girl! Good, good—!" I gagged as a clod of dirt lodged in my throat. *Ick!* I coughed it up, spit it out—*PUH!*—and decided to hold further praise for later.

My partner and I continued our mission, digging side by side, Brigit making far quicker progress than I.

A squeal of glee came from the other side of the wall. "I see paws!" the young woman cried.

"That's my partner!" I called back. "She's a trained K-9."

While Naomi continued to bang on the door of the coop and the chickens clucked and fluttered, Juliette, Brigit, and I continued to dig, our efforts frantic. Soon, the hole was big enough that I could see fingers working on the other side, too.

"I see your hands!" I called.

Eager to see who was on the other side of the wall Brigit put her head down and peered through the hole.

Juliette cried, "Thank you, dog! Keeping digging! Please!"

My partner and I dug, and dug, and dug, and dug. When the hole was nearly a foot deep, a face appeared on the other side, illuminated by the beam of my flashlight, which lay on the ground at my side. The face belonged to the young woman with the dark hair, just as I'd expected.

She blinked against the glare. "Bless you!" she cried, tears streaming down her face. "Bless you for helping me!"

"Can you get through yet?"

She shoved her head into the hole. From my side, all I could see was the top of her scalp, as if she were being reborn into the free world.

She pulled back. "Not yet! It's not big enough yet!"

The three of us continued to dig. The hole was wide enough now, but still lacked a few inches. Brigit continued to send pawfuls of dirt into the air, and I could hear it showering down on the ground behind us.

I looked at the hole again. *It might be deep enough now.*

"Try again!" I called to the young woman.

Again she stuck her head in the hole. Again it didn't quite fit through.

"Turn your head sideways!" I said.

She turned her head and next thing I knew it was on my side of the wall. Brigit licked the side of Juliette's face, washing away the tears. "I'm stuck!" she cried.

"Hold on!"

I dug around her. Brigit did, too. Juliette wiggled and

wriggled and wrestled and wrangled. Eventually, her entire top half was through the hole. The bottom half, however, seemed intent on remaining in the compound. Her butt was stuck.

Brigit and I continued to dig, trying to get under her to remove the dirt impeding her progress. Face contorted in agony and determination, the young woman pushed herself up on her hands, arching her back and pressing her pelvis into the dirt as hard as she could to make room for her rear. Inch by precious inch she pulled herself forward, her skirt sliding down to her hips, until finally her rump broke free of the wall. I stood, grabbed her wrists, and pulled her the rest of the way through.

She rolled onto her back, her face covered in muddy tears Brigit was doing her best to clean away. "I'm free!" Juliette cried, raising her voice and hands to the heavens. "Thank God! I'm free!"

FIFTY-ONE
HOT DIGGEDY DOG

Brigit

Yay! Digging is so much fun!

Usually, Brigit only got to dig in the backyard. She'd dig up grubs for a crunchy, gooey snack. She'd dig a hole to hide her bones in. Sometimes she'd dig because the cool, moist earth underneath the hard, warm top layer felt good on her paws and was nice to lie on. But tonight, she'd gotten to dig an extra big hole. And there were chickens on the other side! Did this mean Megan was going to let her wriggle through and grab a chicken to take home? She sure hoped so!

FIFTY-TWO
FLOWN THE COOP

Father Emmanuel

When he realized the fire seemed a little too coinciden-
al, a little too contained, and that it was taking the fire
department a little too long to put out what was only
a small blaze, Father Emmanuel realized what was
going on. *The fire had been intentionally set as a dis-
raction.* And the only thing anyone might try to dis-
ract him from was the young man and woman he'd
been holding in the compound against their will.

He found Luke right away. Zeke and Jeb flanked the
young man, ensuring he couldn't sneak away. But Juliette was another story. *Where is she?*

He charged toward Sister Margaret. "Where is she?"
he cried. "Where's sister Juliette?"

Sister Margaret seemed taken aback by his forceful
tone. "She's gone to the henhouse, Father. With Sister
Naomi. It was their turn to collect the eggs tonight."

He stormed past the woman and aimed for the
chicken coop, running as fast as he could in his boots
and robe, which seemed determined to trip him up.

As he drew near, he could tell something wasn't

right. Juliette's lantern hung from a hook outside the coop, but its flame had been extinguished. Fingers curled through the wire, and Naomi's face was pressed up against the door. A hair ribbon had been tied around the frame and knotted tightly on the outside, trapping the young woman inside with the boisterous birds.

Squawk-squawk! Cluck-cluck-cluck!

"Father!" Naomi cried. "I'm so glad you're here. Juliette locked me in here and—"

"Where is she?" he barked.

"I don't know," Naomi said, her young face bewildered, her voice softer.

Emmanuel's eyes darted around, looking for signs that might tell him in which direction she'd gone. *Where the hell is she?*

Only God could help her if Emmanuel caught her. There was no way in hell he'd let that little whore bring him down.

A scuffling noise behind the chicken coop caught his attention. He circled the coop just in time to see Juliette's feet disappear through a hole that had been dug under the wall. He could see two furry legs on the other side.

It's that bitch cop and her bitch dog.

He should've known they'd be back. Only God could help them if he got a hold of them, too.

As much as he'd like to settle the score with that cop and her dog, revenge would have to wait. With Juliette now on the outside, it was only a matter of time before law enforcement would be swarming all over the refuge. His only hope was to get out now, before the officers realized he was gone.

He ran to his house as fast as he could with his robe

still doing its best to wrap around his legs. He pulled the ladder and wire cutters out from behind the bushes hiding them. In mere seconds, he'd leaned the ladder against the wall and scaled it to the top, where he used the wire cutters to strip through the rigid strands of razor wire. He didn't bother trying to pull the ladder up and over to climb down on the other side. Instead, he straddled the wall, leaning forward across it, and swung his inside leg over to slide down the other side.

It was a farther drop to the ground than he'd expected. His right ankle was jarred when his feet hit the ground, sending jolts of pain up his leg. He grimaced against the pain and limped away from the wall.

I have to get across the field!

Inspired by the biker the cop had pulled over days earlier, Emmanuel had realized a motorcycle would provide an easy and elusive means of escape. He'd bought a powerful dirt bike and stashed it in the silo, just in case an event like tonight ever transpired. He'd stashed a wad of cash in the saddlebags, too.

It was a perfect plan.

He'd be off and long gone before those stupid cops even began looking for him.

FIFTY-THREE
ESCAPE ROUTE

Megan

"This way!" I motioned for Juliette to follow me. Because it could be dangerous for Juliette to pass by the compound's gate, Summer planned to pick us up on a dirt road on the far side of the church's farmland.

The beam of the flashlight bounced as Juliette, Brigit, and I ran down the trail through the park, emerging onto the field. The back wall of the compound was to our left.

Holy crap! A man was coming over the wall. The robe told me it was Emmanuel, attempting to escape the raid he must have somehow realized was imminent. While Summer was waiting for us across the way, the roads were not blocked.

He could get away.

The thought made me sick and angry. It was time for this manipulative man to face his judgment day.

I motioned across the field. "There's a cop waiting over there to pick us up," I told Juliette. "Keep heading that way. Brigit and I are going to get Emmanuel."

Without waiting for her reply, I turned and ordered

Brigit to come with me. Shifting my flashlight to my left hand, I yanked my baton from my belt and flicked my wrist to extend it. *Snap!* Any funny business, and Father Emmanuel would get a solid whack to his old and new testaments.

Emmanuel jerked along ahead of us with a limping gait. He must have hurt himself coming over that wall. *That's what he gets for making it so tall.*

"Stop right there!" I hollered as we gained on him. "Police!"

He looked our way, the full moonlight illuminating the rage on his face. He didn't stop as ordered. Rather, he turned back and continued to limp across the field, heading to the silo.

Why? Has he stashed something in there? Could it be weapons?

I had no idea. I only knew it was imperative he not reach the structure.

We were forty feet away when I tried again, "Stop! Police!"

Still he didn't stop. It was time to put an end to this. I issued Brigit the order to take him down.

She took off after him, her feet thundering on the ground.

"Stop!" I hollered one last time.

This time he stopped. And he turned. And he raised his arm.

"Noooo!"

FIFTY-FOUR
A SHOT IN THE DARK

Brigit

Brigit had been hoping Megan would issue the order for her to take the man down. She'd felt cheated last week when the guy she'd been chasing fell down on his own.

When she was at just the right distance, she bent her legs in motion and sprang from the ground. She saw a bright light flash and, at the same time, felt something hot and hard enter her chest. She also heard a loud noise that hurt her furry ears. *BANG!*

She wasn't sure what had just happened, and she didn't feel right. But she was going to finish her job. She wasn't going to let Megan down.

FIFTY-FIVE
THE FALL OF A KINGDOM

he Father

ANG!

The sound echoed off the silo and the sanctuary alls as the muzzle flash lit up the enormous dog soar-g through the air toward him. There was a surprised]ueal of pain, then all was dark again.

Did I kill the dog?

The K-9's body hit him with the force of a furry eight train and the next thing he knew he was on his ack. His head snapped backward and slammed against e packed dirt of the field. *Bonk!* Before he could raise is head, the dog had grabbed him by the throat, her ngs sinking into his flesh, stifling the scream that arely managed to squeeze out.

No. She wasn't dead. But the warm, wet liquid seep-g through his robe told him she might be soon. It lso told him he might be able to get away from the dog he struggled hard enough.

He squirmed underneath the injured beast, shoving t her with his hands. He managed to push her off him nomentarily, but as she shifted she tightened her hold,

sinking her fangs deeper into his throat. He felt his sk
tear as he gasped to pull oxygen into his lungs. He f
the darkness closing in, his mind closing down.

Then the dog went limp.

The mouth that had gripped his throat went slac
He gulped air and the fog in his mind dissipated.

Looks like I killed the bitch after all.

He shoved the dog aside and leveraged himself
his feet. He'd just turned to run when another soun
met his ears.

Swish!

What the—?

FIFTY-SIX
OFFICER DOWN

Megan

My baton met Father Emmanuel's head with a solid and satisfying *WHACK!*

The bastard's head rolled on his shoulders and he collapsed in a pile of false piety on the farmland. As much as I wanted to beat the man to death right then and there, my fear for Brigit took me to my knees beside her. Her eyes were closed, her bloody body still.

"Brigit!" I screamed. "Brigit!"

"Is she all right?" Juliette cried, running up to us.

"I don't know!"

Brigit made no response. I put a hand on her chest. Her heart still beat, though the pulse was slow and weak. Her chest rose only barely with her shallow breaths.

I pushed the button on my shoulder-mounted radio. "I need backup by the silo! Now! Officer down!"

The dog might weigh nearly a hundred pounds, but at that instant she felt like a feather as I scooped her up in my arms and took off running with her.

A beam of light bounced across the field as Summ
rushed toward me.

"I've got to get Brigit to the ambulance!" I shoute
"Emmanuel's on the ground behind me."

"I'll get the bastard!" She took off running again

My lungs burned as I ran as fast as my legs wou
take me to the cruiser in the park's lot. I propped B
git's lower half on my thigh as I wrestled the key cha
from my pocket and unlocked the cruiser. I yanked h
door open, put my arm back under her, and slid her in
her enclosure.

I jumped into my seat, started the car, and took c
without buckling my belt, my tires squealing in th
night. *SQUEEEEE!*

The heavy chain stretched across the entrance to th
park wasn't going to stop me. I floored the gas ped
and drove right through it. The chain gave way, th
ends clanking against the sides of the squad car. *Clan
klunk!*

Seconds later, I approached the top of the hill whe
the ambulance waited. I jabbed the button to roll dov
my window. Seth, Frankie, and another firefighter we
standing by the road. Seth held the hose, while Frank
was using a tool to tamp down the flames. As n
cruiser careened to a screeching stop, Seth looked ov
at me.

"Seth!" I screamed. "Brigit was shot! Help her!"

Seth's face flashed with alarm. He handed the ho
to the other firefighter and ran to my car, jerking th
back door open. I jumped out as he pulled Brigit fro
her enclosure and ran with her to the open doors of th
ambulance.

"She's been shot!" I yelled to the paramedics inside. "My dog's been shot!"

They helped Seth lift her into the bay and laid her on a gurney. The white sheets instantly stained red as blood flowed from the open wound in her chest. My partner, my best friend, *my Brigit* lay there, motionless and unresponsive, as one of the paramedics forced her eyelids open and shined a penlight into her eyes.

"No response," he said. "If she's going to have any chance at all, we've got to get her to an emergency vet. Stat."

I grabbed a bar and pulled myself into the ambulance.

Seth backed away. "I'll be there as soon as I can!"

The paramedic slammed the door closed and hollered to the driver. "Go!"

"Where?" he asked.

While one paramedic continued to examine Brigit, the other used his phone to search for the closest emergency animal hospital. "Get to I-20 and head east," he instructed.

I knelt next to the gurney, my hand cupping Brigit's chin. "Fight, girl!" I told her. "You can make it!"

Tears tried to blind me, but I blinked them away. I watched her chest, thankful each time it rose with a breath. *Thank you, God!* I also begged the Almighty to spare her life. *Please, God! Don't take her from me! She doesn't deserve to die!*

The paramedic called the animal hospital to let them know we were on our way. "We've got a police K-9 who's been shot in the chest. She's unresponsive but still breathing."

But as the ambulance raced toward the clinic, its si
ren screaming through the night, Brigit's breaths grew
farther apart and became so shallow they were virtu
ally imperceptible.

The second paramedic put a stethoscope to her ches
and listened. "We're losing her!"

Oh, no! Please, God! No!

He rolled her onto her back, put the ball of his hand:
to her chest, and began compressions.

Terror gripped my mind. *Stay with me, Brigit
Please!* Rage took a turn, too. *If that bastard killed
Brigit,* I thought, *then I hope I killed him!* That whack
I'd delivered had been solid. I'd held nothing back.

The ambulance pulled up to the doors of the clinic
The paramedics flung their doors open and rushed
around to open the bay. As the doors swung open,
could see two people in scrubs rush out of the anima
hospital and run toward us.

They lowered the gurney and whisked Brigit away
leaving me standing in the back of the ambulance. The
paramedic who'd worked on her helped me down, pu
a hand on my shoulder, and gave it a squeeze. "I hope
your partner pulls through."

Tears blinded me and he became a blur. "Thanks fo
everything you've done," I whispered, my throat tigh
with emotion.

They packed up the ambulance and drove off
Though I was terrified of what I might learn inside,
forced my feet to move and walked into the clinic.

The woman at the front desk acknowledged me with
a nod. "They've got your dog in surgery. We'll give you
an update as soon as we know anything. In the mean
time, you can wash up and take a seat."

Wash up?

I glanced down to see that my shirt was drenched in Brigit's blood. My hands were covered in her blood, too. I shuffled zombielike to the bathroom off the foyer. In the mirror, I noticed more of Brigit's blood smeared across my chin. As much blood as I had on me, how much could be left in her veins? Would it be enough to keep her alive?

I turned on the water and watched it turn pink as it took Brigit's blood from my hands. I grabbed a paper towel, wet it, and wiped my chin. I grabbed additional towels and pressed them to my uniform, blotting what blood I could. An odd sense of guilt rippled through me as I placed the towels bearing Brigit's once life-sustaining blood in the trash can.

I returned to the waiting area and sat to wait for what felt like an eternity. At some point, Seth came in and took both the seat next to me and my hand. I was glad he didn't offer any platitudes to try to lift me up. We'd both seen how bad she'd looked. We both knew the chances of her surviving were slim to none.

A half hour later, a veterinarian in scrubs and a surgical mask stepped into the lobby. I rose reflexively, my mouth falling open, too afraid to let the question on my lips come out.

"We removed the bullet," he said, "but it came very close to her heart. She's stable now, but I won't lie to you. It was touch and go for a while in there."

I nodded and bit my lip to keep from bursting into sobs. When I could compose myself, I asked, "Can we see her?"

"Sure."

He led me and Seth to Brigit's recovery room. She

lay on a gurney with metal bars on each side to prevent her from falling off the bed. A tube ran from an IV drip into her front paw, and wires ran from her chest to a heart monitor that displayed her heart rhythm on a screen and emitted a soft *beep* with each beat. Her chest had been shaved bare and a wide, white gauze bandage was wrapped around her. Her fur was damp with acrid-smelling antiseptic, tinges of blood still visible around her sides.

I cupped her jaw loosely, running my thumb over her ear. She'd always liked to have her ears rubbed.

"I'm here, girl," I told her. "You're a good girl. A good, good girl. You're going to be okay." Of course I didn't know whether she was going to be okay or not, but just in case she could hear me I wanted to sound reassuring. I pressed my lips lightly to her snout. "I love you, Briggie."

FIFTY-SEVEN
BLEEPING BEEPS

Brigit

She felt Megan kiss the side of her nose, smelled Megan's sweat and fear, heard her say what a good girl Brigit was. She wanted to open her eyes and look at Megan, but she was too exhausted and drowsy.

"You're a good girl," Megan repeated as she stroked Brigit's ear.

I am a good girl.

Brigit could still taste the man's blood in her mouth. He'd been fun to chase, at least until something hot and hard had hit her in the chest. That had hurt. But now she was feeling no pain.

She drifted off to Megan's mantra. "You're a good, good girl."

FIFTY-EIGHT
COUNT YOUR BLESSINGS

The Father

He shouldn't have shot the dog. He'd have faced charges for kidnapping, he supposed. Maybe false imprisonment for refusing to let Juliette and Luke leave the sanctuary. But now he'd also face charges for killing a police officer. How many years would he get for that? Hell, he'd probably end up with a sentence longer than a typical dog's life span.

The doctor held up the X-ray. "You've got a cranial fracture. Whoever hit you meant business."

A fractured skull. No wonder he had a migraine. That damn cop and her stupid dog had ruined everything.

There would be no going back now.

He only wondered what would happen going forward, what his sentence would be when he got his judgment day.

FIFTY-NINE
RESURRECTIONS AND REUNIONS

Megan

Three hours later, as the sedation wore off, Brigit's eyes fluttered.

A squeal of glee leaped from my throat and I stood from the rolling stool. "She's waking up!"

Seth stood, too, and we hovered over the dog as she blinked against the glare of the overhead light. She tried to raise her head, but could only manage to lift it an inch or two before putting it back down. The blood loss had left her without energy and strength.

I ran my hand over her head and neck, joyful tears welling up in my eyes. "Just rest, girl. Just rest. You're going to be okay."

Brigit released a shuddering breath, opened her mouth, and gave my wrist a loving lick.

With Brigit now stable and sleeping soundly, I checked in with Detective Jackson.

The phone had barely had time to ring before she answered my call. "How's Brigit?"

"She pulled through," I said.

"Thank God!" She breathed hard in relief. "We were all so worried."

The veterinarian had said that my partner would have to stay at the animal hospital another couple of days for observation, but then she could come home to recuperate. I wasn't sure how long it would take before things would return to normal, but I hoped it wouldn't be long.

"What's going on?" I asked Jackson.

"I just got back to the station," she said. "It took us a while to sort everything out at the compound. Father Emmanuel is at the hospital. His skull is fractured, but he's expected to make a full recovery."

While I'd earlier hoped I'd killed the bastard, I had to admit I was now glad he'd lived. I didn't need a kill on my conscience or my work record, and it would be fun to see him dragged through the mud, convicted and sentenced, his sins made public.

"We've got two other men in custody," Jackson said. "The ones that went by Zeke and Jebediah. The baby's parents are here at the station. Can you swing by?"

"Of course."

After making a quick stop at my house so I could change into clean clothes, Seth drove me to the station. My cruiser sat in the lot, waiting for me and Brigit to get back out on patrol together once she'd recovered. One of the other officers must have driven it from the compound back to the precinct. The chain I'd driven through at the park's entrance had left a series of dents along the sides and chipped the paint, but the cosmetic damage shouldn't cost a lot or take much time to fix.

Seth gave me a quick kiss on the cheek before I climbed out. "You sure know how to get a job done."

"Are you saying I'm a good girl?" I put my curved hands up in front of me like paws and let my tongue loll out, pretending to pant. *Heh-heh-heh.*

He reached out to ruffle the hair on the top of my head. "Yep. You're a good girl, Megan. A good, good girl." A naughty grin spread across his face. "If you'd like, I'll treat you to a bone."

"Maybe later," I replied. "There's still work to be done." With that, I returned his kiss and walked into the station.

I found Detective Jackson in her office. Juliette sat upright in one of the chairs. Though her cheeks were stained with fresh tears, her blue eyes were bright with hope. Her hand was clutched in the palm of an attractive young man who sat in the other chair. He had long limbs, short brown hair, and a sickly yellow tinge around one eye, the remnants of the black eye he'd received weeks before. He was the guy I'd seen through my binoculars, the one who'd tried to run to Juliette when she'd been in the garden.

Jackson introduced us. "Officer Luz, this is Luke. He's the baby's father."

Just as I'd suspected.

Luke released Juliette's hand and the two stood from their seats.

Juliette grabbed my hand in both of hers and raised it to her heart. "Thank you!" she cried. "Thank you for saving us from that awful place!"

"No problem." I gave her a smile and a nod.

When she released my hand, Luke took it. "We owe you everything, Officer Luz. You and your partner."

I shook my head. "We were just doing our jobs."

Jackson scoffed but cut me a smile. "That's the understatement of the year."

Maybe so, but I'd only done what seemed right. I whipped out my cell phone and pulled up my camera roll, swiping through it until I found the picture I'd taken of their baby the night she'd been dropped. "I took a photo of your baby the night she was left at the fire station. Would you like to see it?"

"Yes!" Juliette clapped her hands and jumped up and down.

Luke nodded, a big grin on his face.

I held up the screen to show them.

Juliette's hands went to her cheeks as tears flooded her eyes. "There she is!" Instinctively, she reached toward the screen as if to touch her baby. I handed her the phone, and Juliette clutched it as if hanging on to her baby for dear life.

Luke grinned at the screen, a proud papa, before turning to Juliette. "She's just as beautiful as you said she was."

"You never got to see her?" I asked.

Luke's face clouded. "No. Father Emmanuel wouldn't let me near the infirmary. He took the baby away right after the midwife delivered her."

Juliette affirmed Luke's words with a nod and looked up from the screen, her eyes going from me to Jackson. "I know y'all need to ask us questions, and I know our baby is safe, but is there any way we can go see Skye now?"

"Skye?" I asked. "Is that what you named her?"

She nodded. "The sky was the only thing we could

see of the outside world from the church grounds. Looking up at the sky gave us hope."

"It's the perfect name for her," I agreed, "especially since she looks like a little angel." As much as I hated to interrupt her admiring the photo of her baby, I'd need my phone to call the foster parents. I held out my hand. "If you'll hand me my phone, I'll check with the couple who's caring for her, see how soon we can get a visit."

She handed the device to me, and I scrolled through my contacts until I found the number for the O'Neills. It was two in the morning, but after meeting the foster mother earlier and learning what a sweet woman she was, I had no doubt she'd forgive us for the late-night call.

The woman's voice was groggy when she answered. "Hello?"

"Hi, Mrs. O'Neill," I said. "It's Officer Megan Luz. Sorry to call you so late, but we've got some new information on the baby girl you've been fostering."

"What is it?" She sounded wide awake now.

"The baby had been kidnapped."

The woman gasped. "Oh my gosh!"

"The man who dropped her off wasn't her father. We found her real parents only a few hours ago, and they'd love to see her as soon as possible."

"Of course!" she said. "Come as soon as you can."

I gave the couple a thumbs-up so they'd know she'd agreed to the late-night visit. "We're on our way."

Luke and Juliette gathered up their meager belongings and we piled into Jackson's unmarked car. Luke and Juliette sat in the back, while I sat up front and navigated.

On the drive, the detective filled me in on what happened at the compound after I left in the ambulance with Brigit. "Summer kept watch over Father Emmanuel until another ambulance arrived and took him to John Peter Smith," she said, referring to Fort Worth's primary public hospital. "I interviewed Juliette on-site. You were right about her being the baby's mother, obviously. A year ago, Juliette and Luke asked Father Emmanuel for permission to marry, but he refused to let them wed and did his best to keep them apart afterward. He told them if they left the compound, they'd never be allowed back to see their families. He'd make sure they couldn't even communicate with each other either."

Juliette and Luke interjected as the detective went along, describing Father Emmanuel as a control freak who expected complete and unconditional loyalty, and wouldn't tolerate anyone questioning his teachings or methods. Neither Juliette nor Luke toed the party line to his satisfaction, and Father Emmanuel was intent on breaking them, molding them to his will. When he found out the two had somehow managed to get time alone together and that Juliette was pregnant, he was furious.

"He called me a whore," Juliette said. "He told me I'd rot in hell for having a baby out of wedlock. But Luke and I had already committed ourselves to each other, before God, without Father Emmanuel's blessing. As far as we were concerned, we were married. Our baby wasn't a sin. She was a sign of God's love, a gift."

"A blessing," Luke added.

Father Emmanuel felt differently, of course. He considered the baby a sign of their disobedience, a challenge to his authority. After Juliette gave birth, when he told her he was taking the baby for her newborn shots and eye drops, he ordered Zeke to drop the baby at the fire station to punish the young couple.

Juliette's fists balled involuntarily. "I begged Father Emmanuel to let me go with them to the hospital, but he wouldn't let me. He said I needed to rest. I had a really bad feeling about things, but there was nothing I could do to stop them. When they were walking off with Skye, I realized how cold the night was. I asked them to let me get the blanket I'd made for her. While they waited outside the door to the infirmary, I got the idea to sew the message in the blanket. I only had a few seconds to get it done. I wasn't sure it would do any good, that anyone would see it." She gulped back a fresh sob of emotion, and when she spoke again her voice was tight. "Thank God you did." She grabbed my shoulder and gave it a grateful squeeze.

Emotion gripped my vocal chords now, and all I could do was nod. It would have been so easy to overlook the threads, to miss Juliette's critical message. I could only wonder how many other cryptic cries for help were overlooked each day.

Jackson eyed Juliette in the rearview mirror. "Sewing that message was a clever thing to do."

"I suppose it was divine inspiration." Juliette offered a small smile before continuing. "When Father Emmanuel came back, he told me our baby had died at the hospital. I was upset and thought he might be lying to me and I tried to fight back. That's when he threw me into the silo. He knew nobody would find me there or hear me call for help." She shuddered. "It was so dark inside. I lost all track of time. I had no idea how long he kept me there."

My mind recalled the towering, leaning structure on the adjacent farmland, how I'd seen a man climbing down the ladder on its side. Had Juliette been inside at the time? And what kind of sick creep throws a new mother—one whose baby has just been torn from her—into that kind of solitary confinement? It was torture, pure and simple.

Jackson let out a loud breath. "It's amazing you didn't go crazy in there."

"I nearly did," Juliette said. "But I kept telling myself to stay calm, that I'd be no good to myself or my baby if I lost my mind. And I didn't want to let Father Emmanuel win." Her eyes narrowed and she gritted her teeth in determination before continuing. "When he let me out of the silo, I asked to see Skye's body. He told me she'd already been cremated. At that point, I was starting to believe him. I thought maybe I just didn't want to face the truth, that I'd really lost my baby. But a few days later he came to me and asked 'Does your baby have a birthmark on her bottom?' He talked about her like she was still alive, and it made me wonder again if he'd lied to me. She doesn't have a birthmark, but it seemed like the right answer to give him was 'yes,' so that's what I said."

I explained to her that the pretend birthmark was my doing. "We knew from the description the firefighters gave us that Zeke was the one who'd dropped Skye at the station, but we had serious doubts about whether he was the baby's father. A father would know whether his baby has a birthmark. The question was my way of determining if the baby really belonged to Zeke."

Jackson chimed in again. "When Zeke gave the wrong answer, we knew for certain something strange was going on."

"I'd seen you through my binoculars from the rise in the road," I told Juliette. "You were in the garden with an older woman, sprinkling something on the lantana."

Juliette exhaled sharply. "Father Emmanuel gave me a vase filled with what he said were my baby's ashes. The garden was my favorite spot, the place where Luke and I used to meet and talk, so I decided to spread Skye's remains there. Emmanuel wouldn't let Luke come with me. He wouldn't let me do it alone, either. After we asked Father Emmanuel for permission to leave, they kept us apart and always made sure another woman was with me and another man was with Luke. We were under constant watch." She wiped a fresh tear from her eye. "Of course, I know now that those ashes weren't Skye. They'd smelled of cedar. I bet Father Emmanuel just collected them from the fireplace in the manna hall."

What kind of sick, twisted person would do such a thing? Tell a young mother her baby had passed and provide her with fake ashes? A person who belongs in prison for the rest of his life, that's what kind.

"When I saw you," I said, "it struck me that you had the same dark hair and the same blue knit cap as your baby. I figured you were likely the baby's mother. But when we searched the place we couldn't find you. We had no idea where you'd gone."

Realization dawned in her eyes. "That must have

been when they put me and Luke in the silo together. We didn't know why. But Jeb came and got me from the garden and hurried me to the back wall. They had a ladder and made me climb over and rushed me to the silo."

The ladder was probably the same one Father Emmanuel had used to scale the wall earlier.

"It was the same for me," Luke said. "After Zeke grabbed me, he forced me into the silo, too." He cast a loving glance at Juliette. "When I saw that Juliette was in there, I was so happy. At first, anyway. Then Jeb pulled out a gun and said if either of us said a single word, he'd put an end to us both."

"Luckily," Juliette added, "they only kept us there for a few hours that time."

I pointed to Detective Jackson. "You've got her to thank for that. She convinced Zeke and Father Emmanuel that we believed their story, that the baby's mother had abandoned her and left the compound."

Jackson shrugged. "My gut told me we should play along."

Juliette looked from me to the detective. "Whose idea was it to send me the message on the quilt?"

Jackson pointed to me now. "Megan gets all the credit for that maneuver."

I humbly raised my palms. "I was only following your lead, Juliette. I'd come across your bluebonnet blankets at the country store down the road. When I noticed that the blanket was so similar to the one the baby had been wrapped in, I asked the sales clerk where the store got their blankets from. She told me they were made by women in the People of Peace compound. That told me we were on the right track."

She clasped her hands to her chest and choked up when she tried to speak. "You'll never know what it meant to me when the quilt came back and I saw the words on it, offering to help me. For the first time, I had real hope I might get out of that hell, that Luke and I could start a normal life on the outside with our baby."

"Speaking of Luke." Jackson turned her focus to the young man and gestured to his black eye. "How did that come about?"

He put his fingers to his face, as if he'd forgotten all about the bruise in his excitement to be freed. "When Emmanuel first told me the same story about our baby, that she'd had a bad reaction to a shot and passed on, I questioned him. He took my questions as defiance, and told Zeke and Jeb to discipline me."

Though Luke said no more, it was clear the discipline resulted in the horrific bruise. Those two could add assault and battery to the charges they'd be facing.

I asked Juliette and Luke some questions that had been dogging me. "Have you two always lived in the compound?"

"No," Juliette said. "My parents moved us there from Fort Worth when I was ten. They were poor and not well educated and struggled. My father lost his job when the bean factory closed."

The closing of the iconic Ranch Style Beans factory had been a dark day for the city. Residents had grown accustomed to smelling the savory aroma of simmering beans, onions, and garlic when passing the factory. These days, the space served as the home of a whiskey distillery.

"When we were evicted from our apartment," Juliette continued, "we went to a church for help. It was nighttime, and the church was dark and locked up. I'll never forget that night. I could tell my parents were scared, that they didn't know what to do. Father Emmanuel happened to come upon us there and offered help. To my parents, he seemed like a godsend, a savior. He offered them both steady work and a roof over our heads and three meals a day. My parents considered the refuge a paradise, but I didn't like it there. I missed my friends and my school. I didn't like that we couldn't all live together as a family anymore. And I never liked Father Emmanuel. Something about him always seemed weird to me, but my parents wouldn't listen. They thought I was just being a rebellious adolescent. Anytime I brought it up, they'd force me to kneel in the church and pray for hours. After a while, I realized they'd never listen to me. They were caught in Father Emmanuel's web. I gave up even trying to convince them to leave."

Poor Juliette. She was caught in Emmanuel's web, too, though unwillingly.

When she finished, Luke turned his attention from her to me and shared his story. "I was fifteen when my mother took me to the settlement. She'd had drug problems and hadn't been able to get clean. She saw the refuge as a place to get herself together." He closed his eyes for a moment, as if in pain, before opening them again. "She got clean, but she got brainwashed, too. If Father Emmanuel told her to cut out her own heart, she'd happily do it."

Were people so desperate for a savior they were willing to believe anything and anyone? While I could understand having faith in a higher power, I supposed I'd never understand that kind of blind devotion to another human being, a mere mortal. My mind simply didn't work that way. I'd been born with a brain that wondered "what if?," that insisted on examining things from every angle, that accepted little without proof and rarely took things at face value, that sought to discern the motives behind human behavior. Some might call me a cynic or skeptic, but I preferred to think of myself as a truth-seeker.

As we drove, Luke and Juliette leaned forward anxiously in their seats and watched intently out the windows, as if seeing civilization for the first time. I could hardly imagine being confined to a few acres and cut off from the outside when there was a whole world full of possibilities to explore. I hoped these two would make up for lost time and find a happy place for themselves out here.

"How much longer?" Juliette asked after we'd been driving only a short time.

I glanced at the screen of my phone. "Eight minutes."

"That long?" The agonized look on her face said it could never be soon enough.

The detective and I exchanged glances. Though this situation technically didn't constitute an emergency, we'd implicitly agreed in that glance that it was worth bending the rules. I reached into the console and pulled out the detective's temporary beacon. After plugging the ten-foot cord into the cigarette lighter, I unrolled my window, activated the flasher, and slid the flashing light onto the roof of the car, where a strong magnet held it in place.

"Hang on tight!" Jackson called to the couple.

She put the pedal to the metal and in three short

minutes we pulled up in front of the gray brick home where I'd visited the baby previously. On the porch stood Mrs. O'Neill, along with her stocky, brown-haired husband, both wearing pajamas and slippers. The woman held Skye cradled in her arms. Though it had only been a few weeks since the baby had been left at the fire station, and much less since I'd paid them a visit, it was clear she'd grown quite a bit.

The car hadn't even come to a complete stop before Juliette and Luke had thrown their doors open and leaped out. Detective Jackson cut the engine, and we opened our doors as they ran across the grass and up the steps.

"Skye!" Juliette cried. "Mommy and Daddy are here!" She burst into happy sobs as Mrs. O'Neill handed the baby over.

Luke wrapped his long arms around both the baby and his wife, enveloping them in a protective embrace. He, too, began to sob.

Lest the flashing light rouse the neighbors, I un-plugged the beacon and removed it from the roof of the car, returning it to its place in the console. I walked up the front path, waving away a pesky moth that had flown in to powwow with his buddies around the porch light. After greeting the foster mother with a smile and nod, I extended my hand to her husband. "Hi, Mr. O'Neill. I'm Officer Megan Luz."

Jackson introduced herself to the couple, as well. "Detective Audrey Jackson. Nice to meet you folks."

After handshakes were exchanged, the four of us smiled at the couple oohing and aahing over the baby they'd missed so desperately. The little thing was only half awake, her eyes slowly blinking against the glare of the porch light. She was probably wondering why her sweet dreams had been interrupted.

"She's such a good baby," Mrs. O'Neill told Juliette and Luke. "Sleeps well, rarely fusses. Cute, too, as you can see."

"She sure does eat a lot, though." Mr. O'Neill patted his belly and jovially asked, "But who am I to judge?"

Mrs. O'Neill looked from the couple to me and the detective, her face slightly pained and pensive. "What's the plan? Will they be taking the baby with them tonight?"

"Not yet," Jackson said. "Given the unusual circumstances, the court will likely require them to take a blood test to prove they're the baby's parents before Child Protective Services relinquishes custody."

"They will?" Juliette bit her lip. "How long will that take?"

Jackson rested a comforting hand on the young mother's shoulder. "Don't worry. I'm sure they'll move things along as quickly as they can." She removed her hand and addressed the young couple jointly. "Do y'all know anyone outside the compound you can stay with? A friend from before, or maybe a relative in the area?"

Juliette swept her tears away with her fingers and shook her head. "No. The last time I saw any of my friends, I was only ten years old. I don't remember any of their phone numbers or addresses. There's no telling where they might be today. Some of them are probably away at college."

Juliette had missed out on the chance to go to college herself. Heck, in the last ten years, she'd missed out on all kinds of things. The inauguration of the first black president. Twerking. The short-lived Pokemon Go craze. Nearly a dozen iterations of the iPhone. Brexit. The return of straight-leg jeans.

"I might be able to track down a relative," she added, "but last I knew, none of them lived in town. The closest one back then was my aunt in Lampasas."

Lampasas was a two-hour drive to the southwest. Nowhere the young couple could get to tonight, nor a convenient location for them to be able to see their baby until she was released to them.

Luke said, "My mother burned all our bridges before she joined the People of Peace." Unfortunately, that wasn't unusual for someone with a bad drug habit.

Juliette clutched her baby tighter. "I suppose we can go to a shelter until we figure things out."

"You'll do no such thing," Mrs. O'Neill said sweetly. "Our couch folds out into a bed. It might not be the most comfortable thing to sleep on, but it'll do for now. You can stay with us until you sort things out. That will give my husband and me time to adjust, too." She reached out and ran a finger along Skye's cheek. "We're going to miss your little girl. We've grown quite attached to her."

With any luck, another child would become available for the O'Neills soon. They'd certainly make loving parents.

Juliette gave Mrs. O'Neill a soft smile. "Thanks for taking such good care of her."

"It was nothing." Mrs. O'Neill waved a dismissive hand, but the tear in her eye said taking care of Skye had in reality meant everything to her. She opened the door. "Come on in. Let's get y'all settled."

Jackson gestured to her car. "We'll grab their things."

While the two couples took the baby back inside, the detective and I retrieved Juliette and Luke's things from the car. Each of them had a small stack of well-worn clothing. No bag or suitcase. Not a surprise given that they were not allowed to travel outside the compound and would have had no need for luggage once they'd been taken in by the cult. They each had a few toiletries wrapped up in a bath towel. That was it. No electronics. No books. No silly knickknacks or mementos. None of the things people their age normally owned.

Jackson and I carried the things inside and found Luke and Juliette side by side on the couch. Skye was cuddled up against Luke's chest, snoozing away, not a care in the world. The little baby had no inkling of the trauma her parents had gone through. *Maybe that's a good thing.*

After depositing their things on the coffee table, Jackson said, "We'll head out now. Let us know if we can help with anything."

The O'Neills walked us out onto the porch. There, the woman whispered, "I'll admit I'm sad the baby won't be ours now. But I can't even imagine what those two have gone through. I'm glad they'll get to be a family."

Mr. O'Neill issued an *mm-hm* in agreement and pointed to me. "You come across any more babies that need a mom and dad, you let us know."

I gave him a smile. "I sure will."

The department gave me the next few days off so I could be with Brigit at the vet's until she was released and then nurse her back to health at home. I bought her another noisy rubber pig to replace the toy she'd destroyed earlier. The oinking would drive me crazy, but if it made Brigit happy, I'd suck it up. I gave it to her when she was released from the veterinary hospital. She wagged her tail, took the pig in her teeth, and chomped down tight. *Oink!*

Back at home, Brigit recovered quickly and, before we knew it, she was back to harassing squirrels in the backyard as if nothing had ever happened, her shaved chest and the round scar the only signs she'd taken a bullet. But while my partner might be the same, I wasn't sure I ever would be. Seeing Brigit so close to death that night had caused me a raw, helpless heartache like nothing I'd ever experienced. I understood how Juliette must have felt when she'd been told her child had passed away. Knowing Father Emmanuel had put the young mother through that unnecessary agony on purpose, for nothing more than spite, made me want to take my baton to every inch of him.

Once Father Emmanuel was released from the hospital, he was taken directly to the county lockup and charged with kidnapping, false imprisonment, resisting arrest, assault on a police officer, and attempted murder. He wouldn't be getting out of prison any time soon. I hoped he thought of Brigit every time he looked in the mirror and saw her fang scars on his neck. I also hoped he thought of me any time he suffered a headache.

Zeke was also charged for aiding and abetting the kidnapping of Skye. He worked out a plea deal and would serve two years in the state lockup.

Given that it was his first and only charge, Jeb got off relatively lightly, sentenced only to probation and community service for his role in Luke's assault.

With more than enough evidence to convict Father

Emmanuel, I was able to convince Detective Jackson and the district attorney to release the bluebonnet baby blanket from the police department's evidence warehouse and return it to its rightful owner—Skye. Luke and Juliette were tested, and proved to be the baby's biological parents. The state's custody of their baby ended, and she was theirs once again, to have and to hold.

Mr. O'Neill landed Luke a job in the warehouse of a discount furniture company, where he worked as a manager. Knowing Beverly was looking for help in her sewing business, I introduced her to Juliette. Beverly was impressed with Juliette's technique and hired her on the spot as her new assistant. It turned out to be the perfect arrangement for both of them. Beverly allowed Juliette to bring Skye with her to work, and fell in love with the adorable baby, acting as a surrogate grandmother and spoiling Skye rotten with toys and clothes. When Beverly learned that the O'Neills hoped to adopt and would need their nursery on short notice if a baby became available, she invited Luke and Juliette to live with her until they could save up enough funds for an apartment and furnishings of their own. A vacant bedroom was put into use, and the crib Beverly's grandchildren had slept in came out of its retirement in the garage and was put back in service. In addition to helping Beverly with the alterations and custom clothing orders, Juliette continued to make her beautiful bluebonnet quilts and sell them at the country store. Now, though, rather than being forced to turn over the financial fruits of her labor to Father Emmanuel, she got to keep the share she earned.

Because the assets of the People of Peace sanctuary

had been used in crimes, they were forfeited to the
government. The vehicles were seized and sold, and
the city took over the compound to expand the lakeside park and facilities. The adjacent farmland was
purchased by a cattle rancher who promptly tore down
the leaning silo rather than risk the structure falling
over on his land and livestock.

The members of the People of Peace scattered to the
wind, some of them moving on together to another secluded sanctuary in New Mexico, while others recon-
nected with family and friends and decided to rejoin
the society they'd once shunned. Juliette's parents and
Luke's mother were among the latter. They found a
more mainstream church that offered them the spiritual support system they needed, as well as some financial assistance to help get them on their feet. The
social worker who'd picked up Skye from the fire station gave Juliette's father some leads on worker training programs. He'd signed up for classes and was
working hard to gain some new marketable job skills.
Frankie put in a good word for Juliette's mother at the
grocery store where she once worked, and the woman
was given a job as a cashier.

Though their relationship would be recognized as a
valid common-law marriage under Texas law, Juliette
and Luke nevertheless wanted to hold the formal ceremony and celebration they'd been denied when living
in the compound. Juliette spent a week sewing her own
wedding gown, with Beverly giving her expert advice
on the beading. She also made a beautiful ruffled dress
in bluebonnet blue for her daughter for the event. The
pastor of their new church agreed to perform the cer-

-mony in the city's botanical gardens, by the turtle pond. It was a beautiful spot.

I'd introduced Seth to Juliette and Luke shortly after their rescue from the compound. They were glad to meet the man who'd been the first on the outside to see their daughter and ensure she was safe and protected. He'd been invited to the wedding, as had the paramedic Doug Harrison, Detective Jackson, the social worker, the O'Neills, Beverly, and, of course, Juliette's parents and Luke's mother. Brigit had been invited, too, her plus-one being Blast. Seth had brought Ollie along simply so he could get some fresh air and enjoy the crisp autumn day. The wedding was the perfect occasion for me to wear the pretty coral dress and purple jewelry I'd bought from Felicia.

Luke made a handsome groom in a dark gray suit with a light gray shirt and white tie. As he took his place next to the pastor under a sprawling live oak, the rest of us took seats in the lawn chairs we'd brought to sit in.

The procession began with Beverly carrying Skye up the short aisle. Skye was too young and lacked the motor control to actually toss flower petals, but Beverly improvised, taking the baby's hand in her own, plucking pink petals from the basket, and tossing them into the air. Once Beverly had taken a seat on the front row next to Juliette's mother, a flautist from their church launched into a high-pitched rendition of "Here Comes the Bride." We stood as Juliette's father walked her the seven steps up the short aisle, their procession ending long before the song.

We retook our seats as Juliette took her place next

to Luke, a bouquet of artificial bluebonnets in her hand. She gazed up at him, and he looked down at her, their love and devotion written clearly on their happy faces.

"Dearly beloved," began the officiate, "we gather here today to celebrate the marriage of Luke and Juliette . . ." The ceremony continued on until they were pronounced husband and wife, gave each other a warm kiss, and the pastor said, "What God has joined together, let no man put asunder."

Amen to that.

The flautist launched into a short recessional as the newly married couple turned to us, both of them beaming.

Given that Luke and Juliette were not quite twenty-one yet, we toasted their nuptials with plastic glasses of sparkling grape juice kept cold in a rolling cooler. Brigit and Blast served themselves mouthfuls of water lapped up from the turtle pond. After the couple cut their cake, Juliette's mother and I finished the job, handing pieces to each of the guests along with a napkin and fork.

As the celebration wound down, Seth pulled a tennis ball from his pocket, cocked his arm back, and sent it sailing across the long stretch of grass. Blast and Brigit took off after it. My furry, four-legged partner might have recently taken a bullet to the chest, but you'd never know it to watch her now. She easily bested Blast, snatching his ball up in her teeth on the fly, and banking until she headed back in our direction. When she ran past us, Seth and I turned to see where she'd gone. She'd carried the ball to Ollie. Beverly had pulled her lawn chair up next to his. The two looked down and aughed when Brigit dropped the ball at their feet and ssued an insistent *arf,* demanding they throw the ball or her.

I nudged Seth in the ribs and whispered. "You seeing what I'm seeing? Looks like your grandfather and Beverly are hitting it off."

"Ugh," Seth said. "I think I'm going to be sick."

He was only teasing, of course. Frankly, it was high time Ollie got back in the romance game, and we both knew it. He'd pined for his dead wife and retreated from the world long enough. Just like the cult members, it was time he was liberated.

Seth's focus moved from his grandfather to the newlyweds. His eyes narrowed as he watched them. "You ever think about it?" he asked. "Getting married?"

"To Chris Hemsworth?" I said. "All the time."

He cut me an intent look, arching an inquisitive brow. "Anyone else?"

I gave him a sly smile. "Never. You?"

He gave me a sly smile right back. "Not even once."

We were both lying, of course, and we both knew that, too.

When Juliette and Luke were ready to go, the rest of us formed two lines and sent them off amid a colorful shower of dried-flower confetti. Those of us in attendance had pooled our resources and paid for the newlyweds to enjoy a couple of nights at a quaint bed-and-breakfast in Granbury. They'd have fun exploring the historic square, enjoying good food at the town's restaurants, and attending a live show at the theater. I hoped it would mark the beginning of a long and happy marriage for the two of them. They certainly deserved it.

Brigit and I were back at work on Monday, patrolling the streets. The cult case was certainly one of the strangest and most challenging we'd worked so far, and I could only wonder what else lay ahead for my furry partner and me.

I eyed her in the rearview mirror. "Hey, Brig. What do you think our next big case will be? Drugs? Armed robbery? A murder?"

She gave a single wag of her tail as if to say, *Who knows?*

Whatever it might be, we were ready to take it on together.

Look for these other *tails* of romance
and K-9 suspense from Diane Kelly

PAW ENFORCEMENT

PAW AND ORDER

UPHOLDING THE PAW
(an e-original novella)

LAYING DOWN THE PAW

AGAINST THE PAW

ABOVE THE PAW

ENFORCING THE PAW

From St. Martin's Paperbacks